The Rise of European Security Cooperation

One of the most striking developments in international politics today is the significant increase in security cooperation among European Union states. Seth Jones argues that this increase in cooperation, in areas such as economic sanctions, weapons production and collaboration among military forces, has occurred because of the changing structure of the international and regional systems. Since the end of the Cold War, the international system has shifted from a bipolar to a unipolar structure characterized by US dominance. This has caused EU states to cooperate in the security realm to increase their ability to project power abroad and decrease reliance on the United States. Furthermore, European leaders in the early 1990s adopted a 'binding' strategy to ensure long-term peace on the continent, suggesting that security cooperation is caused by a desire to preserve peace in Europe whilst building power abroad.

SETH G. JONES is Adjunct Professor in the Security Studies Program at Georgetown University and Political Scientist at the RAND Corporation. He is a distinguished scholar of European affairs, state-building operations and counterterrorism. Professor Jones was Europe Editor at *The Christian Science Monitor*, is a contributor to *The New York Times*, *The Financial Times*, and *National Interest* and has appeared on the BBC, CNN and other national and international television and radio programmes.

T0370682

The Rise of European Security Cooperation

Seth G. Jones

CAMBRIDGE
UNIVERSITY PRESS

CAMBRIDGE UNIVERSITY PRESS
Cambridge, New York, Melbourne, Madrid, Cape Town,
Singapore, São Paulo, Delhi, Tokyo, Mexico City

Cambridge University Press
The Edinburgh Building, Cambridge CB2 8RU, UK

Published in the United States of America by Cambridge University Press, New York

www.cambridge.org
Information on this title: www.cambridge.org/9780521689854

First published 2007

A catalogue record for this publication is available from the British Library

ISBN 978-0-521-86974-4 Hardback
ISBN 978-0-521-68985-4 Paperback

CONTENTS

Figures and Tables

Acknowledgments

The American author Mark Twain wrote in his book *Life on the Mississippi* that "we write frankly and fearlessly, but then we 'modify' before we print." This book is the product of countless modifications. Numerous colleagues offered frank critiques and comments that forced me to delete or rewrite sections, add new information, and avert pitfalls. Their fingerprints are over every page of this book. While I accepted many of their suggestions, I did not accept all of them. And I alone bear responsibility for any shortfalls that still exist.

There are several people who deserve particular mention. They read drafts of the book, provided excellent comments, and pointed out problems with the argument and evidence more times than I care to remember. They include John Mearsheimer, Charles Glaser, Sebastian Rosato, Charles Lipson, Lloyd Gruber, Michael Freeman, and Dong Sun Lee. I also owe a profound debt of gratitude to Robert Art, Richard Bitzinger, Deborah Boucoyannis, Jasen Castillo, Alexander Downes, Daniel Drezner, Doowan Lee, Susan Rosato, John Schuessler, Jeremy Shapiro, Frank Smith, Duncan Snidal, Alexander Thompson, Alex Wendt, and Joel Westra for providing helpful comments over the course of the research and writing. Thanks also to the University of Chicago's Program on International Security Policy for providing a wonderful intellectual home. I presented various chapters to audiences at the University of Chicago's Program on International Politics, Economics, and Security (PIPES); University of Chicago's Program on International Security Policy; Columbia University; Georgetown University; Stiftung Wissenschaft und Politik; and the RAND Corporation. I owe a special debt of gratitude to Cambridge University Press, especially John Haslam and the anonymous reviewers, for their excellent reviews, helpful comments, and sheer professionalism. And a big thank you to Daniel Byman, who introduced me to Cambridge University Press (and, indirectly, to my wife), and who has been a great friend and colleague.

In addition, I have learned a great deal from several colleagues and friends who shared their experience working on European affairs at the

US State Department, National Security Council, and National Intelligence Council. They include Ambassador James Dobbins, Gregory Treverton, Ambassador Robert Hunter, Earl Anthony Wayne, and Stephen Larrabee. Ambassador Dobbins was kind enough to provide me with the time and resources necessary to finish the book, and has been an excellent mentor and colleague. Thanks to Nora Bensahel, David Brannan, Keith Crane, Stephan de Spiegeleire, David Gompert, John Gordon, Bruce Hoffman, Mark Lorell, Evan Medeiros, Olga Oliker, Andrew Rathmell, Bill Rosenau, Steve Simon, Michael Spirtas, and others at RAND who work on a range of European security issues – and who influenced various parts of this book. I also owe an enormous debt to two wonderful assistants, Karen Stewart and Nathan Chandler, who provided greater support and assistance than they realized.

During the research phase of the book, there were a number of government officials from the US State Department, Defense Department, National Security Council, and intelligence community who were generous in providing time, information, and other assistance in the midst of busy schedules. I would also like to thank those officials from the British, French, German, and Italian governments that I interviewed – often more than once – as well as officials from NATO and the European Union. Since most requested that I not attribute them by name, I decided to avoid attributions to them as a whole.

Finally, my family has been my backbone and rudder. My parents and three brothers – Alex, Josh, and Clark – provided constant support over the years. In addition, I understand more clearly what Mark Twain meant in a speech in 1868, when he asked: "What Sir, would be the people of the earth without woman?" My daughter, Elizabeth, was an endless source of inspiration, especially after late nights working on the computer. My wife, Suzanne, was my most faithful and steady supporter. This book is dedicated to both of them.

1   Introduction

In the late 1930s, shortly before Germany's *blitzkrieg* into Poland and
the beginning of World War II, Western Europe was a labyrinth of defensive walls and fortresses. A traveler journeying eastward from Paris
to Stuttgart would have stumbled across two heavily fortified lines: the
Maginot and Siegfried Lines. In France, the Maginot Line began near
Basel, Switzerland, snaked northward along the Franco-German border,
and ended near the French town of Longuyen. As a reporter for the
British *Daily Express* wrote in May 1933:

I embarked today on a perilous pilgrimage to the battlefields of the next war . . .
No man has yet succeeded in locating the exact positions of the mystery
defences, in gauging their strength, appearance and cost. "Go at your own peril,"
a high official of the War Ministry said to me when I informed him of my
intention . . . Along the scattered line of defences north of Metz, behind Belgium,
where movable forts, strange modern devices with rolls of barbed wire, armaments and guns, travel from place to place, wherever they are needed, like
lumbering tanks, my way lies.[1]

French politicians and military figures – including André Maginot,
French minister of war who directed its construction – conceived the
Maginot Line as an impregnable barrier against any future German
invasion.

It consisted of some fifty large fortifications. At the front were *maisons
fortes*, fortified barracks manned by armed frontier police, whose job
was to delay an enemy's advance and alarm the main defenses. Roughly
a mile behind laid the *avant postes*, large concrete bunkers equipped with
machine guns and 47mm anti-tank guns. They were protected by
stretches of barbed wire to hinder the advance of infantry, anti-personnel
mines, and upright rail sections embedded in concrete to impede tank
movement. Behind the *avant postes* was the main defensive line, the

---

[1] Quoted in Vivian Rowe, *The Great Wall of France: The Triumph of the Maginot Line*
(New York: G.P. Putnam's Sons, 1961), p. 82.

position de résistance. These lines consisted of large forts known as *ouvrages* that were scattered roughly nine miles apart, held over 1,000 troops, and housed artillery ranging from the 75mm gun to the 135mm howitzer. The surface areas were protected by steel-reinforced concrete up to 3.5m thick, a depth capable of withstanding multiple direct hits.[2]

In Germany, the Siegfried Line (or West Wall) began near Basel, crept roughly 400 miles northward along the borders with France, Luxembourg, Belgium, and the Netherlands, and petered out just south of the Waal River. The line included a system of pillboxes, observation and command posts, and bunkers that housed machine guns and anti-tank weapons. Most were constructed of concrete, steel, logs, and filled sandbags. Scattered among them were trenches, minefields, barbed wire, and the infamous "dragon's teeth," large concrete slabs protruding from the earth to obstruct tank movement. As Winston Churchill noted in the late 1930s, the Siegfried Line presented a formidable barrier:

In the dawn of 1938 decisive changes in European groupings and values had taken place. The Siegfried Line confronted France with a growing barrier of steel and concrete, requiring as it seemed an enormous sacrifice of French manhood to pierce. The door from the West was shut.[3]

The heavily fortified walls in eastern France and western Germany are stark reminders of the security competition that plagued Europe in the two centuries prior to World War II. The Napoleonic wars (1803–1815), wars of Italian unification (1859), Seven Weeks' War (1866), Franco-Prussian War (1870–1871), World War I (1914–1918), and World War II (1939–1945) included some of the bloodiest and most destructive wars ever fought.

Today, little more than weeds and rubble are left of these once formidable walls. In fact, a traveler journeying from Paris to Stuttgart today may be forgiven for not realizing that he or she has even crossed borders. The differences between pre-World War II Europe and today are striking. Indeed, Europe has experienced two fundamental transformations in the security realm over the last century. The first was the move from Hobbesian balance-of-power politics and security competition during much of the eighteenth and nineteenth centuries, and half of the twentieth century, to US-led transatlantic cooperation during the

---

[2] On the Maginot Line see Rowe, *The Great Wall of France*; Anthony Kemp, *The Maginot Line: Myth and Reality* (New York: Stein and Day, 1982); J.E. Kaufmann and H.W. Kaufmann, *The Maginot Line: None Shall Pass* (Westport, CT: Praeger, 1997).

[3] Winston S. Churchill, *The Gathering Storm* (Boston: Houghton Mifflin, 1948), pp. 261–2.

Cold War. The second major transformation was the increase in intra-European security cooperation after the end of the Cold War. The latter transformation is the primary focus of this book. Yet a proper understanding of today also requires delving into the sinews of Europe during the Cold War.

The debate about Europe

This book examines one of the most striking developments in international politics today: the significant increase in security cooperation among European Union states since the end of the Cold War. To assess this development, this book offers the most systematic and comprehensive analysis of European security cooperation to date. The increase in European security cooperation today is especially impressive given Europe's bloody and divided history, which is neatly illustrated by the walls and fortresses that carved up the continent between World Wars I and II. It is also striking since security cooperation has continued despite such incidents as the French and Dutch veto of the European Constitution in 2005.[4]

Arguments about Europe tend to fall into two camps. A small minority believe that European security cooperation has increased since the end of the Cold War. Some also believe that Europe is becoming a major global actor. For example, Henry Kissinger argues: "The emergence of a unified Europe is one of the most revolutionary events of our time."[5] Another analysis contends that European security developments are "of revolutionary significance" and will likely "transform the nature of the European Union, its relations with other parts of the word and, in particular, the shape of transatlantic relations."[6] But the vast majority of scholars and policymakers – especially in the United States – are deeply pessimistic that little, if any, meaningful security cooperation has occurred in Europe.

Consequently, this book examines the evolution of European cooperation in the security realm. It asks three sets of questions. First, has there

---

[4] The French and Dutch rejections led some analysts to wonder whether this spelled the eventual demise of the European Union. See, for example, Laurent Cohen-Tanugi, "The End of Europe?" *Foreign Affairs*, Vol. 84, No. 6, November / December 2005, pp. 55–67. On the constitution see the Draft Treaty establishing a Constitution for Europe, European Convention, Brussels CONV 850/03, 18 July 2003.

[5] Henry Kissinger, *Does America Need a Foreign Policy? Toward a Diplomacy for the 21st Century* (New York: Simon & Schuster, 2001), p. 47.

[6] Gilles Andréani, Christoph Bertram, and Charles Grant, *Europe's Military Revolution* (London: Centre for European Reform, 2001), p. 5.

been a significant increase in security cooperation among EU states since the Cold War? Second, if so, why? Why has there been significant cooperation since the end of the Cold War, and why was there comparatively little security cooperation through the European Community during the Cold War? Third, what are the future prospects for security cooperation among EU states? What are the implications for European–American relations?

The main argument can be divided into two parts. First, the evidence clearly shows that there has been a significant increase in European security cooperation since the end of the Cold War. To date, however, there has been virtually no effort to measure this change systematically. A "significant" increase in cooperation means that European states today predominantly cooperate with each other in such areas as imposing economic sanctions for foreign policy goals, developing and producing weapons, and building military forces – rather than unilaterally or with non-European states. It also means that there has been a measurable increase in intra-European cooperation compared to the Cold War. Several examples illustrate the point:

- *Security institutions*: European states established a foreign policy arm of the EU beginning with the Maastricht Treaty (1992). There was no meaningful intra-European security cooperation during the Cold War, as illustrated by such failed attempts as the European Defense Community, Fouchet Plan, and European Political Cooperation.
- *Economic sanctions*: European states impose sanctions for foreign policy goals roughly 78 percent of the time through the European Union. This marks a striking difference from the Cold War, when they sanctioned only 12 percent of the time through the European Community.
- *Arms production*: European states and defense firms largely develop and produce advanced weapons with each other. In some areas, such as missiles and helicopters, research and development occurs almost exclusively at the European rather than the national level.
- *Military forces*: European states have established a rapid reaction military capability, EU battle groups, European Gendarmerie Force, and a political-military structure to project power independently of NATO and the United States. They have also deployed nearly a dozen EU missions to such countries as Macedonia, Bosnia, Democratic Republic of the Congo, Georgia, and Palestinian territory. There were no deployments through the European Community during the Cold War.

To be clear, I use the term "cooperation" rather than integration because European behavior has been intergovernmental, not supranational.

Major foreign policy and defense decisions are still made in European capitals. The European Union is not on the verge of becoming a supranational state, nor is a European army imminent. European states also do not agree on all foreign policy issues, though they agree on many of them. The point, however, is that there has been a quantifiable and largely unrecognized increase in security cooperation among European states since the end of the Cold War.

Second, this cooperation has largely occurred because of the changing structure of the international and regional systems. The international system shifted from a bipolar structure during the Cold War characterized by competition between the United States and Soviet Union, to a unipolar structure after the Cold War characterized by US dominance. This shift caused European states to cooperate in the security realm for two reasons: to increase Europe's ability to project power abroad, and to decrease reliance on the United States. In addition, the regional system in Europe shifted from one with a divided Germany and a dominant US presence during the Cold War, to one with a rapidly declining US presence and a reunified Germany. This shift caused European leaders in the early 1990s to adopt a "binding" strategy to ensure long-term peace on the continent. In sum, security cooperation has been about preserving peace on the continent and building European power abroad.

To test this argument, this book offers a comprehensive approach. It measures cooperation from World War II to the present by examining all major attempts to create a European security institution, all cases in which European states imposed sanctions for foreign policy goals, all cases of transnational weapons collaboration involving European defense firms, and the collaboration of military forces. The finding is unambiguous: European states are increasingly cooperating in the security realm. The likely result will be increasing friction between the United States and Europe in the future. Indeed, some in the US government have strongly opposed security cooperation outside NATO. For instance, the US Department of Defense has stated that it would actively work "to prevent the creation of an EU counterpart to Supreme Headquarters Allied Powers Europe (SHAPE) and a separate 'EU' army."[7]

Consequently, this book challenges two sets of arguments. First, it contends that the deep skepticism about the extent of European security cooperation and the prospects for the future are mistaken. For

---

[7] United States Department of Defense, *Responsibility Sharing Report* (Washington, DC: US Dept of Defense, June 2002), Chapter II, p. 5.

the vast majority of scholars – especially in the United States – security cooperation has been more talk than action. European countries have been just as unwilling as always to coordinate foreign and defense policies. "On foreign policy issues," notes the *Financial Times*, "Europe [is] more unwilling than ever to speak with one united voice."[8] Thomas Risse notes that on foreign policy and defense matters "Europe remains divided, while the US rules."[9] In his book *Of Paradise and Power*, Robert Kagan writes that "the effort to build a European force has so far been an embarrassment to Europeans."[10] Douglas Lemke likewise argues that European states, including France, continue to view NATO as the only viable regional security organization. "The [European Union] Rapid Reaction Force is too small to serve as a counter to U.S. military power and French officials have stated repeatedly that NATO will remain Europe's primary defense organization."[11]

In addition, some argue that the future of Europe will likely be one of competition rather than cooperation. As John Mearsheimer writes: "Without the American pacifier, Europe is not guaranteed to remain peaceful. Indeed, intense security competition among the great powers would likely ensue because, upon American withdrawal, Europe would go from benign bipolarity to unbalanced multipolarity, the most dangerous kind of power structure."[12] These arguments are misplaced. As this study demonstrates, there has been a measurable *increase* in security cooperation in several areas despite the withdrawal of 70 percent of US European Command since 1990, and despite the likelihood that more will withdraw from Europe in the near future.[13] The departure of large numbers of US forces – and European expectations

---

[8] Judy Dempsey, "Result May Not Focus European Minds," *Financial Times*, November 7, 2002, p. 3. See also, for example, Martin Walker, "Walker's World: The EU's Grim Year," *United Press International*, December 31, 2005.

[9] Thomas Risse, "Neofunctionalism, European Identity, and the Puzzles of European Integration," *Journal of European Public Policy*, Vol. 12, No. 2, April 2005, p. 303.

[10] Robert Kagan, *Of Paradise and Power: America and Europe in the New World Order* (New York: Alfred A. Knopf, 2003), p. 53. Walter Russell Mead similarly argues that "Europe's relative decline in world influence will continue at least through the first half of the new century," including its feeble attempt at foreign policy and defense cooperation. Walter Russell Mead, "American Endurance," in Tod Lindberg, ed., *Beyond Paradise and Power: Europe, America and the Future of a Troubled Partnership* (New York and London: Routledge, 2004), p. 163.

[11] Douglas Lemke, "Great Powers in the Post-Cold War World: A Power Transition Perspective," in T.V. Paul, James J. Wirtz, and Michel Fortmann, *Balance of Power: Theory and Practice in the 21st Century* (Stanford, CA: Stanford University Press, 2004), p. 60.

[12] John J. Mearsheimer, "The Future of the American Pacifier," *Foreign Affairs*, Vol. 80, No. 5, September/October 2001, p. 52.

[13] Congressional Budget Office (US Congress), *Options for Changing the Army's Overseas Basing* (Washington, DC: Congressional Budget Office, May 2004).

that the US military presence will be short-lived – should have led to less cooperation in the security realm. Instead, there was more.

Second, it challenges several explanations regarding why cooperation has occurred. European security cooperation is not caused by pressure from domestic and transnational actors on state preferences, as argued by *liberal intergovernmentalists*. This argument, which has its roots in broader liberal theories of international politics, assumes that states' strategic preferences for European cooperation come largely from the efforts of powerful domestic interest groups. Nor is security cooperation primarily a function of efforts to increase the prospects for mutual gain through an international institution, as *institutionalists* argue. European security cooperation is also not caused by the internalization of a *European identity*. This argument assumes that German, French, Italian, and other national identities and security interests have increasingly been transformed into a collective European identity. Finally, cooperation is not caused by *functional spillover* from the economic or other realms.

Part of the problem with the current debate about European security is that the dependent variable is almost never clearly specified or measured. What do we mean by foreign policy or defense cooperation? How do we measure it? How do we know whether European Union states are speaking or acting with "one voice"? The development of the European Union and the subsequent political, economic, and security changes in Europe have led to a sizable – though not always impressive – amount of scholarly work seeking to explain the causes of European cooperation. The bulk of it, however, has focused on explaining cooperation in such areas as economic and monetary affairs. What is perhaps most troubling, though, is the absence of rigorous work that seeks to measure the behavior of European states *over time*. Has there been a change over the past few decades in the coordination of foreign and defense policies? And, if so, why?

An additional problem is one of selection bias. Skeptics often argue that European cooperation is illusory because European states have not devoted sufficient resources to defense in comparison to the United States.[14] But this is a false dichotomy. It is certainly true that the United States has spent significantly more on defense than Europe. But it is unclear why United States capabilities should serve as a benchmark for European security cooperation, especially when European states collectively amass greater military resources than any other state in the world except the United States.

[14] Stephen G. Brooks and William C. Wohlforth, "Hard Times for Soft Balancing," *International Security*, Vol. 30, No. 1, Summer 2005, pp. 72–108.

Social scientists have much to offer here. As Gary King, Robert Keohane, and Sidney Verba argue: "The distinctive characteristic that sets social science apart from casual observation is that social science seeks to arrive at valid inference by the systematic use of well-established procedures of inquiry."[15] With this in mind, this study examines European security since World War II by undertaking a time-series study to measure the extent of security cooperation.

The argument

The major argument is that structural shifts in both the international and European systems have caused a notable increase in EU security cooperation in the post-Cold War era. As used here, "security cooperation" occurs when states adjust their foreign policy and defense behavior to the actual or anticipated preferences of others.[16] States cooperate to realize gains that are unachievable through individual action; policymaking is achieved multilaterally rather than unilaterally.[17]

My aim is to develop a theory that can explain the significant increase in European security cooperation since the end of the Cold War, and offer a useful roadmap for the future. Consequently, this book examines three time periods: past, present, and future. Past evidence strongly indicates that structural factors played a determining role in discouraging European states from pursuing widespread security collaboration through the European Community during the Cold War. Recent evidence suggests that changing structural conditions in the post-Cold War created a strong impetus for states to cooperate through the EU. The evidence from both the past and present suggest that EU security cooperation will increase in the future. In short, the overriding independent variable of this book is the structure of the international and regional systems.

The international system

During the Cold War, the international system was bipolar. It was characterized by security competition across the globe between the United States and Soviet Union. Under these conditions, European

---

[15] Gary King, Robert O. Keohane, and Sidney Verba, *Designing Social Inquiry: Scientific Inference in Qualitative Research* (Princeton, NJ: Princeton University Press, 1994), p. 6.
[16] Robert O. Keohane, *After Hegemony: Cooperation and Discord in the World Political Economy* (Princeton, NJ: Princeton University Press, 1984), p. 51.
[17] See, for example, Walter Mattli, *The Logic of Regional Integration: Europe and Beyond* (New York: Cambridge University Press, 1999), p. 41.

states were primarily concerned about balancing the Soviet Union, and most security cooperation was transatlantic rather than intra-European. NATO was the primary security institution, the United States was a key sanctions partner, and arms collaboration was largely transatlantic rather than intra-European.

However, the structure of the international system shifted from bipolarity to unipolarity when the Soviet Union collapsed, and the United States emerged as the preponderant global power. This structural shift left European states with a series of choices. One was to bandwagon with the United States through NATO and to continue dependence on American power. But the collapse of the Soviet Union eliminated the one issue that had inextricably tied Europe and America together for over four decades: balancing against the Red Army. European states also became increasingly concerned about American power and, with a growing divergence in security interests, wanted to increase their ability to project power abroad and decrease US influence. Power is important because it can make states more secure, and it can increase states' ability to influence, deter, and coerce others. Consequently, the European Union allowed European states to project power abroad and increase autonomy from America.

This action would not have been taken if the US were not so powerful, or if the international system was still bipolar. As French President Jacques Chirac argued, a powerful America reinforces the need for a stronger Europe "politically and economically." "The distance between America and Europe continues to increase," he noted, and this development led "toward a growing consolidation in Europe."[18] In addition, as the *European Security Strategy* pointedly noted: "The point of the Common Foreign and Security Policy and the European Security and Defense Policy is that we are stronger when we act together."[19] This means coordinating foreign and defense policies through the European Union.

In three important areas – economic sanctions, weapons production, and military forces – EU states began to aggregate power in the post-Cold War era. Between 1950 and 1990, European states sanctioned

[18] Christophe Jakubyszyn and Isabelle Mandraud, "Face à l'Amérique de Bush, les responsables politiques misent sur l'Europe," *Le Monde*, November 5, 2004; Pierre Avril, "Les Vingt-Cinq face à leurs limites," *Le Figaro*, November 5, 2004, p. 6; Patrick E. Tyler, "Europe Seeks Unity on New Bush Term," *New York Times*, November 6, 2004, p. A1; Daniel Dombey, "EU Still Split Over Diplomacy with US," *Financial Times*, November 6, 2004, p. 8; "Europe Should Bolster Powers in Face of Strong US," *Agence France Presse*, November 5, 2004.

[19] Council of the European Union, *A Secure Europe in a Better World: European Security Strategy* (Brussels: European Council, December 2003), p. 13.

through the European Community in only two out of seventeen cases (12 percent). Yet between 1991 and 2006 they sanctioned through the EU in twenty-one out of twenty-seven cases (78 percent). Between 1950 and 1989, European defense firms were more likely to cooperate with US defense firms in mergers, acquisitions, and codevelopment and coproduction projects. But since 1990, intra-European defense cooperation has increased in order to compete with such powerful US firms as Boeing and Lockheed Martin. This has included the development of the European Defense Agency to develop European military capabilities, improve defense research and technology, manage cooperative programs, and strengthen the European defense industry. Finally, while European states coordinated their military forces through NATO during the Cold War, they established a European Union rapid reaction force, EU battle groups, and an independent planning capability in the post-Cold War era.

To be sure, European states are not "balancing" against the United States as conventionally defined, since the US does not pose a military threat to Europe. Jeffrey Cimbalo argues, for example, that "there is considerable evidence that EU foreign policy, led by Paris and Berlin, will actively seek to balance . . . US power."[20] Some also argue that European security cooperation is a form of "soft balancing" against the United States.[21] But balancing, as conventionally defined, refers to an attempt by states to build economic and military power to contain an aggressive opponent that directly threatens their security through *military conquest*. The United States does not present a military threat to Europe.

The regional system

In addition, European Union states have cooperated in response to structural shifts in the regional system. During the Cold War, the Soviet

---

[20] Jeffrey L. Cimbalo, "Saving NATO From Europe," *Foreign Affairs*, Vol. 83, No. 6, November/December 2004, p. 115. See also Timothy Garton Ash, "President Kerry and Europe," *Washington Post*, October 24, 2004, p. B7.

[21] Robert J. Art, "Europe Hedges its Security Bets," in Paul, Wirtz, and Fortmann, *Balance of Power Revisited*, pp. 179–213; Barry R. Posen, "ESDP and the Structure of World Power," *The International Spectator*, Vol. 39, No. 1, January–March 2004, pp. 5–17; Robet A. Pape, "Soft Balancing against the United States," *International Security*, Vol. 30, No. 1, Summer 2005, pp. 7–45; T.V. Paul, "Soft Balancing in the Age of U.S. Primacy," *International Security*, Vol. 30, No. 1, Summer 2005, pp. 46–71; Stephen M. Walt, *Taming American Power: The Global Response to U.S. Primacy* (New York: W.W. Norton, 2005), pp. 126–32.

threat and concerns about German revanchism led to a large United States military presence in Europe and the division of Germany. This development was neatly captured in Lord Ismay's famous quip that NATO was critical "to keep the Americans in, the Russians out, and the Germans down." The presence of the "American pacifier" ensured that most security cooperation was transatlantic, rather than intra-European.[22] As noted earlier, NATO was the primary security institution and there was little intra-European cooperation in such areas as sanctions, arms collaboration, and military forces.

But structural shifts at the end of the Cold War increased the likelihood of security cooperation through the European Union. The collapse of the Soviet Union led to dramatic cuts in US forces in Europe and concerns about the US's long-term commitment to – and the relevance of – NATO. The reunification of Germany also created a potentially unstable regional situation, and British and French leaders were deeply concerned that a Germany which opted out of Europe would destabilize the region. Consequently, European states adopted a "binding" strategy in the early 1990s to tie Germany into Europe and increase the likelihood of peace on the continent. Binding Germany ensured peace because German leaders renounced unilateralism and agreed to a number of limitations, such as a reduction in German armed forces and the rejection of nuclear, chemical, and biological weapons. The European Union offered a logical long-term solution. A binding strategy was possible because Germany was a status quo power, and German, French, and British leaders had learned from Europe's troubled history. In short, structural shifts in Europe at the end of the Cold War triggered an increase in security cooperation through the European Union. Cooperation allowed European states to bind Germany and ensure long-term peace on the continent.

This book offers two additional arguments. First, European security cooperation has been – and will likely continue to be – intergovernmental rather than supranational for the foreseeable future. Major EU foreign policy and defense decisions have been made in European capitals rather than in Brussels. Second, Europe's major powers – Germany, France, and Britain – have been the primary motors of security cooperation. Indeed, one of Angela Merkel's first statements as German

---

[22] On the American pacifier see Josef Joffe, "Europe's American Pacifier," *Foreign Policy*, No. 54, Spring 1984, pp. 64–82; John J. Mearsheimer, *The Tragedy of Great Power Politics* (New York: W.W. Norton, 2001), pp. 377, 379, 386–92, 394; Robert J. Art, "Why Western Europe Needs the United States and NATO," *Political Science Quarterly*, Vol. 111, No. 1, Spring 1996, pp. 1–39.

chancellor in 2005 was to remind Europeans that France and Germany remained the key "motors" of European cooperation.[23] Cooperation is thus a function of relative power.

Those who argue that this approach misses the contributions of other member countries tend to overestimate these contributions.[24] Perhaps more importantly, the point is not that other countries never matter, but rather that Germany, France, and Britain matter most. For economic sanctions, they have the largest economies and the most power to wield when trying to coerce or deter other states. For arms production, their arms companies are the largest in Europe: Britain's BAE Systems; France's Thales; and the German, French, and Spanish conglomerate EADS. These companies and their respective national defense ministries have the greatest power in developing and producing advanced weapons and platforms. For military forces, Germany, France, and Britain have the largest defense budgets in Europe and, especially for France and Britain, have the most competent expeditionary military forces.

Neither of these arguments means that France, Germany, and Britain as a group – or even Europe as a whole – always speak with one voice in the security realm. Indeed, it logically follows from the first argument that they may disagree on issues because of the intergovernmental nature of cooperation. As Robert Art concludes:

[W]e must remember that there is as yet no single entity called Europe that speaks with one voice on foreign, security, and defense policy . . . On these issues, Europe still remains a set of nations that retain individual control over their foreign policies and defense establishments and whose national interests on these matters differ.[25]

As examined in more detail in later chapters, French leaders have historically pushed hardest for European security cooperation. German leaders strongly preferred cooperation through NATO during the Cold War, but have increasingly viewed the European Union as the key security, economic, and political organization in Europe. British leaders have historically resisted European security arrangements if they threaten – or appear to threaten – the preponderance of NATO, though

---

[23] Carsten Volkery, "Wie Merkel die Skorpione zaehmte," *Der Spiegel*, December 17, 2005; Marlies Fischer, "Merkel zähmte Blair und Chirac," *Hamburger Abendblatt*, December 19, 2005.

[24] See, for example, Helen Wallace's criticism of Moravcsik in "Review Section Symposium: The Choice for Europe: Social Purpose and State Power from Messina to Maastricht," *Journal of European Public Policy*, Vol. 6, No. 1, March 1999, pp. 155–79; Michael E. Smith, *Europe's Foreign and Security Policy* (New York: Cambridge University Press, 2004), pp. 19–20.

[25] Art, "Europe Hedges its Security Bets," p. 183.

they have increasingly supported a European Security and Defense Policy.

Research design

The research design adopted in this book is straightforward. First, I parsed the dependent variable – security cooperation – into four categories: security institutions, economic sanctions, arms production, and military forces. These categories were chosen because they represent a cross-section of tools states possess in the security realm. The category of *security institutions* includes the creation and development of a European (as opposed to a transatlantic) security institution. *Economic sanctions* cover the coordinated use of sanctions for foreign policy goals, such as ending civil wars or establishing democracy. *Arms production* encompasses collaboration in the arms industry, especially through mergers and acquisitions (M&As) and coproduction and codevelopment projects. Finally, the category of *military forces* includes the establishment and use of joint military and other crisis response forces. What ties them together is that states use them to pursue specific goals in the security realm: security institutions are constructed to balance against external powers or ameliorate the possibility of war; weapons such as fighter jets or precision-guided missiles are manufactured to provide security and project power; economic sanctions are utilized to coerce target states into changing behavior; and military forces are used for coercive or deterrent purposes.

Second, the principal historical evidence I use is the diplomatic history of Europe between 1950 and 2006 – though there is some variation because of access to data. I identified at least 4 major attempts to create a European security institution, 44 cases in which European states imposed sanctions, 482 instances of weapons collaboration, and several cases of military forces. I then deduced trends in the data and, through comparative case studies, examined state motives for deciding whether or not to pursue security cooperation.[26] Case studies offer a useful approach to help understand the motivations of European leaders.[27]

---

[26] In particular see Alexander L. George, "Case Studies and Theory Development: The Method of Structured, Focused Comparison," in Paul Gordon Lauren, ed., *Diplomacy: New Approaches in History, Theory, and Policy* (New York: Free Press, 1979), pp. 43–68.

[27] On the costs and benefits of comparative case studies see David Collier, "The Comparative Method: Two Decades of Change," in Dankwart A. Rustow and Kenneth Paul Erickson, eds., *Comparative Political Dynamics: Global Research Perspectives* (New York: Harper Collins, 1991), pp. 7–31; Charles C. Ragin, "Comparative Sociology and the Comparative Method," *International Journal of Comparative Sociology*, Vol. 22, Nos. 1–2,

As Alexander George and Timothy McKeown argue, they are useful in uncovering "what stimuli the actors attend to; the decision process that makes use of these stimuli to arrive at decisions; the actual behavior that then occurs; the effect of various institutional arrangements on attention, processing, and behavior; and the effect of other variables of interest on attention, processing, and behavior."[28]

This time-series approach should counter the criticism that scholarly work on European security cooperation is methodologically problematic because it is a single case.[29] Single observations can lead to indeterminate results, particularly since they don't control for random error and can make it extremely difficult to determine which of several alternative explanations is the most viable.[30] However, this study includes numerous observations and does not have an N of 1.

Third, I have chosen to examine Europe for several reasons. One is that there has been a significant and largely unprecedented increase in security cooperation since the end of the Cold War. This makes developments in Europe an intriguing puzzle. Charles Kupchan argues that "Europe will soon catch up with America not because of a superior economy or technological base, but because it is coming together, amassing the impressive resources and intellectual capital already possessed by its constituent states." Kupchan notes that in the defense realm Europe's "military presence will mount in the years ahead."[31]

March–June 1981, pp. 102–20; Charles Tilly, "Means and Ends of Comparison in Macrosociology," in Lars Mjoset et al., Comparative Social Research: Methodological Issues in Comparative Social Science, Vol. XVI (Greenwich, CT: JAI Press, 1997), pp. 43–53; Theda Skocpol and Margaret Somers, "The Uses of Comparative History in Macrosocial Inquiry," Comparative Studies in Society and History, Vol. 22, No. 2, 1980, pp. 174–97; Stephen Van Evera, Guide to Methods for Students of Political Science (Ithaca, NY: Cornell University Press, 1997), pp. 49–88.

[28] Alexander L. George and Timothy J. McKeown, "Case Studies and Theories of Organizational Decision Making," in Robert F. Coulam and Richard A. Smith (eds.), Advances in Information Processing in Organizations: A Research Annual, Vol. II (Greenwich, CT: JAI Press, 1985), p. 35.

[29] On Europe and the $N = 1$ debate see James A. Caporaso, Gary Marks, Andrew Moravcsik, and Mark A. Pollack, "Does the European Union Represent an n of 1?" ECSA Review, Vol. 10, No. 3, Fall 1997, pp. 1–5.

[30] See, for example, King, Keohane, and Verba, Designing Social Inquiry, pp. 208–30; John H. Goldthorpe, "Current Issues in Comparative Macrosociology: A Debate on Methodological Issues," in Mjoset et al., Comparative Social Research, pp. 1–26; David Collier and James Mahoney, "Insights and Pitfalls: Selection Bias in Qualitative Research," World Politics, Vol. 49, No. 1, October 1996, pp. 56–91.

[31] Charles A. Kupchan, The End of the American Era: US Foreign Policy and the Geopolitics of the Twenty-First Century (New York: Alfred A. Knopf, 2002), pp. 119, 148. See also Kupchan, "Hollow Hegemony or Stable Multipolarity?" in G. John Ikenberry, ed., America Unrivaled: The Future of the Balance of Power (Ithaca and London: Cornell University Press, 2002), pp. 68–97; Kupchan, "The Travails of Union: The American

Some analysts in the Central Intelligence Agency predict that the European Union will be a unified economic, political, and military actor in 2015, second only to the United States in total power.[32]

Europe also has been – and will continue to be – an area of strategic importance for the United States. This is partly because of the combined power of the EU and the individual power of its major states: Germany, France, and Britain. Furthermore, European history since World War II includes substantial variation in the independent variable (the structure of the international system), as well as substantial variation in the four categories of the dependent variable (security institutions, economic sanctions, arms production, and military forces). Finally, the Treaty on the European Union in 1992 (Maastricht) and subsequent treaties in the post-Cold War era provide an opportunity to study security institutions, a subject that has received inadequate attention in the international relations literature.[33]

Related to this, some readers might question why this book focuses on security cooperation in Europe, and not on other regions. After all, why hasn't the global distribution of power caused other states to cooperate in response to American power? There has not been similar cooperation in Asia, Latin America, the Middle East, or Africa. The answer is straightforward. Europe has been unique because of the nature of European states led by Germany. Regional cooperation in the post-Cold War era is possible because Germany was a status quo power and German, French, and British leaders had learned from Europe's bloody history. European cooperation thus benefited from the decision by its major powers – especially Germany – to pursue multilateral cooperation. Consequently, significant security cooperation in Asia and

---

Experience and its Implications for Europe," *Survival*, Vol. 46, No. 4, Winter 2004/5, pp. 103–20. As William Wallace and Bastian Giegerich conclude: "There has been a remarkable increase in the scale, distance and diversity of external operations by European forces – an increase that has scarcely registered in public debate across Europe, let alone the United States." Bastian Giegerich and William Wallace, "Not Such a Soft Power: The External Deployment of European Forces," *Survival*, Vol. 46, No. 2, Summer 2004, p. 164.

[32] Central Intelligence Agency, *Modeling International Politics in 2015: Potential U.S. Adjustments to a Shifting Distribution of Power* (Washington, DC: Strategic Assessments Group, CIA, 2004).

[33] Notable recent exceptions include G. John Ikenberry, *After Victory: Institutions, Strategic Restraint, and the Rebuilding of Order after Major Wars* (Princeton, NJ: Princeton University Press, 2001); David A. Lake, *Entangling Relations: American Foreign Policy in Its Century* (Princeton, NJ: Princeton University Press, 1999); Helga Haftendorn, Robert O. Keohane, and Celeste Wallander, eds., *Imperfect Unions: Security Institutions over Time and Space* (New York: Oxford University Press, 1999); Emanuel Adler and Michael Barnett, eds., *Security Communities* (New York: Cambridge University Press, 1999).

other regions hinges on the support of potential hegemons such as China. To date, there has been little interest by major powers, including China, for regional cooperation. Absent this support, significant security cooperation is unlikely.

This leaves Europe in a unique situation. The decision by great powers to pursue widespread security cooperation is historically anomalous. States have, of course, created formal military alliances such as NATO and collective security organizations such as the nineteenth-century Concert of Europe. But the breadth of European efforts in the post-Cold War era is largely unprecedented, and the current European Union security project thus presents a very interesting theoretical and empirical puzzle.

Outline of the book

The final section offers a brief outline of the book. Chapter 2 outlines the structural argument and then examines four alternative arguments: (1) there has not been significant security cooperation among EU states; (2) security cooperation has been caused by pressure from domestic actors; (3) security cooperation has been caused by a desire to increase the prospects for mutual gain through international institutions; and (4) security cooperation has been caused by the construction of a European identity.

Chapter 3 examines the structure of the regional system and asks: why was a security arm of the EU created in post-Cold War Europe? Why did it succeed when earlier attempts failed? It then examines four cases: the European Defense Community (1950–1954), the Fouchet Plan (1958–1963), European Political Cooperation (1969–1991), and the Treaty on European Union and beyond (1992–). It finds that while the three earlier attempts failed, a European security arm was finally created as part of the Treaty on European Union for structural reasons.

Chapters 4, 5, and 6 examine the structure of the international system and show that EU states have been motivated by a desire to build and project power in a unipolar world. Chapter 4 asks: why have European states increasingly imposed economic sanctions for foreign policy goals through the EU in the post-Cold War era? Why did they refrain from using the EC during the Cold War? It explores the extent of European security cooperation since 1950 by examining forty-four cases in which European states imposed sanctions. Chapter 5 asks: why has there been a substantial increase in intra-European weapons collaboration in the post-Cold War era? Why was there minimal cooperation during the Cold War? It explores the extent of weapons production collaboration by examining 482 cases of M&As and coproduction and codevelopment projects involving European defense firms. Chapter 6 asks: why have European Union states opted to build a rapid reaction force in the post-Cold War era? It examines the creation of NATO and the establishment of EU military and crisis response forces, and finds that there has been a notable shift in the post-Cold War era toward the establishment of an autonomous EU military capability.

Finally, Chapter 7 uses the arguments developed in this study to assess the future of European security over the next decade and offer policy prescriptions. It concludes that EU security cooperation will likely increase in the future, and predicts that the US–European strategic relationship will be characterized by increasing competition and friction. We now turn to possible explanations of EU security cooperation.

2   Power and security cooperation

It has become *de rigueur* to focus on the European Union as a global economic actor. The introduction of the euro as Europe's common currency and the establishment of a single European market have indeed transformed the European Union into a major economic power. As former German foreign minister Joschka Fischer noted regarding economic and monetary union:

In Maastricht one of the three essential sovereign rights of the modern nation-state – currency, internal security, and external security – was for the first time transferred to the sole responsibility of a European institution. The introduction of the euro was not only the crowning-point of economic integration, it was also a profoundly political act, because a currency is not just another economic factor but also symbolizes the power of the sovereign who guarantees it.[1]

The evidence shows that European states have also increasingly co-operated in the security realm, though it has been intergovernmental rather than supranational. Examples include the creation of a security arm of the European Union, the coordination of economic sanctions for foreign policy goals, rationalization in the European arms industry, and the creation of a rapid reaction military force.

This poses an interesting puzzle. Why has there been a substantial increase in security cooperation among European Union states since the end of the Cold War? Why was there little cooperation during the Cold War? The answer is a function of the changing structure of the regional and international systems. First, EU states have pursued cooperation in such areas as economic sanctions, arms production, and military forces in response to the end of bipolarity and the resulting unipolar structure of the international system. Aggregating power decreases European states' reliance on the United States and increases their ability to project power abroad. Second, European Union states have cooperated to

---

[1] Speech by Joschka Fischer, "From Confederacy to Federation: Thoughts on the Finality of European Integration," Berlin, May 12, 2000 (www.germany-info.org).

ensure peace on the continent and to prevent the rise of Germany as a regional hegemon. This decision has been facilitated by the ability of German, French, and British leaders to "learn" from history.

This chapter is divided into five major sections. First, it outlines the core assumptions. Second, it explores structural changes in the international system, as well as state strategies to deal with a unipolar power. It looks at the European response in three areas: economic sanctions, arms production, and military forces. Third, it examines structural changes in the European system, as well as European strategies in the early 1990s to deal with the rise of Germany and the withdrawal of US forces. Fourth, it explores potential counter-arguments. Fifth, it concludes by summarizing the key arguments and briefly examining them.

Structure and the distribution of power

The ultimate criterion for assessing any argument is the ability to explain real events in the real world. This places a high premium on empirical evidence. In addition, good arguments should also be logically consistent and precise. Other things being equal, arguments that are stated precisely and are internally consistent are preferable to those that are vague or contradictory.[2] The purpose of this chapter is to sketch the logic of my argument and several other competing arguments; the rest of the book then examines the evidence.

I begin by arguing that states seek security and influence in the international system. Policymakers and their populations want to be secure from internal and external threats, and seek to influence others to ensure their safety. Security and influence are not their only goals, but they are generally prerequisites for other goals such as wealth.[3] In addition, states are rational actors. Policymakers are generally aware of their external environment, and they think strategically about how to

---

[2] On how to judge social science arguments and theories, see Stephen M. Walt, "Rigor or Rigor Mortis? Rational Choice and Security Studies," *International Security*, Vol. 23, No. 4, Spring 1999, pp. 5–48.

[3] This assumption has its roots in several key realist arguments. First, the international system is anarchic. This is an ordering principle; it does not mean that the international system is chaotic or disorderly. Rather, it means that there is no world government or authority above states to enforce agreements or guarantee security. Second, states can never know with 100 percent certainty the current and future intentions of others. In the economic realm, most actions are reasonably transparent and information on compliance is often a matter of public record. In the security realm, however, there are limits to transparency and information sharing. States may have an incentive to misrepresent such information, and intentions can change. See, for example, Kenneth Waltz, *Theory of International Politics* (New York: McGraw-Hill, 1979); John J. Mearsheimer, *The Tragedy of Great Power Politics* (New York: W.W. Norton, 2001).

survive in it. They tend to be forward-looking and calculate the best means to assure their survival and security given the actions and reactions of other states.

Consequently, states care a great deal about power, especially the distribution of power. Power in this context refers to material capabilities, and particularly to military and economic assets. Power is important because it can make states more secure, and it can increase their ability to influence others. Conversely, the absence of power decreases the ability of states to do these things, and makes them more reliant on those with greater power. Power is thus relative.[4] Weaker states have a strong incentive to increase their power to ensure survival and increase security. Increasing their power also helps decrease reliance on more powerful states and raises their ability to project power abroad to influence, deter, and coerce others. States may not behave this way all the time. But those who do are more likely to flourish, and those who do not are more likely to suffer. As noted below, states may adopt a wide range of other strategies, such as bandwagoning with more powerful states or passing the buck to others.

The distribution of power in international and regional systems is an important causal variable. Historically, two distributions of power have existed: multipolarity and bipolarity. A multipolar system is one in which there are three or more great powers. It has been the most common pattern. Bipolarity is a system with two great powers, such as the international system during the Cold War with the US and Soviet Union.[5] In the aftermath of the Cold War, the international system moved to yet another distribution of power: unipolarity. With the demise of the Soviet Union, the United States became the most powerful state in the international system.

Structural theories are at best rough predictors of which states will combine capabilities against a dominant power.[6] While structural

---

[4] Joseph M. Grieco, "Anarchy and the Limits of Cooperation: A Realist Critique of the Newest Liberal Institutionalism," *International Organization*, Vol. 42, No. 3, Summer 1988, pp. 485–507.

[5] Among the key works on bipolarity and multipolarity are Karl W. Deutsch and J. David Singer, "Multipolar Power Systems and International Stability," *World Politics*, Vol. 16, No. 3, April 1964, pp. 390–406; Kenneth N. Waltz, "The Stability of a Bipolar World," *Daedalus*, Vol. 93, No. 3, Summer 1964, pp. 881–909; Mearsheimer, *The Tragedy of Great Power Politics*; Waltz, *Theory of International Politics*; Thomas J. Christensen and Jack Snyder, "Chain Gangs and Passed Bucks: Predicting Alliance Patterns in Multipolarity," *International Organization*, Vol. 44, No. 1, Spring 1990, pp. 137–68.

[6] Glenn H. Snyder, *Alliance Politics* (Ithaca, NY: Cornell University Press, 1997); William C. Wohlforth, "The Stability of a Unipolar World," *International Security*, Vol. 21, No. 1, Summer 1999, p. 29; Christensen and Snyder, "Chain Gangs and Passed Bucks," pp. 137–68.

conditions provide the impetus for weaker states to aggregate power, unit-level factors may determine whether – and with whom – a state will aggregate resources.[7] Specifically, participant states must share a certain degree of similarity and trust to overcome fears and to aggregate power. States that have common cultural, political, strategic, or economic similarities and interests may be more likely to cooperate because the barriers and costs of combining resources are lower. But these unit-level factors are at best intervening variables, and structural factors do exert a powerful influence on state behavior. Consequently, focusing predominantly on structure should tell us a lot about security cooperation.

Europe and the international system

During the Cold War, the international system was bipolar. This caused European states to cooperate with the United States to check Soviet power. NATO was the primary security institution, and European states imposed sanctions and built weapons with the United States. However, with the collapse of the Soviet Union in 1991, the international system shifted from bipolarity to unipolarity. A unipolar system is one in which no single state is powerful enough to balance against the dominant power. However, it is not a hegemonic system. It is still possible for a group of second-order powers to act in concert against the dominant power in a unipolar system.[8] The United States became the preponderant global power, and its economic, military, technological, and geopolitical dominance has been historically unprecedented.[9]

"One can't deny that there is henceforth a dominant 'pole,' the United States," noted Hubert Védrine, former French foreign minister. "In this

[7] Christopher Layne, "The Unipolar Illusion: Why New Great Powers Will Rise," *International Security*, Vol. 17, No. 4, Fall 1993, p. 9; Mearsheimer, *Tragedy of Great Power Politics*, p. 335.
[8] Pape, "Soft Balancing against the United States," p. 11.
[9] G. John Ikenberry, ed., *America Unrivaled: The Future of the Balance of Power* (Ithaca and London: Cornell University Press, 2002); Wohlforth, "The Stability of a Unipolar World," pp. 1–36; Layne, "The Unipolar Illusion," pp. 5–51; Kenneth N. Waltz, "Structural Realism after the Cold War," *International Security*, Vol. 25, No. 1, Summer 2000, pp. 5–41; Waltz, "The Emerging Structure of International Politics," *International Security*, Vol. 18, No. 2, Fall 1993, pp. 44–79; Michael Mastanduno, "Preserving the Unipolar Moment: Realist Theories and US Grand Strategy after the Cold War," *International Security*, Vol. 21, No. 4, Spring 1997, pp. 49–88; Samuel P. Huntington, "Why International Primacy Matters," *International Security*, Vol. 17, No. 4, Spring 1993, pp. 68–83.

sense the world is unipolar."[10] This structural shift created an important incentive for European states to pursue security cooperation. European leaders believed that aggregating power was necessary to decrease reliance on the United States and increase their ability to project power abroad. Power and autonomy are important because they make European states more secure and increase their ability, as already stated, to influence, deter, and coerce others. This has been particularly true since American and European security interests steadily began to diverge with the collapse of the Soviet Union. To be clear, aggregating power in response to structural changes must be causally linked with the systemic concentration of power. That is, states would not take these actions if the United States were not so powerful.

States may adopt one of several strategies when confronted with a unipolar international system. First, they can *bandwagon* with the dominant power by allying with it and trying to acquire at least some of the spoils of war. However, there is a significant drawback: bandwagoning fails to check the power of the unipole, and states that pursue this strategy give up any hope of preventing it from gaining power at their expense. This strategy jeopardizes their ability to influence, deter, and coerce others, and makes them dependent on the dominant power. Second, states can adopt a *buckpassing* strategy by refusing multilateral cooperation, pursuing independent foreign and defense policies, and passing to others the task of dealing with the dominant power. This strategy has a similar drawback: it fails to check the dominant power, especially if there is no one to catch the buck. By definition, a unipolar system is one in which no state possesses the capabilities to check the power of the dominant state on its own. Third states can try to *bind* the unipolar power in a multilateral institution.[11] The major problem with this strategy, however, is that it hinges on the willingness of the most powerful state to cooperate. Because of the significant disparity in power between the dominant state and second-order powers, however, the dominant state in a unipolar system is unlikely to agree to a binding strategy. Fourth, states can *balance* against the unipole to protect themselves from attack. As John Mearsheimer argues: "With balancing a great power assumes direct responsibility for preventing an aggressor from

---

[10] Hubert Védrine, *France in an Age of Globalization* (Washington, DC: Brookings Institution Press, 2001), p. 2.

[11] Walt, *Taming American Power*, pp. 144–52; Randall L. Schweller, *Deadly Imbalances: Tripolarity and Hitler's Strategy of World Conquest* (New York: Columbia University Press, 1998), pp. 70–1; Paul W. Schroeder, "Alliances, 1815–1945: Weapons of Power and Tools of Management," in Klaus Knorr, ed., *Historical Dimensions of National Security Problems* (Lawrence, KA: University Press of Kansas, 1976), pp. 227–62.

upsetting the balance of power. The initial goal is to deter the aggressor, but if that fails, the balancing state will fight the ensuing war."[12] States balance when confronted by a great power that poses a military threat.

However, the unique situation at the end of the Cold War presented European states with a somewhat different option. Unlike past preponderant powers, the United States has largely eschewed territorial conquest as a means of increasing power. Imperial Rome, France in the seventeenth century, and Britain in the nineteenth century all conquered territory and created empires while they were the sole great powers.[13] While the US has used military force to overthrow foreign governments, such as in Afghanistan in 2001 and Iraq in 2003, it has generally not expanded its power through conquest and territorial expansion. It never occupied Afghanistan, and it governed Iraq for barely a year before handing control to an interim Iraqi administration.

Some have argued that this is because the United States can no longer produce leading-edge military technologies on its own, which makes a fundamental challenge to the territorial status quo easier to subdue.[14] Others have argued that it is a function of the increasing proliferation of nuclear weapons.[15] Sill others have argued that it is largely a function of the "stopping power of water." Large bodies of water, such as the Atlantic and Pacific oceans for the United States, are formidable obstacles that cause significant power projection problems for the US military.[16] Finally, some have argued that America's liberal democratic political system and willingness to embed itself in institutions make it less likely to engage in conquest.[17] Scholars may argue over which of these arguments is the most convincing. Each, however, has an element of truth and collectively they explain more than any one of them alone. The proliferation of leading-edge military technologies and nuclear

---

[12] Mearsheimer, *The Tragedy of Great Power Politics*, p. 156. On neorealist balancing, also see Waltz, *Theory of International Politics*; Stephen M. Walt, *The Origins of Alliances* (Ithaca, NY: Cornell University Press, 1987); Dale C. Copeland, *The Origins of Major War* (Ithaca, NY: Cornell University Press, 2000).

[13] Layne, "The Unipolar Illusion"; Michael W. Doyle, *Empires* (Ithaca, NY: Cornell University Press, 1986).

[14] Stephen G. Brooks, *Producing Security: Multinational Corporations, Globalization, and the Changing Calculus of Conflict* (Princeton, NJ: Princeton University Press, 2005).

[15] Robert Jervis, *The Meaning of the Nuclear Revolution: Statecraft and the Prospect of Armageddon* (Ithaca, NY: Cornell University Press, 1989).

[16] Mearsheimer, *The Tragedy of Great Power Politics*, pp. 114–28; Stephen M. Walt, "American Primacy: Its Prospects and Pitfalls," *Naval War College Review*, Spring 2002, Vol. 55, No. 2, pp. 9–28.

[17] John M. Owen, IV, "Transnational Liberalism and US Primacy," *International Security*, Vol. 26, No. 3, Winter 2001/02, pp. 117–52; G. John Ikenberry, "Democracy, Institutions, and American Restraint," in *America Unrivaled*, pp. 213–38.

weapons, the stopping power of water, and America's liberal democratic system have all caused the United States to shun territorial conquest. This has meant that most states, including its Cold War allies, have not been militarily threatened by US power and fear US conquest. However, many find themselves deeply at odds with American foreign policy, yet with little power to change or counter it. Former German Chancellor Gerhard Schröder argued that his country would not participate in any "adventure" in Iraq since it was not in Germany's strategic interest. But there was little Germany could do to prevent the US war.[18] While the US does not present a military threat to Europe, it is the structural condition of unipolarity that has caused European states to aggregate power. This is not quite balancing as conventionally defined, since European states do not view America as a military threat.[19]

We now turn to the reason why the structural shift to unipolarity has caused European states to pursue security cooperation. The two logics of increasing power abroad and decreasing superpower dependency are analytically distinct but complementary in pushing European states to cooperate with each other.

Increasing global power

Aggregating power allows smaller states to project greater power in the international system. They lack the resources to project power around the globe on their own and to compete with the preponderant power. Trying to build up sufficient economic or military might by themselves takes far too long, if they could do it all. For instance, some have argued that China is currently balancing against the United States. While this may be true, the economic and military gap between the two is so large that it will take decades for China to become a legitimate pole and check the power of the United States.[20] Indeed, a unipolar system is by definition one in which the preponderant state is significantly more

---

[18] Elizabeth Pond, *Friendly Fire: The Near-Death of the Transatlantic Alliance* (Washington, DC: Brookings Institution Press, 2004); Steven Erlanger, "US Quietly Chides German for his Dissension on Iraq," *New York Times*, August 17, 2002, p. A1.

[19] This strategy has sometimes been called "soft balancing," though the term has invoked more confusion than clarity. T. V. Paul, "Introduction: The Enduring Axioms of Balance of Power Theory and their Contemporary Relevance," in Paul, Wirtz, and Fortmann, *Balance of Power*, pp. 1–28; Robert A. Pape, "Welcome to the Era of 'Soft Balancing,'" *Boston Globe*, March 23, 2003, p. H1; Josef Joffe, "Gulliver Unbound: Can America Rule the World?" Twentieth Annual John Bonython Lecture, Sydney, Australia, August 5, 2003; Christopher Layne, "America as European Hegemon," *National Interest*, No. 72, Summer 2003.

[20] Owen, IV, "Transnational Liberalism and US Primacy," pp. 117–52.

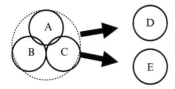

Figure 2.1. Projecting power abroad.

powerful than all others. As a group, however, weaker states are much stronger.

As Figure 2.1 illustrates, states A, B, and C may be better able to project power abroad over other states such as D and E if they aggregate military and economic resources.[21] States want to project power abroad because it increases their security and augments their ability to influence, coerce, and deter others in an anarchic international system.[22] A failure to project power abroad decreases states' ability to provide for their own security. The stronger a state or group of states is in a self-help system, the less likely others are to threaten it or jeopardize its interests.

European states have begun to aggregate resources through the EU to increase power and project it abroad, thus raising their capability of influencing, deterring, and coercing other states. Examples include the increasing use of economic sanctions for foreign policy goals, collaboration in the arms industry, and construction of joint military forces.

First, sanctioning through the EU aggregates power and increases their ability to influence others.[23] The primary aim of sanctions is to

---

[21] Robert Gilpin argues that a primary objective of states is to increase their ability to influence others: "Through the use of threats and coercion, the formation of alliances, and the creation of exclusive spheres of influence, states attempt to create an international political environment and rules of the system that will be conducive to the fulfillment of their political, economic, and ideological interests." Gilpin, *War and Change in World Politics* (New York: Cambridge University Press, 1981), p. 24.

[22] William Curti Wohlforth, *The Elusive Balance: Power and Perceptions during the Cold War* (Ithaca, NY: Cornell University Press, 1993), pp. 12–13.

[23] Richard Haass, "Conclusions: Lessons and Recommendations," in Haass, ed., *Economic Sanctions and American Diplomacy*, pp. 197–212; Thomas O. Bayard, Joseph Pelzman, and Jorge Perez-Lopez, "Stakes and Risks in Economic Sanctions," *The World Economy*, Vol. 6, No. 1, March 1983, pp. 73–87; Jaleh Dashti-Gibson, Patricia Davis, and Benjamin Radcliff, "On the Determinants of the Success of Economic Sanctions: An Empirical Analysis," *American Journal of Political Science*, Vol. 41, No. 2, April 1997, pp. 608–18; Grant W. Gardner and Kent P. Kimbrough, "The Economics of Country-Specific Tariffs," *International Economic Review*, Vol. 31, No. 3, pp. 575–88.

coerce a target government into changing its political behavior by imposing high costs on its economy. Imposing sanctions as a group increases the power of European states, and it augments their ability to punish target countries and improves the effectiveness of sanctions. Adding additional countries to a sanctions regime can limit a target's ability to substitute trade to third countries by decreasing the set of available markets.[24] Consequently, multilateral sanctions can be more effective in inducing economic damage than unilateral sanctions. Individual European countries rarely wield the market power necessary to inflict significant damage through unilateral sanctions.

In addition, a number of sanctions studies have demonstrated that cooperation through international institutions such as the European Union decreases enforcement problems.[25] Trade sanctions generate rents by altering the supply and demand for sanctioned items. This creates an incentive for senders to circumvent sanctions.[26] Sanctions can also generate high political costs on sender states, causing domestic interest groups that are adversely affected to pressure public officials into eliminating or reducing them. Domestic pressure may be so great that policymakers in sender states will be unwilling to bear the costs and opt to defect.[27] Consequently, multilateral sanctions are often difficult to sustain because of enforcement problems. However, sanctioning through institutions can help states overcome enforcement problems by monitoring behavior and doling out side payments to potential defectors. Increased transparency among members allows them to monitor the behavior of sender states better and detect cheating by governments and firms.

Second, aggregating defense resources increases the military and economic power of weaker states. Because of their unrivaled position in the international system, preponderant states tend to feel few restraints. This increases their incentive to assert power around the

---

[24] See, for example, Bayard, Pelzman, and Perez-Lopez, "Stakes and Risks in Economic Sanctions."

[25] Daniel Drezner, "Bargaining, Enforcement, and Multilateral Sanctions: When is Cooperation Counterproductive?" *International Organization*, Vol. 54, No. 1, Winter 2000, pp. 73–102; Lisa Martin, *Coercive Cooperation: Explaining Multilateral Economic Sanctions* (Princeton, NJ: Princeton University Press, 1992). On enforcement problems see also James D. Fearon, "Bargaining, Enforcement, and International Cooperation," *International Organization*, Vol. 52, No. 2, Spring 1998, pp. 269–305.

[26] Bayard, Pelzman, and Perez-Lopez, "Stakes and Risks in Economic Sanctions"; William Kaempfer and Anton Lowenberg, "Unilateral Versus Multilateral International Sanctions: A Public Choice Perspective," *International Studies Quarterly*, Vol. 43, 1999, pp. 37–58.

[27] Edward Mansfield, "International Institutions and Economic Sanctions," *World Politics*, Vol. 47, No. 4, July 1995, pp. 575–605.

globe.[28] Hans Morgenthau argued that "without a state of equilibrium among them, one element will gain ascendancy over the others" and "encroach upon their interests and rights."[29] In the defense industry, a preponderant state's defense firms are likely to have global power and reach in an open international trading system. States will try to expand their arms sales to foreign markets, pursue an arms monopoly, and thereby increase influence over others. These actions create a strong impetus for other states to combine power. In the defense realm, collaboration increases the power and economic competitiveness of weaker states' defense firms.

In a unipolar international system, US military dominance has created a strong impetus for European states to collaborate to increase European economic and defense power. Collaboration increases the global power of European defense firms and allows them to compete more effectively with the United States in terms of arms sales and the spin-offs that defense industries can produce. As John Rose, former chief executive of Rolls-Royce, argued: "Competition for Europe's aerospace industry comes primarily from the US. The US industry is roughly twice the size in terms of employment and turnover . . . The need to strengthen R&D efforts at a European level and to coordinate with national programs is quite simply, essential."[30] Former GEC director Lord Weinstock similarly noted that European companies "have to respond to the changes in America. They are producing giant companies through these mergers. Compared to them BAE and GEC's defence operations are minnows. We have to form companies of sufficient size to compete effectively with them."[31] The cost of not collaborating is straightforward: European states could not compete with the US on the global arms market, and some European defense companies might face extinction.

Third, constructing military joint forces increases the power projection capabilities of European states. The logic is that states are much stronger when they combine military power than when they act unilaterally. Constructing joint military forces merges military resources

---

[28] Robert Jervis, "The Compulsive Empire," *Foreign Policy*, Vol. 137, July/August 2003, pp. 83–7.
[29] Morgenthau, *Politics among Nations*, 169. See also Hans Morgenthau and Kenneth Thompson, eds., *Principles and Problems of International Politics* (New York: Knopf, 1950), 104; Inis L. Claude, *Power and International Relations* (New York: Random House, 1962), 11–39.
[30] John Rose, "New Structure, New Programmes, Bright Future," July 4, 1999, comment on the situation of the aerospace industry at the annual AECMA press conference (www.aecma.org/stats/speech).
[31] Bernard Gray, "Financial Strength is the Issue Not Competition," *Financial Times*, November 4, 1991, 18.

(troops, weapons, and technology) and augments their ability to project power abroad. Combining power also necessitates maximizing efficiency. On the strategic level, militaries have different grand strategies, military doctrines, and force structures. On the operational and tactical level, they may have different command, control, and communications $(C3^3)$ equipment as well as intelligence, surveillance, and reconnaissance (ISR) capacities.[32] Soldiers even speak different languages. Creating multilateral forces with an integrated civilian-military organizational structure can help overcome these problems by forcing participant states to address their differences. Indeed, the process of planning for multilateral operations should force states to coordinate their strategies and doctrines, integrate their forces through training and exercises, and improve the interoperability of their equipment. By establishing a civilian-military organizational structure, militaries also centralize decision-making and increase efficiency.

Europe's major powers created a multilateral EU force and political-military structure to project power abroad. As President Chirac argued in the French journal *Défense nationale*, "the creation of permanent [military] bodies within the European Union will enable it to make decisions and act completely autonomously, whether or not it uses NATO assets, to prevent or manage crises affecting its security."[33] Indeed, European participation in Bosnia, Kosovo, and Afghanistan highlighted the distance between the United States and Europe with regard to medium and high-end expeditionary military forces.[34] EU leaders believed that a failure to coordinate military forces would severely hamper their ability to project power and respond quickly to regional crises. EU external relations commissioner Christopher Patten argued, "Too often in the past, take the Balkans for example, we have just not been able to respond with the efficiency or timeliness that developments in the real world demand."[35]

---

[32] Myron Hura *et al.*, *Interoperability: A Continuing Challenge in Coalition Air Operations*, MR-1235-AR (Santa Monica, CA: RAND, 2002); Thomas S. Szayna *et al.*, *Improving Army Planning for Future Multinational Coalition Operations*, MR-1291-A (Santa Monica, CA: RAND, 2001); Wesley K. Clark, *Waging Modern War: Bosnia, Kosovo, and the Future of Combat* (New York: Public Affairs, 2001); Michele Zanini and Jennifer Morrison Taw, *The Army and Multinational Force Compatibility*, MR-1154-A (Santa Monica, CA: RAND, 2000).

[33] Chirac, "Politique de défense et de sécurité," p. 10.

[34] Frédéric Bozo, "The Effects of Kosovo and the Danger of De-coupling," in Jolyon Howorth and John T. S. Keeler, eds., *Defending Europe: The EU, NATO and the Quest for European Autonomy* (New York: Palgrave Macmillan, 2003), pp. 61–80.

[35] Christopher Patten, "Remarks in the European Parliament," January 17, 2001. Available at (europa.eu.int/comm/external_relations/news/patten/rrf_17_01_01.htm).

Increasing autonomy

Weaker states may also aggregate power in a unipolar system to decrease the likelihood that the dominant power will impose its will on them in areas of strategic importance. This logic is different from the desire to project power abroad, though it is complementary in encouraging European states to cooperate. A preponderant power will invariably elicit concern among others, no matter how benign it may try to be. As Robert Jervis argues: "A hegemon tends to acquire an enormous stake in world order. As power expands, so does a state's definition of its own interests. Most countries are concerned with what happens in their immediate neighborhoods; but for a hegemon, the world is its neighborhood."[36] This inevitably brings it into conflict with the interests and values of others as it becomes increasingly assertive around the globe.

In some cases, the rationale for combining power may involve a fear of territorial conquest by the dominant power. The United States does not present this threat to Europe. In other cases, weaker states may simply want to decrease their dependence on a dominant power. Hans Morgenthau and Kenneth Thompson note that the combination of power "is a universal instrument of foreign policy used at all times by all nations who wanted to preserve their independence in their relations with other nations."[37] As Figure 2.2 illustrates, the logic is that combining power decreases the likelihood that the dominant state will gain ascendancy over weaker states and impose its will on them. In a unipolar international system, States A, B, and C will have a strong incentive to aggregate power to protect themselves from State F, the dominant power. The threat from F may not be a military one. Rather, it may simply be able to influence the policies of smaller states and constrain

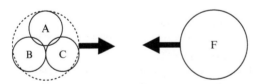

Figure 2.2. Decreasing reliance on a dominant state.

[36] Jervis, "The Compulsive Empire," p. 84.
[37] Morgenthau and Thompson, eds., *Principles and Problems of International Politics*, p. 104.

their ability to make independent decisions in the security realm.[38] For example, the 1823 Monroe Doctrine asserted an American sphere of influence over Latin America, and subsequent US administrations have attempted to prohibit countries within the Western Hemisphere from entering into major strategic relationships with outside powers. If weaker states do not acquire greater power, they may be exploited by the dominant power.[39]

European states have begun to aggregate resources through the EU in part to decrease reliance on the US. First, sanctioning as a bloc increases the power of individual European states and decreases their reliance on the United States. During the Cold War, European states relied on the United States and its economic power when they imposed sanctions for foreign policy goals. The United States was a partner in every case in which a European state participated in multilateral sanctions, except for one: against Turkey in 1981. In the aftermath of the Cold War, however, European security interests increasingly diverged from American interests. This shift increased the impetus to sanction through the European Union and decrease reliance on the United States. Examples include EU sanctions against Austria in 2000, Zimbabwe in 2002, and Uzbekistan in 2005.

Second, European weapons collaboration is preferable because it increases European autonomy and decreases reliance on the United States defense industry.[40] The risk for European states is that a failure to aggregate power may create a reliance on America for defense resources and lead to foreign dependence. Dependence on the US defense industry decreases European security of supply, compromises the viability of European states' defense industrial base, and limits the global competitiveness of its defense firms. Reliance on a preponderant power for weapons and military supplies decreases a state's security by placing

---

[38] See Lake's continuum of security relationships in David A. Lake, *Entangling Relations: American Foreign Policy in Its Century* (Princeton, NJ: Princeton University Press, 1999), pp. 17–34.
[39] Layne, "The Unipolar Illusion," p. 12.
[40] John Deutch, Arnold Kanter, and Brent Scowcroft, "Saving NATO's Foundation," *Foreign Affairs*, Vol. 78, No. 6, November/December 1999, p. 56; Terrence R. Guay, *At Arm's Length: The European Union and Europe's Defence Industry* (New York: St. Martin's Press, 1998), pp. 82–100; Jane Davis Drown, "European Views on Arms Cooperation," in Jane Davis Drown, Clifford Drown, and Kelly Campbell, eds., *A Single European Arms Industry? European Defence Industries in the 1990s* (London: Brassey's 1990), pp. 30–2, 36–40; Burkard Schmitt, *From Cooperation to Integration: Defence and Aerospace Industries in Europe*, Chaillot Paper 40 (Paris: Institute for Security Studies, 2000), pp. 23–8; Jean-Paul Hébert and Laurence Nardon "Concentration des industries d'armement américaines, modèle ou menace?" *Cahier d'études stratégiques*, No. 23 (Paris: CIRPES, 1999), pp. 9–36.

its supply in the hands of someone else. This may be fine under most conditions. But can dependent states always rely on the preponderant power for spare parts and regular access? As a European Commission report concluded, "there is a danger that European industry could be reduced to the status of sub-supplier to prime US contractors, while the key know-how is reserved for US firms."[41] French President Jacques Chirac warned that if Europe fails to aggregate defense resources it risks "vassal status" to a preponderant US.[42]

Third, building an EU rapid reaction military capability increases autonomy and decreases dependence on the US. As Henry Kissinger notes, the "distinctive feature of the European Union military force . . . is to create a capacity to act outside the NATO framework."[43] In general terms, aggregating power by building multilateral forces decreases reliance on the dominant state. In a unipolar international system the dominant power, which possesses superior military capabilities, will use military force to pursue its own interests. As Kenneth Waltz argues, this may conflict with the interests of others. "The powerful state may . . . think of itself as acting for the sake of peace, justice, and well-being in the world. These terms, however, are defined to the liking of the powerful, which may conflict with the preferences and interests of others."[44] While weaker states may not be physically threatened by the dominant state, they may wish for more autonomy. The risk for them is that a failure to aggregate military forces increases the likelihood that they will be dependent on the preponderant power for power projection capabilities. These resources might include aerial refueling, airlift and sealift capabilities for troop transport, and precision-guided munitions, which they might have to rely on others to supply.

In sum, security cooperation has occurred in Europe in the post-Cold War era largely because of structural changes in the international system. The current unipolar system has provided a significant impetus for European states to aggregate resources. Security cooperation through the European Union decreases the US's ability to impose its will on European states. While Europe and America were once inextricably

[41] Commission of the European Communities, *Towards an EU Defence Equipment Policy*, COM 113 Final (Brussels: Commission of the EC, March 2003), p. 11.
[42] Martin Fletcher, "Europe's Galileo Navigation System puts US on the Spot," *The Times*, March 26, 2002. On the US and the European defense industry, see also Alain Richard, "European Defense," Speech at the Symposium of the Association Diplomatie et Défense, April 18, 2001, Washington: Embassy of France in the United States, 2001.
[43] Henry Kissinger, *Does America Need a Foreign Policy? Toward a Diplomacy for the 21st Century* (New York: Simon and Schuster, 2001), p. 34.
[44] Kenneth N. Waltz, "Structural Realism after the Cold War," in Ikenberry, ed., *America Unrivaled*, p. 53.

bound together because they shared a common Soviet threat, this bond no longer exists. European states have increasingly pushed for cooperation with each other. As the European Union's *European Security Strategy* noted:

The end of the Cold War has left the United States in a dominant position as a military actor . . . As a union of 25 states with over 450 million people producing a quarter of the world's Gross National Product (GNP), and with a wide range of instruments at its disposal, the European Union is inevitably a global player. In the last decade European forces have been deployed abroad to places as distant as Afghanistan, East Timor and the [Democratic Republic of Congo]. The increasing convergence of European interests and the strengthening of mutual solidarity of the EU makes us a more credible and effective actor.[45]

This leads to several testable propositions. First, in the post-Cold War era, European states should increasingly impose sanctions through the EU rather than unilaterally or through other forums. This should contrast with the Cold War, when structural conditions provided little impetus to sanction through the European Community. Second, there should be a rise in the percentage of intra-European defense mergers and acquisitions, coproduction projects, and codevelopment projects in the post-Cold War era. This should differ from the Cold War, when weapons collaboration should be largely transatlantic. Third, there should be an increase in military cooperation through the EU in the post-Cold War era, including such aspects as military forces and a political-military organizational structure. This should be different from the Cold War, when most military cooperation should be transatlantic. In all of these cases, aggregating power should be causally linked with the systemic distribution of power. That is, states would not take these actions if the United States were not so powerful.

Europe and the regional system

The changing structure of the regional system in Europe also triggered an increase in security cooperation through the EU. At the end of the Cold War, there were several concerns about the long-term stability of Europe. Germany reunified, the Soviet Union collapsed, and the United States began to withdraw forces from the continent. Specifically, would a powerful and reunited Germany with a revanchist past flex its muscles? To be clear, these concerns about Germany existed primarily in the late

---

[45] Council of the European Union, *A Secure Europe in a Better World: European Security Strategy* (Brussels: European Council, December 2003), p. 1.

1980s and early 1990s, but they had an important impact on European decision-making in its formative years.

Potential hegemons – states that have the potential to be substantially more powerful than their neighbors – induce concern among nearby states because of their power. As German leaders argued before World War I, the growth of Russia presented a challenge to Germany. Referring to a May 1914 meeting with Army Chief of the General Staff Helmut von Moltke, Foreign Secretary Gottlieb von Jagow noted:

The prospects for the future weighed heavily upon him. In two to three years Russia would have finished arming. Our enemies' military power would then be so great that he did not know how he could deal with it. Now we were still more or less of a match for it. In his view there was no alternative but to fight a preventive war so as to beat the enemy while we could still emerge fairly well from the struggle. The Chief of Staff therefore put it to me that our policy should be geared to bringing about an early war.[46]

Wars involving potential hegemons are likely to be destructive. The three most devastating wars in Europe between 1792 and the present – the Napoleonic wars, World War I, and World War II – occurred in multipolar systems with potential hegemons. Indeed, the existence of a potential hegemon is likely to trigger a security dilemma because other states fear it. A security dilemma arises when the efforts a state makes to increase its own security decrease the security of others.[47] Structural changes in Europe at the end of the Cold War created significant concerns among European states about German power. The reunification of Germany, the collapse of the Soviet Union, and the withdrawal of over 70 percent of United States forces caused deep concern among European states. Germany had the economic resources and population to develop a powerful military, and it had a history of hegemonic ambition. British Prime Minister Margaret Thatcher argued that it was important to move "faster towards a federal Europe in order to tie down the German

[46] Quoted in Fritz Fischer, *War of Illusions: German Policies from 1911 to 1914* (New York: Norton, 1975), p. 402.
[47] The security dilemma literature is quite large. Some of the basic works include John Herz, "Idealist Internationalism and the Security Dilemma," *World Politics*, Vol. 2, No. 2, January 1950, pp. 157–80; Robert Jervis, "Cooperation under the Security Dilemma", *World Politics*, Vol. 30, No. 2, January 1978; Charles L.Glaser, "Realists as Optimists: Cooperation as Self-Help," *International Security*, Vol. 19, No. 3, Winter 1994/95, pp. 50–90; Randall L. Schweller, "Neorealism's Status-Quo Bias: What Security Dilemma?" *Security Studies*, Vol. 5, No. 3, Spring 1996, pp. 90–121; Andrew Kydd, "Sheep in Sheep's Clothing: Why Security Seekers Do Not Fight Each Other," *Security Studies*, Vol. 7, No. 1, Autumn 1997, pp. 114–55; Glaser, "The Security Dilemma Revisited," *World Politics*, Vol. 50, No. 1, October 1997, pp. 171–201.

giant."[48] And former French President Valéry Giscard d'Estaing
likewise noted that "we need an organized Europe to escape German
domination."[49]

European states had several options. First, they could have pursued a
buckpassing strategy.[50] They could have refused multilateral cooperation,
pursued independent foreign and defense policies, and opted to "free
ride" on the efforts of other states. The major problem with this strategy
was obvious: it would not have diminished the possibility of a destabilizing security dilemma and the likelihood of war because it would not
have contained German power.[51] European states had already learned
this lesson in the 1930s, when both France and the Soviet Union tried to
pass the buck to each other in the face of the Nazi threat. A second
possibility was *balancing* against Germany. However, states generally
balance when they are faced with a serious military threat. Germany in
1990 did not present a current threat, but a future one. It had a small
military and no nuclear weapons. Third, European states could have
pursued a strategy of *bandwagoning*. Much like buckpassing strategies,
bandwagoning strategies would have failed to check the power of a rising
Germany.

A fourth strategy was to pursue a *binding* strategy.[52] In general, the
fear of future conflict may create a strong impetus for multilateral
cooperation because the cost of security competition can become exorbi-
tantly high for states. Robert Jervis wrote, "What they would lose if the
system broke down into mutual defection and competition is very great
because such a configuration could lead to the renewed threat from the
potential hegemon, or to a very costly war."[53] A binding strategy has
been pursued on a number of occasions. For example, Western European states created NATO for two purposes, what has often been called
"dual containment": to balance against the Soviet Union, and to keep
the Germans down by incorporating them into a security arrangement.[54]

[48] Margaret Thatcher, *The Downing Street Years* (New York: HarperCollins, 1993), p.798.
[49] Quoted in David Marsh, "Final March of the Old Guard," *Financial Times*, April 25, 1994, p. 17.
[50] Barry R. Posen, *Sources of Military Doctrine: France, Britain, and Germany between the World Wars* (Ithaca, NY: Cornell University Press, 1984), pp. 232–3; Christensen and Snyder, "Chain Gangs and Passed Bucks," pp. 137–68.
[51] Jervis, *Perception and Misperception in International Politics* (Princeton, NJ: Princeton University Press, 1976), pp. 84–90.
[52] Schweller, *Deadly Imbalances*, pp. 70–1. See also Schroeder, "Alliances, 1815–1945," pp. 227–62.
[53] Robert Jervis, "From Balance to Concert: A Study of International Security Cooper-ation," *World Politics*, Vol. 38, No. 1, October 1985, p. 78.
[54] On dual containment see G. John Ikenberry, *After Victory: Institutions, Strategic Restraint, and the Rebuilding of Order after Major Wars* (Princeton, NJ: Princeton University Press,

Similarly, one of the primary reasons for bringing Germany into the European Coal and Steel Community (ECSC) was to help bind it and prevent future German hegemony. Prussia, Britain, Austria, and Russia brought France into the Concert of Europe in 1818 to prevent future French aggression.[55] The major problem with this strategy is that it hinges on the potential hegemon's ability to understand the security dilemma and its willingness to ameliorate it. A binding strategy may seem counterintuitive since international systems with severe security dilemmas are highly unstable and often lead to intense competition and war. What incentives might the potential hegemon, let alone other great powers, have to coordinate foreign and defense policies? Moreover, in the face of acute security concerns, how can states be sure that the potential hegemon's intentions are benign?

Potential hegemons have not tended to prefer widespread security cooperation through an international institution. In some cases they simply fail to recognize the existence of a security dilemma. Prior to World War I, for instance, German and Russian militaries adopted a "cult of the offensive" that glorified offensive military strategies and clouded the ability of leaders to recognize the existence of a security dilemma.[56] In other cases, potential hegemons have wanted more than just security; they have also desired to expand their power through conquest.[57] Under what conditions, then, might a potential hegemon be willing to cooperate?

First, it must be a status quo power. That is, it must rule out territorial expansion as a means to achieve such goals as security, power, or wealth.[58] It should desire to preserve the resources it already has and to maintain the status quo, rather than increase its resources at the expense of others. Germany was a status quo power. Randall Schweller

---

2001), pp. 205–10; Thomas A. Schwartz, *America's Germany: John J. McCloy and the Federal Republic of Germany* (Cambridge, MA: Harvard University Press, 1991).

[55] Norman Rich, *Great Power Diplomacy, 1814–1914* (Boston, MA: McGraw-Hill, 1992). Also see Paul W. Schroeder, *The Transformation of European Politics, 1763–1848* (New York: Oxford University Press, 1994), pp. 583–636.

[56] Jervis, *Perception and Misperception in International Politics*, p. 94. On the "cult of the offensive" see also Stephen Van Evera, "The Cult of the Offensive and the Origins of the First World War," *International Security*, Vol. 9, No. 1, Summer 1984, pp. 58–108; Van Evera, *Causes of War: Power and the Roots of Conflict* (Ithaca, NY: Cornell University Press, 1999), pp. 117–239.

[57] Peter Liberman, *Does Conquest Pay? The Exploitation of Occupied Industrial Societies* (Princeton, NJ: Princeton University Press, 1996). See also Halford J. Mackinder, "The Geographical Pivot of History," *Geographic Journal*, Vol. 23, No. 4, April 1904, pp. 421–44.

[58] On the distinction between expansionist and status quo powers, see Glaser, "Realists as Optimists"; Schweller, *Deadly Imbalances*, especially pp. 15–38.

and David Priess argue that "status quo states do not require expansion for their security (if they did, they would not be satisfied with the status quo) and, for them, the benefits of peace far outweigh the costs of not engaging in expansion. If each is confident that all the others feel the same way, institutionalized cooperation . . . may develop."[59] German leaders pushed for security cooperation through the European Union because they were interested in the status quo. Indeed, one of the first steps German leaders took as a result of reunification was to agree in 1990 to several important security limitations as part of the 2+4 settlement on German reunification, Conventional Forces in Europe (CFE) agreement, and German–Polish treaty. Germany agreed to reduce its armed forces; renounce nuclear, chemical, and biological weapons; and recognize the Oder-Neisse border with Poland.

Second, an external event such as a recent war may cause the potential hegemon to "learn" from past experience. By learning I do not mean what some have called "social learning": the identities and interests of states are learned and reinforced through interaction with others.[60] Used in this sense, learning is a process that leads to a change in the identity of actors. Rather, I use learning in a less ambitious way: new information causes a change in the beliefs of state leaders, which in turn leads to a change in behavior. Scholars in American politics have utilized learning models to explain such phenomena as partisan attitudes among voters.[61] Through a process of Bayesian updating, voters utilize information they gather about political parties to update their prior beliefs and form judgments about the ability of the parties to deliver benefits.[62] Consequently, learning refers to the process in which actors update beliefs through the accumulation of new information. In international politics, policymakers may also learn from historical experiences and alter behavior.[63] Examples abound. The "lessons of Munich" have influenced

---

[59] Randall L. Schweller and David Priess, "A Tale of Two Realisms: Expanding the Institutions Debate," *Mershon International Studies Review*, Vol. 41, 1997, p. 22.

[60] Alexander Wendt, *Social Theory of International Politics* (New York: Cambridge University Press, 1999), pp. 326–36.

[61] Christopher Achen, "Social Psychology, Demographic Variables, and Linear Regression: Breaking the Iron Triangle in Voting Research," *Political Behavior*, Vol. 14, pp. 195–211; Alan Gerber and Donald P. Green, "Rational Learning and Partisan Attitudes," *American Journal of Political Science*, Vol. 42, No. 3, July 1998, pp. 794–818.

[62] Bayes's theorem determines the probability of a state of the world being true by calculating the probability that the event and the state will occur, and dividing it by the probability that the event will occur regardless of the state. See, for example, James D. Morrow, *Game Theory for Political Scientists* (Princeton, NJ: Princeton University Press, 1994), pp. 161–87.

[63] For a good summary of learning and international relations see Jack Levy, "Learning and Foreign Policy: Sweeping a Conceptual Minefield," *International Organization*,

numerous leaders ranging from Anthony Eden during the 1956 Suez crisis to Madeleine Albright during the 1990s war in Bosnia. The "lessons of Vietnam" and the "lessons of Somalia" have affected the actions of American policymakers. So may the "lessons of Iraq" following the 2003 overthrow of Saddam Hussein and the subsequent counterinsurgency.

German leaders ultimately learned from history. Policymakers such as Foreign Minister Hans-Dietrich Genscher recognized that other European capitals, especially Paris and London, were concerned about Germany's growing power because of the specter of Adolf Hitler and Germany's past behavior. Consequently, German leaders made a strong push to establish and deepen a security arm of the European Union. Acting through the EU was important because it signaled that German leaders had benign intentions. While it is conceivable that German leaders could have successfully signaled that it had benign intentions and still remained unilateral, acting through the EU enhanced Germany's ability to show that it had benign intentions.[64] Beginning in early 1990, for example, Kohl and Mitterrand strongly pushed for the creation of a security arm of the EU as an important tool to preserve peace in Europe. Both the Germans and the French advocated moving away from NATO as the sole European security institution, reviving the defunct Western European Union (WEU), and eventually incorporating it into the EU by the late 1990s. Kohl and Mitterrand explicitly stated in a draft text to Dutch Prime Minister Ruud Lubbers in October 1991 that the WEU should be a "component" of the European Union.[65]

In sum, Germany was a status quo power at the end of the Cold War, and German, French, and British leaders learned from history. Security cooperation offered an opportunity to ensure peace on the continent, bind Germany into Europe, and learn from the continent's troubled history. This leads to a testable proposition. In the post-Cold War era, European states should increasingly build and develop a European

Vol. 48, No. 2, Spring 1994, pp. 279–312. See also Dan Reiter, "Learning, Realism, and Alliances: The Weight of the Shadow of the Past," *World Politics*, Vol. 46, No. 4, July 1994, pp. 490–526; Robert Jervis, *Perception and Misperception in International Politics*; Jack Snyder, *Myths of Empire: Domestic Politics and International Ambition* (Ithaca, NY: Cornell University Press, 1991).

[64] On signaling see also A.M. Spence, "Job Market Signaling," *Quarterly Journal of Economics*, Vol. 87, No. 3, August 1973, pp. 355–74; James D. Fearon, "Domestic Political Audiences and the Escalation of International Disputes," *American Political Science Review*, Vol. 88, No. 3, September 1994, pp. 577–92; Kydd, "Sheep in Sheep's Clothing," pp. 114–54; Glaser, "Realists as Optimists," pp. 50–90; Fearon, "Signaling Foreign Policy Interests: Tying Hands versus Sinking Costs," *Journal of Conflict Resolution*, Vol. 41, No. 1, February 1997, p. 69.

[65] Richard Corbett, *Treaty of Maastricht: From Conception to Ratification: A Comprehensive Reference Guide* (Harlow: Longman Group, 1993), p. 344.

security institution because of structural conditions: the collapse of the USSR, the withdrawal of US military forces, and the reunification of Germany. This should contrast with the Cold War, when structural conditions provided little impetus for intra-European security cooperation.

Alternative arguments

There are a number of alternative arguments to the one outlined here. Indeed, since the creation of the European Coal and Steel Community (ECSC) in 1951, scholars have struggled to understand and explain the process of European cooperation.[66] Early work by functionalists and neofunctionalists attempted to explain the dependent variable of economic integration, and thus focused on the transactions of economic actors and the supranational capacity needed to regulate these actions.[67] As first posited by such individuals as David Mitrany, functionalism explained integration through a series of "spillovers."[68] When sovereign states engage in specific and deliberate joint activities such as monetary or industrial policy, common cooperation spills over into related areas.[69] However, functional arguments were highly underspecified, particularly regarding the process of spillover.

---

[66] For a concise historical overview of European integration arguments see Ben Rosamond, *Theories of European Integration* (New York: St. Martin's Press, 2000).

[67] On functionalism see the works of David Mitrany, such as *A Working Peace System* (Chicago: Quadrangle Books, 1966); *The Functional Theory of Politics* (New York: St. Martin's Press, 1975). Prominent neofunctionalist works include Ernst B. Haas, *The Uniting of Europe: Political, Social, and Economic Forces, 1950–1957* (Stanford, CA: Stanford University Press, 1958); Leon N. Lindberg and Stuart A. Scheingold, *Regional Integration: Theory and Research* (Cambridge, MA: Harvard University Press, 1971); Leon Lindberg, *The Political Dynamics of European Economic Integration* (Stanford: Stanford University Press, 1963); J.S. Nye, *Peace in Parts: Integration and Conflict in Regional Organization* (Boston: Little, Brown, and Company, 1971); Philippe Schmitter, "Three Neo-Functional Hypotheses about International Integration," *International Organization*, Vol. 23, No. 1, Winter 1969, pp. 161–6.

[68] As Mitrany writes: "The more fields of activity [the group] actively enters, e.g. agriculture, the more acquisitive it tends to become; and in the degree to which it is rounded out it also hardens into a segregated unity." Mitrany, *A Working Peace System*, p. 209. Mitrany argued that the post-World War II world was increasingly becoming one indivisible community and that functionalism would not lead just to regional integration, but to an organized world society. Also see Mitrany, *The Functional Theory of Politics*.

[69] Like many international relations theories, the impetus for functionalism came from a desire to explain an empirical event – in this case, the creation of the European Coal and Steel Community by France, West Germany, Italy, Belgium, the Netherlands, and Luxembourg in 1951. All customs, tariffs, and quotas in the coal and steel industries – as well as artificial distortions of competition (such as cartels) – were forbidden, and key economic policy decisions were transferred from member states to the Community. See,

In order to put more flesh on the causal logic of functionalist arguments, "neofunctionalists" attempted to make the theory more rigorous. Neofunctionalism began from the premise that the key actors were not policymakers but "the economic technician, the planner, the innovating industrialist, and trade unionist."[70] These actors provided the crucial impetus for the coordination of economic policies in strategic economic sectors such as coal and steel. In order to facilitate cooperation, a supranational high authority was necessary to oversee the integration process.[71] The integration of specific economic sectors and the role of the high authority created functional pressures to coordinate policies in related areas. A number of mechanisms affected the possibility of spillover: the linkage of related tasks, the level of transactions among states, and the degree of socialization among political decision-makers.[72] Finally, neofunctionalists believed that political loyalties would gradually shift away from the nation-state and toward the supranational institution, as economic integration and institutionalization deepened.

However, there were at least two major problems with neofunctionalism. First, neofunctionalist arguments were teleological. They were unable to explain variation in the dependent variable and answer such questions as: under what conditions would spillover occur, and under what conditions would it stall? The logic of the theory *ipso facto* assumed that integration would gradually expand. As Ernst Haas conceded in *The Obsolescence of Regional Integration Theory*, neofunctionalist models were unable to explain change in the level of integration.[73] This critique was particularly apropos in the 1960s, when French President Charles de Gaulle rejected certain aspects of European integration because it

for example, Walter Hallstein, *Europe in the Making* (London: George Allen & Unwin, 1972).

[70] Haas, *The Uniting of Europe*, p. xix.

[71] On critiques of neofunctionalism see Andrew Moravcsik, "The European Constitutional Compromise and the Neofunctionalist Legacy," *Journal of European Public Policy*, Vol. 12, No. 12, April 2005, pp. 349–86; Walter Mattli, "Ernst Haas's Evolving Thinking on Comparative Regional Integration: Of Virtues and Infelicities," *Journal of European Public Policy*, Vol. 12, No. 12, April 2005, pp. 327–48; Rosamond, *Theories of European Integration*, pp. 50–73; Mattli, *The Logic of Regional Integration* (New York: Cambridge University Press, 1999), pp. 23–8.

[72] J.S. Nye, "Comparing Common Markets: A Revised Neo-Functionalist Model," *International Organization*, Vol. 24, No. 4, Autumn 1970, pp. 796–835; Philippe Schmitter, "Three Neo-Functional Hypotheses about International Integration," *International Organization*, Vol. 23, No. 1, Winter 1969, pp. 161–6.

[73] Ernst B. Haas, *The Obsolescence of Regional Integration Theory* (Berkeley, CA: Institute of International Studies, 1975). Haas's book should not be read, however, as a complete rejection of neofunctionalism. Rather, he argued that while there were problems with the argument, some of the theory's core concepts nonetheless possessed considerable explanatory power.

conflicted with French national interests. Second, neofunctionalism focused on the dependent variable of economic integration. As neofunctionalists admitted, the theory had little to say about the security realm. Haas, for instance, recognized that security cooperation was a substantially different animal. Functionalist arguments and their focus on economic actors were of little help in understanding cases of security cooperation such as NATO because of the importance of security concerns.

Where does this leave us? The rest of this section considers four alternative arguments. The first contends that security cooperation is largely illusory. The other three offer competing explanations for European security cooperation: pressure from domestic actors; international institutions; and the construction of a European identity.

The illusion of security cooperation

European security cooperation is unlikely to occur because of nationalism and balance-of-power politics, and the withdrawal of American forces will lead to security competition

A prominent alternative argues that there has not been – nor will likely be – meaningful European security cooperation. European states may cooperate from time to time, as they did during the Cold War.[74] But they rarely agree on major foreign policy issues, and are unwilling to cooperate in such "high politics" areas as weapons production and military forces. Cooperation is unlikely for at least two reasons.

The first is that nationalism and balance-of-power politics makes significant cooperation unlikely. Leaders and their constituents will be unwilling to give up sovereignty over security issues. Stanley Hoffman, for example, argued that "in areas of key importance to the national interest, nations prefer the certainty, or the self-controlled uncertainty,

---

[74] Such skeptical arguments are particularly prevalent in the United States. See, for example, Mearsheimer, *The Tragedy of Great Power Politics*, pp. 360–402; Mearsheimer, "Back to the Future: Instability in Europe after the Cold War," *International Security*, Vol. 15, No. 1, Summer 1990, pp. 5–56; Philip Gordon, "Europe's Uncommon Foreign Policy," *International Security*, Vol. 22, No. 3, Winter 1997/98, pp. 74–100; Robert J. Art, "Why Western Europe Needs the United States and NATO," *Political Science Quarterly*, Vol. 111, No. 1, Spring 1996, pp. 1–39; Carsten Tams, "The Functions of a European Security and Defence Identity and its Institutional Form," in Helga Haftendorn, Robert O. Keohane, and Celeste Wallander, eds., *Imperfect Unions: Security Institutions over Time and Space* (New York: Oxford University Press, 1999), pp. 80–103; Zbigniew Brzezinski, "Living with a New Europe," *The National Interest*, No. 60, Summer 2000, pp. 17–29; Stanley Hoffmann, "Obstinate or Obsolete? The Fate of the Nation-State and the Case of Western Europe," in Joseph S. Nye, ed., *International Regionalism: Readings* (Boston: Little, Brown and Company, 1968), pp. 177–230.

of national self-reliance, to the uncontrolled uncertainty of the untested blender . . . Russian roulette is fine only as long as the gun is filled with blanks."[75] The logic is that nationalism will inhibit substantial cooperation in Europe because the two are inherently conflictual. Populations and leaders will stymie efforts to pursue sustained foreign policy and defense cooperation because it would force them to sacrifice national interests. The de Gaulle era in France is perhaps the clearest historical instance in which nationalism trumped efforts to pursue greater regional cooperation. In addition, this argument interprets the French and Dutch vetoes of the EU Constitution as an example of the triumph of nationalism. As Paul Révay, European director of the Trilateral Commission, noted: "Today's politicians have lost all sense of idealism regarding the European integration project and – after a decade of raging intergovernmentalism – are driven essentially by naked nationalism."[76]

The second reason is that peace and cooperation in Europe today are wholly a function of the "American pacifier." The complete withdrawal of American forces from the continent would trigger security competition among European states and a return to balance-of-power politics. For instance, Robert Art contends that "if the Americans removed their security blanket from Europe . . . the Western European states could well return to the destructive power politics that they had just spent the last forty-five years trying to banish from their part of the continent."[77] The logic is that since states continue to operate in an international system that is anarchic, they will be unwilling to pursue sustained security cooperation because of fears of cheating and concerns about relative gains.[78] The presence of American forces since World War II removed the structural cause of conflict and ameliorated the condition of anarchy in Europe. As Alain Crémieux's novel *Quand les "Ricains" repartiront* suggests, an American withdrawal would remove the security guarantee and lead to severe competition among European states.[79]

This leads to several testable propositions. First, there should be little or no meaningful security cooperation through the European Union.

---

[75] Hoffmann, "Obstinate or Obsolete?" p. 199.
[76] Paul Révay, *After the "No's": Getting Europe Back on Track* (Brussels: Friends of Europe, 2005), p. 52.
[77] Art, "Why Western Europe Needs the United States and NATO," pp. 5–6.
[78] Grieco, "Anarchy and the Limits of Cooperation," pp. 485–507; John J. Mearsheimer, "The False Promise of International Institutions," *International Security*, Vol. 19, No. 3, Winter 1994/95.
[79] Alain Crémieux, *Quand les "Ricains" repartiront: Le journal imaginaire du nouveau millénaire* (Boofzheim, France: ACM, 2000). On a discussion of the book, see David S. Yost, "Transatlantic Relations and Peace in Europe," *International Affairs*, Vol. 78, No. 2, April 2002, pp. 277–300.

There should not be an increase in cooperation in such areas as military forces, arms production, or sanctions for foreign policy goals among EU states. Second, the lack of security cooperation should be caused by nationalist sentiments and a refusal to give up sovereignty in the foreign policy and defense realm, as well as by balance-of-power considerations among European states. Third, the withdrawal of United States forces and the rise of Germany should trigger an increase in security competition among European states. As Mearsheimer argues, "on close inspection the evidence shows that security competition and the threat of great-power war remain facts of life in Europe."[80]

Liberalism and domestic politics

European security cooperation is caused by pressure from domestic and transnational actors on state preferences

The next alternative is that European states have pursued cooperation in response to pressure from a variety of domestic coalitions and social actors. This argument is best laid out by Andrew Moravcsik in his book *Choice for Europe*.[81] The logic is that states' strategic preferences for cooperation come largely from the efforts of powerful domestic and transnational interest groups, who influence government policies to further their economic interests. Decisions are ultimately made through a series of European-level intergovernmental bargains. This argument has its roots in broader liberal theories of international politics.[82] There are at least three core assumptions of liberal theories. First, the fundamental actors are rational individuals and domestic groups who organize

---

[80] Mearsheimer, *Tragedy of Great Power Politics*, pp. 377–8.
[81] Andrew Moravcsik, *The Choice for Europe: Social Purpose and State Power from Messina to Maastricht* (Ithaca, NY: Cornell University Press, 1998). Also see Moravcsik, "De Gaulle between Grain and Grandeur: The Political Economy of French EC Policy, 1958–1970 (Parts I and II)," *Journal of Cold War Studies*, Spring and Fall 2000. While Moravcsik has not been optimistic about the prospects for European security cooperation, the logic of his argument is still relevant. See Moravcsik, "How Europe Can Win without an Army," *Financial Times*, April 3, 2003, p. 19.
[82] On liberal theory see Moravcsik, "Liberal International Relations Theory: A Scientific Assessment," in Colin Elman and Miriam Fendius Elman, eds., *Progress in International Relations Theory* (Cambridge, MA: MIT Press, 2003); Moravcsik, "Taking Preferences Seriously: A Liberal Theory of International Politics," *International Organization*, Vol. 51, No. 4, Autumn 1997, pp. 513–53; John M. Owen, IV, *Liberal Peace, Liberal War: American Politics and International Security* (Ithaca, NY: Cornell University Press, 1997), ch. 1; Michael W. Doyle, *Ways of War and Peace: Realism, Liberalism, and Socialism* (New York: W.W. Norton, 1997); Lisa L. Martin, *Democratic Commitments: Legislatures and International Cooperation* (Princeton, NJ: Princeton University Press, 2000).

and lobby to promote their interests. Second, states are representative institutions that are subject to influence and capture by domestic coalitions and social actors. The state is not a single rational actor but a "conglomerate of coalitions and interests, representing individuals and groups."[83] State policy is formulated by the preferences and social power of individuals and groups in civil society that enter the political realm. As John Owen argues: "If elites of one ideology control foreign policy, the state will follow one set of strategic preferences; if no ideology dominates, the state's policy will be incoherent."[84] Variation in the nature of political institutions helps define which groups influence the national interest. Third, the configuration of state preferences shapes state behavior in the international system. Liberals view the distribution of preferences – rather than capabilities (realism) or ideas (constructivism) – as the systemic characteristic that shapes state strategies.

Turning to Europe, the liberal argument is that European security cooperation is largely a function of pressure from powerful domestic and societal groups in an interdependent global economy. In such areas as the production of weapons, economic sanctions, and the creation of joint military forces, European cooperation is a response to pressure from domestic groups. For example, cooperation in the European weapons industry is largely a function of pressure from domestic arms firms who are motivated to maximize their private economic gains.[85] Moravcsik argues that in defense collaboration "the decisive variable explaining which negotiations succeed and which fail is the global market position of domestic arms-producing firms."[86] This argument assumes that collaboration is a function of pressure from domestic arms firms on state preferences.

---

[83] Doyle, *Ways of War and Peace*, p. 19.

[84] Owen, IV, "Transnational Liberalism and US Primacy," p. 122.

[85] Andrew Moravcsik, "Arms and Autarky in Modern European History," *Daedalus*, Vol. 120, No. 4, Fall 1991, pp. 23–45; Moravcsik, "Armaments among Allies: European Weapons Collaboration, 1975–1985," in Peter B. Evans, Harold K. Jacobson, and Robert D. Putnam, *Double-Edged Diplomacy: International Bargaining and Domestic Politics* (Berkeley: University of California Press, 1993), pp. 128–67; Moravcsik, "The European Armaments Industry at the Crossroads," *Survival*, Vol. 32, No. 1, January/February 1990, pp. 65–85; Jonathan B. Tucker, "Partners and Rivals: A Model of International Collaboration in Advanced Technology," *International Organization*, Vol. 45, No. 1, Winter 1991, pp. 83–120; Andrew D. James, "The Prospects for a Transatlantic Defence Industry," in Schmitt, ed., *Between Cooperation and Competition*, pp. 93–122; John Lovering, "Which Way to Turn? The European Defense Industry after the Cold War," in Anne R. Markusen and Sean S. Costigan, eds., *Arming the Future: A Defense Industry for the 21st century* (New York: Council on Foreign Relations Press, 1999), pp. 363–366; Terrence Guay and Robert Callum, "The Transformation and Future Prospects of Europe's Defence Industry," *International Affairs*, Vol. 78, No. 4, 2002, pp. 757–76.

[86] Moravcsik, "Armaments among Allies," p. 136.

Furthermore, European states have cooperated to impose sanctions because of domestic pressure from powerful interest groups and rent-seeking coalitions.[87] Sanctions offer an opportunity for governments to "do something" about a foreign state's activities, satisfying both interest groups and protectionist coalitions. Therefore "intense domestic pressure, particularly in democratic states, to 'do something' can persuade the government in the sanctioning nation to respond by imposing sanctions."[88] Finally, the construction of joint military forces by European Union states is largely a function of the influence of domestic elites. As John Owen argues, the creation of an EU rapid reaction force has been motivated by the desire of liberal elites "to carry out liberal foreign policy more efficiently" in countries such as Germany, France, and Britain.[89]

This leads to a fairly straightforward proposition: security cooperation should be tied to the preferences of domestic actors. An increase in cooperation should be caused by pressure from domestic actors such as arms firms, powerful domestic producer groups, military leaders, lobbying organizations, and domestic elites. The incentives for policy coordination should be particularly strong when joint action can have positive effects for powerful domestic producer groups.

Institutions and cooperation

European security cooperation has been caused by a desire to increase the prospects for mutual gain through an international institution

Another alternative builds on the assumptions of liberal institutional arguments, and contends that foreign policy and defense cooperation is caused by a desire for mutual gain among European states. European states have been motivated to establish a security arm of the European Union because they share numerous common interests. As economic and foreign policy issues became increasingly entangled during the Cold War, European states became more likely to cooperate to manage the mutual costs and benefits of these issues. In addition, as

---

[87] On sanctions and domestic politics see Ivan Eland, "Economic Sanctions as Tools of Foreign Policy," in David Cortright and George Lopez, eds., *Economic Sanctions: Panacea or Peacebuilding in a Post-Cold War World?* (Boulder, CO: Westview Press, 1995); Richard N. Haass, "Sanctioning Madness," *Foreign Affairs*, Vol. 76, No. 6, November/December 1997, pp. 74–85; M.S. Daoudi and M.S. Dajani, *Economic Sanctions: Ideals and Experience* (Boston, MA: Routledge & Kegan Paul, 1983); Robin Renwick, *Economic Sanctions*, No. 45 (Cambridge, MA: Center for International Affairs, 1983).

[88] Eland, "Economic Sanctions as Tools of Foreign Policy," p. 29.

[89] Owen, "Transnational Liberalism and US Primacy," p. 142.

"new institutional" arguments have noted, the binding characteristics of an EU security arm generated path-dependent effects that have promoted greater cooperation.

Liberal institutional arguments have focused on the creation of international institutions as vehicles to overcome coordination and collaboration problems.[90] To illustrate the difficulties of cooperation in international politics, they have relied on what Thomas Schelling refers to as "mixed-motive games" – games that include both mutual dependence and conflict.[91] Perhaps the most famous example is the Prisoner's Dilemma, which concludes that common interests and the prospect of collective gain may be insufficient to induce cooperation. Since the payoffs for cheating in a cooperative arrangement can be high, there is a substantial incentive to defect. These arguments are reinforced by the collective goods literature, which finds that rational individuals will often not act to achieve their common interests because of the "free rider" problem.[92] Under certain conditions, individuals are better off *not* contributing to the provision of a collective good, but are better off free riding – letting others bear the costs of organization. The result is the absence of cooperation and a world in which all are worse off than if they had contributed equally to the provision of the good.[93]

To overcome these problems, international institutions can improve the prospects for cooperation between states by providing a forum for repeated interaction, increasing the collection and availability of information, reducing transaction costs, helping solve distribution problems, and, as a result, reducing uncertainty.[94] Since

[90] Arthur Stein, "Coordination and Collaboration: Regimes in an Anarchic World," *International Organization*, Vol. 36, No. 2, Spring 1982, pp. 299–324; Robert Axelrod and Robert O. Keohane, "Achieving Cooperation under Anarchy: Strategies and Institutions," *World Politics*, Vol. 38, No. 1, October 1985, pp. 226–54; Kenneth Oye, "Explaining Cooperation under Anarchy: Hypotheses and Strategies," *World Politics*, Vol. 38, No. 1, October 1985, pp. 1–24; Duncan Snidal, "Coordination versus Prisoners' Dilemma: Implications for International Cooperation and Regime," *American Political Science Review*, Vol. 79, No. 4, December 1985, pp. 923–42; Lisa L. Martin and Beth A. Simmons, "Theories and Empirical Studies of International Institutions," *International Organization*, Vol. 52, No. 4, Autumn 1998, pp. 729–57.
[91] Thomas C. Schelling, *The Strategy of Conflict* (Cambridge, MA: Harvard University Press, 1960), p. 89.
[92] Mancur Olson, *The Logic of Collective Action: Public Goods and the Theory of Groups* (Cambridge, MA: Harvard University Press, 1965).
[93] Also see Russell Hardin, "Collective Action as an Agreeable n-Prisoners' Dilemma," *Behavior Science*, Vol. 16, September 1971.
[94] On interaction (folk theorem) see James W. Friedman, "A Non-cooperative Equilibrium for Supergames," *Review of Economic Studies*, Vol. 38, No. 1, pp. 1–12; Drew Fudenberg and David K. Levine, *The Theory of Learning in Games* (Cambridge, MA: MIT Press, 1998); Robert Axelrod, *The Evolution of Cooperation* (New York: Basic

decentralized cooperation is difficult to achieve and frequently short-lived, institutions can help promote cooperation and make it more resilient.[95] In the security realm, for example, some argue that collective security organizations such as the Concert of Europe have fostered cooperation by increasing the availability of credible information between participants, developing norms and rules that regularize the behavior of participating states, and decreasing uncertainty by generating expectations of future behavior.[96] In addition, once institutions are established, they often experience feedback effects. States and other actors often hold conflicting preferences, and these preferences or interests can be shaped by institutions. Today's decisions can influence tomorrow's behavior because institutions can have "path-dependent" or "lock-in" effects, which effectively limit the capacity of actors to control the change. This is a core feature of "new institutional" theories of cooperation.[97] Consequently, institutions can help promote greater international cooperation.

Turning to Europe, some argue that European states have created a European security institution to increase the prospects for mutual gain. European states increasingly share numerous common interests because of their history, geography, and liberal democratic systems.[98]

Books, 1984). On information see Axelrod and Keohane, "Achieving Cooperation under Anarchy"; Helen V. Milner, *Interests, Institutions, and Information* (Princeton, NJ: Princeton University Press, 1997). On transaction costs see Oliver E. Williamson, *The Economic Institution of Capitalism: Firms, Markets, Relational Contracting* (New York: Free Press, 1985); Paul R. Milgrom, Douglass C. North, and Barry R. Weingast, "The Role of Institutions in the Revival of Trade: The Law Merchant, Private Judges, and the Champagne Fairs," *Economics and Politics*, Vol. 2, No. 1, pp. 1–23. On distribution problems see James D. Morrow, "Modeling the Forms of International Cooperation: Distribution versus Information," *International Organization*, Vol. 48, No. 3, Summer 1994, pp. 387–423; Fearon, "Bargaining, Enforcement, and International Cooperation," pp. 269–305.

[95] For work on variations in types of institutions, see Barbara Koremenos, Charles Lipson, and Duncan Snidal, "The Rational Design of International Institutions," *International Organization*, Vol. 55, No. 4, Autumn 2001, pp. 761–99.

[96] Charles A. Kupchan and Clifford A. Kupchan, "Concerts, Collective Security, and the Future of Europe," *International Security*, Vol. 16, No. 1, Summer 1991, pp. 114–61; Helga Haftendorn, Robert O. Keohane, and Celeste Wallander, eds., *Imperfect Unions: Security Institutions over Time and Space* (New York: Oxford University Press, 1999).

[97] See, for example, Douglas C. North, *Institutions, Institutional Change, and Economic Performance* (New York: Cambridge University Press, 1990); Paul Pierson, "When Effect Becomes Cause: Policy Feedback and Political Change," *World Politics*, Vol. 45, No. 4, July 1993, pp. 595–628; Brian Arthur, "Competing Technologies, Increasing Returns, and Lock-In by Historical Events," *Economic Journal*, Vol. 99, March 1989, pp. 116–31.

[98] Roy H. Ginsberg, *Foreign Policy Actions of the European Community: The Politics of Scale* (Boulder, CO: Lynne Rienner, 1989); Jeffrey J. Anderson and John B. Goodman, "Mars or Minerva? A United Germany in a Post-Cold War Europe," in Robert O. Keohane,

As economic and foreign policy issues became increasingly entangled, European states became more likely to cooperate to manage the costs and benefits of those issues. Complete national autonomy became harder to sustain, and states recognized the potential for mutual gain. A security arm of the European Union facilitated cooperation by increasing information flows, reducing transactions costs, resolving distribution problems, and permitting repeated interaction among states. Furthermore, as Michael Smith argues, institutionalized foreign policy cooperation dating back to the late 1960s has helped promote greater cooperation through a path-dependent process. Smith argues, "The specific institutional reforms of EU foreign policy largely reflected endogenous, path-dependent processes" that began with European political cooperation.[99] Consequently, the constraining characteristics of an EU security arm have generated increasing returns that make it path-dependent and difficult to terminate. Institutions create relations and commitments between participants and institutions that raise the costs of change.[100]

This is different from my argument in several ways. I argue that the *independent variable* is the structure of the regional and international systems. Structural conditions at the end of the Cold War, including concerns about a reunified and powerful Germany, played the critical role in causing greater European security cooperation. Institutional arguments assume that institutions have an independent impact on state preferences and interests. I disagree. I contend that institutions are merely an intervening variable in the process and are essentially "arenas for acting out power relationships."[101] The key independent variable is thus the structure of the international and regional systems. Furthermore, the preferences of the major European powers – especially Germany, France, and Britain – are the primary motors of cooperation. Cooperation is thus a function of relative power.

In addition, I argue that the *timing* of cooperation is tied to structural changes at the end of the Cold War. Most institutional arguments, such

Joseph S. Nye, and Stanley Hoffmann, eds., *After the Cold War: International Institutions and State Strategies in Europe, 1989–1991* (Cambridge, MA: Harvard University Press, 1993), p. 23.

[99] Michael E. Smith, *Europe's Foreign and Security Policy* (New York: Cambridge University Press, 2004), p. 176.

[100] Ikenberry, *After Victory*, pp. 69–72; Celeste Wallander, "Institutional Assets and Adaptability: NATO after the Cold War," *International Organization*, Vol. 54, No. 4, Autumn 2000, pp. 705–35.

[101] Tony Evans and Peter Wilson, "Regime Theory and the English School of International Relations: A Comparison," *Millennium: Journal of International Studies*, Vol. 21, No. 3, Winter 1992, p. 330.

as that by Michael Smith, contend that cooperation occurred much earlier and for different reasons. For example, Smith argues that "the growing prospect of the first enlargement of the EU in the late 1960s, and the beginning of the final stage of the Common Market project, led the EU heads of government" to begin foreign policy cooperation in 1969.[102] Consequently, structure had little, if anything, to do with the increase in European cooperation. And it began in the late 1960s and early 1970s, rather than at the end of the Cold War.

Finally, I argue that international institutions such as NATO have not ameliorated concerns about *American power*. In fact, quite the opposite is true. Most institutionalists believe that European states should not be alarmed by American power because it has been "institutionalized" through Western security institutions. As John Ikenberry argues, institutions such as NATO have placed "constraints on the United States and its partners, thereby mitigating fears of domination or abandonment."[103] I disagree. The evidence strongly suggests that NATO was largely a manifestation of the bipolar distribution of power in Europe during the Cold War. It was this balance of power, not NATO *per se*, that was critical to maintaining stability on the continent.[104] As explained in more detail later in this chapter, the evidence indicates that NATO has not curbed US power, and US policymakers have consistently operated outside NATO and contrary to the interests of key European powers.

Institutional arguments lead to at least three testable propositions. First, the European Union should have an independent impact on state preferences and interests, including Germany, France, and Britain. Institutions, not structure, should be the key independent variable. Second, the timing of European security cooperation should correlate with the establishment of European Political Cooperation beginning in 1969, rather than as a result of structural changes at the end of the Cold War. European Political Cooperation should not be merely a "gentlemen's dining club," as some have argued, but an example of substantive foreign policy cooperation.[105] Third, European states should not be concerned about American power because it has been institutionalized through such organizations as NATO.

[102] Smith, *Europe's Foreign and Security Policy*, p. 68.
[103] G. John Ikenberry, "Democracy, Institutions, and American Restraint," in Ikenberry, ed., *America Unrivaled*, p. 227.
[104] Mearsheimer, "The False Promise of International Institutions," pp. 13–14.
[105] William Wallace and David Allen, "Political Cooperation: Procedure as Substitute for Policy," in Helen Wallace, William Wallace, and Carole Webb, eds., *Policy-Making in the European Communities* (London: John Wiley & Sons, 1977), p. 237.

A European identity

European security cooperation is caused by the construction of a European identity

The final explanation focuses on the consolidation of a European identity.[106] Decades of interaction through the ECSC and the European Community caused a change in the interests and identity of European states. German, French, Italian, and other national identities and interests have increasingly been transformed into a collective European identity. Furthermore, the instability that plagued Europe for the last several centuries has given way to a "security community" – a community in which the possibility of war and security competition among European states no longer exists. In short, security cooperation through the European Union has occurred because of the constitution of a European identity.

Social constructivists make several general assumptions relevant for European cooperation. First, the identity and interests of states are socially constructed. The way states behave toward each other is not a function of how the world is structured or by the political make-up of states, but instead is largely determined by how individuals think and talk about politics. This is captured by Alexander Wendt's phrase that "anarchy is what states make of it."[107] Discourse is the motor that drives international politics.

Second, state interests and identities are influenced by constitutive effects. As John Searle illustrates, the creation of traffic rules was caused by an increase in the number of cars on the road, higher levels of traffic, and a greater number of fender-benders. But chess rules "are constitutive of chess in the sense that playing chess is constituted in part

---

[106] On constructivism and Europe see Craig Parsons, *A Certain Idea of Europe* (Ithaca, NY: Cornell University Press, 2003); Frank Schimmelfennig, *The EU, NATO and the Integration of Europe: Rules and Rhetoric* (New York: Cambridge University Press, 2003); Ole Waever, "Insecurity, Security, and Asecurity in the West European Non-War Community," in Emanuel Adler and Michael Barnett, eds., *Security Communities* (New York: Cambridge University Press, 1998), pp. 69–118; Waever, "Integration as Security: Constructing a Europe at Peace," in Charles A. Kupchan, ed., *Atlantic Security: Contending Visions* (New York: Council on Foreign Relations, 1998), p. 48; Peter J. Katzenstein, ed., *Tamed Power: Germany in Europe* (Ithaca, NY: Cornell University Press, 1997); Thomas U. Berger, "Norms, Identity, and National Security in Germany and Japan," in Katzenstein, ed., *The Culture of National Security: Norms and Identity in World Politics* (New York: Columbia University Press, 1996), pp. 317–56; Jeffrey T. Checkel, "Social Construction and Integration," *Journal of European Public Policy*, Vol. 6, No. 4, 1999, pp. 545–60.

[107] Alexander Wendt, "Anarchy is What States Make of It: The Social Construction of Power Politics," *International Organization*, Vol. 40, 1987, pp. 335–70.

by acting in accord with the rules."[108] Chess rules were clearly not created to prevent wooden chess pieces from colliding. Rather, the rules allow us to play chess; they are constitutive of the game. On a similar note, constructivists argue that state interests and identities are constituted through interaction in the international system. It is not a causal process – or at least not *just* a causal process – but is dependent on social knowledge and discourse. Shared rules and discourses have constitutive effects. What made the Soviet Union but not Canada a threat to the United States, or Iraq but not Israel, was the way in which US leaders constituted a "threat."[109] The discourse of US national security – rather than sheer military capabilities – caused the Soviet Union and Iraq to be viewed as threatening.[110]

Third, states can develop a collective identity and redefine their interests and identity as part of a group. Sociologists, political scientists, and others have done similar work in examining the phenomena of nationalism and ethnic violence.[111] States may adopt – or internalize – a collective identity in which national identity evolves into a broader, regional one through a process of socialization. In particular, states may develop what Karl Deutsch referred to as a security community: a group of states in which "there is real assurance that the members of that community will not fight each other physically, but will settle their disputes in some other way."[112] One of the ways this can happen

---

[108] John R. Searle, *The Construction of Social Reality* (New York: Free Press, 1995), p. 28. See also John Gerard Ruggie, "What Makes the World Hang Together? Neo-utilitarianism and the Social Constructivist Challenge," *International Organization*, Vol. 52, No. 4, Autumn 1998, p. 871.

[109] David Campbell, *Writing Security* (Minneapolis: University of Minnesota Press, 1992).

[110] Robert G. Herman, "Identity, Norms, and National Security: The Soviet Foreign Policy Revolution and the End of the Cold War," in Peter J. Katzenstein, ed., *The Culture of National Security: Norms and Identity in World Politics* (New York: Columbia University Press, 1996), pp. 271–316; Thomas Forsberg, "Power, Interests, and Trust: Explaining Gorbachev's Choices at the End of the Cold War," *Review of International Studies*, Vol. 24, No. 4, October 2000, pp. 603–21; Rey Koslowski and Friedrich Kratochwil, "Understanding Change in International Politics: The Soviet Empire's Demise and the International System," in Richard New Lebow and Thomas Risse-Kappen, eds., *International Relations Theory and the End of the Cold War* (New York: Columbia University Press, 1995), pp. 127–66; Robert D. English, *Russia and the Idea of the West: Gorbachev, Intellectuals, and the End of the Cold War* (New York: Columbia University Press, 2000).

[111] See, for example, Benedict Anderson, *Imagined Communities: Reflections on the Origin and Spread of Nationalism* (New York: Verso, 1991); Ernest Gellner, *Nations and Nationalism* (Ithaca, NY: Cornell University Press, 1983); Ronald Grigor Suny, *The Revenge of the Past: Nationalism, Revolution, and the Collapse of the Soviet Union* (Stanford, CA: Stanford University Press, 1993).

[112] Deutsch divides security communities into two categories: amalgamated and pluralistic. Amalgamated security communities are those in which there is a formal merger

is through interaction in international institutions, which can consciously or unconsciously lead to a coalescing of the interests and identity of states.[113] Used in this sense, institutions have an independent effect on actors. Over time, states may develop a collective identity because institutions promote the diffusion of ideas to participant states.

Turning to Europe, constructivists argue that the process of European interaction since the European Coal and Steel Community transformed the identities and interests of European states. As Ole Waever argues: "Decades of economic integration and efforts to construct a collective political space have succeeded in creating a nascent European polity, which in turn infuses the identity of national states and shapes how those states define their national interests."[114] Interaction over time caused states to internalize a European identity and interests, though they have developed somewhat differently in such countries as Britain, France, and Germany.[115] Indeed, self-interest was transformed from competing national interests – German *vs.* French *vs.* Italian interests – to a sense of "we-ness" among Europeans. This process was largely constitutive; change occurred because European states internalized a new identity and set of interests. As Frank Schimmelfennig notes, "the international relations of Europe have been thoroughly transformed in the process of European integration . . . by the Europeanization of state identities."[116] Germany is singled out as the clearest example of identity change.[117]

between two or more units that were previously independent – such as the United States. Pluralistic security communities, however, are those in which there is a reassurance that separate units will not fight each other, but where the legal independence of the units is preserved. Contemporary Europe might be an example of this category. See Karl W. Deutsch et al., *Political Community and the North Atlantic Area: International Organization in the Light of Historical Experience* (Princeton, NJ: Princeton University Press, 1957), p. 5.

[113] Judith Goldstein and Robert O. Keohane, eds., *Ideas and Foreign Policy: Beliefs, Institutions, and Political Change* (Ithaca, NY: Cornell University Press, 1993); Adler and Barnett, *Security Communities*.

[114] Waever, "Integration as Security," p. 48. See also Thomas Christiansen, Knud Erik Jorgensen, and Antje Wiener, "The Social Construction of Europe," *Journal of European Public Policy*, Vol. 6, No. 4, 1999, pp. 528–44.

[115] Thomas Risse, "A European Identity? Europeanization and the Evolution of Nation-State Identities," in Maria Green Cowles, James Caporaso, and Thomas Risse, *Transforming Europe: Europeanization and Domestic Change* (Ithaca, NY: Cornell University Press, 2001), pp. 198–216; Jonathan Mercer, "Anarchy and Identity," *International Organization*, Vol. 49, No. 2, Spring 1995, pp. 229–52. On self-interest see also Wendt, *Social Theory of International Politics*, pp. 238–43.

[116] Schimmelfennig, *The EU, NATO and the Integration of Europe*, p. 84.

[117] Katzenstein, ed., *Tamed Power*; Thomas U. Berger, "Norms, Identity, and National Security in Germany and Japan," in Katzenstein, ed., *The Culture of National Security*, 317–56; Andrei S. Markovits and Simon Reich, *The German Predicament: Memory and*

52   The rise of European security cooperation

While it once projected power through brute military and economic might, Germany now exercises "soft" power and seeks such goals as security and wealth through institutions rather than through naked aggression.[118] Germany has supported European cooperation because it has internalized European norms, not because German leaders have been motivated by strategic or instrumental reasons.

In the security realm, the daily interaction of European diplomats beginning with European Political Cooperation (EPC) in the late 1960s had an important impact. By the early 1990s, a European identity had been internalized to such a degree that it became necessary to establish a security arm of the European Union, that became the Common Foreign and Security Policy (CFSP). Kenneth Glarbo argues, "Social integration is emerging as the natural historical product of the day-to-day practices of political co-operation. Diplomats and national diplomacies have internalized, in particular, the formal requirements of a CFSP."[119] The construction of a collective identity among European states spilled over into the foreign policy and defense realms and created a need for security cooperation. Indeed, regular interaction among European leaders was critical in the development of common security interests and a European – as opposed to a transatlantic – security institution.

The result has been the creation of a European security community.[120] The security dilemma that was prevalent in Europe in the first half of the twentieth century no longer exists, and war between European states is not a realistic possibility. Indeed, security concerns have been aggregated as a European problem rather than as a German, French, or Italian problem. In place of concerns about the intentions of other states and fears of vulnerability to external aggression, Europe has developed what Alexander Wendt refers to as a Kantian culture.

Power in the New Europe (Ithaca, NY: Cornell University Press, 1997); Martin Marcussen, Thomas Risse *et al.*, "Constructing Europe? The Evolution of French, British, and German Nation State Identities," *Journal of European Public Policy*, Vol. 6, No. 4 1999, pp. 614–33; Adrian Hyde-Price and Charlie Jeffery, "Germany in the European Union: Constructing Normality," *Journal of Common Market Studies*, Vol. 39, No. 4, November 2001, pp. 689–717.

[118] On "soft" power see also Joseph S. Nye, *Bound to Lead: The Changing Nature of American Power* (New York: Basic Books, 1990).

[119] Kenneth Glarbo, "Wide-Awake Diplomacy: Reconstructing the Common Foreign and Security Policy of the European Union," *Journal of European Public Policy*, Vol. 64, No. 4, 1999, pp. 649–50. On the importance of interaction and European integration see Checkel, "Social Construction and Integration," pp. 545–60.

[120] On Europe as a security community see Deutsch, *Political Community and the North Atlantic Area*; Ole Waever, "Insecurity, Security, and Asecurity in the West European Non-War Community," in Adler and Barnett, *Security Communities*, pp. 69–118.

European states have internalized common norms and values to such a degree that the security of others is not only viewed as related to their own, but "as literally being their own."[121] War among European states has gradually been squeezed out as a concern, and security has been internalized by individual states to mean "European."

This leads to several propositions. First, since European states have created a security community, there should be a notable absence of mutual security concerns. States have internalized a collective identity, and security is now conceived of as a regional matter. Even Germany, Europe's most powerful state, should be viewed as unthreatening because it has internalized European norms. Second, we should expect to find an increase in "Europeanness" among European states at the end of the Cold War and in the early post-Cold War years. Since the Treaty on the European Union was a turning point in the creation of an EU security arm, we should find a notable increase in the internalization of a European collective identity among national leaders, foreign policy elites, and perhaps European populations. Third, security cooperation should not be an instrumental strategy pursued by national leaders to maximize goals such as power, security, or wealth. Rather, it should reflect the internalization of a European identity and European interests.

Conclusion

Each of the alternative arguments offers some useful insights into why European states are increasingly cooperating in the security realm, and these are summarized in Table 2.1. As the case studies show, however, EU security cooperation has largely been a function of structural conditions. First, EU states have pursued cooperation in such areas as economic sanctions, arms production, and military forces in response to US power. Combining power increases the ability of European states to project power abroad and decreases the ability of the US to impose its will on them. Second, European Union states pursued security cooperation in the early 1990s through the EU to ensure long-term peace in the region and to prevent the rise of a hegemonic Germany. Evaluating theories is, of course, never dichotomous. The aim here is not to prove that one theory can entirely explain European security cooperation, but to assess the relative importance of various factors. This is what Imre Lakatos refers to as a three-cornered fight between rival

---

[121] Wendt, *Social Theory of International Politics*, p. 305.

Table 2.1. *Summary of main arguments*

Argument	Assumptions	Testable propositions
Structure and Power	• States care a great deal about the distribution of power	• Security cooperation should be correlated with structural changes in the international and regional systems
Illusion of Security Cooperation	• Nationalism remains a powerful force in Europe • US military presence in Europe keeps peace	• There should be no meaningful security cooperation • The withdrawal of US forces should increase security competition in Europe
Domestic Politics	• States are subject to influence by domestic actors • Decisions made through intergovernmental bargains	• Security cooperation should be tied to the preferences of domestic actors
Institutions	• Institutions can improve the prospects for cooperation • Once established, institutions are "path-dependent"	• The EU should have an independent impact on state preferences and interests • Timing of cooperation should correlate with the establishment of European Political Cooperation • Institutions should dampen concern about US power
European identity	• Identity and interests of states are socially constructed • States and populations can develop a collective identity	• There should be a notable absence of security concerns in Europe • There should be a significant increase in "Europeanness" at the end of the Cold War

theories and empirical evidence, and what caused him to conclude that there "is no falsification before the emergence of a better theory."[122] The chapter concludes by briefly examining one additional issue – NATO – which is dealt with more extensively in virtually every chapter of the book. While European states are increasingly cooperating through the European Union, there is nonetheless some evidence of bandwagoning with the United States through NATO.[123] Despite the collapse of the Soviet Union, NATO has expanded its membership to include Poland, Hungary, the Czech Republic, Bulgaria, Estonia, Latvia, Lithuania, Romania, Slovenia, and Slovakia.

---

[122] Imre Lakatos, "Falsification and the Methodology of Scientific Research Programmes," in Lakatos and Alan Musgrave, eds., *Criticisms and the Growth of Knowledge* (New York: Cambridge University Press, 1970), p. 119
[123] Barry R. Posen, "ESDP and the Structure of World Power," *The International Spectator*, Vol. 39, No. 1, January–March 2004, pp. 9–10.

It has also created the NATO Response Force for expeditionary operations, its doctrine has become more expansive, and it played notable roles in Bosnia, Kosovo, and Afghanistan. Bandwagoning is particularly apropos with the British, who have supported both NATO and ESDP. As British Prime Minister Tony Blair argued: "We believe that a flexible, inclusive approach and effective links to NATO are essential to the success of ESDP. We will not agree to anything which is contradictory to, or would replace, the security guarantee established through NATO."[124] In short, some might argue that NATO is still the premier European security organization or, at the very least, that it continues to play an important role in European security.

As discussed in more detail in Chapter 3, however, European states have expressed at least two concerns with NATO. The first is the United States long-term commitment to Europe. These concerns were reinforced by the American decision to bypass NATO during the combat phase in Afghanistan, the transatlantic tensions that resulted from the 2003 war in Iraq, and the United States decision to decrease the number of military forces and bases in Europe after the 2003 Iraq War. Along these lines, Blair articulated this fear of abandonment in noting that "Americans are too ready to see no need to get involved in affairs of the rest of the world . . . We understand that this is something we have no right to take for granted and must match with our own efforts. That is the basis for the recent initiative I took with President Chirac of France to improve Europe's own defense capabilities."[125] The second concern is that European states have little real autonomy in NATO, since the United States remains the preponderant power. This is, in part, why former German Chancellor Gerhard Schröder argued: "As part of the European Union, Germany today feels that it shares responsibility for international stability and order . . . NATO's presence in Afghanistan has highlighted how helpful its military organization can be even in distant crises. However, it is no longer the primary venue where transatlantic partners discuss and coordinate strategies."[126]

These concerns have caused European states to increasingly look toward the European Union as the primary security institution in Europe.

[124] James Blitze and Jean Eaglesham, "UK May Clash with EU Partners over Defense," *Financial Times*, September 10, 2003, p. 4.
[125] Tony Blair, "Doctrine of the International Community," A speech to the Economic Club of Chicago, April 22, 1999.
[126] Gerhard Schröder, Speech on the 41st Munich Conference on Security Policy (Berlin: Chancellor's Office, February 2005).

The next four chapters of the book compile substantial qualitative and quantitive evidence to support this trend. NATO still exists – and may continue to exist – as a transatlantic defense organization, even though it increasingly resembles Oscar Wilde's Dorian Gray. It appears youthful and robust as it grows older, but is becoming ever more infirm. The North Atlantic Treaty will likely remain in force, NATO may even continue to issue upbeat communiqués and conduct joint training exercises, and the Brussels bureaucracy may keep NATO's webpage updated – so long as NATO isn't actually asked to do much else.[127]

---

[127] Stephen M. Walt, "The Ties that Fray: Why Europe and America are Drifting Apart," *The National Interest*, No. 54, Winter 1998/99, pp. 3–11.

3   Security institutions

Why was a security arm of the European Union created in post-Cold War Europe? Why did it succeed when earlier attempts failed to create a viable institution? Standing before a crowded Bundestag on November 28, 1989, barely a year before German reunification, the then Chancellor Helmut Kohl made a rather bold promise to Germans and Europeans. "We have always regarded the process leading to the recovery of German unity to be a European concern," he said. "It must, therefore, also be seen in the context of European integration."[1] Over the next decade, German leaders played a pivotal role in the construction of a European security arm tied to the European Union. Past efforts such as the European Defense Community, the Fouchet Plan, and European Political Cooperation failed to create a European – as opposed to a transatlantic – security institution. But this was different. German leaders strongly favored and helped create an EU security arm as part of the Treaty on European Union (1992), and pressed for deeper EU security cooperation at Amsterdam (1997), Helsinki (1999), Nice (2001) and beyond. Germany's behavior and the variation in European security institutions pose an interesting puzzle.

This chapter explains why European states have constructed an EU security institution in the post-Cold War era – what I call a "binding" strategy – and why they failed to do so during the Cold War. In order to do this, this chapter lays out the conditions under which states might choose a binding strategy. That choice is mainly a function of the structure of the regional system. Specifically, European security cooperation is inversely correlated with American power in Europe: the lower the American military presence in Europe, the greater the

---

[1] "A Ten-Point-Programme for Overcoming the Division of Germany and Europe," Chancellor Helmut Kohl, speech in the German Bundestag, November 28, 1989, quoted in Frank Elbe and Richard Kiessler, *A Round Table with Sharp Corners: The Diplomatic Path to German Unity* (Baden-Baden, Germany: Nomos Verlagsgesellschaft, 1996), p. 226.

impetus for EU security cooperation to ameliorate a potential security dilemma. It is also correlated with German power: the greater the power of Germany, the greater the impetus for cooperation. During the Cold War, the large US military presence in Europe and division of Germany dampened security concerns. This changed at the end of the Cold War for two reasons: (1) Germany reunified in 1990; and (2) the United States dramatically cut its military forces in Europe. However, Germany was a status quo power and learned from history. German, British, and French leaders ultimately calculated that cooperation through the European Union was the optimal strategy to achieve peace and security.

To test the argument, this chapter examines four cases since World War II in which European states attempted to create a security institution. An institution is defined as a set of rules that specify how states should behave. The four cases include: the European Defense Community (1950–1954); the Fouchet Plan (1958–1963); European Political Cooperation (1969–1991); and the Treaty on European Union (1991–). These cases were chosen for several reasons: they represent the most important attempts to create a European security institution following World War II; they allow for variation in the existence of a security institution (the dependent variable); and they allow for variation in the structure of the system (the independent variable).

The chapter then briefly explores alternative arguments. Constructivists argue that the creation of a European security institution has been caused by the internalization of a European identity. The logic is that decades of interaction have caused European states to internalize regional rather than national identities and interests. EU states have now established a "security community" in which competition and war are no longer plausible. Some argue that the success and failure of European institutions have largely been a function of domestic coalitions and social actors. Still others argue that the prospects for mutual gain through an international institution can best explain the variation in security institutions. Finally, some argue that there is not – nor will be – substantial EU security cooperation because nationalism is deeply ingrained in European countries. Security competition, rather than cooperation, will be the wave of the future. The inability of all European states to adopt a common position on the 2003 US war in Iraq illustrates the point. The *Financial Times* notes, "Take the common foreign policy, including defense. The European split over Iraq has wreaked havoc with the progress that had been made."[2]

---

[2] Quentin Peel, "The Failure of Blair's European Policy," *Financial Times*, May 6, 2003, p. 21.

Consequently, this chapter is divided into six parts. First, it examines options for building security institutions, and outlines the conditions under which states might adopt a binding strategy. Second, it examines the failed efforts to create a European defense community in the early 1950s. Third, it explores Charles de Gaulle's unsuccessful attempt in the 1960s to create a European security institution as part of the Fouchet Plan. Fourth, it looks at failed efforts to create a security institution through European political cooperation in the late 1960s and early 1970s. Fifth, it examines changes initiated by the Treaty on European Union negotiated at Maastricht. And sixth, it concludes by examining the alternative arguments.

Options for building security institutions

States have traditionally pursued multilateral cooperation in the security realm by balancing against a threatening state through an alliance, bandwagoning with the source of danger, or buckpassing to others. However, states have pursued another option that has generally been overlooked. They sometimes attempt to incorporate a potential threat into an institution – what I call binding. Since there are substantial barriers to security cooperation through an international institution, we should expect it to occur only under rare conditions. This section argues that there are two major conditions for a binding strategy. The first is a potential security dilemma that may trigger major war. The second condition is that the threatening state must be a status quo power and it must have learned from history.

The first condition arises when the existence of a potential security dilemma might lead to major war. A security dilemma arises when the efforts a state makes to increase its own security decrease the security of others.[3] Security dilemmas are especially likely in situations where there is a potential hegemon – a state that is substantially more powerful than its neighbors and has the potential to dominate them. Potential hegemons induce fear among nearby states because of their considerable

---

[3] The security dilemma literature is quite large. Some of the basic works include John Herz, "Idealist Internationalism and the Security Dilemma," *World Politics*, Vol. 2, No. 2, January 1950, pp. 157–80; Robert Jervis, "Cooperation under the Security Dilemma"; Charles L. Glaser, "Realists as Optimists: Cooperation as Self-Help," *International Security*, Vol. 19, No. 3, Winter 1994/95, pp. 50–90; Randall L. Schweller, "Neorealism's Status-Quo Bias: What Security Dilemma?" *Security Studies*, Vol. 5, No. 3, Spring 1996, pp. 90–121; Andrew Kydd, "Sheep in Sheep's Clothing: Why Security Seekers Do Not Fight Each Other," *Security Studies*, Vol. 7, No. 1, Autumn 1997, pp. 1114–54; Glaser, "The Security Dilemma Revisited," *World Politics*, Vol. 50, No. 1, October 1997, pp. 171–201.

power. States encountering a potential hegemon have a number of options. First, they can pursue a buckpassing strategy.[4] They can decline multilateral cooperation and "free ride" on the efforts of other states. However, the most significant cost of this strategy is that it does little to decrease the possibility of a security dilemma and the likelihood of major war.[5] A second possibility is balancing against the potential hegemon. States that choose to balance commit themselves to contain their opponent by aggregating power and forming an alliance.[6] States balance when confronted by a great power that poses a military threat. Third, states may pursue a strategy of bandwagoning with the potential hegemon. Those that opt to bandwagon commit themselves to join their opponent by allying with it.[7] However, bandwagoning strategies can be costly because they put the security and survival of a state at risk if the potential hegemon becomes too strong.

The fourth strategy is to pursue cooperation with the hegemon through a multilateral institution. I refer to this as binding.[8] The fear of future conflict may create a strong incentive for multilateral cooperation through an institution since competition may be too costly for states. This is clearly not bandwagoning. States that opt to bandwagon abandon any hope of preventing the potential hegemon from gaining power, and they join forces to acquire at least a portion of the spoils of victory. This strategy has been pursued on several occasions. In addition to balancing against the Soviet Union, NATO was designed in Lord Ismay's words to "keep the Germans down" by incorporating Germany

---

[4] Barry R. Posen, *Sources of Military Doctrine: France, Britain, and Germany between the World Wars* (Ithaca, NY: Cornell University Press, 1984), pp. 232–3; Thomas J. Christensen and Jack Snyder, "Chain Gangs and Passed Bucks: Predicting Alliance Patterns in Multipolarity," *International Organization*, Vol. 44, No. 2, Spring 1990, pp. 137–68.

[5] Robert Jervis, *Perception and Misperception in International Politics* (Princeton, NJ: Princeton University Press, 1976), pp. 84–90.

[6] Kenneth N. Waltz, *Theory of International Politics* (New York: McGraw-Hill, 1979); Hans J. Morgenthau, *Politics among Nations: The Struggle for Power and Peace* (New York: Alfred A. Knopf, 1963); John J. Mearsheimer, *The Tragedy of Great Power Politics* (New York: W. W. Norton, 2001); Ernst B. Haas, "The Balance of Power: Prescription, Concept, or Propaganda?" *World Politics*, Vol. 5, No. 4, July 1953, pp. 442–77. On balancing against threat (rather than power), see Stephen M. Walt, *The Origins of Alliances* (Ithaca: Cornell University Press, 1987).

[7] Walt, *The Origins of Alliances*, pp. 17–49.

[8] This strategy is similar to what Randall Schweller terms "binding" and what Paul Schroeder refers to as "pactas de contrahendo." Randall L. Schweller, *Deadly Imbalances: Tripolarity and Hitler's Strategy of World Conquest* (New York: Columbia University Press, 1998), pp. 70–1; Paul W. Schroeder, "Alliances, 1815–1945: Weapons of Power and Tools of Management," in Klaus Knorr, ed., *Historical Dimensions of National Security Problems* (Lawrence, KA: University Press of Kansas, 1976), pp. 227–62.

into a regional security institution.[9] Similarly, France was brought into the Concert of Europe in 1818 by Prussia, Britain and Austria in order to prevent it from becoming a potential hegemon again. The major problem with this strategy, however, is that it hinges on the potential hegemon's willingness to cooperate.

In the second condition the potential hegemon must understand the security dilemma and be willing to go to considerable lengths to ameliorate it. Potential hegemons have not tended to prefer widespread security cooperation through an institution. In some situations, such as before World War I when Germany and Russia adopted a "cult of the offensive," states may fail to recognize a security dilemma.[10] In other instances, potential hegemons have sought to expand their power through conquest.[11] A potential hegemon may be willing to cooperate through an institution if it is a status quo power.[12] It must rule out territorial expansion as a means to achieve such goals as security, power, or wealth and prefer to maintain the resources it already has. Changes since World War II such as the introduction of nuclear weapons have caused foreign conquest to be unappealing and costly for states.[13] Furthermore, an exogenous event such as a major war may cause the potential hegemon to learn from history and prefer the status quo. Policymakers may alter their behavior because of historical experience.[14]

---

[9] On dual containment see G. John Ikenberry, *After Victory: Institutions, Strategic Restraint, and the Rebuilding of Order after Major Wars* (Princeton, NJ: Princeton University Press, 2001), pp. 205–10; Thomas A. Schwartz, *America's Germany: John J. McCloy and the Federal Republic of Germany* (Cambridge, MA: Harvard University Press, 1991).

[10] Jervis, *Perception and Misperception in International Politics* (Princeton: Princeton University Press, 1976), p. 94. On the "cult of the offensive" see also Stephen Van Evera, "The Cult of the Offensive and the Origins of the First World War," *International Security*, Vol. 9, No. 1, Summer 1984, pp. 58–108; Van Evera, *Causes of War: Power and the Roots of Conflict* (Ithaca, NY: Cornell University Press, 1999), pp. 117–239.

[11] Peter Liberman, *Does Conquest Pay? The Exploitation of Occupied Industrial Societies* (Princeton, NJ: Princeton University Press, 1996). Also see Halford J. Mackinder, "The Geographical Pivot of History," *Geographic Journal*, Vol. 23, No. 4, April 1904, pp. 421–44.

[12] On the distinction between expansionist and status quo powers, see Glaser, "Realists as Optimists"; Randall L. Schweller, *Deadly Imbalances: Tripolarity and Hitler's Strategy of World Conquest*, (New York: Columbia University Press, 1998), especially pp. 15–38.

[13] Robert Jervis, *The Meaning of the Nuclear Revolution: Statecraft and the Prospect of Armageddon* (Ithaca, NY: Cornell University Press, 1989).

[14] For a good summary of learning and international relations see Jack Levy, "Learning and Foreign Policy: Sweeping a Conceptual Minefield," *International Organization*, Vol. 48, No. 2, Spring 1994, pp. 279–312. Also see Dan Reiter, "Learning, Realism, and Alliances: The Weight of the Shadow of the Past," *World Politics*, Vol. 46, No. 4, July 1994, pp. 490–526; Robert Jervis, *Perception and Misperception in International Politics*; Jack Snyder, *Myths of Empire: Domestic Politics and International Ambition* (Ithaca, NY: Cornell University Press, 1991).

Indeed, the lessons of Munich, Vietnam, Somalia, and Iraq have influenced numerous American policymakers. A recent history of great power war may cause leaders to pursue such options as security cooperation through an international institution if it translates into greater security. To summarize the hypotheses, we should expect the following:

- The smaller the US military presence in Europe and the greater the power of Germany, the greater the possibility of a security dilemma because of Germany's power and past behavior.
- The greater the willingness of Germany to ameliorate it through an institution, the greater the likelihood of regional security cooperation.

European defense community (1950–1954)

In the immediate aftermath of World War II, one of the critical issues for Western policymakers was how to ensure long-term stability in Western Europe. Of particular importance, of course, was how to solve the "German problem" and to answer the pivotal question: what was the optimal strategy to ensure a democratic Germany allied to the West, but safeguard against a revival of German militarism? As NSC 160, the Eisenhower administration's position paper on Germany, highlighted, Germany was critical for a variety of reasons: it was one of the most powerful European states west of the Soviet Union; it was a major zone of potential conflict between the Western powers and the Soviets; and it had a recent history of aggression.[15] There were at least four potential options:

- Buckpassing
- Balancing against Germany
- NATO
- European defense community.

First, the default strategy was buckpassing. Western powers could have refused multilateral cooperation, pursued independent foreign and defense policies, and perhaps created bilateral alliances to protect their security. This is the strategy they had pursued for much of European history.[16] In the United States there was substantial

---

[15] United States Department of State, "United States Position with Respect to Germany, August 17, 1953," in *Foreign Relations of the United States 1952–1954*, (hereafter *FRUS* and date), Vol. VII, *Germany and Austria* (Washington, DC: Government Printing Office, 1986), pp. 510–20.
[16] This is similar to what Josef Joffe refers to as "balancing à la Britain": refrain from becoming entangled in multilateral organizations or alliances, but prevent the rise

opposition to American involvement in multilateral cooperation on the continent, much like its strategy during the interwar years. Former President Herbert Hoover, echoing the sentiments of supporters such as Senator Robert Taft, warned that US entanglement in Europe "would be the graveyard of millions of American boys and would end in the exhaustion of this Gibraltar of Western Civilization."[17] In Europe, French and British leaders could have severely limited Germany's economic and military power, established an alliance to protect themselves against future German aggression, but refused to construct an institution. This was particularly popular among some French politicians who later defeated the EDC: Western Germany should be deprived of any bargaining position and refused all forms of rearmament. The Communist Party, for example, condemned any integration of Germany into a European institution and supported all those who wished "to avert the deadly danger of a reconstitution of the Germany army."[18]

A second option was balancing against Germany through an alliance. This is the strategy European states had pursued for much of their recent history.[19] There was some support in Europe for severely limiting Germany's economic and military power, establishing an alliance to protect against future German aggression, but refusing to incorporate Germany in an institution.[20] However, there were problems with both strategies. The US and West European states believed that one of the most significant threats to their security would be for western Germany to ally with the USSR. "The consequences for Europe as well as for Germany would be disastrous," noted British Foreign Secretary Anthony Eden, "if Germany fell within the Soviet orbit, either directly or gradually via neutralization."[21] Neither unilateralism nor balancing

of a European hegemon. Josef Joffe, "'Bismarck' or 'Britain'? Toward an American Grand Strategy after Bipolarity," *International Security*, Vol. 19, No. 4, Spring 1995, pp. 94–117.

[17] "Our National Policies in this Crisis," Broadcast from New York City, December 20, 1950, in Herbert Hoover, *Addresses upon the American Road: 1948–1950* (Stanford, CA: Stanford University Press, 1951), p. 205. Also see Robert A. Taft, *A Foreign Policy for Americans* (Garden City, NY: Doubleday, 1951), pp. 82–102; John Lewis Gaddis, *Strategies of Containment: A Critical Appraisal of Postwar American National Security Policy* (New York: Oxford University Press, 1982), pp. 117–25.

[18] Jacques Fauvet, "Birth and Death of a Treaty," in Daniel Lerner and Raymond Aron, eds., *France Defeats the EDC* (New York: Frederick A. Praeger, 1957), p. 142.

[19] Joffe, "'Bismarck' or 'Britain'?" pp. 94–117.

[20] Jacques Fauvet, "Birth and Death of a Treaty," p. 142.

[21] Anthony Eden, *Full Circle* (Boston, MA: Houghton Mifflin, 1960), p. 174. In 1951 Dean Acheson argued that "if the decision is made to abandon Germany, that country and its people will fall to the other side and that will make the whole problem unmanageable." Memorandum by Acheson, July 6, 1951, *FRUS 1951*, Vol. III, *European Security and the German Question*, p. 813.

were a strong safeguard against this. Moreover, as the interwar period demonstrated, neither could keep Germany down for ever. While European leaders were opposed to an independent German national army and a German general staff, they believed that a realistic and acceptable defense of Western Europe necessitated active and willing German military participation.[22] As US high commissioner for Germany, John McCloy, argued, European security required getting Germany "enmeshed" in a security institution.[23]

A third alternative option was to bind Germany into NATO. The North Atlantic Treaty, which was signed on April 4, 1949, excluded Germany. British leaders in particular supported German membership in NATO because they were wary of joining a supranational European institution and believed that American participation was necessary to contain German power.[24] This meant that British policy should be geared toward trying "to lead the integration movement away from exclusively European ideas towards an Atlantic community, including Germany" because the "U.S. commitment in Europe is desirable."[25] A number of French leaders, however, were opposed to rearming Germany through NATO, and in theory were opposed to rearming Germany *at all*.[26] If it had to be done, as the Americans, British, and Germans demanded, it should be done in a European institution that would place the Germans under supranational command. This leads to our final option.

Fourth, Germany could be incorporated into a European security institution, which became known as the European Defense Community (EDC). In the economic realm, the French had already spearheaded a

[22] "Report by the North Atlantic Military Committee," December 1950, *FRUS 1950*, Vol. III, p. 539.

[23] Meeting of United States ambassadors at Rome, March 22–24, 1950, *FRUS 1950*, Vol. III, *Western Europe* p. 817.

[24] Eden, *Full Circle*, pp. 44, 65, 168, 171. See also Foreign and Commonwealth Office, *Documents on British Policy Overseas*, ed. Roger Bullen and M. E. Pelly (London: Her Majesty's Stationery Office, 1986), pp. 7–13, 457–62, 488–90, 587–94, 742–4. Hereafter *DBPO*.

[25] Memorandum for the Permanent Under Secretary's Committee, 9 June 1951, *DBPO*, Series II, Vol. I, p. 594.

[26] During the ratification debate on the North Atlantic Treaty in the French National Assembly, Robert Schuman argued: "Germany is unarmed and will remain unarmed . . . It is unthinkable that she should be allowed to joint the Atlantic Pact as a nation empowered to defend or help defend other nations." Jean Monnet, *Memoirs* (Garden City, NY: Doubleday, 1978), p. 337. Schuman also warned US policymakers that German rearmament *in any form* would be very unpopular with the French public and members of the French parliament, especially since France was still militarily weak. Minutes of meeting between French, British, and United States foreign ministers and their High Commissioners for Germany, September 14, 1950, *FRUS 1950*, Vol. III, *Western Europe*, pp. 296–301.

plan in 1950 to incorporate Germany into a European economic institution by creating the European Coal and Steel Community. As Jean
Monnet argued, a giant step toward precluding "German industrial domination" was to "place the whole of Franco-German coal and steel production under an international Authority open to the participation of the
other countries of Europe."[27] The military equivalent to the European
Coal and Steel Community was the EDC. As Monnet noted in a confidential memorandum to René Pleven in October 1950, the French needed
to find a way to keep the Germans tied down in a European security
institution:

[T]he solution of the German problem in its military aspect [should] be sought
in the same spirit and by the same methods as for coal and steel: the establishment of a European Army with a single High Command, a single organization,
unified equipment and financing, and under the control of a single supranational
authority (German units would gradually be integrated into this initial
nucleus).[28]

As US Secretary of State Dean Acheson noted: "During the summer of
1951 I had come to the conclusion that the best way to an adequate
German contribution lay in strong support of the French proposal for a
European defense community."[29] The Eisenhower administration,
which took office in January 1953, was particularly supportive of the
EDC and European security cooperation efforts.[30]

The EDC treaty, which was signed on May 27, 1952 by the Federal
Republic of Germany, Belgium, France, Italy, Luxembourg, and the
Netherlands, was designed to integrate the militaries of its respective
members by creating a supranational security institution with common
armed forces and a common budget.[31] It established a commissariat that

---

[27] Monnet, *Memoirs*, pp. 292, 295.   [28] Ibid., p. 346.
[29] Dean Acheson, *Present at the Creation: My Years in the State Department* (New York:
W.W. Norton, 1969), p. 557.
[30] Dulles argued that "no real effort had been made to get the EDC treaties before the
parliaments of the Western European countries until Eisenhower had become President
and had thrown his weight behind this great project." Moreover, he noted that "there
was no hope for Europe without integration." Memorandum of National Security
Council discussion, August 13, 1953, *FRUS 1952–54*, Vol. VII, p. 502. See also Dwight
D. Eisenhower, *The White House Years: Mandate for Change, 1953–1956* (Garden City,
NY: Doubleday, 1963), pp. 398–404.
[31] As the introduction to the treaty highlights: "Resolved to contribute to the maintenance of
peace, particularly by ensuring the defense of Western Europe against any aggression . . .
a *supranational* European organization is the most appropriate means of reaching
this goal with all the necessary rapidity and effectiveness." "The European Defense
Community Treaty, May 27, 1952," in United States, Department of State, *American
Foreign Policy 1950–1955: Basic Documents*, Vol. I (Washington, DC: Government
Printing Office, 1957), pp. 1107–8. Emphasis added.

was vested with executive powers, and it shared several bodies such as a common assembly and court of justice with the European Coal and Steel Community. More importantly, it created an integrated European army consisting of a unified command, as well as conscripted and volunteer soldiers wearing a common European uniform.[32] The EDC was designed to allow Germany to rearm by binding it into a regional institution. Member states would contribute forty-three divisions to the general military pool: fourteen from France, twelve each from Italy and West Germany, and the remainder from the Benelux countries. However, it would be integrated into NATO. Article 2 clearly stated that the EDC was created "within the framework of the North Atlantic Treaty," and Article 18 noted that its military forces would be under the control of NATO's supreme allied commander.[33] However, in August 1954 the French National Assembly rejected the EDC by a vote of 319 to 264. West Germany was admitted into NATO following the October 1954 Paris accords, and Britain extended membership to West Germany and Italy in its nascent Western European Union project.

What explains the failure of the EDC? Most historical accounts of the collapse of the EDC focus exclusively – or nearly exclusively – on ideational or domestic politics factors.[34] Some argue that the failure of the EDC was largely a function of domestic politics, especially the economic interests of domestic coalitions,[35] with the replacement of French Third Force leaders in 1952 by a conservative coalition with different domestic concerns leading to the EDC's defeat. Others argue that the failure was largely due to ideational factors. For example, Craig Parsons argues that "only the cross cutting ideas of traditional, confederal, and community models explain the pattern of French positions

---

[32] As Article 10 explained, member states were prohibited from recruiting or maintaining national armed forces with a few exceptions. They could possess military forces: (1) to use in non-European territories; (2) to participate in international missions such as those directed by the United Nations; (3) to protect their chief of state. "The European Defense Community Treaty," pp. 1110–11.

[33] The supreme allied commander of NATO was authorized to ensure that the European Defense Forces were organized, equipped, trained, and prepared for duty – and would command their forces. Specifically, Article 18 of the EDC treaty states: "During wartime, the competent Supreme Commander of the North Atlantic Treaty Organization shall exercise with regard to the Forces provided for above the full powers and responsibilities of Supreme Commanders, such as these are conferred upon him by his terms of reference." "The European Defense Community Treaty," pp. 1112–13.

[34] See, for example, Lerner and Aron, *France Defeats the EDC*; Fursdon, *The European Defence Community*.

[35] Paul Pitman, "France's European Choices," Ph.D dissertation, Columbia University, New York, 1998.

on the EDC."[36] While these factors are undoubtedly important, they ignore the broader forces that contributed to the collapse of the EDC: structural conditions largely caused the EDC's collapse.[37]

The security dilemma was ameliorated by the massive US military presence and long-term commitment to Europe. At the core of US policy toward Western Europe was a desire to incorporate Germany into the Atlantic Alliance – whether directly through NATO or indirectly through the EDC.[38] Either way, the US wanted a determining role in European security affairs for the foreseeable future.[39] Charles Spofford, US deputy representative on the North Atlantic Council, argued that US power was critical to balancing the Soviet Union and containing Germany; European states were simply too weak. Consequently, it would be "dangerous to permit development of any thought of NATO defense framework as being temporary in comparison with European framework. Believe it important, therefore, that European army developments be considered as permanently rather than temporarily within NATO framework."[40]

By the early 1950s, US leaders were committed to keeping large numbers of military forces in Europe for the long term.[41] President Eisenhower remarked, for example, that the United States would keep military forces in Europe "as long as the need existed," including in Germany.[42] As Figure 3.1 illustrates, the number of US forces rose

[36] Craig Parsons, *A Certain Idea of Europe* (Ithaca, NY: Cornell University Press, 2003), p. 82

[37] On structure and the rationale for establishing the EDC, see William Hitchcock, *France Restored: Cold War Diplomacy and the Quest for Leadership in Europe, 1944–1954* (Chapel Hill, NC: University of North Carolina Press, 1998).

[38] On the importance of making the EDC an integral part of NATO see Acheson to diplomatic offices, January 29, 1951, *FRUS 1951*, Vol. III, p. 761. Spofford to Acheson, July 8, 1951, *FRUS 1951*, Vol. III, p. 821; Acheson and Lovett to Truman, July 30, 1951, *FRUS 1951*, Vol. III, pp. 849–52; meeting between Truman and Pleven, January 30, 1951, *FRUS 1951*, Vol. IV, *Europe: Political and Economic Relations*, p. 325; Chiefs of Mission meeting, October 2, 1952, *FRUS 1951*, Vol. III, pp. 652–5; Conant to Dulles, November 13, 1953, *FRUS 1952–54*, Vol. VII, pp. 553–5.

[39] There was some discussion during the early Eisenhower administration that the failure of the EDC might lead to an eventual American withdrawal from Europe. Perhaps the most noted example is John Foster Dulles's comment that the demise of the EDC "would compel an agonizing reappraisal of basic American policy." This was largely rhetorical, as demonstrated by Germany's swift entrance into NATO and the continuation of American build-up after the EDC's rejection. See, for example, Edward Fursdon, *The European Defence Community: A History* (New York: St. Martin's Press, 1980), pp. 230–4.

[40] Spofford to Acheson, July 8, 1951, *FRUS 1951*, Vol. III, p. 822.

[41] See, for example, memorandum of conversation between Lewis and Krekeler, November 18, 1953, *FRUS 1952–54*, Vol. VII, p. 556.

[42] Eisenhower, *The White House Years*, p. 400.

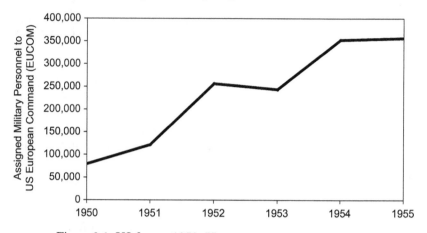

Figure 3.1. US forces, 1950–55.
Source: Nelson, *A History of U.S. Military Forces in Germany*, p. 81.

rapidly after 1950. By 1955 the US military presence increased an astounding 350 percent, demonstrating an irrevocable commitment to the defense of Western Europe. Furthermore, the US also contributed $8.8 billion between 1951 and 1955 to military buildup in Europe, and in 1953 the Eisenhower administration's "New Look" strategy led to the deployment of tactical nuclear weapons in Western Europe.[43]

By extending a security guarantee to Europe, the United States solved the security dilemma. At the heart of such a dilemma is the assumption that the anarchic nature of international politics – the absence of a supranational authority – forces states to protect themselves from external aggression. Since it can be difficult to know the intentions of other states and since states may misrepresent information, "one state's gain in security often advertently threatens others."[44] The American security guarantee to Europe removed this structural cause of conflict and ameliorated the condition of anarchy. The presence of several hundred thousand US military forces, along with nuclear weapons, meant that there was little reason to fear other Western European states. Rather

---

[43] On military aid see US Department of State, *Semiannual Report of the Secretary of Defense, January 1 to June 30, 1954* (Washington: Government Printing Office, 1955), p. 50. On US conventional and military forces in Europe during the early 1950s, see William P. Mako, *U.S. Ground Forces and the Defense of Central Europe* (Washington, DC: The Brookings Institution, 1983), pp. 10–16; Daniel J. Nelson, *A History of U.S. Military Forces in Germany* (Boulder, CO: Westview Press, 1987), pp. 37–59.

[44] Jervis, "Cooperation under the Security Dilemma," p. 170.

than relying on themselves, European states could rely on the American military for security.[45]

Most European governments supported a substantial American presence in Europe. As noted earlier, British leaders preferred a long-term US commitment to Europe. American military forces – rather than simply financial aid – were necessary to preserve peace in Europe and contain Germany, in addition to balancing against the Soviet Union.[46] The British thus refused to participate in the EDC. The establishment of the EDC, they feared, might cause the US to lose interest in Europe, revert to the isolationism of the interwar years, and trigger a severe security dilemma. "[European integration] is something which we know, in our bones, we cannot do," argued British Foreign Secretary Anthony Eden in a January 1952 speech at Columbia University. "We know that if we were to attempt it, we should relax the springs of our action in the Western Democratic cause and in the Atlantic Association which is the expression of that cause."[47] German, Dutch, Belgian, and a number of other European leaders seconded the importance of American forces.[48]

Structural conditions directly contributed to the collapse of the EDC for several reasons. To begin with, the British decision to support NATO rather than the EDC meant that France would be the only major power left to tie Germany down. French President Pierre Mendès-France argued that the absence of Britain had a deleterious impact on his government's ability to pass the EDC.[49] This is partly why he exclaimed moments after the defeat of the EDC that "the axiom of French policy must be to stick to Great Britain."[50] Furthermore, a

---

[45] Josef Joffe, "Europe's American Pacifier," *Foreign Policy*, No. 54, Spring 1984, esp. pp. 66–9.

[46] Jebb to Younger, 12 September 1950, *DBPO, 1950*, Series II, Vol. III, pp. 28–31; Cabinet meeting held at 10 Downing Street, 16 November 1950, *DBPO, 1950*, Series II, Vol. III, pp. 263–6.

[47] Speech by British Foreign Secretary Anthony Eden at Columbia University, New York, January 11, 1952, in Denise Folliot, ed., *Documents on International Affairs, 1952* (New York: Oxford University Press, 1955), pp. 43–4. British leaders also opposed the EDC because they refused to give up sovereignty in the security realm to a supranational institution.

[48] See, for example, Dirk U. Stikker, *Men of Responsibility: A Memoir* (New York: Harper & Row, 1965), pp. 303–4; Paul-Henri Spaak, *The Continuing Battle: Memoirs of a European, 1936–1966* (London: Weidenfeld and Nicolson, 1971), p. 150; Konrad Adenauer, *Memoirs, 1945–53* (Chicago: Henry Regnery, 1966), p. 320.

[49] "Le débat parlementaire sur les accords de Londres," 7 October 1954, in Pierre Mendès-France, *Oeuvres complètes III: Gouverner c'est Choisir 1954–1955* (Paris: Gallimard, 1986), pp. 390–1. See also "Le débat sur la ratification de la C.E.D.," 29 août 1954, ibid., p. 290.

[50] Reports of MM Jules Moch, Max Lejeune, and M. Triboulet, August 28 and 29, 1954, *J. O. Assemblée Nationale*, pp. 4454–73.

number of EDC opponents in the French Assemblée Nationale were not against the idea of German rearmament *per se*. Rather, they believed that the EDC was not the best institution; without Britain and the United States it would revive a barely disguised Wehrmacht, and Germany would increasingly dominate the EDC.[51] As Charles de Gaulle asked: "How could the memory of [Germany's] ambition, her audacity, her power and her tyranny be effaced from people's memories – an ambition which only yesterday had unleashed a military machine capable of crushing with one blow the armies of France and her allies."[52] In the aftermath of the EDC, France's speedy agreement to rearm a sovereign West Germany and incorporate it into NATO was only possible because of the American security guarantee. With the presence of American – as well as British – forces, European states would be secure from German revanchism. In sum, as Daniel Lerner argues, "it was precisely the American guarantee which gave France security at minimal cost and made possible the rejection of EDC on rational grounds of self-interest."[53]

The American military presence in Europe had largely solved the security dilemma, and the division of Germany only reinforced it. Germany could not become a potential hegemon. Both superpowers were wary that a reunified Germany might ally with the other side, and division was preferred over other alternatives.[54] By 1949, the German division was more or less complete; West Germany approved its Basic Law and Bonn was chosen as the country's capital. There were few tears shed following Germany's division, as French author François Mauriac wryly summed up: "I love Germany so dearly that I hope there will always be two of them." The efforts by German leaders to reassure Europeans that it understood the security dilemma were extraneous: German power was mitigated by American power. German Chancellor Konrad Adenauer repeatedly argued that Germany was a status quo power and must be enmeshed in a regional security institution to prevent it from becoming dangerous and to alleviate the fears of European states.

---

[51] Reports of MM Jules Moch, Max Lejeune, and M. Triboulet, August 28 and 29, 1954, *J.O. Assemblée Nationale*, pp. 4379–401; pamphlet "Contre le traité actuel de la C.E.D. pour la liberté de vote et l'unité fraternelle du parti" published at the end of March 1954 by the opponents of EDC. For an overview of the EDC debate see Stanley Hoffmann, "The Postmortems," in Lerner and Aron, *France Defeats EDC*, pp. 165–96.

[52] Charles de Gaulle, *Memoirs of Hope: Renewal 1958–62, Endeavour 1962–* (London: Weidenfeld and Nicolson, 1971), p. 172.

[53] Daniel Lerner, "Reflections on France in the World Arena," in Lerner and Aron, *France Defeats the EDC*, p. 216.

[54] John Lewis Gaddis, *We Now Know: Rethinking Cold War History* (New York: Oxford University Press, 1997), pp. 135–8.

"One must never forget that between Bonn and Paris lie the gigantic graveyards of Verdun." Germany must pursue a policy of "Germany in Europe" and encourage "a spirit of truly European cooperation."[55] Such statements were doubtlessly helpful. But American power largely negated the possibility of a security dilemma.

Fouchet Plan (1958–1963)

Not long after the return to power of French President Charles de Gaulle in 1958, European states began a serious debate over creating a European security institution based on the plans of Christian Fouchet, the French ambassador to Denmark. Some recent scholars such as Andrew Moravcsik have argued that the Fouchet Plan was largely a "sideshow."[56] But the evidence suggests otherwise.[57] De Gaulle had high hopes for the Fouchet Plan because he was becoming vexed with NATO. Perhaps the core issue centered on the United States' unwillingness to support the nationalization of European nuclear forces. In the event of a war with the Soviet Union in Europe, the United States wanted to retain control of the launch of nuclear weapons. This presented at least two questions for France: could the French be sure that the United States would react quickly to Soviet aggression? As de Gaulle told Eisenhower in September 1959:

In the course of the two world wars, America was France's ally, and France . . . has not forgotten what she owes to American help. But neither has she forgotten that during the First World War, that help came only after three long years of struggle which nearly proved mortal for her, and that during the Second she had already been crushed before you intervened.[58]

Moreover, in the event of a nuclear war, how much control would France have over the initiation and conduct of the war? If a nuclear war erupted in Western Europe, "France ran the risk of being committed without even knowing it."[59] Among de Gaulle's other concerns with

---

[55] Adenauer, *Memoirs*, pp. 364–5.

[56] Andrew Moravcsik, "De Gaulle Between Grain and Grandeur: The Political Economy of French EC Policy, 1958–1970 (Part I)," *Journal of Cold War Studies*, Vol. 2, No. 2, Spring 2000, pp. 3–43. Also see Moravcsik, *The Choice for Europe: Social Purpose and State Power from Messina to Maastricht* (Ithaca, NY: Cornell University Press, 1998), p. 177.

[57] See the responses to Moravcsik and the Fouchet Plan by Marc Trachtenberg, Stanley Hoffmann, and Jeffrey Vanke in *Journal of Cold War Studies*, Vol. 2, No. 3, Fall 2000.

[58] De Gaulle, *Memoirs of Hope*, p. 214. Moreover, he told American journalist C.L. Sulzberger that "the United States will not fight for us." C.L. Sulzberger, *The Last of the Giants* (New York: Macmillan, 1970), p. 61.

[59] Memorandum of conversation between Eisenhower and de Gaulle, September 2, 1959, *FRUS 1958–60*, Vol. VII, *Western Europe*, p. 260.

NATO was that it was too narrowly limited to the security of the North Atlantic. He preferred to establish a security institution with a much broader scope that addressed important security issues in such areas as the Middle East and North Africa.[60]

With the initiation of a NATO crisis, what options did European states have? There were at least three possible ones:

- Unilateralism
- NATO
- Fouchet Plan.

First, the default strategy was unilateralism. By the late 1950s, for example, France was considering the possibility of a unilateral foreign policy. It began to move in this direction by exploding its first nuclear bomb in February 1960, pursuing an independent nuclear weapons program, withdrawing the French Mediterranean Fleet from NATO in March 1959, and ultimately withdrawing from NATO's integrated military arm in 1966.[61] Unilateralism, however, was problematic for most European states because it triggered the security dilemma that the US had already resolved. Who would protect Western Europe against a Soviet conventional or nuclear attack? How could European states be sure that Germany would remain a benign power in the future? In short, a unilateral foreign and defense policy was problematic for European states because it aggravated the security dilemma.

Second, European states – including France – could have continued with NATO. We know through hindsight, of course, that NATO was the preferred option because it ensured that a large American military presence would remain in Western Europe. However, it is worth remembering that by 1960 there were serious tensions in the Atlantic Alliance. As Marc Trachtenberg argues: "This conflict between the United States and the European allies on the nuclear issue was a basic source of tension, but it is important to see it in context: the western political system as a whole was in disarray, and the problems were growing."[62]

---

[60] Letter from President de Gaulle to President Eisenhower, September 17, 1958, *FRUS 1958–60*, Vol. VII, pp. 81–3. This concern about broadening the scope of security cooperation is apparent in the series of tripartite negotiations between France, Britain, and the United States. See, for example, discussions during the tripartite talks, *FRUS 1958–60*, Vol. VII, pp. 128–44, 156–9, 160–2, 164–81.

[61] In withdrawing his Mediterranean Fleet, de Gaulle pointed out that the United States and Great Britain had, after all, "taken steps to prevent the greater part of their naval forces from being integrated in NATO." Press Conference held by General de Gaulle, March 25, 1959, *Major Addresses, Statements and Press Conferences of General Charles de Gaulle, May 19, 1958–January 31, 1964* (New York: French Embassy, 1964), p. 49

[62] Trachtenberg, *A Constructed Peace*, p. 238.

Third, European states also considered establishing a European security institution anchored by the six states participating in the European Economic Community ("the Six"): France, Belgium, Italy, Luxembourg, West Germany, and the Netherlands. This became known as the Fouchet Plan and was named after Christian Fouchet, the French ambassador to Denmark, who was tasked with chairing the committee to develop a European security institution.[63] Between 1958 and 1961, leaders of the Six held a series of general meetings to discuss the need for greater political cooperation.[64] They were capped by the Fouchet Plan, which consisted of several draft treaties: a first draft was presented by the French to the committee in November 1961; a second revised draft was submitted by the French in January 1962; and a counter draft treaty was prepared by the five other delegations in January 1962.

The first draft called for the establishment of a new European institution termed the "Union of the European Peoples" to coordinate foreign policy. It was explicitly *not* supranational and aimed "to bring about the adoption of a common foreign policy" and to strengthen "the security of Member States against any aggression by adopting a common defence policy."[65] Decision-making would be intergovernmental: heads of state would meet every four months to coordinate foreign and defense policies, foreign ministers were expected to meet at least every four months, and a European political commission was to prepare and implement the decisions of European leaders. Foreign Ministers of the Six continued to meet throughout the winter to revise the draft treaty, particularly the relationship between the Union and NATO.

In January 1962, Fouchet introduced a second French draft that was unilaterally revised by de Gaulle. The French president refused to

[63] For general accounts of the Fouchet negotiations see Robert Bloes, *Le "Plan Fouchet" et le problème de l'Europe politique* (Bruges: Collège d'Europe, 1970); Pierre Gerbert, "In Search of Political Union: The Fouchet Plan Negotiations (1960–62)," in Roy Pryce, ed., *The Dynamics of European Union* (New York: Croom Helm, 1987), pp. 105–29; Susanne J. Bodenheimer, *Political Union: A Microcosm of European Politics, 1960–1966* (Leiden: A. W. Sijthoff, 1967), pp. 76–102; Alessandro Silj, *Europe's Political Puzzle: A Study of the Fouchet Negotiations and the 1963 Veto* (Cambridge, MA: Center for International Affairs, 1967).
[64] See, for example, de Gaulle's remarks on May 31, 1960 and September 5, 1960. Address by President Charles de Gaulle, May 31, 1960, *Major Addresses, Statements and Press Conferences of General Charles de Gaulle*, p. 78; Press Conference held by General de Gaulle, September 5, 1960, ibid., pp. 92–3.
[65] European Parliament, *Towards Political Union: A Selection of Documents* (General Directorate of Parliamentary Documentation and Information, 1964), p. 12. De Gaulle believed that political union in Europe was "utopian," but wanted France to have more political weight. Christian Fouchet, *Mémoires d'hier et de demain: Au service du Général de Gaulle* (Paris: Plon, 1971), p. 197.

include a reference to NATO, widened the scope of the institution to include economic responsibilities, and added two new bodies: a committee of foreign ministers and a committee of ministers of education.[66] In response to the French draft, the delegations from Belgium, Italy, Luxembourg, West Germany, and the Netherlands prepared a third draft treaty that was notably different in several ways: it added a clause on the importance of NATO to European security; deleted any reference to cooperation in the realm of economics; and introduced a Court of Justice.[67] Despite continued negotiations throughout the winter and spring, the Fouchet Plan folded by April 1962. Negotiations in Paris among foreign ministers of the Six ended in a stalemate, and no date was fixed for further ministerial discussions of a draft treaty.

What explains the failure of the Fouchet Plan and the attempt to create a European security institution in the early 1960s? Again, structural factors played a critical role. The major reason was the continued US military presence in Europe, which mitigated the security dilemma. There was little demand for a security institution in the early 1960s because the United States military presence in Europe continued to resolve the security dilemma. As Figure 3.2 highlights, the US kept well over 300,000 military personnel in EUCOM (European Command) in the late 1950s and early 1960s. Furthermore, the United States continued to possess a robust nuclear arsenal in Europe that included strategic aircraft (such as B-52s and B-47s), missiles (such as *Atlas*, *Titan*, and *Minuteman*), ballistic submarines (such as *Polaris*), and tactical nuclear weapons that were deployed into NATO land forces (such as the *Honest John* at brigade and divisional levels, and *Corporal* and *Redstone* at corps and army levels).[68]

With such flashpoints as the crisis over Berlin, which continued with varying degrees of intensity until the end of 1962, the United States was willing to make a long-term commitment to Europe. As President Kennedy reminded Adenauer in 1961, the United States intended "to maintain and even increase its forces."[69] The US's conventional and nuclear capabilities, as well as its long-term commitment to

---

[66] See, for example, Fouchet, *Mémoires d'hier et de demain*, pp. 369–71.

[67] This draft included two different variants on the institution's relationship to NATO. The Dutch proposed that the adoption of a common defense policy should be formed "within the framework of the Atlantic Alliance," while the other four delegations proposed that it be worded "as a contribution towards strengthening the Atlantic Alliance." *Towards Political Union*, p. 20.

[68] International Institute for Strategic Studies, *The Military Balance, 1962–63* (London: IISS, 1963), pp. 9–21.

[69] Memorandum of conversation between Kennedy and Adenauer, April 12, 1961, *FRUS 1961–63*, Vol. XIII, *Western Europe and Canada*, p. 275.

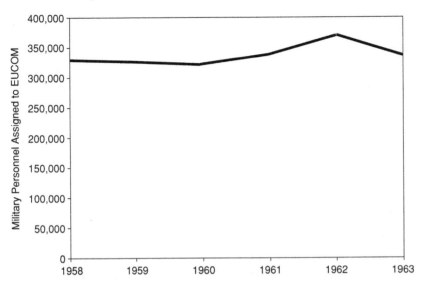

Figure 3.2. US forces, 1958–63.
Source: Nelson, *A History of U.S. Military Forces in Germany,* p. 81.

Europe, mitigated the security dilemma. It prevented the rise of a rearmed and revanchist Germany, and protected Western Europe from a Soviet attack. In sum, the American security guarantee removed the structural cause of conflict in Europe and ameliorated the condition of anarchy.

In the absence of a potential security dilemma, there was little need to push for a European security institution. Indeed, the fundamental reason for the Belgian and Dutch refusal to support the Fouchet Plan, the Italians' tepid endorsement, and eventually the somewhat ambivalent attitude of the Germans was the plan's impact on NATO – and, more specifically, on US involvement in Europe.[70] The Dutch delegation objected to any discussions on European defense outside NATO, and, as noted earlier, inserted a clause into one of the drafts stating that any common European defense policy must remain "within the framework of the Atlantic Alliance."[71] Belgian foreign minister Spaak similarly noted that he was deeply concerned that the Fouchet Plan might lead to a departure of the United States and perhaps even

[70] Frédéric Bozo, *Two Strategies for Europe: De Gaulle, the United States, and the Atlantic Alliance* (New York: Rowman and Littlefield, 2001), pp. 77–82.
[71] *Towards Political Union,* p. 36.

Britain from continental Europe.[72] In their counterproposal to de
Gaulle's unilateral draft in January 1962, the five other delegations
explicitly stipulated that the Union should not interfere with NATO,
but should strengthen it. De Gaulle, of course, was acutely aware of
these sentiments and somewhat despairingly acknowledged that one
of the core reasons why the bulk of the Six rejected the Fouchet
Plan was because "in the state of Cold War which existed in the world,
everything for them was subordinated to the desire for American
protection."[73]

Much like the European defense community in the 1950s, the need
for German leaders to understand the security dilemma was largely
moot. The US security guarantee solved the dilemma. Moreover,
Germany remained a divided country and was a potential hegemon. In
fact, German leaders directly contributed to the downfall of the Fouchet
Plan. Following de Gaulle's unilateral revisions, German leaders became
concerned that the Fouchet Plan might threaten NATO. Along with
Belgium, Italy, Luxembourg, and the Netherlands, they argued for the
inclusion of a clause stating that one objective of the Union should be
"the adoption of a common defence policy as a contribution towards
strengthening the Atlantic Alliance."[74] At a meeting with de Gaulle in
February 1962, Adenauer demanded that the Fouchet plan "pay solemn
homage to the Atlantic Alliance."[75]

European political cooperation (1969–1991)

In the late 1960s and early 1970s, discussions about reducing American
forces on the continent – termed "mutually balanced force reduction"
(MBFR) – helped jumpstart negotiations about European cooperation
in foreign policy and defense. In a meeting with German Chancellor
Willy Brandt in April 1970, for example, President Richard Nixon began
by asking what the chancellor's "principal objections were to a substantial
reduction of the American military presence in Europe."[76] Nixon
said that while he was opposed to withdrawing troops from Europe,

---

[72] Paul-Henri Spaak interview with *Le Soir* in *A Retrospective View of the Political Year in
Europe, 1962* (Paris: Western European Union Assembly, General Affairs Committee),
pp. 30–2. On the Dutch see Bodenheimer, *Political Union*, pp. 76–102.
[73] De Gaulle, *Memoirs of Hope*, p. 199.
[74] *Towards Political Union*, pp. 26, 36.
[75] See the account in Jean Lacouture, *De Gaulle: The Ruler, 1945–1970* (New York:
W.W. Norton, 1991), p. 349.
[76] Willy Brandt, *People and Politics: The Years 1960–1975* (Boston, MA: Little, Brown and
Company, 1976), p. 285.

he was under tremendous domestic political pressure from Congress. In particular, US Senator Mike Mansfield introduced an amendment to the Draft Extension Act that would halve US forces in Europe. Mansfield believed that drastic cuts in American forces would save money and force European states to take more responsibility for their own defense.[77] Consequently, European states had several options:

- Unilateralism
- NATO
- European political cooperation.

First, they could have pursued unilateralism. As usual, the French were good candidates. Though Charles de Gaulle was replaced by Georges Pompidou in 1969, there were still strong unilateralists in the French government such as Defense Minister Michel Debré and Prime Minister Jacques Chaban-Delmas. As explicated in the 1972 *Livre blanc sur la défense nationale* (White Paper on national defense), French policymakers refused to reintegrate French military forces into NATO's military command and to compromise on France's independent *force de frappe* (nuclear strike force).[78] Within a few years, France's nuclear force was bolstered by the deployment of tactical nuclear weapons, intermediate-range missiles on the windswept Plateau d'Albion in south-eastern France, and strategic submarines.[79] The problem – as even the French recognized – was that a return to unilateralism for *all* European states would have been highly destabilizing. The reason, of course, is that no one wanted a unilateral Germany, which would have triggered a security dilemma.

Second, European states could have continued with NATO as the preeminent security institution and kept a large contingent of US military forces on the continent. Again, we know through hindsight that NATO was the preferred option among European leaders. However, it was not *ipso facto* inevitable. As already noted, the Nixon Administration was under severe domestic pressure to cut US forces in Europe

---

[77] See, for example, Mansfield's statement on the floor of the Senate on September 13, 1968. "The Situation in Czechoslovakia and U.S. Forces in Europe," Reports of Senator Mike Mansfield to the Committee on Foreign Relations, Y4.F76/2:V67/14 (Washington, DC: US Government Printing Office, 1968), pp. 13–16.

[78] French Ministry of Defense, *Livre blanc sur la défense nationale* (Paris: Ministère de la Défense Nationale, June 1972). Also see Philip H. Gordon, *A Certain Idea of France: French Security Policy and the Gaullist Legacy* (Princeton, NJ: Princeton University Press, 1993), pp. 70–8.

[79] In 1974, for example, France had ballistic missile submarines with M-1 missiles, SSBS S-2 intermediate-range ballistic missiles, and Mirage IVA bombers. International Institute for Strategic Studies, *The Military Balance, 1974–1975* (London: IISS, 1974), p. 21.

drastically, and NATO itself was, in Henry Kissinger's words, "in urgent need of revision."[80] In his "Year of Europe" speech Kissinger explicitly encouraged greater European cooperation: "We will continue to support European unity. Based on the principles of partnership, we will make concessions to its further growth."[81]

Third, European states could have created a European security institution – that eventually became known as "European political cooperation" (EPC).[82] Discussions began during the European summit conference at the Hague in December 1969, when the heads of state "agreed to instruct the Ministers for Foreign Affairs to study the best way of achieving progress in the matter of political unification."[83] EPC consisted of several stages: the Luxembourg Report (1970), the Copenhagen Report (1973), the London Report (1981), and the Single European Act (1986).

Following the Hague summit's directive, Belgian political director Vicomte Davignon was given the task of producing a report that laid the groundwork for a new institution of foreign policy cooperation. Davignon's report, which was approved at the Luxembourg Conference of Foreign Ministers on October 27, 1970, was strikingly minimal in its suggestions. Noting that European efforts "ought first to concentrate specifically on the coordination of foreign policies," the Luxembourg report concluded that the foreign affairs ministers should meet at least every six months.[84] It was notable for its paucity of both substance and supranational involvement. EPC was not integrated into the European Community; it operated as an intergovernmental process separate from the treaties of Rome and Paris. The Copenhagen Report, which was approved on July 23, 1973, likewise made little progress. It increased the frequency of meetings involving foreign affairs ministers

[80]   Henry Kissinger, *Years of Upheaval* (Boston: Little, Brown and Company, 1982), p. 134. On the crisis within NATO see Lewis Gaddis, *Strategies of Containment*, pp. 332–3.

[81]   Kissinger, *Years of Upheaval*, p. 153.

[82]   For general works on European Political Cooperation see Simon J. Nuttall, *European Political Co-operation* (New York: Oxford University Press, 1992); Panayiotis Ifestos, *European Political Cooperation: Towards a Framework for Supranational Diplomacy?* (Brookfield, VT: Avebury, 1987); Alfred Pijpers, Elfriede Regelsberger, and Wolfgang Wessels, *European Political Cooperation in the 1980s: A Common Foreign Policy for Western Europe?* (Boston: Martinus Nijhoff, 1988); David Allen, Reinhardt Rummel, and Wolfgang Wessels, *European Political Cooperation: Towards a Foreign Policy for Western Europe* (Boston, MA: Butterworth Scientific, 1982).

[83]   Western European Union Assembly, "Communiqué issued after the conference in the Hague," December 2, 1969, *A Retrospective View of the Political Year in Europe, 1969* (Paris: General Affairs Committee, Western European Union Assembly, 1970), p. 144.

[84]   The Davignon (Luxembourg) Report, in Christopher Hill and Karen E. Smith, eds., *European Foreign Policy: Key Documents* (New York: Routledge, 2000), p. 76.

to every three months, introduced a "correspondents group" tasked with the rather daunting job of implementing political cooperation and studying problems of organization, and established the COREU telex network to increase information-sharing between European capitals. By the mid 1970s, however, it was clear that EPC was largely a pipedream. Belgian Prime Minister Léo Tindemans tellingly wrote in 1975:

Why has the European concept lost a lot of its force and initial impetus? I believe that over the years the European public has lost a guiding light, namely the political consensus between our countries on our reasons for undertaking this joint task and the characteristics with which we wish to endow it.[85]

For the next fifteen years EPC remained stagnant despite some beleaguered attempts to revive it. In October 1981 the London Report offered several token changes. For example, it created a small body of foreign policy officials to assist the European Community when dealing with third countries. Often referred to as the "troika principle," it was inspired by the desire for the now ten European states to speak with a single voice: "Third countries will increasingly express the desire to enter into more or less regular contact with [the Ten]. It is important that the Ten should be able to respond effectively to these demands . . . and that they should speak with one voice in dealings with them."[86] In February 1986 the Single European Act, which is largely remembered for introducing the Single European Market, introduced several modest foreign policy changes. As its name suggests, the Act was referred to as "single" because it covered both the European Community and the EPC in one legal text, though it importantly did not integrate EPC directly into the European Community.[87] Moreover, it replaced the troika of foreign policy officials with a secretariat for EPC based in Brussels. Despite these steps, however, EPC was not, as some have argued, a "profoundly important step towards political unity."[88] While it did cause an increase in information-sharing between European capitals, it did not lead to the creation of a viable European security institution. As one senior British diplomat has noted: "EPC was really just an opportunity

[85] Léo Tindemans, "Report on European Union," December 29, 1975, in Hill and Smith, *European Foreign Policy*, p. 100.
[86] The London Report, October 13, 1981, in Hill and Smith, *European Foreign Policy*, p. 117.
[87] This step was important because it left the door open for a more explicit linking between security and non-security issues. See, for example, Nuttall, *European Political Cooperation*, p. 252.
[88] Ifestos, *European Political Cooperation*, p. 151. Also see Michael E. Smith, *Europe's Foreign and Security Policy* (New York: Cambridge University Press, 2004).

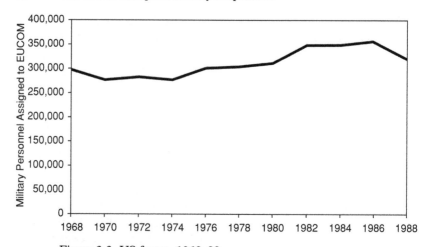

Figure 3.3. US forces, 1968–88.
Source: Nelson, *A History of U.S. Military Forces in Germany*, p. 103; *The Military Balance, 1974–1975* through *The Military Balance, 1988–1989*; *Military Presence: U.S. Personnel in NATO Europe*, p. 3; Author's estimates.

to increase information exchanges between European capitals. It was not a serious attempt at cooperation."[89]

What explains the failure of EPC and the attempt to create a European security institution in the early 1970s? The massive US military presence in Europe continued to ameliorate the security dilemma. In the face of strong pressure from Capitol Hill to reduce US force levels in Europe drastically, the Nixon Administration remained committed to European security. Kissinger made it clear in his "Year of Europe" speech that while he encouraged Europeans to share more of the defense burden, "we will not disengage from our solemn commitments to our allies. We will maintain our forces and not withdraw from Europe unilaterally."[90] These words were supported by plenty of evidence. As Figure 3.3 highlights, US forces remained around or above 300,000 throughout the 1970s and 1980s. As usual, American conventional forces were backed by a powerful nuclear deterrent. The Soviet Union continued to present a formidable nuclear and conventional threat to Western Europe and the United States, and US policymakers were firmly committed to remaining in Europe for the foreseeable future.

---

[89] Author's interview with senior official, British Foreign and Commonwealth Office, London, January 31, 2001.
[90] Kissinger, *Years of Upheaval*, p. 153.

Moreover, most European leaders supported a substantial American presence in Europe and believed that NATO was the only viable security institution for the future they foresaw. As the 1971/72 German *White Paper* argued: "The maintenance of a global balance of forces remains a necessity. To that end, an adequate counterweight to the military power of the Soviet Union and the Warsaw Pact must be maintained in Europe . . . A substantially undiminished presence of the United States in Europe is prerequisite to a stable peace in Europe."[91] European leaders such as Willy Brandt reassured American policymakers that they wanted American forces to stay. The British and French shared this view, and argued that a unilateral reduction in US forces would unnecessarily decrease security on the continent.[92] Consequently, there was little incentive to create a viable European security institution such as European Political Cooperation. The American guarantee ameliorated the security dilemma in Europe. Germany remained a divided power and the US military presence solved the dilemma. Nevertheless, German leaders did not shy away from arguing that they were a status quo power and denouncing their country's past behavior, particularly the Nazi era. "No reservations, no whitewash," Brandt remarked in May 1968. "Neo-Nazism and nationalism are a betrayal of our country and nation."[93]

Toward Maastricht and beyond (1991–)

Structural changes at the end of the Cold War began a fundamental shift in European security. The collapse of the USSR, European concerns about an American withdrawal, and the reunification of Germany created a potential security dilemma in Europe. There were at least four plausible options:

- Balance against Germany
- Collective security through the Organization for Security and Co-operation in Europe (OSCE)

---

[91] *White Paper 1971/1972: The Security of the Federal Republic of Germany and the Development of the Federal Armed Forces* (Bonn: Federal Minister of Defence, 1971/1972), p. 6. See also *White Paper 1979: The Security of the Federal Republic of Germany and the Development of the Federal Armed Forces* (Bonn: Federal Minister of Defence, 1979).

[92] Brandt, *People and Politics*, p. 303. On US forces in Europe see also pp. 260, 285, 288. In an address to the National Press Club on April 10, 1970, Brandt remarked that "close relations with the United States are considered as [*sic*] number one priority in foreign affairs and that the presence of U.S. forces in our country continues to be regarded as vital" (p. 288).

[93] Ibid., p. 152.

- Continuation of NATO
- Creation of an EU security arm.

First, with the demise of the Soviet Union, European states could have refrained from relying on an any security institution – including NATO – for regional stability, and opted to balance against German power.[94] The major problem with this strategy, however, was that it was unlikely to curb the German threat. If possible, Europe's major powers – France, Britain, and Germany – preferred to prevent a destabilizing security dilemma. French and British leaders argued that they would balance against Germany if it refused to enmesh itself in a European institution. At a meeting with German Foreign Minister Hans-Dietrich Genscher in late 1989, for example, French President François Mitterrand bluntly warned: "If German unification was to occur in a Europe that ultimately made no real progress, then the European partners, who in the future were going to face 80 million Germans, would probably be looking for a counterweight."[95] Thus, balancing against Germany was a realistic option only if Germany refused multilateral cooperation.

Second, European states could have chosen a collective security institution along the lines of the nineteenth-century Concert of Europe.[96] As Charles and Clifford Kupchan argued, for example, European states could have adopted a two-tiered concert centered around Britain, France, Germany, and perhaps the United States and Russia.[97] The logical organization was the Conference on Security and Cooperation in Europe, which expanded into the 55-member Organization for Security and Cooperation in Europe (OSCE) in 1995 and included member countries from Europe, North America, and Central Asia. However, the OSCE was unlikely to prevent a security dilemma since most collective security organizations have been far too weak and unwieldy.[98]

---

[94] Some realists predicted that the collapse of the Soviet Union would cause the United States to withdraw from the continent, leading to a return to balance-of-power politics in Europe. See, for example, John J. Mearsheimer, "Back to the Future: Instability in Europe after the Cold War," *International Security*, Vol. 15, No. 1, Summer 1990, pp. 5–56. On NATO's dim future see Stephen M. Walt, "The Ties that Fray: Why Europe and America are Drifting Apart," *The National Interest*, No. 54, Winter 1998/99, pp. 3–11.

[95] Haus-Dietrich Genscher, *Rebuilding a House Divided: A Memoir by the Architect of Germany's Unification* (New York: Broadway Books, 1998), p. 308. Also see Zelikow and Rice, *Germany Unified and Europe Transformed*, pp. 47, 97–98, 207.

[96] This option was preferred by Soviet leaders and German Foreign Minister Hans-Dietrich Genscher. See Genscher, *Rebuilding a House Divided*, pp. 362–4, 392–3, 460–2.

[97] Charles A. Kupchan and Clifford A. Kupchan, "Concerts, Collective Security, and the Future of Europe," *International Security*, Vol. 16, No. 1, Summer 1991, pp. 114–61.

[98] For a critique of collective security organizations see John J. Mearsheimer, "The False Promise of International Institutions," *International Security*, Vol. 19, No. 3, Winter 1994/95, pp. 26–37; Charles L. Glaser, "Why NATO is Still Best: Future Security

Furthermore, the expansion of the OSCE was not caused by the fear of a united Germany; most policymakers recognized that the organization was too weak to accomplish that objective. Rather, the OSCE's goal was much more modest and included such functions as monitoring elections in transitioning European countries and lobbying for greater human rights and freedom of the press.[99] US Secretary of State James Baker, who was involved in the German unification negotiations, was explicitly clear that the organization "was not the appropriate place for determining Germany's future."[100]

Third, European states could have continued utilizing NATO as the continent's only viable security institution.[101] As already noted, NATO played a crucial role in ameliorating the security dilemma during the Cold War, and American conventional and nuclear power served as the lynchpin. British policymakers led by John Major were particularly supportive of the continued preeminence of NATO.[102] Indeed, NATO expanded eastward in 1999 to include Poland, Hungary, and the Czech Republic, and added seven more Eastern European countries in 2004.[103] As will be discussed in more detail later, there was an important cost to relying on NATO: it was unclear how long the United States would remain in Europe. With the collapse of the Soviet Union, NATO's *raison d'être*, there were serious doubts about the US's long-term commitment. Despite American verbal reassurances that it would remain a continental power, many European leaders nevertheless believed that the absence of the Soviet threat and increasing US security concerns in the Middle East and Asia would eventually lead to an

Arrangements for Europe," *International Security*, Vol. 18, No. 1, Summer 1993, pp. 5–50; Joseph Joffe, "Collective Security and the Future of Europe: Failed Dreams and Dead Ends," *Survival*, Vol. 34, No. 1, Summer 1992, pp. 36–50.

[99] Organization for Security and Co-operation in Europe, *OSCE Handbook* (Vienna: OSCE, 2000), pp. 12–17.

[100] Zelikow and Rice, *Germany Unified and Europe Transformed*, p. 177.

[101] See, for example, Glaser, "Why NATO is Still Best"; Stephen Van Evera, "Primed for Peace: Europe after the Cold War," *International Security*, Vol. 15, No. 3, Winter 1990/91, pp. 7–57; Charles A. Kupchan, "Reconstructing the West: The Case for an Atlantic Union," in Kupchan, ed., *Atlantic Security: Contending Visions* (New York: Council on Foreign Relations, 1998), pp. 64–91. This would have meant changing the purpose of NATO from a security institution committed to balancing against the Soviet Union to an institution with broader goals, such as preserving regional security and promoting democracy. NATO has, of course, attempted to do this. See, for example, Celeste Wallander, "Institutional Assets and Adaptability: NATO after the Cold War," *International Organization*, Vol. 54, No. 4, Autumn 2000, pp. 705–35.

[102] John Major, *John Major: The Autobiography* (New York: HarperCollins Publishers, 1999), p. 586.

[103] See, for example, Ronald D. Asmus, *Opening NATO's Door: How the Alliance Remade Itself for a New Era* (New York: Columbia University Press, 2002), p. xxv.

American withdrawal. The expansion of NATO in 1999 did not dispel concerns about US withdrawal, which were reinforced by the American decision to bypass NATO during the 2001–2002 war in Afghanistan, the transatlantic tensions that resulted from the 2003 war in Iraq, and the US decision to withdraw from additional bases in Western Europe. Thus, NATO by itself was not a reliable long-term solution.

The fourth option was to create a security arm of the European Union. This offered a long-term solution to the security dilemma by keeping Germany enmeshed in a security institution. Consequently, European states pushed ahead on two tracks: a common foreign and security policy (CFSP), and a European security and defense policy (ESDP). Efforts to build a CFSP began in the late 1980s during the preliminary negotiations for the Treaty on European Union, which was signed in Maastricht in February 1992. Maastricht established CFSP as one of the three pillars of the EU. This marked a significant change because it brought foreign policy for the first time within the framework of the European Union.[104] Maastricht also urged member states to define and conform to "common positions" and to implement "joint actions" in areas where member states had important interests in common such as the Balkans, the Mediterranean, and Russia. The 1997 Amsterdam Treaty introduced several institutional reforms. It established "common strategies" in areas where member states had joint interests.[105] More importantly, Article 26 created a high representative for CFSP to improve the coordination and centralization of foreign policymaking.[106] The high representative was equipped with a policy planning and early warning unit to monitor international security developments, provide assessments of potential crises, and produce policy option papers. Amsterdam also led to the appointment of European diplomatic envoys to areas of geostrategic importance such as the Balkans and the Middle East.

[104] As Title V, Article J.1 stated: "The Union and its Member States shall define and implement a common foreign and security policy, governed by the provisions of this Title and covering all areas of foreign and security policy." Treaty on European Union, in Richard Corbett, *Treaty of Maastricht: From Conception to Ratification: A Comprehensive Reference Guide* (Harlow, Essex: Longman Group, 1993), pp. 429–30. Also see Simon J. Nuttall, *European Foreign Policy* (New York: Oxford University Press, 2000), pp. 273–4.

[105] "Common Strategy of the European Union on Russia," April 4, 1999; "European Council Common Strategy on Ukraine," December 11, 1999; "Common Strategy of the European Council on the Mediterranean Region," June 19, 2000 (http://ue.eu.int/pesc/strategies/en.htm).

[106] On centralization see Barbara Koremenos, Charles Lipson and Duncan Snidal, "The Rational Design of International Institutions," *International Organization*, Vol. 55, No. 4, Autumn 2001, pp. 771–2.

The second track was the establishment of a coordinated defense capability for peacekeeping operations through ESDP. In December 1998 the Franco-British summit at St Malo added a common defense policy to the second pillar.[107] As British Prime Minister Tony Blair and French President Jacques Chirac argued: "the [European] Union must have the capacity for autonomous action, backed up by credible military forces."[108] A permanent political-military structure was established at the 1999 Helsinki summit to oversee future peacekeeping operations conducted by a European Union rapid reaction force.[109] EU states created a political and security committee, chaired by the high representative for CFSP, to exercise political control and strategic direction of EU military operations. It also established a military committee, composed of the respective defense ministers and represented by their delegates, to provide the Political and Security Committee with military advice and recommendations on all military matters within the EU. Finally, a military staff was created to conduct EU peacekeeping operations and provide early warning, situation assessment, and strategic planning for operations.[110]

In sum, Maastricht marked the beginning of a fundamental shift in European security by creating a foreign policy and defense arm of the European Union. Bolstered by later developments at Amsterdam, St Malo, Helsinki, Nice, and beyond, Maastricht succeeded where the European Defense Community, the Fouchet Plan, and European political cooperation failed. As discussed in more detail in Chapter 6, these organizational developments facilitated the deployment of EU-led military and civilian operations to Bosnia, Macedonia, Congo, Palestinian territory, Georgia, and a number of other countries around the world.[111]

---

[107] Perhaps the first allusion to Britain's change in policy toward an EU role in defense was at the informal European summit at Pörtschach, Austria on October 24–25, 1998. At the press conference, Blair noted that there was a strong British willingness "for Europe to take a stronger foreign policy and security role."

[108] Franco-British Summit, St Malo, France, December 3–4, 1998 in Maartje Rutten, ed., *From St. Malo to Nice: European Defence, Core Documents* (Paris: Institute for Security Studies, May 2001), pp. 8–9. Emphasis added. As one senior State Department official noted: "St. Malo took us completely off guard, and, frankly, some time to recover from." Author's interview with senior United States State Department official, January 31, 2001. Also see US Secretary of State Madeleine Albright's response to the St Malo accord several days later: "The Right Balance Will Secure NATO's Future," *The Financial Times*, December 7, 1998.

[109] European Council, Helsinki, December 10–11, 1999.

[110] As of this writing it is not clear whether the European Union will have an independent military planning staff, or whether that will be done in conjunction with NATO's Supreme Headquarters Allied Powers Europe (SHAPE).

[111] Council of the European Union *Presidency Report on ESDP*, 15678/05 (Brussels: European Council, December 2005).

Indeed, one of the truly remarkable features of Maastricht was that any security institution at all was established given the failures over the past forty years.

Why was a security arm of the European Union created in post-Cold War Europe when earlier attempts failed? The answer is straightforward. German reunification and concerns about an American withdrawal created a potential security dilemma in Europe. But German leaders understood the dilemma and were willing to ameliorate it through the EU. In the end, German, British, and French leaders learned from history and calculated that cooperation through the European Union was the optimal strategy to achieve regional peace and security.

To begin with, the reunification of Germany and the fear of an American withdrawal created a potential security dilemma in Europe. German reunification significantly increased Germany's power. Its population increased 27 percent from 63 million in 1990 to 80 million in 1991, and its gross domestic product increased over 20 percent from 1990 to 1991.[112] By 1991, Germany had the largest population and gross domestic product in Europe, causing notable concern among European leaders. In Britain, Prime Minister Margaret Thatcher was deeply worried about Germany because of its increased power and historical behavior. She argued that "a reunified Germany is simply too big and powerful to be just another player within Europe. Moreover, Germany has always looked east as well as west . . . Germany is thus by its very nature a destabilizing rather than a stabilizing force in Europe."[113] During a visit to Moscow in September 1989 she told Soviet President Mikhail Gorbachev that "we were rather apprehensive" about reunification, a sentiment that was shared by the Soviet leader.[114] At the Strasbourg European Council meeting in December, she held two private meetings with French President François Mitterrand on Germany. At one of the meetings, she pulled out a map depicting past configurations of Germany and noted that, thankfully, both France and Britain now "had the will to check the German juggernaut."[115] In March 1990 Thatcher held a confidential discussion at Chequers, her country residence, on the implications of German reunification. While most participants agreed that contemporary Germany was different from

---

[112] Organization for Economic Cooperation and Development, *Quarterly Labour Force Statistics, No. 4* (OECD, 2001), p. 190; data also provided by the Federal Statistics Office of Germany.
[113] Margaret Thatcher, *The Downing Street Years* (New York: HarperCollins, 1993), p. 791.
[114] Thatcher, *The Downing Street Years*, p. 792. According to Thatcher, Gorbachev responded by stating that he was not in favor of German reunification.
[115] Ibid., p. 797.

Nazi Germany, there were nonetheless perceptible concerns about its future behavior:

> Given that a much larger and more powerful Germany would soon be upon us, we had to consider what sort of European framework would be most likely to encourage the benign effects and diminish the adverse consequences . . . We wanted Germany to be constrained within a security framework which had the best chance of avoiding a resurgence of German militarism.[116]

French leaders were equally worried about German reunification. At a May 1989 meeting with George Bush in Kennebunkport, Maine, Mitterrand argued that reunification was only one of two possible causes of great-power war in Europe (the other was German acquisition of nuclear weapons).[117] Alluding to the appeasement of Germany before World War II, Mitterrand noted to Thatcher in 1989: "We find ourselves in the same situation as the leaders in France and Britain before the war, who didn't react to anything. We can't repeat Munich!"[118] Like the British, French leaders were deeply worried about reunification because Germany was a potential hegemon with a revisionist past.

European states were also deeply worried about an American withdrawal from the continent. In the absence of the Soviet Union it was not clear how long American forces would remain in Europe, and most European leaders were skeptical that the United States would stay for the long term. Statements from Capitol Hill and prominent international relations experts weren't reassuring. At a 1992 conference in Munich, for instance, Senator William Cohen argued that the prevailing view in the United States was that NATO was "no longer necessary, relevant or affordable," and that it would most likely become "mainly a European organization."[119] The US Defense Department's 1993 *Bottom-Up Review* argued that America's major security concerns were in the Middle East and Asia rather than Europe, and thus required building military forces to combat such states as Iraq and North Korea.[120]

---

[116] Participants at Chequers included Prime Minister Thatcher, Foreign Secretary Douglas Hurd, Lord Dacre, Charles Powell, Norman Stone, Timothy Garton Ash, George Urban, Fritz Stern, and Gordon Craig. The minutes were recorded by Powell, the prime minister's private secretary. See "What the PM learnt about the Germans," *The Independent*, July 15, 1990.

[117] Notes from the meeting were taken by one of Mitterrand's closest advisers, Jacques Attali. See Attali, *Verbatim: Tome 3, Chronique des années 1988–1991* (Paris: Fayard, 1995), p. 241. See also Zelikow and Rice, *Germany Unified and Europe Transformed*, p. xiii.

[118] Attali, *Verbatim*, p. 369.

[119] Marc Fisher, "Europeans Told of US Isolationism," *The Washington Post*, February 10, 1992, p. A1.

[120] *Report on the Bottom-Up Review* (Washington, DC: United States Department of Defense, October 1993).

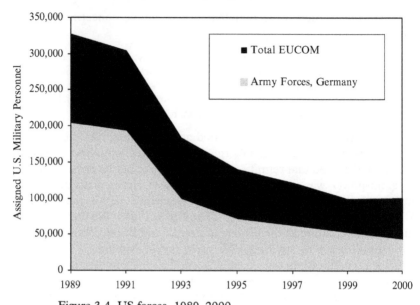

Figure 3.4. US forces, 1989–2000.
Source: IISS, *The Military Balance 1989–90* through *2000–01*.

A drastic reduction of American forces was promulgated by a number of other members of Congress and former statesmen, including Henry Kissinger.[121] State Department analysts were also pessimistic about the prospects for keeping US troops in Germany.[122]

As Figure 3.4 illustrates, US forces dropped precipitously in the post-Cold War era. In 1989 United States European Command (EUCOM) included 326,000 military personnel, of which 202,000 were army personnel and 40,300 were air force personnel stationed in the Federal Republic of Germany. By 2000 EUCOM had dropped nearly 70 percent to 100,000, the army presence in Germany dropped almost 80 percent to 42,200, and the air force presence in Germany dropped 63 percent to 14,880.

---

[121] Henry A. Kissinger, "A Memo to the Next President," *Newsweek*, September 19, 1988, pp. 34–41; "Report on NATO Calls on US to Cut its Forces by Two-Thirds," *The New York Times*, March 2, 1991; Ian Murray, "US Threatens to Abandon NATO Over Trade Talks," *The Times (London)*, February 10, 1992.

[122] The assessment came from Burleigh to Kimmitt, "Maintaining US Forces in a United Germany – An Uphill Battle," April 11, 1990. Zelikow and Rice, *Germany Unified and Europe Transformed*, p. 247.

This led to serious concerns in European capitals – especially Paris – about the long-term commitment of the United States.[123] In February 1990, Mitterrand argued that both NATO and the Warsaw Pact would probably not be around for much longer and that the "main thing, for me, is for Europe to take up its true place in the world again after the self-destruction of two world wars. In short, I expect Europeans to keep in mind, as I do, a paraphrase of that well-known expression, 'Let Europe take care of itself.'"[124] Surely, NATO would not disappear in the short term. But could a substantial US presence be assured for ten years? Twenty years? Thirty years? If not, it would be critical to maximize French security and tie the Germans down in a security institution. There needed to be a long-term solution. As one US staff member on the Bush administration's NSC noted:

The most striking impression I derived from my many conversations is the nearly total absence of the US in the mid- and long-term calculations of French policymakers. So convinced do the French seem that the US will rapidly withdraw its forces from Europe that they are thinking, and at times acting, as if we were already gone.[125]

Moreover, German officials preferred a US commitment to Europe but wondered how long the United States would remain engaged there. American intelligence reports supported this argument, and noted that Hans-Dietrich Genscher viewed NATO as existing only for the short term.[126] According to one senior British diplomat: "There was a palpable sense among European leaders in the early 1990s that the US might not be a long-term player. This perception was critical to the creation of CFSP."[127] Indeed, it was clear to senior American officials at the State Department, Defense Department, and National Security Council that Europe was deeply worried about the US commitment.[128]

---

[123] Author's interviews with senior official, French Ministry of Defense, June 19, 2001; senior official, British Foreign and Commonwealth Office, January 31, 2001; senior official, German Ministry of Defense, May 9, 2001.

[124] "German Reunification: Interview with President Mitterrand," February 14, 1990 (Washington, DC: Embassy of France, 1990).

[125] The message was written by NSC staffer Adrian Basora and was titled "What Happened to the Spirit of Kennebunkport?," February 20, 1990. Zelikow and Rice, *Germany Unified and Europe Transformed*, p. 206.

[126] Ibid., p. 175.

[127] Author's interview with senior official, British Foreign and Commonwealth Office, January 31, 2001.

[128] Author's interviews with Robert Hunter, United States Ambassador to NATO (1993–8), May 9, 2001; Earl Anthony Wayne, Director for Western European Affairs, National Security Council (1991–3), May 8, 2001; correspondence with John Hamre, Under Secretary of Defense (1993–7), April 30, 2001.

As John Hamre, US under secretary of defense, noted: "The concern of American withdrawal from the continent was felt most heavily by the British, followed by the Germans. The French were 'convinced' the United States would withdraw and argued they needed European security cooperation to be in place when that occurred."[129]

German leaders pushed for security cooperation through the European Union because they were interested in the status quo. One of the first steps German leaders took as a result of reunification was to agree to several important limitations as part of the 2+4 settlement on Germany reunification: the Conventional Forces in Europe (CFE) agreement, and the German–Polish treaty. Germany agreed to reduce its armed forces to 370,000 (including land, air, and sea forces); renounce nuclear, chemical, and biological weapons; recognize the Oder-Neisse border with Poland; and amend article 23 of the Basic Law, which was written to note: "With a view to establishing a united Europe, the Federal Republic of Germany shall participate in the development of the European Union . . . To this end the Federation may transfer sovereign powers by a law with the consent of the Bundesrat."[130] Germany's past behavior affected the country's foreign policy decision-making process. As Genscher noted in 1989 regarding questions about the Oder-Neisse line: "Fifty years ago the Polish people became the victim of a war that was started by Hitler's Germany. It shall know that we Germans will not question its right to live within secure borders, not now or in the future, by making territorial demands. The wheel of history will not be turned back."[131] The existence of a security dilemma was clearly apparent to German leaders, who understood that they might face a balancing coalition if they did not become integrated into Europe. In particular, they recognized that the specter of Adolf Hitler and Germany's past behavior caused other Europeans to be concerned about Germany's future intentions.[132]

Acting through the European Union was important because it signaled that German leaders had benign intentions. When French

---

[129] Correspondence with John Hamre, Under Secretary of Defense (1993–7), April 30, 2001.

[130] Basic Law for the Federal Republic of Germany.

[131] Genscher, *Rebuilding a House Divided*, p. 3. Genscher refers to Hitler numerous times in his memoirs in the context of overcoming Germany's belligerent history. See pp. 15–16, 18–19, 60, 71, 76, 82–3, 184–5, 194–5, 197, 200, 287, 331, 400, 441, 490, 559.

[132] On Germany and "collective memory" see Andrei S. Markovits and Simon Reich, *The German Predicament: Memory and Power in the New Europe* (Ithaca, NY: Cornell University Press, 1997).

President François Mitterrand warned that a reunified Germany which did not bind itself into Europe would likely trigger a balancing coalition, German Foreign Minister Hans-Dietrich Genscher replied that "those counterweights would not be necessary if European integration was progressing along the lines we hoped for."[133] Frank Elbe, one of Genscher's top aides, and journalist Richard Kiessler noted that the structural changes at the end of the Cold War placed Germany in a precarious situation. Since German unilateralism would have been destabilizing, Kohl's government believed that working through the EU signaled that Germany was a status quo power:

The following principle will now apply more strongly than during the four decades of the Cold War: Germany cannot and must not pursue a singular approach to foreign policy. It remains bound in processes of cooperative decision-making. Germany must remain the locomotive of a process that shall lead Europe to unity. Otherwise this Germany could . . . provoke tendencies "to readjust the balance" – to the disadvantage of the Germans.[134]

Indeed, Germany became one of the prime motors of a security arm of the European Union. This was first apparent during the Maastricht negotiations, when Germany strongly pursued a binding strategy and was perhaps the most "integrationist" of the major European powers. The impetus for establishing CFSP as a pillar of the European Union came from the Germans and the French. Kohl initiated the push by arguing in mid 1989 that the German Bundestag wanted progress on foreign policy in exchange for progress on economic and monetary affairs.[135] In early 1990, Kohl and Mitterrand met several times to discuss German reunification and European cooperation. In April 1990 they wrote a letter arguing that the European Council should begin preparing for an intergovernmental conference on political union to define and implement a common foreign and security policy.[136] German and French preferences were further outlined in a series of papers by French Foreign Minister Roland Dumas and German Foreign Minister Genscher, which promulgated the importance of CFSP and the eventual incorporation of a military arm of the EU.[137] Both the Germans and the

[133] Genscher, *Rebuilding a House Divided*, p. 308.
[134] Elbe and Kiessler, *A Round Table with Sharp Corners*, p. 206.
[135] Moravcsik, *The Choice for Europe*, p. 447.
[136] "Kohl–Mitterrand letter," April 20, 1990, in Corbett, *Treaty of Maastricht*, p. 126.
[137] See, for example, Colette Mazzucelli, *France and Germany at Maastricht: Politics and Negotiations to Create the European Union* (New York: Garland Publishing, 1997), p. 138; George Ross, *Jacques Delors and European Integration* (New York: Oxford University Press, 1985), pp. 94–5.

French advocated moving away from NATO as the sole European security institution, reviving the defunct Western European Union (WEU), and eventually incorporating it into the EU by the late 1990s. Kohl and Mitterrand explicitly stated in a draft text to Dutch Prime Minister Ruud Lubbers in October 1991 that the WEU should be a "component" of the European Union.[138]

German leaders continued to press for further deepening of the European Union's security arm over the next decade. In particular, they strongly supported the creation of a high representative for CFSP during the Amsterdam negotiations, and have played a leading role in the construction of an EU rapid reaction force.[139] Following the December 1998 Franco-British summit at St. Malo, Germany held the EU presidency and pushed hard to extend the St. Malo initiative to an EU-wide framework. This was done at the Cologne summit in June 1999, which began the development of military capabilities for European Union states.[140] German leaders have also supported the creation of a European Union Foreign Minister as part of a new EU Constitution.

In sum, security cooperation through the European Union has been inversely correlated with American power in Europe: the lower the American military presence and commitment to the continent, the greater the incentive for cooperation through the EU to ameliorate a potential security dilemma. It has also been correlated with German power: the greater the power of Germany, the greater the impetus for cooperation. While it is difficult to disentangle these two structural factors, the significant withdrawal of US forces from Europe was probably most important. If Germany had reunified but the number of US troops remained at approximately 300,000, the significant American presence would probably have been sufficient to ameliorate a potential security dilemma. On the other hand, a significant decline in the number of US forces but the continuation of a divided Germany may still have triggered some concerns about German revanchism.

---

[138] Corbett, *Treaty of Maastricht*, p. 344.

[139] German Presidency Paper, Bonn, February 24, 1999, in Maartje Rutten, ed., *From St. Malo to Nice: European Defence, Core Documents*, Chaillot Paper 47 (Paris: Institute for Security Studies, May 2001), pp. 14–16; Germany's proposal at the informal meeting of EU foreign ministers in Eltville, March 13–14, 1999, ibid., pp. 17–19; Mark Mazower, "An Answer to the German Question," *Financial Times*, November 30, 2000, p. 15.

[140] European Council, Cologne, June 3–4, 1999, in Rutten, *From St. Malo to Nice*, pp. 41–5. See also Gilles Andréani, Christoph Bertram, and Charles Grant, *Europe's Military Revolution* (London: Centre for European Reform, 2001), pp. 21–2.

Conclusion

Table 3.1 shows the results of the four cases. The variation in European security institutions is largely a function of the structure of the system. The collapse of the USSR, reunification of Germany, and withdrawal of US forces from Europe set in motion a chain of events that led to an increase in EU security cooperation. EU states pursued a "binding" strategy to ensure internal peace on the continent and prevent the rise of a hegemonic Germany. This strategy was possible because Germany was a status quo power and Europe's major powers had learned from history.

There are several potential counter-arguments. First, some might argue that there is not – nor will be – substantial security cooperation in Europe. The logic is that nationalism and balance-of-power politics will stymie efforts to pursue sustained foreign policy and defense cooperation among European states. While European cooperation may be possible in areas of "low politics" such as economics, states will not concede sovereignty in the security realm. Security competition among European states, rather than cooperation, is more likely to be the wave of the future. However, the historical evidence demonstrates that this argument is problematic for several reasons. One is that United States forces dropped substantially in the post-Cold War era, but European states reacted contrary to these predictions. European leaders pushed

Table 3.1. *Summary of institutions, 1945–present*

Security institution	Years	Potential security dilemma	Reason	Outcome
European Defense Community	1950–1954	No	• Large US presence • Germany divided	Defeated in French Assembly
Fouchet Plan	1958–1963	No	• Large US presence • Germany divided	Rejected by European states
European Political Cooperation	1969–1991	No	• Large US presence • Germany divided	Failed to become viable, rejected by European Community
Treaty on European Union	1992–	Yes	• Decline in US presence • Germany reunified	Established an EU security arm

for more cooperation, rather than less. Between 1989 and 2000 United States European Command (EUCOM) dropped nearly 70 percent, and the US army presence in Germany dropped almost 80 percent. The withdrawal of American forces and the reunification of Germany *did* trigger fears of security competition. Yet European states responded by creating (and then deepening) a security arm of the European Union, rather than pursuing competition with each other. Furthermore, there is no evidence that EU states have engaged in security competition. As the data in the remainder of this study demonstrate, intra-European cooperation has *increased* in the post-Cold War era in such areas as economic sanctions, defense production, and even military forces.

Others might argue, second, that the creation of a security institution has been caused by the internalization of a European identity. Through interaction and decades of cooperation, states have internalized European interests and identities. In addition, European security cooperation has led to the creation of a "security community" in Europe and the absence of mutual security concerns. This argument runs into several problems as well. To begin with, there is little or no quantitative evidence of a change in the identity of European populations or elites. If identity is the critical independent variable, we should expect to find a shift in the level of "European-ness" over the course of the 1980s and early 1990s. Unfortunately, there is little evidence. *Eurobarometer* data in the 1980s and early 1990s are inconclusive. If anything, they show that for two of Europe's most significant powers – Germany and France – sentiments of European-ness actually *decreased* by the early 1990s for general populations.[141] As one study notes: "Our empirical analysis makes clear that, whatever the tendencies and processes involved, it is too soon to speak of the internalization of identities. For the present, a

---

[141] Between 1982 and 1992, respondents were asked similar forms of the question: "Do you ever think of yourself not only as (nationality) citizen but also as a citizen of Europe?" First, the increase in the number of Germans who answered "never" is particularly startling: 18 percent in 1982, 27 percent in 1985, 42 percent in 1987, 44 percent in 1989, 50 percent in 1991 and 59 percent in 1992. Second, the number of French who answered "never" dipped a bit and then increased slightly: 37 percent in 1982, 32 percent in 1985, 47 percent in 1987, 40 percent in 1989, 40 percent in 1991 and 47 percent in 1992. Third, as we might expect, the number of British who answered "never" was quite high and showed very little change: 72 percent in 1982, 74 percent in 1983, 70 percent in 1985, 66 percent in 1987, 69 percent in 1989, 69 percent in 1991, and 71 percent in 1992. See Commission of the EC, *Eurobarometer*, issues in June 1982 (vol. 17), June 1983 (vol. 19), December 1985 (vol. 24), December 1986 (vol. 26), June 1987 (vol. 27), June 1990 (vol. 33), June 1991 (vol. 35), December 1991 (vol. 36), and June 1992 (vol. 37).

European identity is a vanguard phenomenon."[142] Some might respond that identity change has occurred predominantly – or solely – at the elite level, but there is likewise no convincing evidence that European elites experienced a substantial change in identity in the 1980s and 1990s. With little or no variation in European-ness, how can we explain change? In addition, it is hard to swallow the argument that European states have adopted a Kantian culture when security concerns were substantial, particularly in the early 1990s. Primary sources clearly indicate that both French and British leaders were worried about a reunified Germany that reverted to unilateralism.

Third, some institutionalists might argue that European political cooperation helped promote greater cooperation through a path-dependent process. Substantial foreign policy cooperation began in late 1969 through European political cooperation, and then gradually deepened through a process that involved information-sharing among technical specialists, norm and rule creation, the development of permanent organizations in the EU, and governance mechanisms to oversee EU foreign policies. As one study concludes, European political cooperation was substantive cooperation that "resulted in a gradual but persistent expansion of the EU's political relationships with third states and with many other regional and international organizations."[143] Unfortunately, there is little evidence that EPC was any thing more than a talking shop. This makes it virtually impossible to explain the timing of European cooperation at the end of the Cold War, since it was not a function of path dependency. There is nearly unanimous consensus among those who have examined EPC that it was not substantive.[144] European states did not change their foreign policy and defense behavior in any meaningful way, and NATO remained the only viable security institution. Other than cheap talk, little else went on. As one participant in the EPC negotiations recalled: "So we meet, eat well, and exchange

[142] Sophie Duchesne and André-Paul Frognier, "Is there a European Identity?" in Oskar Niedermayer and Richard Sinnott, eds., *Public Opinion and Internationalized Governance* (New York: Oxford University Press, 1995), p. 223. See also Timothy Garton Ash, "Is Britain European?" *International Affairs*, Vol. 77, No. 1, January 2001, pp. 1–13.
[143] Smith, *Europe's Foreign and Security Policy*, p. 240.
[144] Nuttall, *European Political Cooperation*; Moravcsik, *The Choice for Europe*; Hill and Smith, *European Foreign Policy*; Pijpers, Regelsberger, and Wessels, *European Political Cooperation*; William Wallace and David Allen, "Political Cooperation: Procedure as Substitute for Policy," in Helen Wallace, William Wallace, and Carole Webb, eds., *Policy-Making in the European Communities* (London: John Wiley & Sons, 1977).

views; and if we disagree, then *tant pis*, we will return to the question when we meet again."[145]

Fourth, some argue that domestic politics played a key role in explaining the success and failure of European security institutions, especially the economic interests of domestic coalitions. For example, the replacement of French Third Force leaders in 1952 by a conservative coalition with different domestic concerns led to the European Defense Community's defeat in 1954.[146] As Craig Parsons demonstrates, however, this argument is deeply flawed. The French debate about the EDC was remarkable because of the *absence* of agreement among domestic political groups. "No political majority, bureaucratic elite, or interest group coalition had driven the transformation of the Pleven Plan into the EDC . . . Business, bureaucrats, and the military were all divided."[147] Nor were domestic coalitions a major influence in the defeat of the Fouchet Plan and EPC, or the establishment of a security arm at Maastricht. In sum, identity and institutional or intergovernmental bargaining arguments do not provide a better explanation of European security cooperation than structural factors. The next chapter turns to cooperation in economic sanctions.

---

[145] Wallace and Allen, "Political Cooperation: Procedure as Substitute for Policy," in Wallace, Wallace, and Webb, eds., *Policy-Making in the European Communities*, p. 237.
[146] Pitman, "France's European Choices."
[147] Parsons, *A Certain Idea of Europe*, p. 75.

4   Economic sanctions

Why have European states increasingly imposed economic sanctions
for foreign policy goals through the European Union? Why did they
refrain from imposing sanctions through the European Community
(EC) during the Cold War?[1] Economic sanctions have become an important foreign policy tool for states. Since the end of the Cold War, they
have been used for a host of foreign policy goals ranging from discouraging the proliferation of weapons of mass destruction to improving
human rights conditions. One study notes that there were fifty cases of
economic sanctions in the 1990s – a jump of 36 percent over the 1980s,
22 percent over the 1970s, and 58 percent over the 1960s.[2] Furthermore,
great powers such as the United States, Russia, and Japan have been
particularly prone to using them.[3]

In Europe, the major powers – Britain, France, and Germany – have
increasingly imposed economic sanctions through the European Union,
rather than unilaterally or multilaterally through other forums. This
chapter examines all economic sanctions cases between 1950 and 2006
in which a European state was a primary sender. It finds that between
1950 and 1990 European states sanctioned through the EC in two out of
seventeen cases (12 percent). Since 1991, however, they have imposed
economic sanctions through the European Union in twenty-one of
twenty-seven cases (78 percent), an increase in both the percentage
and the aggregate number of cases. As one EU document notes:
"Sanctions . . . represent one of the main non-military instruments that

---

[1] I use European Community, rather than European Economic Community (EEC), for
simplification. The distinction is insignificant for the purposes of this chapter.
[2] See Gary Clyde Hufbauer, Kimberly Ann Elliot, and Jeffrey J. Schott's "Chronological
Summary of Economic Sanctions for Foreign Policy Goals, 1914–99." (http://www.iie.
com/topics/sanctions/sanctions-overview.htm).
[3] Richard N. Haass, "Introduction," in Haass, *Economic Sanctions and American Diplomacy*
(New York: Council on Foreign Relations, 1998), p. 1.

the European Union has employed to pressure countries to defuse a crisis or adopt a certain course of action."[4]

What explains this variation? I argue that it is mainly a function of the structure of the international system. In the bipolar Cold War system, European states were concerned about balancing the Soviet Union. This meant that they were more likely to cooperate with the United States than with each other to impose multilateral sanctions to further Cold War strategic interests. In a number of cases, individual European states also imposed unilateral sanctions against countries where they had colonial interests. However, this changed in the post-Cold War period with the transition to a unipolar system. European states have imposed sanctions through the European Union as part of a broader strategy to increase Europe's global power and autonomy. Sanctions have become a way to leverage European economic power in the foreign policy realm. As Joseph Nye concludes: "On questions of trade and influence . . . Europe is the equal of the United States."[5] In dealing with a host of critical issues such as weapons of mass destruction, terrorism, and immigration, European states have argued that sanctioning through the EU is the most effective option because it allows them to combine power.[6]

This chapter is divided into five sections. First, it defines several key terms and outlines the major options that states have when imposing economic sanctions. Second, it discusses the data and potential coding problems. Third, it broadly examines European sanctioning behavior since World War II and shows that there has been a dramatic change in the post-Cold War era. Fourth, it fleshes out the causal logic of the argument by briefly examining two cases: British sanctions against Uganda from 1972 to 1979, and EU and US sanctions against Yugoslavia from 1991 to 1995. Fifth, it concludes by evaluating several potential counter-arguments.

---

[4] "European Union Sanctions Applied to Non-Member States" (Washington, DC: Delegation of the European Commission to the United States, 2002). See (www.eur union.org/legislat/Sanctions.htm).
[5] Joseph S. Nye, *The Paradox of American Power* (New York: Oxford University Press, 2002).
[6] Judy Dempsey, "EU Ministers Seek Consensus on Weapons," *Financial Times*, April 14, 2003, p. 10; Council of the European Union, *Basic Principles for an EU Strategy against Proliferation of WMD* (Brussels: Council of the EU, June 2003); Donald G. McNeil, Jr., "European Union Expands its List of Terrorist Groups, Requiring Sanctions and Arrests," *The New York Times*, December 29, 2001, p. B3; Lisbeth Kirk, "The European Union Will Sanction Third Countries," *EU Observer*, June 13, 2002.

Options for imposing sanctions

This section lays out the options states have when imposing economic sanctions for foreign policy goals, and explains why they may opt to impose multilateral sanctions through an international institution. Following the work of Gary Clyde Hufbauer, Jeffrey Schott, and Kimberly Ann Elliott, the "sender" refers to the principal author (or authors) of the sanctions and the "target" refers to the recipient.[7] The focus of this chapter is on economic sanctions for foreign policy goals. Economic sanctions are defined as the deliberate withholding of the flow of goods, services, or capital with a target state to coerce it into changing its behavior.[8] Sanctions are designed to change the behavior of targets by imposing high costs. EU documents have been explicit about this, arguing that sanctions "are imposed by the EU to bring about a change in policy or activity by the target country, part of country, government, entities, or individual."[9] States may take a variety of actions, such as terminating foreign aid and loans, restricting foreign trade and investment, freezing financial assets, or embargoing weapons.[10] Furthermore, foreign policy goals refer to a variety of objectives such as:

- Ending weapons of mass destruction (WMD) programs
- Establishing or restoring democracy
- Improving human rights conditions
- Ending a civil or interstate war
- Helping topple a foreign leader or destabilize a government.

---

[7] The target is generally a single state, though there are two sets of exceptions. First, non-state actors involved in civil wars have been the targets of sanctions. A good example is the 1992 sanctions imposed by Germany, the US, and the UN against the Khmer Rouge in Cambodia. The UN and the US also imposed sanctions in 1993 against UNITA, which was involved in a civil war against the government of Angola. Second, a group of states has occasionally been the target in a sanctions episode. In 1956 the US placed sanctions on both the United Kingdom and France to withdraw from Suez. However, the vast majority of targets – including every one in this study – are single states.

[8] See Robert A. Pape, "Why Economic Sanctions Do Not Work," *International Security,* Vol. 22, No. 2, Fall 1997, pp. 93–4. Hofbauer, Schott, and Elliot *Economic Sanctions Reconsidered* (Washington, DC: Institute for International Economics, 1990); Richard D. Farmer, "Costs of Economic Sanctions to the Sender," *The World Economy,* January 2000, Vol. 23, No. 1, pp. 93–117.

[9] Council of the European Union, *Guidelines on Implementation and Evaluation of Restrictive Measures, (Sanctions) in the Framework of the EU Common Foreign and Security Policy,* 15579/03 (Brussels: European Council, December 2003), p. 5.

[10] I have included arms embargoes – the deliberate withholding of weapons and weapons systems – in the definition of economic sanctions because arms are a traded good, and states that impose arms embargoes generally do so to seek to coerce targets into changing their behavior.

This definition does not include trade wars, in which states impose economic sanctions on target states to coerce them into agreeing to more favorable terms of trade.[11] These cases are excluded because the purpose of trade wars is to change the target's economic policies, not political behavior. Thus, for example, EU trade sanctions against the US over steel tariffs are excluded because they were designed to achieve economic objectives. This step is consistent with the literature on sanctions.[12]

State options

Economic sanctions represent an important and sometimes effective instrument in a state's foreign policy toolbox.[13] States have a number of options when imposing sanctions. First, they can impose them *unilaterally*. Under these conditions, there is only one sender state. Examples include Soviet sanctions against Yugoslavia in 1948 to rejoin the Soviet sphere of influence and destabilize the Tito government; United States sanctions against Cuba in 1960 to undermine the government of Fidel Castro; and Australian sanctions against France in 1983 to stop the latter's nuclear testing in the South Pacific.

Second, states can impose sanctions *multilaterally*. This involves cases where there are two or more sender states and can include at least two types. One involves the imposition of sanctions through an international institution such as the United Nations, the League of Nations, or the European Union. Historical examples abound: United Nations sanctions against South Africa in 1962 to end apartheid; League of Nations sanctions against Greece in 1925 to withdraw from Bulgarian territory; and European Union sanctions against Algeria in 1992 to establish democracy. The other type includes the imposition of economic sanctions in the absence of an international institution. Historical examples include British and United States sanctions against Iran in 1951 to

---

[11] John C. Conybeare, *Trade Wars: The Theory and Practice of International Commercial Rivalry* (New York: Columbia University Press, 1987).

[12] See, for example, Pape, "Why Economic Sanctions Do Not Work," pp. 93–8. See also such definitions as Drezner, *The Sanctions Paradox: Economic Statecraft and International Relations* (New York: Cambridge University Press, 1999), pp. 2–3; James M. Lindsay, "Trade Sanctions as Policy Instruments: A Re-Examination," *International Studies Quarterly*, Vol. 30, 1986, pp. 154–5; Hofbauer *et al.*, *Economic Sanctions Reconsidered*.

[13] David A. Baldwin, *Economic Statecraft* (Princeton, NJ: Princeton University Press, 1985); Michael Mastanduno, "Economic Statecraft, Interdependence, and National Security: Agendas for Research," in Jean-Marc F. Blanchard, Edward D. Mansfield, and Norrin M. Ripsman, eds., *Power and the Purse: Economic Statecraft, Interdependence, and National Security* (Portland, OR: Frank Cass, 2000), pp. 288–316.

reverse the nationalization of oil facilities and destabilize the Mossadeq government; British, French, and United States sanctions against Egypt in 1956 to ensure passage through the Suez Canal and coerce Egypt into compensating for the nationalization of the canal; and French and United States sanctions against Niger in 1996 to restore democracy. In sum, states can impose economic sanctions for foreign policy goals either unilaterally or multilaterally; the latter can include sanctions with or without an international institution.

Why multilateral sanctions?

Under what conditions will states impose multilateral sanctions through an international institution? The evidence in Europe suggests that the shift to unipolarity created a strong impetus for European states to impose multilateral sanctions through the EU to increase European power and autonomy. In short, the structure of the international system has played the fundamental role in greater EU sanctions cooperation.

Cooperation through international institutions such as the European Union can increase power by raising the punishment against target states. The aim of sanctions is to coerce the target government into changing its political behavior by imposing high costs on its economy. Cutting off trade does not *ipso facto* affect the target country's terms of trade; target states can redirect – or substitute – their trade to other markets. For most traded goods, there are several countries that can serve as alternative sources of supply and demand for a sanctioned state. Target states have a strong incentive to take whatever steps they can to circumvent sanctions.[14] For instance, Iran was effectively able to blunt the impact of US sanctions by reconfiguring its trade patterns over time and increasing trade with Japan and other Asian countries.[15] Consequently, what is important is the elasticity of substitution. The cooperation of other countries can limit a target's ability to redirect trade to third countries by decreasing the set of available markets.[16] By increasing the number of trading partners and potential trading partners in the sanctioning group, multilateral sanctions can be more effective than

---

[14] Jonathan Kirshner terms this "robustness." Kirshner, "The Microfoundations of Economic Sanctions," *Security Studies*, Vol. 6, No. 3, Spring 1997, pp. 39–40.

[15] Meghan L. O'Sullivan, *Shrewd Sanctions: Statecraft and State Sponsors of Terrorism* (Washington, DC: Brookings Institution Press, 2003), pp. 45–99.

[16] See, for example, Thomas O. Bayard, Joseph Pelzman, and Jorge Perez-Lopez, "Stakes and Risks in Economic Sanctions," *The World Economy*, Vol. 6, No.1, March 1983, pp. 73–87.

unilateral sanctions in inducing economic damage.[17] Individual senders rarely wield the market power necessary to inflict significant damage through unilateral sanctions. As Michael Mastanduno argues: "Multilateral sanctions allow the senders to maximize the effectiveness of economic pressure, whether selective or comprehensive."[18]

In addition, a number of sanctions studies have demonstrated that cooperation through international institutions such as the European Union decreases enforcement problems.[19] It is generally understood that trade sanctions generate rents by altering the supply and demand for sanctioned items. This creates an incentive for sender states and affected companies to circumvent sanctions.[20] The prospect of losing rents may be particularly high for firms such as oil producers that depend on front-end investments in resources or business contacts.[21] Sanctions can be costly for sender states because they impinge on trade and threaten the economies of scale that result from increased specialization.[22] Sanctions can also generate high political costs on sender states; domestic interest groups that are adversely affected may pressure public officials to eliminate or reduce them.[23]

[17] Richard N. Haass, "Conclusions: Lessons and Recommendations," in Haass, ed., *Economic Sanctions and American Diplomacy* (New York: Council on Foreign Relations, 1998), pp. 197–212; Bayard, Pelzman, and Perez-Lopez, "Stakes and Risks in Economic Sanctions"; Jaleh Dashti-Gibson, Patricia Davis, and Benjamin Radcliff, "On the Determinants of the Success of Economic Sanctions: An Empirical Analysis," *American Journal of Political Science*, Vol. 41, No. 2, April 1997, pp. 608–18; Grant W. Gardner and Kent P. Kimbrough, "The Economics of Country-Specific Tariffs," *International Economic Review*, Vol. 31, No. 3, pp. 575–88; John Galtung, "On the Effects of International Economic Sanctions: With Examples from the Case of Rhodesia," *World Politics*, Vol. 19, No. 3, April 1967, pp. 378–416; Hofbauer, Schott, and Elliot, *Economic Sanctions Reconsidered*, pp. 98–103.

[18] Mastanduno, "Economic Statecraft, Interdependence, and National Security," p. 296.

[19] Daniel Drezner, "Bargaining, Enforcement, and Multilateral Sanctions: When is Cooperation Counterproductive?" *International Organization*, Vol. 54, No. 1, Winter 2000, pp. 73–102; Lisa Martin, *Coercive Cooperation: Explaining Multilateral Economic Sanctions* (Princeton, NJ: Princeton University Press, 1992); Anne C. Miers and T. Clifton Morgan, "Multilateral Sanctions and Foreign Policy Success: Can Too Many Cooks Spoil the Broth?" *International Interactions*, Vol. 28, 2002, pp. 117–36. On enforcement problems also see James D. Fearon, "Bargaining, Enforcement, and International Cooperation," *International Organization*, Vol. 52, No. 2, Spring 1998, pp. 269–305;

[20] Bayard, Pelzman, and Perez-Lopez, "Stakes and Risks in Economic Sanctions," pp. 73–87; William Kaempfer and Anton Lowenberg, "Unilateral versus Multilateral International Sanctions: A Public Choice Perspective," *International Studies Quarterly*, 1999, Vol. 43, pp. 37–58.

[21] Farmer, "Costs of Economic Sanctions to the Sender," pp. 98–9.

[22] Richard D. Farmer, *The Domestic Costs of Sanctions on Foreign Commerce* (Washington, DC: Congressional Budget Office, 1999).

[23] Edward Mansfield, "International Institutions and Economic Sanctions," *World Politics*, Vol. 47, No. 4, July 1995, pp. 575–605.

In short, multilateral sanctions are often difficult to sustain because of enforcement problems. As Daniel Drezner argues: "The dilemma for potential sanctioners is that even if all actors are better off with the imposition of multilateral sanctions, individual actors are even better off if they unilaterally defect while everyone else cooperates."[24] For instance, in Angola the United Nations experienced substantial enforcement problems in trying to coerce UNITA to stop the trade of "conflict diamonds."[25] In the late 1990s a series of embarrassing press reports detailed repeated sanctions violations in Antwerp, Belgium where an estimated 80 percent of the world's rough diamonds and more than 50 percent of polished diamonds passed through.[26] As the UN's "Fowler Report" stated: "The Panel found that the extremely lax controls and regulations governing the Antwerp market facilitate and perhaps even encourage illegal trading activity."[27]

However, international institutions can increase the potency and effectiveness of sanctions by decreasing enforcement problems.[28] Increased transparency and information-sharing among members allows them to monitor better the behavior of sender states. This makes it easier to detect and punish governments or companies that defect from the sanctions coalition, especially if there is support from powerful states. During the sanctions against Yugoslavia in the early 1990s, for example, the European Union established Sanctions Assistance Missions (SAMs) to monitor traffic into and out of Yugoslavia and document suspected violations. International institutions can also help sender states overcome enforcement problems by giving carrots, such as financial aid, to potential defectors. Or they can punish defecting states – and threaten to punish wavering ones. During the Falklands War, for example, the

[24] Drezner, "Bargaining, Enforcement, and Multilateral Sanctions," p. 83.
[25] For the European Union sanctions, see Council Regulation (EC) No. 1705/98, OJ L 215, 1.8.98; Common Position (97/759/CFSP), OJ L 309, 12.11.1997; Common Position (98/425/CFSP), OJ L 190, 4.7.1998.
[26] Blaine Harden, "U. N. Sees Violation of a Diamond Ban by Angola Rebels," *New York Times*, p. A1; Carola Hoyos, "UN Report on Angola Rebels Questioned," *Financial Times*, p. 10. See also Human Rights Watch, *Angola Unravels: The Rise and Fall of the Lusaka Peace Process* (New York: Human Rights Watch, 1999); United Nations, *Final Report of the Monitoring Mechanism on Angola Sanctions*, S/2000/1225 (New York: UN, December 2000); Global Witness, *Conflict Diamonds: Possibilities for the Identification, Certification and Control of Diamonds* (London: Global Witness, May 2000).
[27] United Nations, *Final Report of the UN Panel of Experts on Violations of Security Council Sanctions against Unita: The "Fowler Report,"* S/2000/203 (New York: UN, March 2000).
[28] Drezner, "Bargaining, Enforcement, and Multilateral Sanctions"; Martin, *Coercive Cooperation*:; Miers and Morgan, "Multilateral Sanctions and Foreign Policy Success," pp. 130–1.

European Community deterred Ireland from defecting from the arms embargo by threatening to eliminate European Community benefits.[29] Sanctioning through an institution can also be a good deterrent. By making it easier to monitor the compliance of sender states, sanctioning through institutions can also deter future defectors.

Sanctioning as a bloc also decreases European reliance on the United States. During the Cold War, European states relied on the United States and its economic power when they imposed sanctions for foreign policy goals. The United States was a partner in virtually every case in which a European state participated in multilateral sanctions. In the aftermath of the Cold War, however, European security interests increasingly diverged from American interests. This shift increased the impetus to sanction through the European Union and decrease dependence on United States economic power. Indeed, EU states imposed sanctions against the United States in 1996 in response to US extra-territorial laws regarding Cuba, Iran, and Libya.[30]

Finally, sanctioning through the European Union has been a function of relative power.[31] In general, the most powerful states in an international institution play a determining role in the decision to impose multilateral sanctions through such an institution in order to increase their relative power. Multilateral sanctions can be attractive to states because they provide an opportunity to aggregate economic might, reduce enforcement problems, and increase the economic and political costs on targets. Even though smaller states may possess a common interest in imposing sanctions through an international institution, domestic pressure and economic repercussions may make it difficult for some to continue cooperating. In order to persuade other sender states to enact sanctions and prevent defection, powerful states can utilize both sticks and carrots – threats and incentives – as coercive measures.[32] Indeed, when sanctions are imposed through an international institution, we should expect to find a major power (or powers) taking

---

[29] Martin, *Coercive Cooperation*, pp. 131–68.

[30] The US laws were the National Defense Authorization Act for Fiscal Year 1993; Cuban Democracy Act 1992, sections 1704 and 1706; Cuban Liberty and Democratic Solidarity Act of 1996; and the Iran and Libya Sanctions Act of 1996. See Council Regulation (EC), No. 2271/96 of 22 November 1996.

[31] On relative power see Joseph M. Grieco, "Anarchy and the Limits of Cooperation: A Realist Critique of the Newest Liberal Institutionalism," *International Organization*, Vol. 42, No. 3, Summer 1988, pp. 485–507; Stephen D. Krasner, "Global Communications and Power: Life on the Pareto Frontier," *World Politics*, Vol. 43, April 1991, pp. 336–66; Lisa L. Martin, "Interests, Power, and Multilateralism," *International Organization*, Vol. 46, No. 4, Autumn 1992, pp. 765–92.

[32] Martin, *Coercive Cooperation*, pp. 36–8.

an entrepreneurial or leadership role among the senders. The use of economic sanctions to coerce states successfully requires significant economic resources, which great powers are more likely to possess. In the absence of support from powerful states, multilateral sanctions through an international institution are much more difficult.

In sum, the increase in EU sanctions during the post-Cold War era has been a function of the changing structure of the international system. There was little rationale to sanction through the European Community during the Cold War. The international system was bipolar, and European states were primarily concerned with balancing the Soviet Union and coordinating policies with the United States. However, this changed following the collapse of the USSR and the emergence of a US-dominated international system. The shift from bipolarity to unipolarity increased the impetus of European states to aggregate power and sanction through the European Union.

To summarize the hypotheses, we would expect the following:

• During the Cold War, there would be little sanctioning through the European Community because the international system was bipolar; European states would be primarily concerned about imposing multilateral sanctions with the US to balance the Soviet Union.
• During the post-Cold War era, there would be a notable increase in the percentage of EU sanctions as part of a strategy to aggregate power in a unipolar international system.

The sanctions data

In order to test this argument, I have gathered data on every sanctions case between 1950 and 2006 in which a European state was a sender. The data include cases in which European states sanctioned unilaterally, multilaterally through the EC or EU, or multilaterally through other forums.

There are several potential problems with the coding. First, the distinction between unilateral and multilateral sanctions is not always clear-cut. For example, states may impose sanctions first, and then seek approval and/or support from an international institution. This is what Lisa Martin focuses on in her study of the Falkland Islands conflict between Britain and Argentina in 1982.[33] Britain was able to drum up sanctions cooperation from the European Community during the Falkland Islands conflict, but only after it broke diplomatic relations

[33] *Ibid.*, pp 131–68.

with Argentina and imposed unilateral sanctions. I coded this as a case of unilateral rather than EC sanctions because Britain initiated unilateral sanctions first – and then sought multilateral support to supplement its actions. In 1986 the French government coerced New Zealand into releasing two secret service agents imprisoned for sinking the Greenpeace ship *Rainbow Warrior* when it threatened to veto the adoption of a vital butter quota by the European Community. The New Zealand government subsequently caved in to French demands. New Zealand Prime Minister David Lange lamented, "We've got thousands of dairy farmers out there going broke. They haven't been able to pay their mortgages for the last two quarters. If we took a poll of dairy farmers on the spy agreement, I know what the result would be."[34] Since France's EC butter threat came after unilateral sanctions had already been imposed on a number of other New Zealand products such as fish and kiwi fruit, I coded France as the sender rather than the EC.

In short, I coded the EC and EU as a primary sender when European states collectively imposed sanctions from the beginning of the case. Though one or several states may initiate the move to consider sanctions, they are initially imposed through the institution. Thus, the EU is coded as a sender in the 1998 Yugoslavia case because European states specifically opted to impose sanctions through the EU from the outset. The difference between the two types hinges on timing: did a state seek cooperation *after* it acted, or were sanctions employed *from the beginning* through an international institution? This sets a high bar for sanctions cooperation since I focus only on the primary sender.

Second, there are also potential coding problems when changes occur during a sanctions episode. If the sender's demands change or a new set of sanctions is imposed in response to developments in the target state, how should this be coded? As one case? Separate cases? Departing from Hofbauer *et al.* somewhat, I parsed sanctions against the same target into distinct cases according to whether either the senders' demands changed or new sanctions were imposed following developments in the target state. Thus, I divided sanctions against Indonesia (1991–99 and 1999–2000) and Yugoslavia (1991–1995 and 1998–) into separate cases because the demands were different.[35] And I parsed sanctions

---

[34] Dai Hayward, "Lange Says Trade More Vital than Spies' Fate," *Financial Times*, July 11, 1986, p. 3.

[35] For the sanctions against Yugoslavia 91–1, Hofbauer *et al.* code the sender as the United Nations. However, a careful inspection of the timing demonstrates that the EU imposed sanctions first – followed by the United States and the United Nations.

against Burma/Myanmar (1988–1996 and 1996–) into separate cases because new sanctions were imposed following new human rights violations.

Third, it is important to control for United Nations sanctions. European Union sanctions would be epiphenomenal if they were imposed only after UN sanctions were imposed. For instance, in 1997 the EU sanctioned Libya, but only after the United Nations imposed sanctions to restore democracy. In this case, EU sanctions were imposed as part of much broader UN Security Council sanctions.[36] I have tried to control for this problem by focusing on the issue of timing. In cases where EU sanctions chronologically followed UN sanctions I code the UN as the sender, and cases where EU sanctions came first I code as EU sanctions. Table 4.1 lays out the data.

Europe's historical record

The primary finding is that European states have increasingly imposed economic sanctions through the European Union in the post-Cold War era, rather than unilaterally or multilaterally through other forums. This marks a notable change from the Cold War. As Table 4.2 highlights, between 1950 and 1990 European states sanctioned through the European Community only twice out of seventeen cases. Since 1991, however, they have utilized the European Union in 78 percent of cases. As Figure 4.1 illustrates, the contemporary trend is clear: when European states impose economic sanctions for foreign policy goals, they increasingly do it through the European Union. By the current decade, all sanctions cases in which a European state was a primary sender were being done through the EU.

The primary reason is the change in the structure of the international system. During the Cold War, European states were likely to coordinate multilateral sanctions with the United States to balance the Soviet Union. However, the shift to American preponderance in the post-Cold War era caused European states to aggregate power in such areas as economic sanctions to decrease reliance on the US and increase the effectiveness of sanctions. We now briefly examine the Cold War and post-Cold War eras.

---

[36] The EU's common position on Libya noted that the UN was the primary sender. See Common Position (97/826/CFSP), OJ L 344, 15.12.1997.

Table 4.1. *Foreign policy sanctions by European states, 1950–2006*

Primary sender(s)	Target country	Years	Goal of sender(s)
UK and US	Iran	1951–1953	• Reverse the nationalization of oil facilities • Destabilize Mossadeq government
Spain	United Kingdom	1954–1985	• Gain sovereignty over Gibraltar
UK, France, and US	Egypt	1956	• Ensure passage through Suez Canal • Compensate for nationalization of Suez
France	Tunisia	1957–1963	• Halt support to Algerian rebels
NATO allies	East Germany	1961–1962	• Protect West Berlin
France	Tunisia	1964–1966	• Settle expropriation claims
UK	Rhodesia	1965–1979	• Establish majority rule by black Africans
UK	Malta	1971	• Reinstitute defense agreement
UK	Uganda	1972–1979	• Stop expulsion of Asians • Reverse nationalization of UK companies
EC	Turkey	1981–	• Restore democracy
UK	Argentina	1982	• Withdraw troops from Falkland Islands
Netherlands and US	Suriname	1982–1991	• Improve human rights • Limit alliance with Cuba and Libya
France	New Zealand	1986	• Release French secret service agents
West Germany, US, and Japan	Burma/Myanmar	1988–1996	• Improve human rights • Restore democracy
UK and US	Somalia	1988–	• Improve human rights • End civil war
EC	China	1989	• Improve human rights in the wake of the Tiananmen Square crackdown
Belgium, France, and US	Zaire/Congo	1990–1997	• Establish democracy
EU and US	USSR	1991	• Restore Gorbachev government
UK, Netherlands, and US	Indonesia	1991–1999	• Improve human rights • End conflict in East Timor
EU and US	Yugoslavia	1991–1995	• End conflict in Bosnia and Croatia • Improve human rights in Bosnia
EU and US	Togo	1992–	• Establish democracy • Improve human rights
UK and US	Malawi	1992–1993	• Establish democracy • Improve human rights
EU	Algeria	1992–1994	• Establish democracy
Germany, UN, and US	Cambodia (Khmer Rouge)	1992–	• Support peace plan (Paris accords)
EU	Equatorial Guinea	1993–1997	• Establish democracy • Improve human rights
EU and US	Guatemala	1993	• Oppose coup • Restore democracy
EU and US	Nigeria	1993–1998	• Improve human rights • Establish democracy

Table 4.1. (*cont.*)

Primary sender(s)	Target country	Years	Goal of sender(s)
Greece	Macedonia	1994–1995	• Change name of country • Remove star of Vergina • Alter constitution
Greece	Albania	1994–1995	• Release jailed ethnic Greeks
EU, US, and Japan	Gambia	1994–1998	• Restore democracy
EU	Turkey	1995	• Improve human rights
France and US	Niger	1996–1997	• Restore democracy
EU, US, and Japan	Burma/Myanmar	1996–	• Improve human rights • Restore democracy
EU	United States	1996	• Counteract the effects of US extra-territorial laws regarding Cuba, Iran, Libya
EU and US	Yugoslavia	1998–	• Improve human rights in Kosovo • End conflict in Kosovo
EU and US	Indonesia	1999–2000	• Accept UN peacekeeping force in East Timor • Withdraw Indonesian troops
EU	Austria	2000	• Remove Jörg Haider from leadership role • Prevent Freedom Party from joining government
EU	Zimbabwe	2002–	• Establish democracy • Improve human rights
EU and US	Moldova (leadership of Transnistrian region)	2003–	• End conflict and negotiate peace accord
EU	Belarus	2004–	• Investigate disappearance of opposition leaders, journalist
EU	Macedonia	2004–	• Punish those engaged in violent activities that challenge the Framework Agreement
EU	Sudan	2004	• End conflict
EU	Croatia	2004	• Hand over Ante Gotovina to the International Criminal Tribunal for the former Yugoslavia
EU	Uzbekistan	2005	• Improve human rights • Conduct inquiry into 2004 Andijan events

Table 4.2. *Summary of sanctions by European states, 1950–2006*

Years	N	Unilateral	Multilateral, Not EC/EU	EC/EU	% Through EC/EU
Cold War (1950–90)	17	7	8	2	12%
Post-Cold War (1991–)	27	2	4	21	78%

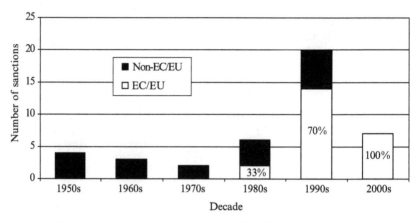

Figure 4.1. Number of sanctions by decade.

The absence of EC sanctions

During the Cold War, the European Community was a primary sender only twice.[37] Since it played no significant role in foreign policymaking, European states did not instinctively turn to the EC to impose economic sanctions for foreign policy goals. In fact, the data show that when European states imposed multilateral sanctions during the Cold War, the United States was a partner in virtually every case. The US, rather than other European states, was the natural ally. This was largely a function of the bipolar structure of the international system, which caused European states to coordinate foreign policy with the US to balance against the Soviet Union. European states also imposed unilateral sanctions in a number of cases where they had colonial interests. When considering sanctions throughout the Cold War, European states had three general choices:

• Unilateral sanctions
• Multilateral sanctions other than through the EC.
• Multilateral sanctions through the EC.

First, Europe's major powers could have employed unilateral sanctions. Indeed, they did in nearly half of the cases during the Cold War,

---

[37] The European Community did participate in a handful of sanctions cases during the Cold War as a secondary sender. Examples include economic sanctions against Iran in 1980 in response to the American hostage crisis (the US was the primary sender), the Soviet Union in 1982 (the US was the primary sender), Argentina in 1982 during the Falklands War (Britain was the primary sender), South Africa in 1986 (the US was the primary sender), and Libya in 1986 (the US was the primary sender).

and usually in cases where they had colonial interests. Spain sanctioned
Britain in 1954 over Gibraltar; France sanctioned Tunisia in 1957 and
1964, as well as New Zealand in 1986; and Britain sanctioned Rhodesia
in 1965, Malta in 1971, Uganda in 1972, and Argentina in 1982. Nearly
all of these cases involved conflicts over former colonies or territorial
disputes, increasing the difficulty of getting significant cooperation from
other EC states.[38] For example, when Rhodesia declared independence
from Britain in 1965, the latter took a number of actions such as terminating the export of arms, ceasing all foreign aid, halting Rhodesia's access
to London's capital market, and banning purchases of Rhodesian sugar
and tobacco.[39] But despite some British efforts, European support was
not forthcoming. France claimed that the Rhodesian conflict was not a
threat to international peace and "was solely the concern of the United
Kingdom, whose colony it is."[40] Furthermore, when France sanctioned
Tunisia in 1957, Britain directly undermined France by offering economic and military assistance to the Tunisian government to prevent it
from turning to the USSR for aid.[41] In 1972 the British not only failed to
obtain EC support for sanctions against Uganda after President Idi
Amin expelled 50,000 Ugandans with British passports, but France
and West Germany increased trade with, and economic aid and military
assistance for, the former British colony.

Second, European states could have imposed multilateral sanctions
through forums other than the EC. This happened in almost half the
cases. In most instances, this was because there was a mutual desire to
balance the Soviet Union and limit its influence throughout the globe.
Britain and the US sanctioned Iran in 1951; Britain, France, and the US
sanctioned Egypt in 1956; NATO sanctioned East Germany in 1961;
West Germany, the US, and Japan sanctioned Burma in 1988; the
Netherlands and the US sanctioned Suriname in 1982; and Britain
and the US sanctioned Somalia in 1988. It is striking that the United

[38] Exceptions included British sanctions against Argentina, which received support from
most EC countries, and French sanctions against New Zealand, which involved a threat
to veto the adoption of a vital EC butter quota.
[39] Harry R. Strack, *Sanctions: The Case of Rhodesia* (Syracuse, NY: Syracuse University
Press, 1978); David M. Rowe, "Economic Sanctions Do Work: Economic Statecraft
and the Oil Embargo of Rhodesia," in Jean-Marc F. Blanchard, Edward D. Mansfield,
and Norrin M. Ripsman, *Power and the Purse: Economic Statecraft, Interdependence, and
National Security* (London: Frank Cass, 2000), pp. 254–87; Galtung, "On the Effects of
International Economic Sanctions," pp. 378–416.
[40] Quoted in M. S. Daoudi and M. S. Dajani, *Economic Sanctions: Ideals and Experience*
(Boston, MA: Routledge & Kegan Paul, 1983), p. 80. On France and Rhodesian
sanctions see also Strack, *Sanctions*, p. 19; A. G. Mezerik, *Rhodesia and the United
Nations*, Vol. XII (New York: International Review Service, 1966), p. 64.
[41] Hofbauer *et al.*, *Economic Sanctions Reconsidered*, pp. 173–7.

States was a multilateral sanctioning partner in each of these cases. For example, as the CIA's history of US and British efforts to overthrow the Mossadeq government in Iran notes, cooperation on economic sanctions and covert action was motivated by Cold War concerns: "The policy of both the US and UK governments requires replacement of Mossadeq as the alternative to certain economic collapse in Iran and the eventual loss of the area to the Soviet orbit."[42] Britain, the United States, and France sanctioned Egypt following Nasser's seizure of the Suez Canal in July 1956. Egypt's control of the canal gave the Soviet Union, which was providing financial and military assistance to Egypt, considerable influence over a major economic lifeline to Western Europe. A substantial amount of oil flowed through the canal, and Prime Minister Anthony Eden noted that he "did not want to see Soviet influence expand in Africa."[43] Moreover, the US and Netherlands sanctioned Suriname in December 1982 following the overthrow of Henck Chin-A-Sen because of concerns that the new government's relationship with Cuba – and hence the Soviet Union – was too close.[44] Finally, NATO's decision to sanction East Germany in 1961 following the construction of the Berlin Wall was inextricably tied to the US–Soviet conflict over Germany.[45]

Third, Europe's major powers could have imposed multilateral sanctions through the European Community. However, they almost never did. The only exceptions were the European Community's decision to sanction Turkey in 1981 and China in 1989. Following the September 1980 military intervention in Turkey and the suspension of democratic institutions, the EC suspended approximately $600 million in aid the following year and demanded that Turkey restore democracy.[46] European Community states also imposed sanctions against China in 1989 to coerce "Chinese authorities to stop the executions and to put an end to the repressive actions against those who legitimately claim their

---

[42] "'London' Draft of the TPAJAX Operational Plan," in Donald N. Wilber, *Overthrow of Premier Mossadeq of Iran* (Washington: Central Intelligence Agency, March 1954), reproduced in Appendix B.

[43] Anthony Eden, *Full Circle: The Memoirs of Anthony Eden* (Boston, MA: Houghton Mifflin, 1960), p. 468.

[44] Walter Ellis, "Concern over Surinam's Future," *Financial Times*, December 16, 1982, p. 4; Warren Hoge, "In Suriname 'They Make You Full of Holes, Man,'" *New York Times*, January 28, 1983, p. A2; Andrew Whitley, "Circuitous Route to an Independent Surinam," *Financial Times*, April 22, 1983, p. 4.

[45] On the conflict over Berlin see, for example, John Lewis Gaddis, *We Now Know: Rethinking Cold War History* (New York: Oxford University Press, 1997), pp. 143–51; Marc Trachtenberg, *A Constructed Peace: The Making of the European Settlement, 1945–1963* (Princeton: Princeton University Press, 1999), pp. 251–351.

[46] EC Resolution Doc. 1–765/91; Doc. 1–5/82; European Parliament Resolution 8.7.1982. See also, for example, Ihsan D. Dagi, "Democratic Transition in Turkey, 1980–93: The Impact of European Diplomacy," *Middle Eastern Studies*, Vol. 32, No. 2, April 1996, pp. 124–41.

democratic rights." The European Community further asked China "to respect human rights and to take into account the hopes for freedom and democracy deeply felt by the population."[47] But these cases were outliers. European states largely refrained from imposing sanctions through the EC during the Cold War. Under Article 113 of the Treaty of Rome, the EC had competence over common commercial policy. But it had little or no foreign policy role.[48] The European Defense Community and de Gaulle's Fouchet Plan failed to materialize, and European Political Cooperation was left outside the EC's legal order. The EC dealt only with economic, commercial, and agricultural matters. Indeed, European states were primarily concerned about the Soviet threat, and the United States was the most likely multilateral sanctions partner.

The EU as a sanctions power

In the post-Cold War era, however, there was a substantial change. With the collapse of the Soviet Union and the emergence of the US as the dominant global power, European states increasingly sanctioned through the EU. They imposed sanctions through the EC only twice (12 percent) during the Cold War. But they have done it twenty-one times (78 percent) since 1990. This has primarily been a function of the structural shift to unipolarity. European states have imposed sanctions through the European Union as part of a broader strategy to aggregate power. Leaders have been motivated to sanction through the EU to increase their autonomy and enhance the effectiveness of sanctions. In the post-Cold War era, EU states have possessed three major options:

- Unilateral sanctions
- Multilateral sanctions other than through the EU
- Multilateral sanctions through the EU.

First, Europe's major powers could have sanctioned unilaterally. This happened twice: Greek sanctions against Macedonia in 1994 and against Albania in 1994. In the Macedonian case, the Greek government imposed sanctions to coerce the Macedonian government into changing the name of its country, removing the star of Vergina from its flag, and altering the constitution.[49] In the Albanian case, Greece imposed

[47] Declaration of European Council, Madrid, June 26, 1989.
[48] Sebastian Bohr, "Sanctions by the United Nations Security Council and the European Community," *European Journal of International Law*, Vol. 4, No. 2, 1993, pp. 256–68.
[49] Nikolaos Zahariadis, "Nationalism and Small-State Foreign Policy: The Greek Response to the Macedonian Issue," *Political Science Quarterly*, Vol. 109, No. 4, Autumn 1994, pp. 647–67; Victor Roudometof, "Nationalism and Identity Politics in

114   The rise of European security cooperation

unilateral sanctions to coerce the Albanian government into releasing five imprisoned ethnic Greeks.[50] However, these cases were outliers, and neither involved a major European power. In fact, no major EU power has imposed unilateral sanctions in the post-Cold War era. This marks a significant shift from the Cold War, when unilateral sanctions by such major powers as France and Britain constituted nearly half the cases.

Second, European states could have imposed multilateral sanctions other than through the EU. This occurred 16 percent of the time. The UK, Netherlands, and the US imposed sanctions against Indonesia in 1991, though the EU eventually replaced the UK and Netherlands as the primary sender in 1999. There were four additional cases: Belgian, French, and US sanctions against Zaire/Congo in 1990; UK and US sanctions against Malawi in 1992; German, UN, and US sanctions against Cambodia in 1992; and French and US sanctions against Niger in 1996. The percentage of multilateral sanctions imposed through forums other than the EU was significantly smaller than during the Cold War, when it had been at nearly 50 percent, a reflection of the structural shift from bipolarity to unipolarity. This is largely because there was no longer a need to balance the Soviet Union.

Third, European states could have sanctioned through the European Union.[51] In the post-Cold War era they sanctioned through the EU 78 percent of the time. These cases included sanctions against Algeria, Austria, Belarus, Burma/Myanmar, Croatia, Equatorial Guinea, Gambia, Guatemala, Indonesia, Macedonia, Moldova, Nigeria, Soviet Union, Sudan,

the Balkans: Greece and the Macedonian Question," *Journal of Modern Greek Studies*, Vol. 14, No. 2, 1996, pp. 253–301; John Shea, *Macedonia and Greece: The Struggle to Define a New Balkan Nation* (Jefferson, NC: McFarland & Company, 1997), pp. 278–310; Evangelos Kofos, "Greek Policy Considerations over FYROM Independence and Recognition," in James Pettifer, ed., *The New Macedonian Question* (New York: St. Martin's Press, 1999), pp. 226–62; Virginia Tsouderos, "Greek Policy and the Yugoslav Turmoil," *Mediterranean Quarterly*, Vol. 4, No. 2, Spring 1993, pp. 1–13.
[50] "Greece v. Albania," *Economist*, September 17, 1994, p. 59; "Greece Hits Out at Albania," *The Independent*, August 27, 1994, p. 7; "Greece Clamps Down after Spy Convictions," *Agence France Presse*, September 8, 1994.
[51] There has been little published work on the European Union and economic sanctions. For some exceptions see Ian Anthony, "Sanctions Applied by the European Union and the United Nations," *SIPRI Yearbook 2002: Armaments, Disarmament and International Security* (New York: Oxford University Press, 2002), pp. 203–28; Michael Merlingen, Cas Mudde, and Ulrich Sedelmeier, "The Right and the Righteous? European Norms, Domestic Politics and the Sanctions against Austria," *Journal of Common Market Studies*, Vol. 39, No. 1, March 2001, pp. 59–77; Commission of the European Communities, *Communication from the Commission on Conflict Prevention* (Brussels: Commission European, November 2001), p. 24; Fiona Palmer, "European Sanctions and Enforcement: European Law Meets the Individual," *The Cambrian Law Review*, No. 28, 1997, pp. 45–67; André Kalbermatter, *Sanctions Practice of the EC* (Zurich: Wenger Vieli Belser, 1999).

Togo, Turkey, United States, Uzbekistan, Yugoslavia, and Zimbabwe. In the aftermath of the Soviet collapse, European states established a number of articles as part of the Maastricht Treaty to facilitate the adoption, suspension, or termination of economic sanctions for foreign policy goals.[52]

EU sanctions generally require the adoption of a common position under Article 15 of the 1992 Maastricht Treaty establishing the European Union. As an instrument of the Common Foreign and Security Policy, the European Council must adopt a common position. When economic sanctions are imposed on a third country, implementation is governed by Article 301 or Article 60 of the Treaty establishing the European Community. When sanctions target persons, groups, and entities which are not directly linked to the regime of a third country, Articles 60, 301, and 308 of the Treaty establishing the European Community apply. Arms embargoes constitute a separate case. Although trade in manufactured goods falls under exclusive Community jurisdiction, Article 296 of the Treaty establishing the European Community allows for an embargo relating to military goods to be implemented by member states using national measures. It is therefore common practice that arms embargoes are imposed by a common position and enforced on the basis of export control legislation of member states.[53] In practice, this means that the decision to impose sanctions is made by national leaders within the European Council, who adopt a common position or joint action that specifies the sanctions objectives. For most types of economic sanctions, the next step is for the European Commission to prepare a regulation containing specific measures to implement the political decision.[54] This ensures that the decision and authority to sanction is retained by member states – and not by the EU itself.

The increase in the number and percentage of EU sanctions has largely been a function of the structure of the international system. As EU High Representative Javier Solana has argued, a critical reason for increased European sanctions cooperation has been "the radical change

---

[52] These are not binding provisions. Member states have opt-out clauses if they believe that participation in a sanctions case violates their security. Article 296 states, for example, that "any Member State may take such measures as it considers necessary for the protection of its security which are connected with the production of or trade in arms, munitions and war material." Article 296 (ex Article 223), Treaty Establishing the European Community.

[53] For example, Article 60 notes that "a Member State may, for serious political reasons and on grounds of urgency, take unilateral measures against a third country with regard to capital movements and payments." Article 60 (ex Article 73g), Treaty Establishing the European Community.

[54] Anthony, "Sanctions Applied by the European Union and the United Nations," pp. 203–28.

in the strategic environment of Europe after the disintegration of the Soviet Union."[55] To begin with, European leaders have sanctioned through the EU because it allows them to conduct autonomous actions. In a unipolar international system, sanctioning through the EU gives European states an important foreign policy option when (1) the United States is not interested in acting; or (2) the United States and Europe have different strategic interests. As one EU document noted: "In the framework of the EU Common Foreign and Security Policy, sanctions or restrictive measures have over recent years become a regularly used policy instrument, either in the form of *autonomous* EU sanctions or as sanctions implementing certain Resolutions of the Security Council of the United Nations."[56]

For example, despite US reluctance to sanction Zimbabwe in 2002, EU countries nonetheless imposed sanctions. British leaders contended that EU sanctions would be more economically devastating than unilateral British sanctions. This marked a notable shift from their strategy nearly forty years earlier, when they unilaterally sanctioned Zimbabwe's predecessor, the British colony of Rhodesia.[57] Dutch leaders adopted a similar strategy, noting: "We are in the process of studying what measures can be taken and these include sanctions. However we would prefer any measures [to be decided] on a European scale."[58] Christopher Patten, former European Union external relations commissioner, concluded that sanctioning through the EU allows European states to wield significant power:

Fragmented policy-making by states and institutions vying for the limelight has been a recipe for vacillation. The alternative is to weld all our efforts into a strategic stance; to take a long-term view on how the EU's collective power and influence can be mobilized on behalf of our values . . . The Union has . . . developed quite an arsenal of sanctions and restrictive measures. These range from restrictions on visits and diplomatic contacts through the suspension of aid or trade privileges to fully-fledged sanctions or embargoes, stopping trade, blocking transport and freezing financial assets and transactions.[59]

[55] Javier Solana, "Decisions to Ensure a More Responsible Europe," *International Herald Tribune*, January 14, 2000.
[56] European Commission, *Common Foreign and Security (CFSP) Sanctions* (Brussels: European Commission, 2004).
[57] Andrew Grice, "Post-Election Zimbabwe: Britain to Press EU for Wider List of Sanctions," *The Independent*, March 15, 2002, p. 15.
[58] "Netherlands Considering Sanctions on Zimbabwe in EU Context," *Agence France Presse*, March 20, 2002.
[59] Christopher Patten, "The Future of the European Security and Defense Policy (ESDP) and the Role of the European Commission," speech at the conference on the Development of a Common European Security and Defense Policy, Berlin, December 16, 1999.

Furthermore, in light of impending EU sanctions against Burma, former British Foreign Secretary Robin Cook argued: "I am bound to say I think actually it would be pointless for Britain itself to try and apply its own economic sanctions . . . We are upholding the European Union approach to Burma."[60] The reason was that the total amount of Burma's trade with the European Union was four times greater than with Burma's single largest EU trading partner, Germany.[61]

Sanctioning through the EU has also helped ameliorate enforcement problems.[62] EU and US sanctions against Yugoslavia beginning in 1991 had a devastating impact on the Yugoslav economy and were important factors in reaching a negotiated settlement at Dayton. The EU's decision to establish Sanctions Assistance Missions decreased enforcement problems against defectors such as Greece, and was important in improving the sanctions' effectiveness. EU and US sanctions against Guatemala in 1993 contributed to the demise of President Jorge Serrano, who fled to El Salvador when the military refused to support his coup.[63] The arms embargo against Indonesia by the EU and US was supported by all sender states – including France and Britain, Europe's largest arms-exporting countries – and was important in coercing Indonesia into accepting a UN-led peacekeeping force in East Timor.[64] Finally, EU sanctions against Austria in 2000 had broad support throughout the European Union – especially among Europe's major powers such as Britain, France, and Germany – and were important in Jörg Haider's decision to step down as leader of Austria's far-right Freedom Party.[65]

[60] Interview given by the British Foreign Secretary, Robin Cook, for BBC Radio, May 14, 1998.

[61] The economic data are for 1996, the first year of EU sanctions. International Monetary Fund, *Direction of Trade Statistics Yearbook, 1998* (Washington, DC: IMF, 1998), pp. 517–18.

[62] On the EU and enforcement problems, see Council of the European Union, *Guidelines On Implementation and Evaluation of Restrictive Measures*.

[63] "European Commission Suspends Aid to Guatemala," *European Report*, No. 1863, June 2, 1993; "EC Welcomes Return to Constitutional Order in Guatemala," *European Report*, No. 1865, June 9, 1993; "U.S. Suspends Aid to Guatemala," *Agence France Press*, May 27, 1993; "United States to Resume Aid to Guatemala," *Agence France Presse*, June 7, 1993.

[64] As London's *Independent* argued: "In an effort to force Indonesia into agreeing to an international peacekeeping force, the EU, along with the US, cut off its arms exports. The pressure worked. The military pulled out of East Timor, the peacekeepers went in and peace was restored." Richard Lloyd Parry, "Indonesian Army Will Use EU Arms in Creeping Coup," *The Independent*, January 18, 2000, p. 12.

[65] Speaking to journalists in Vienna following Haider's decision to step down, Austrian Chancellor Wolfgang Schuessel "suggested that Haider resigned the party leadership to deflect the international criticism that has subjected the new government to repeated diplomatic snubs and massive protests by Austrians opposed to the far right's

In sum, in the post-Cold War era European states sanctioned through the EU in 78 percent of cases; they have increasingly imposed economic sanctions for foreign policy goals through the European Union. This change has been caused by the structural shift at the end of the Cold War. The data also show that European states have chosen to use economic sanctions more often than ever before. This finding supports much of the recent sanctions literature, which argues that states in general have increasingly opted to use economic sanctions for foreign policy objectives.[66]

Case studies of European sanctions

This section offers two case studies to flesh out the causal logic of the argument: British sanctions against Uganda from 1972 to 1979, and EU and US sanctions against Yugoslavia from 1991 to 1995. These cases were chosen for several reasons: they include variation in the amount of sanctions cooperation among EC and EU states (the dependent variable); they include variation in the structure of the international system (the independent variable); and they are two of the most prominent sanctions cases involving European states since World War II. In order to understand the motivations of European leaders, I gathered information from several sources: statements from government leaders in newspapers; European Union and national government documents; and memoirs.

British sanctions against Uganda (1972–1979)

Britain was the dominant power in Uganda from the 1890s until the early 1970s. It provided Uganda with considerable economic and military aid through the early 1970s, first as a British protectorate and then following independence in 1962. Britain supplied armored personnel carriers (APCs) to the Ugandan military, provided training to President Idi Amin's army and intelligence services, and was Uganda's largest trading partner.[67] In 1971 Uganda's trade with Britain totaled

---

anti-immigrant and anti-European-unity policies." Carol J. Williams, "Haider's Resignation Doesn't Ease Pressure," *Los Angeles Times*, March 1, 2000, p. A6.

[66] Drezner, *The Sanctions Paradox*; Hofbauer et al., *Economic Sanctions Reconsidered*; Haass, *Economic Sanctions and American Diplomacy*.

[67] Stockholm International Peace Institute, *SIPRI Yearbook 1972* (New York: SIPRI, 1972), p. 133; International Monetary Fund, *Direction of Trade, Annual 1971–77* (Washington, DC: IMF, 1971), pp. 262, 302; T. Avirgan and M. Honey, *War in Uganda: The Legacy of Idi Amin* (Westport, CN: Hill, 1982), pp. 8–11.

$118 million, a figure greater than its trade with all African countries *combined* and nearly double that of its next largest trading partner, the United States.[68] However, the British–Ugandan relationship began to decline in the early 1970s. In an August 1972 speech to Ugandan troops, Amin announced that he was expelling roughly 50,000 Asians with British passports. "I am going to ask Britain to take over responsibility for all Asians in Uganda who are holding British passports because they are sabotaging the economy of the country," he noted. "I want the economy to be in the hands of Ugandan citizens, especially black Ugandans."[69] Amin then expelled Richard Slater, the British high commissioner in Uganda, in November. He then nationalized thirty-five British companies, such as Mitchell Cotts and British-American Tobacco, in December 1972.[70]

Amin's actions caused a furor both within the Heath government and among members of the British House of Commons. As *The Times* of London reported: "Seldom have MPs been so united as they were today in their condemnation of General Amin's latest decree nationalizing British-owned companies in Uganda."[71] British Prime Minister Edward Heath eventually responded by canceling a £10 million loan to Uganda, ending a technical aid program worth £1.7 million, withdrawing more than 800 officers working on technical assistance projects, banning all military aid, and breaking off diplomatic relations in 1974 following the murder of British citizen Dora Bloch.[72] The sanctions were designed to stop the expulsion of Asians, reverse the nationalization of British companies, and destabilize the Amin government. In 1978, the United States assisted Britain by imposing a trade embargo against Uganda.[73] However, the sanctions failed to achieve their foreign policy objectives. They neither coerced President Amin into changing his

---

[68] *Direction of Trade, Annual 1971–77*, p. 262.
[69] "Uganda Says No Room for 40,000 Asians with British Passports," *The Times*, August 5, 1972, p. 1.
[70] Iain Grahame, *Amin and Uganda: A Personal Memoir* (New York: Granada, 1980), p. 141; Amii Omara-Otunnu, *Politics and the Military in Uganda, 1890–1985* (New York: St. Martin's Press, 1987), pp. 121–2.
[71] Hugh Noyes, "Wave of Anger against General Amin in the Commons," *The Times*, December 20, 1972, p. 1.
[72] "Speech by Sir Alec Douglas-Home on BBC Television, 31 August 1972," in D. C. Watt and James Mayall, *Current British Foreign Policy: Documents, Statements, Speeches 1972* (London: Temple Smith, 1972), pp. 595–7; Edward Heath, *The Course of My Life: My Autobiography* (London: Hodder and Stoughton, 1998), p. 457; George Clark, "£10n Loan to Uganda Cancelled by Britain," *The Times*, December 1, 1972, p. 1.
[73] Steven J. Fredman, "U.S. Trade Sanctions against Uganda: Legality under International Law," *Law and Policy in International Business*, Vol. 11, No. 3, 1979, pp. 1149–91.

behavior nor, contrary to Hufbauer, Schott, and Elliott's assertions, destabilized his government.[74]

Why did British policymakers fail to sanction through the European Community? In a bipolar international system, it was difficult for British leaders to get EC cooperation on sanctions against a British colony, especially when there was no Cold War security issue at stake. Britain's initial response was to coerce Amin into changing his mind through diplomacy and to build multilateral support if possible. As Heath noted: "At first, we did our utmost, via diplomatic channels, to try to persuade Amin to change his mind, both through making representation to him and by encouraging other Commonwealth countries to put pressure on him."[75] Heath sought the support of Commonwealth and European countries, and sent Geoffrey Rippon, chancellor of the duchy of Lancaster, to negotiate with Amin. There was a strong normative rationale for EC states to cooperate. The Amin government was one of the most barbaric and undemocratic African regimes in the twentieth century, and somewhere between 250,000 and 500,000 Ugandans were murdered during his eight-year regime.[76] However, Heath's attempt to gain multilateral support came up empty-handed. In a letter to United States representative Stephen J. Solarz, British Foreign Secretary David Owen remarked that there was "no sign of general support within the [European] Community for the institution of a trade embargo."[77] Britain was unable to garner EC support *despite* a strong normative rationale for employing sanctions.[78]

European states had little incentive to pursue EC foreign policy cooperation; NATO was the primary security institution in Europe. Despite Henry Kissinger's prodding to establish greater EC cooperation in his 1973 "Year of Europe" speech, no progress was made in the security realm.[79] European Political Cooperation (EPC) was largely a talking shop for European states and was not formally integrated into the EC. Indeed, there was "a virtually unanimous view" among European

---

[74] Hofbauer et al. argue that the sanctions were fairly successful in destabilizing the Amin regime, and they give it twelve on a scale from one (outright failure) to sixteen (significant success). Hofbauer et al., *Economic Sanctions Reconsidered*. In this respect, I agree with Pape's assessment of the Uganda case. See Pape, "Why Economic Sanctions Do Not Work," p. 112.
[75] Heath, *The Course of My Life*, pp. 456–7.
[76] Avirgan and Honey, *War in Uganda*, pp. 3–27; Henry Kyemba, *A State of Blood: The Inside Story of Idi Amin* (London: Corgi Books, 1977).
[77] Judith Miller, "When Sanctions Worked," *Foreign Policy*, No. 39, Summer 1980, p. 124.
[78] Britain was not admitted to the EC until January 1973.
[79] Henry Kissinger, *Years of Upheaval* (Boston: Little, Brown and Company, 1982), pp. 128–94.

states that in the EC "there must be no fixed economic commitments such as sanctions, made for reasons of international politics."[80] Despite American pressure, for example, Britain failed to secure EC sanctions against Syria in 1986 following the attempt by Nezar Hindawi to place a bomb on an El Al aircraft at Heathrow Airport.[81]

This paucity of security cooperation among EC states had a severe drawback for the Ugandan sanctions: it made it impossible for Britain to enforce them. Europe's major powers such as France and Germany actually *increased* trade, economic aid, and military assistance with Uganda. French trade with Uganda increased from $17.1 million in 1973 to $65.1 million in 1979, German trade increased slightly from $33.6 million to $34.1 million, EC trade increased from $179.1 million to $236.4 million, and US trade increased from $65.0 million to $77.8 million.[82] Moreover, during the 1970s France sold anti-tank missiles and armored cars to Uganda, Italy sold helicopters, and even the US sold transport aircraft and Bell helicopters.[83] There was also considerable speculation that the French provided Mirage fighter jets to Uganda through Libya, and that French companies such as Intercontinental Technology exported explosives, surveillance equipment, and weapons to the Ugandan military.[84] Finally, until mid 1977 the EC gave financial aid to Uganda to compensate for shortfalls in export earnings.

The lack of EC support also made it difficult for the British government to prevent defections by British companies. After all, the sanctions created rents that other states and firms took advantage of. A number of British companies supplied goods and military equipment to Uganda during the sanctions period. For example, regular C-130 Hercules cargo flights from Entebbe, Uganda to Stansted airport in Essex, England – which became known as the "whisky shuttles" – transported tea and coffee from Uganda, and carried back alcohol, clothing, and electronic equipment such as radios and televisions. There is some evidence that a

---

[80] Christopher Hill, ed., *National Foreign Policies and European Political Cooperation* (London: Royal Institute of International Affairs, 1983), p. 191. Also see Panayiotis Ifestos, *European Political Cooperation: Towards a Framework of Supranational Diplomacy?* (Brookfield, VT: Avebury, 1987), pp. 236–8.

[81] Mastanduno argues, for example, that CoCom's strategic embargo of the Soviet Union and its allies was ineffective from 1969 to 1979, and mixed at best from 1980 to 1989. Michael Mastanduno, *Economic Containment: Cocom and the Politics of East–West Trade* (Ithaca, NY: Cornell University Press, 1992) pp. 143–309.

[82] IMF, *Direction of Trade Yearbook, 1980*, pp. 371–2.

[83] *SIPRI Yearbook 1974*, p. 281; *SIPRI Yearbook 1976*, p. 273; *SIPRI Yearbook 1977*, pp. 341–2.

[84] Mahmood Mamdani, *Imperialism and Fascism in Uganda* (Nairobi: Heinemann Educational Books, 1983), pp. 68–9; *SIPRI Yearbook 1976*, p. 341; Avirgan and Honey, *War in Uganda*, p. 21.

telecommunications firm headquartered in Cambridge, England illegally exported radio equipment for ship-to-shore and air-to-ground communications,[85] while, according to Amnesty International, a Leicester-based firm provided radio communications systems and surveillance equipment to the Ugandan government.[86] There is also evidence to suggest that a security equipment company registered in the Isle of Man exported telephone-tapping devices, night-vision equipment, and anti-bomb blankets to Uganda.[87]

Finally, Uganda was able to redirect the bulk of its economic and military trade to a number of other countries, particularly the Soviet Union, Libya, and Kenya. Amin reacted to British sanctions by turning to the Soviet Union for military assistance. After several meetings between Ugandan and Soviet defense officials, the first batch of Soviet arms under the new agreement was delivered in November 1973. It included T-34/T-54 (main battle) tanks, APCs (armored personnel carriers), small arms, bombs, rockets, and MiG fighter aircraft. Subsequent Soviet shipments included more APCs, MiGs, tanks, air-to-air missiles, helicopters, and trucks.[88] Libya steadily became a helpful intermediary for military aid coming from such countries as the Soviet Union and France. Libyan leader Muammar Qaddafi also gave Uganda a $25 million loan and additional dispersals through a joint Libyan–Ugandan Development Bank.[89] In the economic realm, Uganda turned to Kenyan suppliers as the major source of imports. In 1973 Uganda imported $63.7 million worth of goods from Kenya, just shy of the value of imports from all industrial countries combined ($74.6 million).[90]

In sum, Britain failed to impose EC sanctions against Uganda because there was no major Cold War interest at stake. Uganda was a former British protectorate. In the absence of EC sanctions, other European

---

[85] Avirgan and Honey, *War in Uganda*, pp. 18–20.

[86] Amnesty International, *Tools of Repression for the Likes of Amin?* (London: Amnesty International, July 1979).

[87] On other British exports to Uganda see Malcolm Brown, "Lorry Sales to Uganda Disturb MP," *The Times*, July 9, 1977, p. 4; "Debate on Exports to Uganda Refused," *The Times*, July 12, 1977, p. 9.

[88] Gad W. Toko, *Intervention in Uganda: The Power Struggle and Soviet Involvement* (Pittsburgh: University Center for International Studies, 1979), pp. 69–76; Mamdani, *Imperialism and Fascism in Uganda*, pp. 68–70; *SIPRI Yearbook 1974*, p. 281; *SIPRI Yearbook 1976*, p. 273; *SIPRI Yearbook 1977*, pp. 341–2.

[89] Qaddafi likely wanted to eradicate the influence of Israel in Uganda, which had been a major supplier of military aid through the early 1970s. In 1972 Amin expelled Israeli military advisers from Uganda, broke off diplomatic relations, and terminated their military relationship. Avirgan and Honey, *War in Uganda*, pp. 10–11.

[90] IMF, *Direction of Trade Yearbook 1980*, p. 371.

states and the US actively subverted the sanctions, and Uganda was able to redirect its trade to other countries.

EU sanctions against Yugoslavia (1991–1995)

In the early 1990s, the European Union and the United States imposed crippling sanctions on the Federal Republic of Yugoslavia following the outbreak of war.[91] In June 1991, fighting erupted when Croatian and Slovenian leaders declared independence from the Socialist Federal Republic of Yugoslavia. By March 1992, the war spread to Bosnia-Herzegovina. In early April, Bosnian President Alija Izetbegovic ordered the mobilization of all police and reserve units in the capital city of Sarajevo, and the Serb Democratic Party issued a covert call for Serbs to evacuate the city. On April 6, Serbs began shelling Sarajevo. The next day Serb forces crossed the Drina River into Bosnia and began the siege of the Muslim cities of Zvornik, Visegrad, and Foca. By mid April Bosnia was engulfed in war.[92]

The European Union took the lead diplomatic role in trying to broker a settlement between the warring parties from 1991 to 1994 through a series of peace proposals: the Carrington–Cutileiro Plan (March 1992), the Vance–Owen Peace Plan (May 1993), the Owen–Stoltenberg Plan (September 1993), and the EU Action Plan (December 1993). To augment the diplomatic track, the EU imposed a graduated series of economic sanctions that were supplemented by sanctions from the United States and the United Nations. As Table 4.3 highlights, the first set began in early July 1991 when the EU suspended all weapons sales and deliveries to Yugoslavia and called for an end to the fighting.[93] The UN Security Council followed suit in September by adopting Resolution 713, which imposed an arms embargo on Yugoslavia.[94] In November

---

[91] For simplification purposes I use European Union (EU) throughout this section, rather than switching back and forth between the EU and the European Community (EC). Of course, the Treaty on the European Union was not signed by the foreign and finance ministers of the member states until February 1992.

[92] For general books on the war see Steven L. Burg and Paul S. Shoup, *The War in Bosnia-Herzegovina: Ethnic Conflict and International Intervention* (Armonk, NY: M. E. Sharpe, 1999); Laura Silber and Allan Little, *Yugoslavia: Death of a Nation* (New York: Penguin Books, 1997).

[93] Roger Boyes, "EC Imposes Total Arms Embargo on Yugoslavia," *The Times*, July 6, 1991.

[94] S/Res/713, September 25, 1991. Paragraph 6 stated that "all States shall, for the purposes of establishing peace and stability in Yugoslavia, immediately implement a general and complete embargo on all deliveries of weapons and military equipment to Yugoslavia."

Table 4.3. *EU sanctions against Yugoslavia, 1991–1995*

Date	Type of sanctions
July 1991	• Arms embargo
September/	• Trade concessions
November 1991	• Textiles imports
	• Economic aid
May 1992	• Partial trade embargo
	• Export credits
	• Scientific and technological cooperation
April 1993	• Financial assets of Yugoslav government
	• Transshipment of goods through Yugoslavia
	• Transit through any state of vessels owned by or registered in Yugoslavia
	• Inclusion of Bosnian Serbs
September 1994	• Some sanctions lifted, such as the ban on sporting and cultural events
November 1995	• Sanctions lifted except for "outer wall"

1991, the EU suspended trade concessions, banned imports of Yugoslav textiles, and deleted Yugoslavia from a list of eastern European aid recipients. This translated into a loss of $900 million in promised EU economic assistance.[95]

In May 1992, EU countries broadened the sanctions by imposing a partial embargo on trade with Belgrade, freezing export credits, and suspending all forms of scientific and technological cooperation.[96] Once again, the purpose was to coerce the Serbs into ending the fighting. As one EU diplomat noted: "The Serbian economy is already close to collapse, with inflation approaching 100 percent annually. These additional measures will bite very hard indeed and must cause the Serbian government to think again about its expansionist strategy elsewhere in the former Yugoslavia."[97] EU actions were followed by UN Security

[95] Council Regulation (EEC) No. 3302/91, OJ L 315, 15.11.91; Council Regulation (EEC) No. 3301/91, OJ L 315, 15.11.91; Council Regulation (EEC) No. 3300/91, OJ L 315, 15.11.91. Also see William D. Montalbano, "Yugoslavia Hit by Trade Sanctions," *Los Angeles Times*, November 9, 1991, p. A1. Also see Judy Dempsey, "Yugoslavia's Economy 'Faces Collapse by Christmas,'" *Financial Times*, November 9, 1991, p. 2.

[96] Council Regulation (EEC) No. 1433/92, OJ L 151, 3,6,92; Council Regulation (EEC) No. 1432/92, OJ L 151, 3.6.92.

[97] John Palmer, "European Community Bans Trade with Serbia," *The Guardian*, May 28, 1992, p. 6.

Council Resolution 757, which banned all international trade with Yugoslavia, prohibited air travel, blocked financial transactions, banned sports and cultural exchanges, and suspended scientific and cultural cooperation.[98] NATO also began a naval blockade of Yugoslavia to enforce the sanctions, and it declared the right to stop and search vessels in the Adriatic Sea suspected of carrying contraband to Serbia and Montenegro.

In early 1993, sanctions were tied to the success of the Vance–Owen Peace Plan, led by European envoy David Owen and UN envoy Cyrus Vance. The plan's rejection by the Bosnian Serbs in April 1993 triggered a new level of sanctions. They included a freeze on Yugoslav government financial assets, a ban on the transshipment of goods through Yugoslavia, and a prohibition on transit through any state of vessels owned by or registered in Yugoslavia.[99] Furthermore, the sanctions targeted the Bosnian Serbs. In November 1995, the sanctions were finally lifted after Milosevic signed the Dayton Accords. However, an "outer wall" of sanctions was kept in place that prohibited Yugoslavia from membership in the World Bank and the International Monetary Fund.

Why did European states decide to impose sanctions through the European Union? The push for EU sanctions was caused by the structural shift in the international system. Sanctioning through the EU increased the autonomy of European states and enhanced the effectiveness of sanctions.

First, EU sanctions increased the autonomy of European states and decreased their reliance on the United States. When the first set of European sanctions was imposed in July 1991, the Soviet Union had largely collapsed and European states were negotiating the Maastricht Treaty. Within a few months European leaders signed the Maastricht Treaty and established a security arm of the EU, which included legal provisions for the enactment of economic sanctions on foreign states. James Gow notes in his study of Western diplomacy and the Balkan wars that the "real mainspring of EC involvement" in Yugoslavia was "the nascent Common Foreign and Security Policy (CFSP) of the EC Member States, as they prepared for the Maastricht Summit in

---

[98] S/Res/757, May 30, 1992. One loophole in Resolution 757 was Paragraph 6, which permitted the transshipment of commodities and products through the territory of Yugoslavia. Also see S/Res/787, November 16, 1992.

[99] These sanctions were primarily imposed through UN Security Council Resolution 820. S/Res/820, April 17, 1993. On the European response see Lionel Barber, Laura Silber, and Philip Stephens, "EC Backs New Serbian Sanctions," *Financial Times*, April 26, 1993, p. 16.

December 1991."[100] For European leaders, coordinating diplomacy and economic sanctions regarding Yugoslavia was an important step in acting autonomously. "We have seen the [European] community has the capacity to act together at a time of international crisis," stated British Prime Minister John Major in 1991.[101] Indeed, the shift to unipolarity increased the impetus to increase European power and influence in the face of American preponderance. Italian Foreign Minister Gianni de Michelis declared that the United States and Moscow had been informed – but not consulted – about the European mission to Yugoslavia.[102] Moreover, as Luxembourg Foreign Minister Jacques Poos stated in June 1991: "It is not up to the Americans. [Yugoslavia] is a European country. It is up to the European Community to try to set up a dialogue."[103]

The Bush and early Clinton administrations supported a lead EU role since they did not want to become involved in Yugoslavia. As Brent Scowcroft, Bush's national security adviser, recalled: "Eagleburger and I were the most concerned here about Yugoslavia. The President and Baker were furthest on the other side. Baker would say 'We don't have a dog in this fight.' The President would say to me once a week 'Tell me what this is all about.'"[104] Furthermore, Richard Holbrooke, chief architect of the Dayton Accords, pointedly notes that "American policy makers did not wish to get involved in Yugoslavia, and many considered the situation insoluble . . . For the first time since World War II, Washington had turned a major security issue entirely over to the

[100] James Gow, *Triumph of the Lack of Will: International Diplomacy and the Yugoslav War* (New York: Columbia University Press, 1997), p. 48.
[101] Maureen Johnson, "European Community Leaders Elated at Yugoslav Cease-fire," *Associated Press*, June 29, 1991. Also see "From Dutch Aide, Determined Optimism on EC Presidency," *International Herald Tribune*, July 1, 1991; Howard LaFranchi, "EC Deals with Crisis, Unity Plans," *Christian Science Monitor*, July 1, 1991, p. 3.
[102] Ian Traynor and Michael White, "Shuttle Mission Gets Crash Course in Balkan Realities," *The Guardian*, July 1, 1991.
[103] Raf Casert, "EC Sends Peace Delegation, Sets Aid Freeze," *Associated Press*, June 28, 1991. Poos became the brunt of jokes throughout Europe and the United States for his premature statement that "this is the hour of Europe, not the hour of the Americans." For Poos's statement see Annika Savill and Donald Macintyre, "EC Dispatches Peace Mission to Belgrade," *The Independent*, June 29, 1991, p. 1; David Gardner, "EC Dashes Into its Own Backyard," *Financial Times*, July 1, 1991, p. 2.
[104] Silber and Little, *Yugoslavia*, p. 201. In his memoirs Baker noted: "It was time to make the Europeans step up to the plate and show that they could act as a unified power. Yugoslavia was as good a first test as any." James A. Baker III, *The Politics of Diplomacy* (New York: G. P. Putnam's Sons, 1995), p. 483. On the Bush Administration's policy see also David C. Gompert, "The United States and Yugoslavia's Wars," in Richard H. Ullman, ed., *The World and Yugoslavia's Wars* (New York: Council on Foreign Relations, 1996).

Europeans."[105] In the absence of American interest in Yugoslavia, the option of imposing European Union sanctions was important. It gave European states the ability to punish Yugoslavia's economy, which relied on trade with Europe, without relying on American participation.

Second, European leaders favored sanctioning through the EU because it would increase European power and terms-of-trade effects on Yugoslavia. As we might expect, the imposition of sanctions created an incentive for defection. Of particular concern for the European Union was one of its own members: Greece. The Balkans geographically separated it from Europe, and a substantial amount of Greece's trade passed through Yugoslavia on its way to Eastern and Western Europe. Greece claimed that it had suffered a trade loss of $2.6 billion during the first six months of 1992 alone, as well as $500 million in lost revenue from tourism during 1992.[106] The sanctions forced trucks to take longer routes to Europe through Bulgaria and Romania, which increased the driving time by as much as 24 hours and the freight costs by perhaps 20 percent.[107]

In order to overcome monitoring problems, the European Union created Sanctions Assistance Missions (SAMs) with the help of the Conference on Security and Cooperation in Europe. The SAMs consisted of a network of customs officials dispatched to states that bordered Yugoslavia: Bulgaria, Hungary, Romania, Albania, Croatia, and Macedonia.[108] Customs officials at each of the SAMs were positioned at key border crossing points where they monitored traffic into and out of Yugoslavia and documented suspected violations. The objective was to verify shipping documents and deter violators from sending sanctioned goods into Yugoslavia. Furthermore, the EU established a sanctions assistance missions communications center (SAMCOMM) in Brussels and appointed a sanctions coordinator to oversee it. SAMCOMM was fitted with a computerized satellite communications system that linked its headquarters in Brussels to the United Nations

---

[105] Richard Holbrooke, *To End a War* (New York: Random House, 1998), pp. 26–9.

[106] "Greece Seeks EC Tourist Compensation for Yugoslav Crisis," *Agence France Presse*, June 1, 1993; "Greece Suffers $2.6 billion Loss from UN Embargo on Serbia," *Xinhua News Agency*, June 4, 1993.

[107] Kerin Hope, "Greek Exporters Fear Heavy Losses," *Financial Times*, April 28, 1993, p. 3; Mark Milner, "Serbia Sanctions Squeeze Greece," *The Guardian*, May 1, 1993, p. 1.

[108] On the Sanctions Assistance Missions see United Nations Security Council, *Letter Dated 24 September 1996*, S/1996/776; David Cortright and George A. Lopez, *The Sanctions Decade: Assessing UN Strategies in the 1990s* (Boulder, CO: Lynne Rienner, 2000), pp. 68–72.

sanctions committee in New York.[109] It was designed to facilitate the communication and coordination of information on sanctions violations between SAMs and the national authorities of host countries. SAMCOMM also followed up on suspected breaches of sanctions and established evaluation reports.

The SAMs fingered Greece as one of the most egregious violators of the sanctions, particularly its oil exports to Yugoslavia. European Commissioner for Mediterranean Affairs Abel Matutes presented a report to EU foreign ministers in December 1992 "showing the Greeks were pouring oil into Serbia by road, rail, and sea."[110] Armed with information from SAMs, European Union officials charged that tanker trucks carried illegal shipments of oil from Greece to Bulgaria, Albania, Macedonia, and Romania, where they were transferred to other vehicles and driven into Yugoslavia. Indeed, a leaked European Commission report drafted by SAM monitors charged Greece with violating the sanctions by transporting oil to Serbia through Albania.[111] In many cases, false documents were used to indicate an end-user other than Yugoslavia. Oil shipments were suspected of reaching Yugoslavia either directly from such Greek ports as Thessaloniki, or indirectly through intermediary ports in Albania. SAMCOMM also reported that other products such as oak timber were being illegally exported from Greece to Yugoslavia. Finally, the Greek government was suspected of permitting the establishment in Greece of front companies for banned Yugoslav businesses. As the US State Department summed up:

There are several areas of concern in Greek sanctions enforcement, including the activities of the Serbian Consulate in the northern city of Thessaloniki, the presence of Serbian front companies in Greece, the intermittent use of the oil pre-verification system and the number of Greek goods reaching Serbia via third countries.[112]

The Sanctions Assistance Missions played an important role in monitoring traffic coming into and out of Yugoslavia, documenting suspected

---

[109] David Hughes, "SATCOM Network Helps UN Spot Sanction Violations," *Aviation Week & Space Technology*, Vol. 140, No. 122, p. 70.
[110] "Greece Accused over Serb Sanctions," *Press Association*, December 8, 1992. See also "Greek Smugglers Breaching Yugoslavia Embargo," *Agence France Presse*, December 9, 1992; "UN Authorizes Naval Blockade against Serbia," *Los Angeles Times*, November 17, 1992, p. A1; Nikos Konstandaras, "Flow of Greek Fuel to Former Yugoslavia Could Be Cut," *Associated Press*, November 13, 1992.
[111] "Greece Denies Sanctions-Busting Charge," *United Press International*, October 25, 1995.
[112] US Department of State, *Report on Greek Enforcement of UN Sanctions against Serbia*, 95/06/02 (Washington, DC: US Dept of State, 1995).

violations, and providing information to European states. This allowed the EU and the US to pressure Greece – as well as other neighboring states – into reducing defections by taking such measures as the establishment of a system of checks on petroleum exports.[113]

Furthermore, the EU had substantial economic clout, and it was in a much better position than the United States to punish Yugoslavia through sanctions. The EU had provided a significant amount of foreign assistance to Yugoslavia prior to the war, and it was coordinating the Group of 24 industrial countries' Yugoslav assistance program of $4.1 billion.[114] In 1991, European Union trade with Yugoslavia totaled $19.8 billion, compared to only $1 billion for the United States.[115] European leaders thus supported EU sanctions because they could effectively punish Yugoslavia by aggregating economic power. Indeed, while Yugoslavia's economy was already in dire shape when the EU imposed sanctions in 1991, the sanctions undoubtedly made the situation worse. The economy contracted by 26 percent in 1992 and 28 percent in 1993. Real income decreased by 50 percent, and industrial production shrank 22 percent in 1992 and 37 percent in 1993. Automobile production fell from 97,000 cars in 1991 to 6,900 in 1994. Unemployment officially increased to 23 percent in 1993, though some Serbian economists calculated that it was closer to 40 percent. Inflation skyrocketed to 122 percent in 1991, 9,000 percent in 1992, and a startling 100 trillion percent by the end of 1993.[116] Perhaps unsurprisingly, numerous Yugoslav shopkeepers abandoned the dinar and replaced it with the German mark or resorted to bartering.

The conventional literature on Yugoslavia derides the economic sanctions as either wholly ineffective or counterproductive in ending the conflict.[117] As Susan Woodward argues: "The sanctions, by isolating areas inhabited by Serbs from outside sources of information and

---

[113] Eddie Koch, "Greece Accused of Aiding Sanctions Busters," *Inter Press Service*, July 26, 1993; Nikos Konstandaras, "Flow of Greek Fuel to Former Yugoslavia Could Be Cut," *Associated Press*, November 23, 1992.

[114] Gow, *Triumph of the Lack of Will*, p. 49.

[115] *Direction of Trade Statistics Yearbook 1998*, pp. 188–9.

[116] Economic figures are from US Department of State, *UN Sanctions against Belgrade: Lessons Learned for Future Regimes* (Washington, DC: US Dept of State, June 1996), pp. 1–3.

[117] Susan L. Woodward, *Balkan Tragedy: Chaos and Dissolution after the Cold War* (Washington, DC: Brookings Institution,1995), pp. 289–94, 384–8; Woodward, "The Use of Sanctions in Former Yugoslavia: Misunderstanding Political Realities," in David Cortright and George A. Lopez, eds., *Economic Sanctions: Panacea or Peacebuilding in a Post-Cold War World?* (Boulder, CO: Westview Press, 1995), pp. 141–51; Sonja Licht, "The Use of Sanctions in Former Yugoslavia: Can They

commerce, weakened the external pressures for and internal causes of a policy of peace."[118] However, this conclusion is incorrect. A substantial amount of evidence from Western diplomats involved in the peace negotiations demonstrates that sanctions played a pivotal role in the Yugoslav decision to cut a deal at Dayton in November 1995. Indeed, sanctions were effective because they significantly contributed to a change in Yugoslav policy. As Warren Zimmermann, US ambassador to Yugoslavia, argues: "Milosevic's desire to get the sanctions lifted would give us a bargaining chip; three years later that chip was to play an important role in Milosevic's decision to end the Bosnian war."[119] During the November 1995 Dayton negotiations, Richard Holbrooke contends that lifting the sanctions was a top priority for Milosevic. At a November 16 meeting with US National Security Adviser Tony Lake, Milosevic triggered a "heated debate" over lifting the sanctions. Holbrooke writes, "Milosevic knew that in real terms suspension of the sanctions would give him what he needed most, immediate relief for his people."[120] Holbrooke's view is supported by others involved in the negotiating process, such as European envoy David Owen.[121]

In sum, European states imposed sanctions through the European Union because of the structural shift in the international system. Sanctioning through the EU increased the ability of European states to act autonomously of the United States. It also enhanced the effectiveness of sanctions by making it easier to monitor and crack down on defecting countries, such as Greece.

Assist in Conflict Resolution?" in David Cortright and George A. Lopez, *Economic Sanctions: Panacea or Peacebuilding in a Post-Cold War World?* (Boulder, CO: Westview, 1995), pp. 153–60; Misha Glenny, *The Fall of Yugoslavia: The Third Balkan War* (New York: Penguin, 1999), pp. 210–12; Steven L. Burg, "The International Community and the Yugoslav Crisis," in Milton J. Esman and Shibley Telhami, eds., *International Organizations and Ethnic Conflict* (Ithaca, NY: Cornell University Press, 1995), p. 245; Reneo Lukic and Allen Lynch, *Europe from the Balkans to the Urals: The Disintegration of Yugoslavia and the Soviet Union* (New York: Oxford University Press, 1996), pp. 300–1.

[118] Woodward, *Balkan Tragedy*, p. 386.

[119] Warren Zimmermann, *Origins of a Catastrophe* (New York: Random House, 1996), p. 213.

[120] Holbrooke, *To End a War*, p. 282. Holbrooke also noted that the US's "main bargaining chip with Milosevic had been the economic sanctions . . . The sanctions had seriously damaged Serbia's economy, and Milosevic wanted them ended" (p. 4).

[121] David Owen writes: "We had to tighten every area of sanctions, for there was much economic intelligence showing that Milosevic was becoming really worried about the Serbian economy." David Owen, *Balkan Odyssey* (New York: Harcourt Brace, 1995), p. 142. On the affect of sanctions see also pp. 49, 133, 142–3, 160, 163, 216, 243, 308–11, 398–9.

Conclusions

One implication of this finding is that the deep skepticism that meaningful security cooperation has occurred in post-Cold War Europe is misplaced.[122] Rather, there has been a striking change in the behavior of
European states since the end of the Cold War. They have increasingly
opted to impose sanctions through the European Union, rather than
unilaterally or through other multilateral forums. Indeed, it is particularly noteworthy that EU sanctions cooperation has been led by
European great powers.

There are at least three potential counter-arguments. First, some
might argue that sanctions cooperation is largely irrelevant because
sanctions do not "work." Robert Pape, for instance, contends that
"economic sanctions have little independent usefulness for pursuit of
non-economic goals."[123] The logic is that economic sanctions are ineffective because target states are able to endure substantial amounts of
punishment rather than succumb to the demands of foreigners. Instead
of coercing states into changing their behavior, sanctions often have the
opposite result: they create a "rally around the flag" effect among populations, as the US sanctions on Fidel Castro's Cuba demonstrate.[124]
Leaders may also be able to shift the sanctioning costs away from key
supporters, as Saddam Hussein did in Iraq.[125]

However, this criticism is misplaced here. The primary focus is why
states cooperate – or don't cooperate – in imposing sanctions. We are

[122] John J. Mearsheimer, *The Tragedy of Great Power Politics* (New York: W. W. Norton,
2001), pp. 360–402; Mearsheimer, "Back to the Future: Instability in Europe after the
Cold War," *International Security*, Vol. 15, No. 1, Summer 1990, pp. 5–56; Philip
Gordon, "Europe's Uncommon Foreign Policy," *International Security*, Vol. 22,
No. 3, Winter 1997/98, pp. 74–100; Robert J. Art, "Why Western Europe Needs the
United States and NATO," *Political Science Quarterly*, Vol. 111, No. 1, Spring 1996,
pp. 1–39; Carsten Tams, "The Functions of a European Security and Defence Identity
and its Institutional Form," in Helga Haftendorn, Robert O. Keohane, and Celeste A.
Wallander, eds., *Imperfect Unions: Security Institutions over Time and Space* (New York:
Oxford University Press, 1999), pp. 80–103; Zbigniew Brzezinski, "Living with a New
Europe," *The National Interest*, No. 60, Summer 2000, pp. 17–29.
[123] Pape, "Why Economic Sanctions Do Not Work," p. 93. See also Pape, "Why
Economic Sanctions Still Do Not Work," *International Security*, Vol. 23, No. 1,
Summer 1998, pp. 66–77; T. Clifton Morgan and Valerie L. Schwebach, "Fools
Suffer Gladly: The Use of Economic Sanctions in International Crises," *International
Studies Quarterly*, Vol. 41, No. 1, March 1997, pp. 27–50; Galtung, "On the Effects of
International Economic Sanctions," pp. 378–416.
[124] Susan Kaufman Purcell, "Cuba," in Haass, *Economic Sanctions and American
Diplomacy*, pp. 35–56.
[125] David Cortright and George A. Lopez, *The Sanctions Decade: Assessing UN Strategies in
the 1990s* (Boulder, CO: Lynne Rienner, 2000), pp. 37–61; Eric D. K. Melby, "Iraq,"
in Haass, *Economic Sanctions and American Diplomacy*, pp. 107–28.

primarily interested in deducing what factors have motivated European leaders to sanction through the European Union. The major dependent variable is the amount of sanctions cooperation, not the effectiveness of sanctions. Still, a substantial amount of statistical and empirical research demonstrates that sanctions have sometimes been effective in coercing a change in target behavior – either by themselves or in tandem with other foreign policy tools.[126] Obviously, sanctions are not always effective. Two examples from this study demonstrate that they can help states achieve important foreign policy goals. One is when, in 1986, France successfully used economic sanctions to coerce New Zealand into releasing French secret service agents imprisoned for bombing the Greenpeace ship *Rainbow Warrior*.[127] The second is the evidence from Western policymakers involved in the Bosnian peace negotiations that strongly suggests EU and US sanctions played an important role in coercing Slobodan Milosevic to reach an agreement at Dayton in November 1995.

A second possible argument is that EU cooperation is a result of the construction of a common identity.[128] The logic is that decades of interaction through the European Coal and Steel Community and EC caused a change in the interests and identity of European states. They have increasingly imposed sanctions through the European Union because of the construction of a European identity. In the post-Cold War era, European states have sanctioned through the EU to coerce target states into abiding by European norms of appropriateness on such issues as democracy and human rights.[129] Constructivists have used the case of

---

[126] Drezner, "The Hidden Hand of Economic Coercion," *International Organization*, Vol. 57, Summer 2003, pp. 643–59; Drezner, *The Sanctions Paradox*; Baldwin, *Economic Statecraft*; David M. Rowe, *Manipulating the Market: Understanding Economic Sanctions, Institutional Change, and the Political Unity of White Rhodesia* (Ann Arbor, MI: The University of Michigan Press, 2001); Baldwin, "The Sanctions Debate and the Logic of Choice," *International Security*, Vol. 24, No. 3, Winter 1999/2000, pp. 80–107; Jean-Marc F. Blanchard and Norrin M. Ripsman, "Asking the Right Question: When Do Economic Sanctions Work Best?" in Blanchard, Mansfield, and Ripsman, *Power and the Purse*, pp. 219–53.

[127] "The Butter Did It," *Economist*, July 12, 1986, p. 44; Dai Hayward, "Lange Says Trade More Vital than Spies' Fate," *Financial Times*, July 11, 1986, p. 3.

[128] Merlingen, Mudde, and Sedelmeier, "The Right and the Righteous?," pp. 59–77. On constructivism and sanctions see also Neta C. Crawford and Audie Klotz, *How Sanctions Work: Lessons from South Africa* (New York: St. Martin's Press, 1999).

[129] In explaining shared European interests, Anthony Smith argues: "So what is common to all Europeans? . . . What are these partially shared traditions and heritages? They include traditions like Roman law, political democracy, parliamentary institutions, and Judeo-Chistian ethics, and cultural heritages like Renaissance humanism, rationalism and empiricism, and romanticism and classicism." Anthony D. Smith, "National Identity and the Idea of European Unity," *International Affairs*, Vol. 68, No. 1, January 1992, p. 70. Also see Peter J. Katzenstein, "United Germany in an Integrating Europe," in Katzenstein, ed., *Tamed Power: Germany in Europe* (Ithaca,

EU sanctions against Austria in 2000 as evidence for their argument. European Union states imposed sanctions against Austria because of the inclusion of Jörg Haider's far-right Freedom Party (FPO) in the government. As one article notes:

Clearly, there was a consensus among the governments of the EU 14, shaped by their common identity, that the FPO deviated from accepted standards of political conduct. To act collectively to defend the norms on which their common identity is based, then seems clearly to conform to standards of appropriateness.[130]

Consequently, the decision to impose sanctions through the EU in the post-Cold War era has been a function of a common identity and shared norms of appropriateness.

However, as the previous chapter argued, there is little evidence that the identity of European leaders or populations changed at the end of the Cold War. This makes it difficult to connect identity causally with a change in sanctions behavior. Europeans have long shared many of the norms of appropriateness identified by constructivists, such as democratic and humanitarian norms. As Martha Finnemore argues, by 1868 almost every country in Europe had signed the Geneva Convention, which detailed a variety of humanitarian protections for wounded soldiers and noncombatants.[131] Furthermore, democratic peace arguments have noted that all Western European states have been democracies since at least World War II. The empirical data summarized in Table 4.1 above shows that European states consistently failed to cooperate in the sanctions realm throughout the Cold War, despite the existence of common norms of appropriateness and clear humanitarian and democratic rationales. Perhaps the most extreme example is Britain's inability to persuade EC states to impose sanctions against Idi Amin's Uganda, which, as we have seen, was one of the most savage dictatorships of the twentieth century. Focusing on a single case – such as EU sanctions against Austria – creates a selection bias problem. Indeed, somewhat ironically, since Haider's party had been elected *democratically*, European actions violated one of the norms they were trying to uphold.

NY: Cornell University Press, 1997), pp. 1–48; Timothy Garton Ash, "Is Britain European?" *International Affairs*, Vol. 77, No. 1, January 2001, pp. 1–13.
[130] Merlingen, Mudde, and Sedelmeier, "The Right and the Righteous?", p. 65.
[131] Martha Finnemore, *National Interests and International Society* (Ithaca, NY: Cornell University Press, 1996), pp. 69–88.

A third possible counter-argument is that the increase in EU sanctions cooperation is a function of pressure from domestic economic actors.[132] The logic is that European governments have increasingly imposed economic sanctions for foreign policy goals because of an increase in pressure from domestic interest groups and rent-seeking coalitions. As Clifton Morgan and Valerie Schwebach argue: "Sanctions can be imposed and maintained only when a sufficiently powerful coalition of domestic political actors within the sending state hopes to gain more on the issue under dispute than will be lost due to the sanctions."[133] By sanctioning a foreign state's activities, governments can demonstrate that they are "doing something" and satisfy idealist interest groups. Leaders are sometimes faced with an unpleasant dilemma if the actions of a target state violate norms of behavior. Using military force may be politically costly, especially if the target state is not strategically important to the sender. But doing nothing may be costly as well because it creates the impression of a weak or callous leader. Consequently, Ivan Eland concludes that "intense domestic pressure, particularly in democratic states, to 'do something' can persuade the government in the sanctioning nation to respond by imposing sanctions to meet goals other than target compliance."[134] In sum, European states have increasingly sanctioned through the EU in the post-Cold War era because of a rise in pressure from domestic actors.

However, the domestic politics argument is problematic. Most importantly, statistical tests have demonstrated that there is no correlation between the initiation of sanctions and pressure from domestic actors. As Daniel Drezner argues: "The domestic politics approach does not explain the initiation of sanctions attempts; senders do not initiate coercion attempts in response to domestic pressure, but rather from a rational calculation of the sender's interests in the international system."[135] Furthermore, there is no evidence of a significant shift in

---

[132] Ivan Eland, "Economic Sanctions as Tools of Foreign Policy," in Cortright and Lopez, eds., *Economic Sanctions*, pp. 29–42; Richard Haass, "Sanctioning Madness," *Foreign Affairs*, Vol. 76, No. 6, November/December 1997, pp. 74–85; Daoudi and Dajani, *Economic Sanctions*; Robin Renwick, *Economic Sanctions*, No. 45. (Cambridge, MA: Center for International Affairs, 1983); Dale C. Copeland, "Trade Expectations and the Outbreak of Peace," *Security Studies*, Vol. 9, Nos. 1–2, Autumn 1999-Winter 2000, pp. 15–58; Mastanduno, "Economic Statecraft, Interdependence, and National Security," pp. 306–9; Morgan and Schwebach, "Economic Sanctions as an Instrument of Foreign Policy," pp. 27–50; Blanchard and Ripsman, "Asking the Right Question," pp. 219–53.

[133] Morgan and Schwebach, "Economic Sanctions as an Instrument of Foreign Policy," p. 253.

[134] Eland, "Economic Sanctions as Tools of Foreign Policy," p. 29.

[135] Drezner, *The Sanctions Paradox*, p. 128.

the preferences or strategies of European domestic actors in the post-Cold War era. Nor is there evidence that European leaders became more vulnerable to the domestic pressures of some interest groups. In sum, the absence of a statistical correlation between sanctions initiation and domestic actors, and the absence of evidence of a shift in pressure from domestic actors, undermines the domestic politics argument. We now turn to the arms industry.

5   Arms production

Why has there been a substantial increase in European arms cooperation in the post-Cold War era? Why was there minimal cooperation during the Cold War? Over the last decade the European Union's major powers have increasingly collaborated in the production of advanced weapons. Several examples illustrate the point. In Germany the air force's modernization program includes the Eurofighter Typhoon ground attack combat aircraft, which is equipped with Taurus stand-off missiles for high-precision ground attack. In France the A400M transport aircraft, revamped Tiger attack helicopter, and Scalp sea-launched land attack missile are major components of the military's procurement program. And Britain's modernization program includes the Eurofighter Typhoon and Storm Shadow air-to-surface missile. All of these weapons have something significant in common: they have been developed and produced in collaboration with other European defense companies.

Other developments in Europe reinforce the extent of cooperation. In some areas, such as missiles, research and development occur almost exclusively at the European level through the transnational European firm MBDA. Two companies account for Europe's helicopter business: Eurocopter (a division of the transnational firm EADS) and Agusta Westland (which combined the helicopter capabilities of Italy's Finmeccanica and the UK's GKN). In December 2005, the European Union launched the first of thirty satellites for its Galileo global navigation satellite system. In addition, the merger of German, French, and Spanish defense firms to create the transnational European defense firm EADS was hailed as one of the "grand bargains that [is] building the New Europe."[1] The European Union's establishment of a European defense agency to coordinate procurement programs has further increased the prospect of an integrated European defense market.

---

[1] Karen Lowry Miller, "Now Ready to Take Off?" *Newsweek*, October 25, 1999, p. 70.

The data collected in this chapter show that European states and defense firms are increasingly collaborating in defense production. This marks a striking contrast with the Cold War, when EU states and defense firms were much more likely to collaborate with the United States and US defense firms. It also contrasts with European collaboration in non-defense sectors, since European firms have been increasingly likely to collaborate globally rather than regionally.[2] What explains this variation? To answer the question, this chapter has three objectives.

First, it argues that the changing structure of the international system explains the shift to intra-European collaboration in the post-Cold War era. During the bipolar Cold War, European states were primarily concerned about balancing the Soviet Union. Collaboration was thus largely transatlantic rather than intra-European. However, this changed at the end of the Cold War. In a unipolar international system, EU states led by Germany, France, and Britain have coordinated the development and production of weapons, as well as pursued intra-European mergers and acquisitions (M&As) to decrease reliance on the United States and increase their ability to project power abroad.[3]

As Klaus von Sperber, Germany's director of international armaments affairs, has argued: "The biggest fear among EU states, including Germany, is not being competitive with the United States. This drives us to collaborate in the defense industry."[4] The chief executive officers of Europe's three largest defense firms – BAE Systems, EADS, and Thales – similarly argued that "industry in Europe is under enormous competitive pressure from the United States. With US defense [research

[2] Grazia Ietto-Gillies, Meloria Meschi, and Roberto Simonetti, "Cross-Border Mergers and Acquisitions: Patterns in the EU and Effects," in Chesnais, Ietto-Gillies, and Simonetti, eds., *European Integration and Global Corporate Strategies* (New York: Routledge, 2000), pp. 52–70; Rajneesh Narula, "Strategic Technology Alliances by European Firms Since 1980: Questioning Integration?" in Chesnais, Ietto-Gillies, and Simonetti, eds., *European Integration and Global Corporate Strategies*, pp. 178–91.

[3] On discussions of weapons production and US power, see Terrence R. Guay, *At Arm's Length: The European Union and Europe's Defence Industry* (New York: St. Martin's Press, 1998), pp. 82–100; Jane Davis Drown, "European Views on Arms Cooperation," in Drown, Clifford Drown, and Kelly Campbell, eds., *A Single European Arms Industry? European Defence Industries in the 1990s* (London: Brassey's, 1990), pp. 30–2, 36–40; Burkard Schmitt, *From Cooperation to Integration: Defence and Aerospace Industries in Europe*, Chaillot Paper 40 (Paris: Institute for Security Studies, 2000), pp. 23–8; Jean-Paul Hébert and Laurence Nardon, *Concentration des industries d'armement américaines: Modèle ou menace?* Cahiers d'études stratégiques, No. 23 (Paris: CIRPES, 1999), pp. 9–36; Christopher Cornu, "Fortress Europe – Real or Virtual?" in Burkard Schmitt, ed., *Between Cooperation and Competition: The Transatlantic Defence Market*, Chaillot Paper 44 (Paris: Institute for Security Studies, 2001), pp. 65–9.

[4] Klaus von Sperber, "NATO and EU Military Integration," Lecture at the Center for Strategic and International Studies, Washington, DC, June 16, 2005.

and technology] investment running at around eight times that of Europe's fragmented total and with substantial growth in the Pentagon's vast procurement budget in a heavily protected national market, American industries are reaching new heights." They continued that intra-European defense cooperation is critical because European governments and industry do not "wish to see indigenous defense technology overtaken or dependence on foreign technologies become a necessity."[5]

Second, in order to test the argument, this chapter adopts two methodological approaches: it compiles an arms production data set; and it uses a case study methodology. It utilizes the Defense Budget Project's globalization database to examine 482 cases of interstate collaboration involving European defense firms between 1961 and 2000. The data includes three types: M&As, coproduction projects, and codevelopment projects. Of particular interest is identifying trends in the data. Were European states and defense firms more likely to pursue defense collaboration with firms from Europe, the United States, or other regions? And why? It also adopts a case study methodology to understand the motivation of French, German, and British leaders, and examines primary and secondary sources. Examples include documents from the French procurement agency (Délégation ministérielle de l'armement), German defense White Papers, British Ministry of Defence documents, and EU defense documents such as the *Strategic Aerospace Review for the 21st Century*.

Third, it briefly explores counter-arguments. Domestic politics arguments, such as those by Andrew Moravcsik and Jonathan Tucker, concentrate on the economic interests of domestic arms firms.[6] A second alternative is that the increase in intra-European defense collaboration has been caused by the construction of a European identity. Decades of interaction through the ECSC and European Community caused European states to internalize a common identity, which led to the

---

[5] Denis Ranque, Philippe Camus, Rainer Hertrich, and Mike Turner, "The New European Defense Agency: Getting above the Clouds," June 24, 2004 (www.baesystems.com/newsroom/2004/jun/150604news1.htm).

[6] Andrew Moravcsik, "Arms and Autarky in Modern European History," *Daedalus*, Vol. 120, No. 4, Fall 1991, pp. 23–45; Moravcsik, "Armaments among Allies: European Weapons Collaboration, 1975–1985," in Peter B. Evans, Harold K. Jacobson, and Robert D. Putnam, *Double-Edged Diplomacy: International Bargaining and Domestic Politics* (Berkeley: University of California Press, 1993), pp. 128–67; Moravcsik, "The European Armaments Industry at the Crossroads," *Survival*, Vol. 32, No. 1, January/February 1990, pp. 65–85; Jonathan B. Tucker, "Partners and Rivals: A Model of International Collaboration in Advanced Technology," *International Organization*, Vol. 45, No. 1, Winter 1991, pp. 83–120.

construction of common security interests and the need for defense cooperation.

The article is divided into five sections. First, it lays out states' procurement options and sketches the argument. Second, it briefly examines the defense production data. Third, it explores coproduction, codevelopment, and M&A developments during the Cold War. Fourth, it analyzes changes in the European defense industry since the end of the Cold War. Fifth, it evaluates the alternative arguments and addresses other potential criticisms.

Defense procurement options

National governments, not defense firms, play the most important role in determining the shape of defense industries.[7] Ministries of Defense are the only – or at least the major – buyers of weapons, and consequently are able to wield substantial power on the demand side of the market. This marks a strong contrast with most non-defense markets. Defense firms generally don't develop equipment and then attempt to sell it to their governments. Rather, governments and defense departments collect classified information about foreign capabilities and threats, devise a grand strategy to curb those threats, and then equip themselves accordingly.[8] There is also an asymmetry of information between the government and industry. Products are normally unavailable to competitors for examination and analysis because of national security concerns, giving defense departments substantial control over diffusion in the industry. In sum, governments have enormous power to determine the size of their domestic defense industry, structure, entry and exit, prices, and ownership.[9]

The influence of governments is particularly significant regarding transnational activity. For example, mergers and acquisitions involving

[7] On defense economics see Keith Hartley, *NATO Arms Co-operation: A Study in Economics and Politics* (London: Allen & Unwin, 1983); Todd Sandler and Keith Hartley, *The Political Economy of NATO: Past, Present, and into the 21st Century* (New York: Cambridge University Press, 1999); Sandler and Hartley, *The Economics of Defense* (New York: Cambridge University Press, 1995); Gavin Kennedy, *The Economics of Defence* (London: Faber and Faber, 1975); Kennedy, *Defense Economics* (New York: St. Martin's Press, 1983); Frederic M. Scherer, *The Weapons Acquisition Process: Economic Incentives* (Boston: Division of Research, Graduate School of Business Administration, Harvard University, 1964).
[8] Kenneth Flamm, "Redesigning the Defense Industrial Base," in Ann R. Markusen and Sean S. Costigan, eds., *Arming the Future: A Defense Industry for the 21st Century* (New York: Council on Foreign Relations Press, 1999), pp. 224–46.
[9] Sandler and Hartley, *The Economics of Defense*, p. 114.

foreign firms require the consent of the government to prevent the export of critical technologies. Arms exports require special permission to protect national security and ensure that they are consistent with foreign policy objectives.[10] Governments may even wish to prevent the export of weapons or technology to allied countries because of concern that it will find its way to adversaries.[11] In short, governments play the central role *vis-à-vis* transnational activity because of security concerns.[12]

This is not to say that firms are insignificant. They play an important role in the shape of defense industries by performing the research, development, and production tasks of weapons procurement, and they help make decisions on whether or not – and with whom – to collaborate. In the early 1990s, for instance, the US Department of Defense under William Perry strongly encouraged consolidation of the American defense industry through less stringent anti-trust enforcement, subsidies for merged companies, civil–military integration programs, and direct communication with defense executives. However, it left specific M&A details – such as which firms would merge – to the defense firms themselves to decide.[13] Consequently, national governments play a determining role in the size and shape of defense industries as well as the degree of international collaboration, but defense firms still play an important role.

State options

States have three general options when procuring weapons and systems. As summarized in Table 5.1, they can develop and produce weapons domestically (autarky); cooperate in the development and production of weapons (collaboration); and purchase from abroad (foreign dependence).

First, states may choose *autarky*. They can design and produce weapons domestically, either through a nationalized defense industry or through private firms that are domestically owned. Realists have

---

[10] Kennedy, *The Economics of Defence*, p. 132.
[11] See, for example, the tension between the United States and Israel over arms transfers. Duncan Clarke, "Israel's Unauthorized Arms Transfers," *Foreign Policy*, No. 99, Summer 1995, pp. 89–109.
[12] Scherer, *The Weapons Acquisition Process*, p. 2.
[13] Erik Pages, "Defense Mergers: Weapons Cost, Innovation, and International Arms Industry Cooperation," in Anne R. Markusen and Sean Costigan, eds., *Arming the Future: A Defense Industry for the 21st Century* (New York: Council on Foreign Relations Press, 1999), pp. 207–23.

Table 5.1. *Summary of procurement options*

Options	Characteristics
Autarky	Weapons developed and produced domestically
Collaboration	Weapons developed and produced with foreign nations and defense firms. Can include: • M&As • Coproduction • Codevelopment
Foreign dependence	All or most weapons and technology imported

long noted that in an anarchic international system, states will prefer autarky and self-sufficiency to cooperation. Kenneth Waltz argues, "In a self-help system, considerations of security subordinate economic gain to political interest. Defense spending, moreover, is unproductive for all and unavoidable for most. Rather than increased well-being, their reward is in the maintenance of their autonomy. States compete, but not by contributing their individual efforts to the joint production of goods for their mutual benefit."[14] States may prefer autarky when procuring weapons because it ensures security of supply, sustains a strong defense industrial base, and maintains national technological capabilities.[15] Chinese leaders learned this when the USSR abruptly cut off military aid in the early 1960s and Western countries imposed an arms embargo after the 1989 Tiananmen Square incident.[16]

Great powers have historically been as autarkic as possible in weapons procurement.[17] As E. H. Carr argues in *The Twenty Years Crisis*, autarky in arms production was one of the aims of early mercantilists, and has

[14] Kenneth N. Waltz, *Theory of International Politics* (New York: McGraw-Hill, 1979), p. 107.
[15] Stephen G. Brooks, *Producing Security: Multinational Corporations, Globalization, and the Changing Calculus of Conflict* (Princeton, NJ: Princeton University Press, 2005); Trevor Taylor and Keith Hayward, *The UK Defence Industrial Base: Development and Future Policy Options* (Washington: Brassey's Defence Publishers, 1989), p. 67.
[16] Richard A. Bitzinger, *Towards a Brave New Arms Industry?* Adelphi Paper 356 (London: Oxford University Press, 2003), p. 12; Bates Gill and Taeho Kim, *China's Arms Acquisitions from Abroad: A Quest for 'Superb and Secret Weapons'* (New York: Oxford University Press, 1995), pp. 8–47.
[17] In Western Europe an obvious exception is the period following World War II, when states such as France, Britain, and West Germany relied on the United States for money, supplies, and weapons to rebuild their defense industries and equip their militaries.

been for states for centuries.[18] Following the rise of the modern French nation-state, for example, the state assumed monopoly control over the extraction and sale of saltpeter, as well as the production of such items as gunpowder, hand weapons, firearms, and heavy armaments such as artillery and mortars.[19] In the United States the push for self-sufficiency goes as far back as the Revolutionary War, when Alexander Hamilton in his *Report on the Subject of Manufactures* recommended the development of a domestic industrial base to avoid excessive reliance on foreign suppliers.[20] Successive US administrations in the eighteenth, nineteenth, and twentieth centuries relied on either nationally owned facilities or private US industry to produce weapons.[21] In both cases, the suppliers were almost always domestic.

Since World War II the United States has continued to be largely autarkic in weapons procurement, relying on American defense firms for weapons procurement.[22] It is important to recognize that even great powers cannot be purely autarkic. The constraining factor is access to necessary raw materials. As Robert Gilpin argues, the rise of professional armies required the acquisition of vital war materials such as timber for ships or saltpeter for gunpowder, some of which could only be acquired by importing them.[23] In the modern era, great powers may be forced to import some leading-edge commercial technology such as microprocessors in the construction of advanced weapons systems.[24]

Second, at the other end of the spectrum, states may pursue a procurement policy of *foreign dependence*. In order to maximize efficiency,

---

[18] E. H. Carr, *The Twenty Years' Crisis: 1919–1939* (New York: Harper & Row, 1964), pp. 120–1.

[19] Edward A. Kolodziej, *Making and Marketing Arms: The French Experience and Its Implications for the International System* (Princeton, NJ: Princeton University Press, 1987), pp. 3–53.

[20] Alexander Hamilton, "Report on the Subject of Manufacturers," in Harold C. Syrett, ed., *The Papers of Alexander Hamilton* (New York: Columbia University Press, 1966), pp. 230–341.

[21] Aaron L. Friedberg, *In the Shadow of the Garrison State: America's Anti-Statism and its Cold War Grand Strategy* (Princeton, NJ: Princeton University Press, 2000), pp. 245–95.

[22] Theodore H. Moran, "The Globalization of America's Defense Industries: Managing the Threat of Foreign Dependence," *International Security*, Vol. 15, No. 1, Summer 1990, pp. 57–99; Jacques S. Gansler, *Defense Conversion: Transforming the Arsenal of Democracy* (Cambridge, MA: MIT Press, 1995), pp. 43–50; Gansler, "Needed: A U.S. Defense Industrial Strategy," *International Security*, Vol. 12, No. 2, Autumn 1987, pp. 45–62; US Department of Defense, *Final Report of the Defense Science Board Task Force on Globalization and Security* (Washington: Dept of Defense, 1999).

[23] Robert Gilpin, "Economic Interdependence and National Security in Historical Perspective," in Klaus Knorr and Frank N. Trager, eds., *Economic Issues and National Security* (Lawrence, KA: Allen Press, 1977), p. 29.

[24] Keith Hayward, "The Globalisation of Defence Industries," *Survival*, Vol. 42, No. 2, Summer 2001, pp. 115–32.

states can import all or most weapons and technology from abroad. Weaker states are generally forced to adopt a policy of foreign dependence because they lack the ability to be autarkic. Wealth is a key factor and includes the size of a state's population and the level of its wealth.[25] Wealth includes such factors as abundance of natural resources, level of industrialization, and technological development. States need a substantial amount of resources, technology, and personnel to build weapons. This is particularly true in the modern era because the high cost of advanced weapons makes it either difficult or impossible for small powers to develop and produce on their own.[26] Development and production costs of modern fighter aircraft can be exorbitant. Consider the Lockheed Martin Joint Strike Fighter, whose development and production costs are estimated to exceed $300 billion over twenty-five years.[27]

Manufacturing complex modern weapon systems, platforms, and systems such as aircraft and missiles demands a level of skills that only the most industrialized countries can achieve.[28] Third-world and many industrializing states simply don't have the money, technological capabilities, and resources necessary to build advanced systems, and consequently are dependent on foreign weapons and technology. For these states, foreign dependence may be most efficient because it allows them to devote scarce resources to commercial, rather than defense, industries. Indeed, a strategy of foreign dependence entails the adoption of a free-market approach, at least with allies.

Third, states may pursue a policy of transnational *collaboration*. This entails the design and production of weapons in cooperation with foreign nations and defense firms. There are at least three types of transnational

[25] This definition of power is sometimes referred to as "latent power." See John J. Mearsheimer, *The Tragedy of Great Power Politics* (New York: W. W. Norton, 2001), pp. 43, 55–82.
[26] Kolodziej, *Making and Marketing Arms*, p. 141. On rising costs see Hartley, *NATO Arms Co-operation*, p. 30; Michael Brzoska and Peter Lock, eds., "Restructuring of Arms Production in Western Europe: Introduction," in Brzoska and Lock, eds., *Restructuring of Arms Production in Western Europe* (New York: Oxford University Press, 1992), pp. 4–5; Gansler, "Needed: A US Defense Industrial Strategy," pp. 45–62.
[27] The Joint Strike Fighter estimates are based on 3,000 aircraft configured in conventional takeoff and landing (CTOL) variant, short takeoff and vertical landing (STOVL) variant, and carrier variant (CV). Target flyaway costs for each variant are approximately $28 million for the CTOL, $30–$35 million for the STOVL, and $31–$38 million for the CV in 1994 dollars. See John Birkler *et al.*, *Assessing Competitive Strategies for the Joint Strike Fighter: Opportunities and Options*, MR-1362-OSD/JSF (Santa Monica, CA: RAND, 2001), p. 2.
[28] Klauss Knorr, "Military Strength: Economic and Non-economic Bases," in Knorr and Trager, eds., *Economic Issues and National Security*, p. 185.

collaboration: mergers and acquisitions, coproduction projects, and codevelopment projects.

- Mergers and acquisitions (M&As) – the merger with, or outright purchase of, a foreign defense firm. M&As generally include the purchase of company shares up to gaining majority control.
- Coproduction – shared production and assembly of a weapon, class of weapons, or weapon part.[29] Defense contractors from participant countries purchase the same equipment and jointly produce the weapon.
- Codevelopment – the joint design, engineering, and production of a weapon, class of weapons, or weapons part. Codevelopment involves two or more firms agreeing to a common requirement, sharing research and development costs, and combining national orders.

Why multilateral collaboration?

Under what conditions will states pursue a strategy of multilateral defense collaboration? Significant interstate collaboration has been rare among great powers. However, the existence of a unipolar international system may create a strong impetus for eligible states to collaborate on defense production for two reasons: it decreases reliance on the preponderant state, and it increases states' ability to project power abroad. Eligible states are those that have the military and economic capabilities to become great powers.

Decrease reliance

The first reason weaker states may aggregate power is to decrease reliance on the preponderant state. The risk for weaker states is that a failure to aggregate power may create a reliance on the preponderant state for defense resources and lead to foreign dependence. Dependence decreases security of supply, compromises the viability of a state's defense industrial base, and limits the global competitiveness of its defense firms. Reliance on a preponderant power for weapons and

---

[29] I have excluded *licensed production* – the transnational sale or transfer of the rights to manufacture a weapon, class of weapons, or weapons part to a foreign country – from the definition of "coproduction" because it is more properly folded into the category of "foreign dependence." Licensing involves the production of a foreign firm's equipment by a purchasing nation under license in its own country. Examples include Canadian, Japanese, and European production of the American F-104 fighter, as well as Japanese production of the American F-15.

military supplies decreases a state's security by placing its supply in the hands of someone else. This may be fine under most conditions. But can dependent states always rely on the preponderant power for spare parts and regular access?

European collaboration decreases reliance on the US and its defense industry. The concern is that a failure to collaborate would make Europe reliant on the US for advanced weapons, platforms, and systems when conducting military operations. This is particularly acute in some areas, such as global positioning systems, in which the US controls supply. The evidence in Europe is unambiguous. As a European Commission report concluded, "there is a danger that European industry could be reduced to the status of sub-supplier to prime US contractors, while the key know-how is reserved for US firms."[30] Failure to aggregate defense resources, French President Jacques Chirac warned, risked "vassal status" to a preponderant US.[31] As another European Commission document noted regarding the Galileo global navigation satellite system:

> Galileo will underpin the common European defense policy that the Member States have decided to establish. There is no question here of coming into conflict with the United States . . . If the EU finds it necessary to undertake a security mission that the US does not consider to be in its interest, it will be impotent unless it has the satellite navigation technology that is now indispensable. Although designed primarily for civilian applications, Galileo will also give the EU a military capability.[32]

In other areas, such as missile systems or fighter aircraft, European states might have to rely on the US for spare parts. Or the US might simply refuse to sell some weapons or systems to it in the future.

The 1991 Persian Gulf War, 1995 war in Bosnia, and 1999 war in Kosovo were stark reminders that European countries were largely dependent on US power to conduct even modest military operations.

---

[30] Commission of the European Communities, *Towards an EU Defence Equipment Policy*, COM (2003) 113 Final (Brussels: European Commission, March 2003), p. 11.

[31] Martin Fletcher, "Europe's Galileo Navigation System Puts US on the Spot," *Times*, March 26, 2002. On the US and the European defense industry, also see Alain Richard, "European Defense," Speech at the Symposium of the Association Diplomatie et Defense, April 18, 2001, Washington: Embassy of France in the United States, 2001.

[32] Commission of the EC, *Galileo: The European Project on Radio Navigation by Satellite* (Brussels: European Commission, Directorate General for Energy and Transport, March 2002). Also see Dee Ann Divis, "Military Role for Galileo Emerges," *GPS World*, Vol. 13, No. 5, p. 10. On the military uses of Galileo see also Commission of the EC, *Space: A New European Frontier for an Expanding Union* (Brussels: European Commission, 2003); Michael A. Taverna, "European Union's New Space Role Could Help Meet Military Goals," *Aviation Week & Space Technology*, Vol. 153, No. 22, November 27, 2000, p. 29; "Military Pushes for Galileo," *Aviation Week & Space Technology*, Vol. 156, No. 7, February 18, 2002, p. 28.

For example, the British House of Commons Defence Committee concluded in its report on the lessons of Kosovo that the operation demonstrated how reliant Europe was on US power.[33] The British Ministry of Defense's document *European Defence* argued that Europe should develop its own regional defense capabilities: "As the lessons of Kosovo showed . . . European nations need significantly to improve their military capabilities. They should not continue to depend so heavily on the United States in dealing with crises in and around Europe. Europe needs to improve its ability to act in circumstances where NATO is not engaged."[34]

Increase power

The second reason why weaker states may aggregate resources is that it increases their military and economic power. Because of their unrivaled position in the international system, preponderant states tend to feel few restraints. This increases their incentive to assert power around the globe.[35] The threat from the dominant power may not be a military one. Rather, it may simply be able to influence the policies of smaller states and constrain their ability to make independent decisions. Indeed, Lord Castlereagh, UK foreign Secretary between 1812 and 1822, referred to the maintenance of a just equilibrium between states to prevent one of them from unduly influencing and imposing its will upon the others.[36] In the defense industry, a preponderant state's defense firms are likely to have global power and reach in an open international trading system. States will try to expand their firms' sales to foreign markets, pursue an arms monopoly, and thereby increase influence over

[33] UK House of Commons, Defence Committee, *Lessons of Kosovo*, Fourteenth Report (London: HMSO, 2000), para. 313. Also see Elizabeth Pond, "Kosovo: Catalyst for Europe," *Washington Quarterly*, Vol. 22, No. 4, pp. 77–92; Christopher Layne, "Death Knell for NATO? The Bush Administration Confronts the European Security and Defense Policy," *Policy Analysis*, No. 394, April 4, 2001; Mary Elise Sarotte, *German Military Reform and European Security*, Adelphi Paper 340 (London: International Institute for Strategic Studies, 2001), p. 54; Gilles Andréani, Christoph Bertram, and Charles Grant, *Europe's Military Revolution* (London: Centre for European Reform, 2001), pp. 8–11.
[34] *European Defence*, Paper No. 3 (London: Ministry of Defence, 2001). On British policymakers and the US/NATO commitment, also see Andréani, Bertram, and Grant, *Europe's Military Revolution*, p. 11; *Defence Policy 2001* (London: HMSO, 2001), para. 19; Miskimmon, "Recasting the Security Bargains," p. 90.
[35] Robert Jervis, "The Compulsive Empire," *Foreign Policy*, Vol. 137, July/August 2003, pp. 83–7.
[36] Lord Castlereagh cited in Lenox A. Mills and Charles H. McLaughlin, *World Politics in Transition* (New York: Holt, 1956), pp. 107–8.

others. These actions create a strong impetus for other states to combine power. In the defense realm, collaboration increases the power and competitiveness of weaker states and defense firms, especially relative to the dominant power.[37]

In a unipolar international system, US military dominance creates a strong impetus for European states to pursue defense collaboration to increase European power through military and economic cooperation. The cost of not collaborating is straightforward: they could not compete with the US Defense Department and defense companies on the global arms market, and some European defense companies might face extinction. As French Defense Minister Michèle Alliot-Marie has argued, "at a time when the United States is resolutely leading the space revolution with impressive capabilities and China has begun to invest in the development and use of such systems, the Europeans must together take up the challenge of space." She continued that "the importance of space technology today calls for an effort comparable to that which led to the emergence of nuclear power in the 1960s. As we have seen in the recent armed conflicts, in Kosovo as well as in Iraq, space-based technology is increasingly at the heart of modern military systems."[38]

Collaboration improves competitiveness by decreasing research and development costs, spreading design and development costs and risks among several partners, and reducing duplication. Spreading fixed costs over a larger output and among a number of firms reduces the average per unit R&D component. Collaboration also leads to economies of scale. Larger firms and longer production runs help achieve economies of scale and lower unit production costs. In addition, collaboration among defense firms can increase learning curves.[39] Employees and managers engaged in the production of highly complex weapons systems require substantial experience before they learn to work efficiently. This

[37] Richard A. Bitzinger, "Globalization in the Post-Cold War Defense Industry: Challenges and Opportunities," in Markusen and Costigan, eds., *Arming the Future*, pp. 305–33; Sandler and Hartley, *The Political Economy of NATO*; Derrick J. Neal and Trevor Taylor, "Globalisation in the Defence Industry: An Exploration of the Paradigm for US and European Defence Firms and Implications for Being Global Players," *Defence and Peace Economics*, Vol. 12, 2001, pp. 337–60; Michael Oden, "Cashing In, Cashing Out, and Converting: Restructuring of the Defense Industrial Base in the 1990s," in Markusen and Costigan, eds., *Arming the Future*, pp. 74–105; Moravcsik, "The European Armaments Industry at the Crossroads"; Alan G. Draper, *European Defence Equipment Collaboration: Britain's Involvement, 1957–87* (New York: St. Martin's Press, 1990), p. 51; Hartley, *NATO Arms Co-operation*, pp. 41–68.
[38] Michèle Alliot-Marie, "Défense et espace: l'Europe en marche," *Le Figaro*, 27 décembre 2004, p. 10.
[39] Moravcsik, "The European Armaments Industry at the Crossroads," p. 67; Hartley, *NATO Co-operation*, pp. 52, 60.

creates a learning curve. The logic is that the more frequently labor and management perform a specific task, the more efficient they will become at that task. Finally, collaboration can increase interoperability and standardization. Interoperability refers to the degree to which different weapons, equipment, and forces are compatible.[40] Standardization refers to the degree to which there is a common standard of weapons, tactics, training, and support. Low levels of interoperability and standardization can severely hamper the ability of militaries to fight effectively together by complicating command, control, communications, intelligence, surveillance, and reconnaissance.[41]

If EU states and defense firms have aggregated resources in response to structural conditions, we should expect to see at least two developments. First, we should see an increase in intra-European defense collaboration in the post-Cold War era. This should contrast with European collaboration during the Cold War, which would have been transatlantic; balancing the Soviet Union was their primary focus. Second, intra-European collaboration should be causally linked with power, especially US power. That is, European states would not take these actions if the United States – and US defense firms – were not as powerful. To sum up, we should expect the following:

• During the Cold War, transnational weapons collaboration would largely be transatlantic rather than intra-European. Since the international system was bipolar, European states and defense firms would be primarily concerned about balancing the USSR and collaborating with the United States.
• During the post-Cold War era, transnational collaboration should largely be intra-European. Since the international system is unipolar, European states should be concerned about United States power and increasingly collaborate with each other.

The defense production data

The next step is to examine the data on European weapons production. I used the Defense Budget Project's globalization database to compile

---

[40] Hartley, *NATO Arms Co-operation*, pp. 13–15; Myron Hura, *et al.*, *Interoperability: A Continuing Challenge in Coalition Air Operations*, MR-1235-AF (Santa Monica, CA: RAND, 2000), pp. 7–15; Mark A. Lorell and Julia Lowell, *Pros and Cons of International Weapons Procurement Collaboration*, MR-565-OSD (Santa Monica, CA: RAND, 1995), p. 7.

[41] Hura, *Interoperability*; Wesley K. Clark, *Waging Modern War: Bosnia, Kosovo, and the Future of Combat* (New York: Public Affairs, 2001).

data on all cases ($N = 478$) of collaboration involving European defense firms between 1961 and 2000 in the following areas: M&As, coproduction projects, and codevelopment projects.[42] Since I am particularly interested in examining trends in transnational weapons collaboration, the cases were divided into three categories: intra-European, European–US, and European–other. This allows us to see which firms European defense companies collaborated with.

First, *intra-European* includes transnational collaboration among defense firms from European Community and European Union countries. Collaboration involving defense firms from such European countries as Switzerland were excluded if they were not members of the EC or EU, and were coded as "European–other." Examples of intra-European collaboration include cases of bilateral cooperation such as Thomson-CSF's (France) acquisition of Link-Miles (Britain) in the 1980s, as well as multilateral cooperation such as German, Italian, and British cooperation in developing and producing the Tornado multirole fighter aircraft in the 1970s. Second, *European–US* involves collaboration between defense firms from the United States and EU countries.[43] Separating out collaboration between European and American defense firms is necessary because it allows us to examine whether military cooperation among NATO countries affected weapons collaboration. Again, I included cases of bilateral cooperation such as Raytheon's (US) acquisition of Anschuetz (Germany) in the 1990s, as well as multilateral cooperation such as NATO collaboration on Seasparrow surface-to-air missiles in the 1960s. Third, *European–other* refers to bilateral and multilateral collaboration between defense firms from EU countries and other regions: Asia, Latin America, Africa, the Middle East, and Eastern Europe.

However, there are at least two limitations with the data. First, they do not include domestic M&As and coproduction and codevelopment projects. It might be interesting to know, for example, the total number of M&As within Germany between 1961 and 2000. This would allow us to examine how often German firms merged with or acquired other German firms, and to compare these figures with transnational M&As. As far as I am aware, this information does not exist. Since the data do

---

[42] I thank Richard Bitzinger for generously giving me access to the Defense Budget Project's Globalization Database. I made a notable modification to it. The database defined "European" quite broadly to include NATO countries (such as Turkey) and those that did not belong to either NATO or the EC/EU (such as Russia). Since this study is interested only in members of the European Community and European Union, I defined "European" to include only EC and EU countries.
[43] I also included Canadian defense firms in this category to capture NATO cooperation.

not include information on domestic activity, they have little to say about whether European states are becoming more or less interdependent. However, this is not a major problem; the primary focus of this chapter is on transnational defense cooperation. When European states and defense firms choose to collaborate abroad, with whom are they collaborating?

Second, the data does not include the monetary value of M&As and coproduction and codevelopment projects. While it would be useful to have this information, much of it does not exist. For M&As in which both companies are private firms, there are no requirements to report specific information about the deal, including financial data. For M&As involving a combination of public and private firms, the likelihood that financial data will be publicly available varies depending on the size of the M&A and company preferences. The data also does not include the value of coproduction and codevelopment projects. These values are not included because they present enormous measurement problems. The total cost of transnational weapons and systems incorporates an amalgam of research, development, and production costs from multiple countries that span the life of the project, and the data are often classified and unavailable. While it would be helpful to have the value of collaboration cases, it is not a significant problem. Examining the number of cases and the motivations of European leaders should provide a fairly reliable picture of the European defense industry.

Cold War cooperation

As Figure 5.1 illustrates, European defense firms were more likely to collaborate with American defense firms on coproduction and codevelopment projects than with other European firms during the Cold War. In addition, European defense firms were more likely to consolidate with American than European firms through mergers and acquisitions. The reason is largely tied to the structure of the international system.

During the bipolar Cold War when European states were concerned about balancing the Soviet Union, they were more likely to cooperate with the United States to improve NATO interoperability and standardization in case of a war with the Soviet Union. The emerging parity in strategic forces between the US and USSR meant that NATO countries needed to rely on a coordinated military capability to meet a surprise Soviet attack. Germany's 1970 *White Paper* argued, "West Berlin, which has frequently enough been subject to political pressure by the Soviet Union and her allies, is particularly vulnerable. It is under a permanent threat."

Coproduction and codevelopment projects

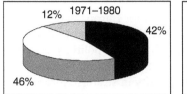 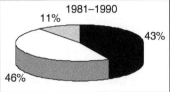

Mergers and acquisitions

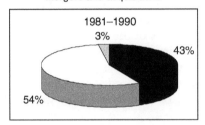

Figure 5.1. Cold War defense cooperation.

The effectiveness of the Alliance is contingent upon the harmonization of military resources which, in turn, permits their coordinated employment in case of an emergency; national elements alone will not do.[44]

In addition, transatlantic defense collaboration helped tie the United States to Europe. British leaders, for example, preferred a long-term US commitment to Europe to balance Soviet power; European states were too weak to do it by themselves. The importance of collaboration with the US was seconded by German, Dutch, Belgian, and a number of other European leaders.[45] In order to make US promises more credible, this meant US participation in collaborative defense projects, mergers and acquisitions, as well as the presence of US military forces.

---

[44] Federal Minister of Defence, *White Paper 1970: The Security of the Federal Republic of Germany and the Development of the Federal Armed Forces* (Bonn: Federal Minister of Defence, 1970), 20–1, 25.
[45] Jebb to Younger, September 12, 1950, *DBPO, 1950*, Series II, Vol. III, pp. 28–31; Cabinet meeting held at 10 Downing Street, November 16, 1950, *DBPO, 1950*, Series II, Vol. III, pp. 263–6. Also see, for example, Dirk U. Stikker, *Men of Responsibility: A Memoir* (New York: Harper & Row, 1965), pp. 303–4; Paul-Henri Spaak, *The Continuing Battle: Memoirs of a European, 1936–1966* (London: Weidenfeld and Nicolson, 1971), p. 150; Konrad Adenauer, *Memoirs, 1945–53* (Chicago: Henry Regnery, 1966), p. 320.

Collaborative projects

During the Cold War there was no prospect for European military action outside of NATO. Neither the European Defense Community nor the Fouchet Plan was ever ratified, and European political cooperation remained largely a pipedream. As US Secretary of Defense Harold Brown argued, however, the emerging parity in strategic forces between the US and USSR meant that NATO countries needed to rely on a coordinated military capability to meet a surprise Soviet attack. This would allow NATO countries "to ensure continuation of a credible NATO defense at a cost that can be economically and politically sustained in each of the countries of the Alliance."[46] Consequently, transnational collaboration during the Cold War was largely transatlantic. In the late 1980s, there was a notable increase in the total number of transnational coproduction and codevelopment projects as defense budgets began to decline. But European firms were still more likely to collaborate with US firms.

In 1949, NATO established a military production and supply board to coordinate production, standardization, and technical research in the weapons industry. After a number of modifications, this body became the Defense Production Committee in 1954 to supervise joint production programs and promote the standardization of weapons. In the late 1960s, NATO established the Conference of National Armaments Directors to promote transatlantic projects and exchange information on operational requirements and national equipment plans. The result of this collaboration included at least fourteen NATO projects by 1976, such as the Jaguar and Tornado aircraft, Milan missile, and RAM air defense system. Other examples included German–American codevelopment of the RAM air defense system and British–American codevelopment of the Harrier fighter aircraft.

In France, the government supported limited NATO codevelopment and coproduction projects to counter Soviet military power.[47] The government's Délégation ministérielle de l'armement (DGA) was responsible for defense procurement, industrial liaison, and equipment

---

[46] Harold Brown, press conference on May 6, 1977. Reprinted in *Survival*, Vol. 19, No. 4, July/August 1977, p. 179.

[47] On French armaments policy see Marc Cauchie, "Coopération internationale dans le domaine des armaments," *Défense nationale*, June 1980, pp. 25–42; Marc Defourneaux, "France and a European Armament Policy," *NATO Review*, No. 5, 1979, pp. 19–25; Defourneaux, "Indépendance nationale et coopération internationale en matière d'armements," *Défense nationale*, February 1979, pp. 35–48; Defourneaux, "Coopération et indépendance technologique," *Défense nationale*, March 1983, pp. 105–18.

collaboration, and largely determined the shape of the French defense industry. As Army General Guy Méry argued, NATO cooperation in a war with the Soviet Union would pose a number of problems, such as "[difficulty of] differences in procedures, equipment and tactical methods, which leads us to seek a certain interoperability of forces and to carry out exercises with Allied forces which are also extremely beneficial for training our own units."[48] French military scholars have generally argued that France's political and military leaders pursued a grand strategy driven by a desire to retain national independence and military autonomy, exemplified by de Gaulle's establishment of a nuclear *force de frappe* and partial withdrawal from NATO in 1966.[49] However, this is somewhat misleading. French leaders still believed that cooperation with NATO was important to balance against the Soviet Union. In particular, this meant that it was important to pursue collaborative projects with Alliance members – including the United States.

Examples of French involvement in transatlantic cooperation included the Multiple Launch Rocket System, a mobile automatic all-weather system used as NATO's standard rocket; the NH-90, a multirole medium helicopter designed as NATO's helicopter for the 1990s; and the CFM turbofan engine, produced jointly by France's SNECMA and the US's General Electric and used to power the KC-135 refueling tanker.[50] The rationale for collaborative projects was to improve NATO's fighting efficiency through interoperability or standardization. The DGA's Marc Cauchi argued,

We see only benefits in interoperability. This is why it constitutes one of the linchpins of France's armaments policy, and why we supported . . . the creation of the ad hoc committee for interoperability in the North Atlantic Council. For operational efficiency, the number-one aim of the equipment of our national armed forces, interoperability, so long as it is implemented at the right level, does surely guarantee the ability to conduct combined operations.[51]

---

[48] General Guy Méry, "Une armée pour quoi faire et comment?" *Défense nationale*, June 1976, p. 17. Also see Méry, "French Defence Policy," *Survival*, Vol. 18, No. 5, September/October 1976, p. 227.

[49] On French military policies during the Cold War see Philip H. Gordon, *A Certain Idea of France: French Security Policy and the Gaullist Legacy* (Princeton, NJ: Princeton University Press, 1993); Philip G. Cerny, *The Politics of Grandeur: Ideological Aspects of De Gaulle's Foreign Policy* (New York: Cambridge University Press, 1980).

[50] For the MLRS see *Jane's Weapons Systems, 1987–88* (London: Jane's Publishing, 1988), pp. 128–9. For the NH-90 see *Jane's All the World's Aircraft, 2002–2003* (London: Jane's Information Group, 2003), pp. 255–8. For the CFM turbofan engine see *Jane's Aero-Engines* (London: Jane's Information Group, 2002).

[51] Address by Ingénieur Général Marc Cauchi, Paris, March 3, 1977. The text is reprinted in *Survival*, Vol. 19, No. 4, July/August 1977, pp. 182.

Furthermore, while there were some successful intra-European codevelopment and coproduction projects such as the HOT, MILAN, and ROLAND family of missiles, these were generally designed to serve NATO military functions. For instance, the HOT missile was a heavy anti-tank weapon developed by France and Germany to fulfill a NATO requirement for missiles that could be launched from helicopters and armored or unarmored vehicles.[52] Since French procurement decisions were largely a function of the military's strategic goals, defense firms played a subsidiary role.

British leaders were also willing to pursue limited transatlantic collaboration in weapons procurement to improve NATO power and efficiency. British Secretary of State for Defence Roy Mason argued that the advantage of weapons collaboration was substantial:

> By means of longer production runs, and the development of European industries to adapt to such production runs, we should be able to manufacture equipment at much more competitive prices, and the forces of NATO would thereby achieve standardization of equipment far more quickly and more cost effectively than by any other method.[53]

This view dovetailed with Britain's grand strategy during the Cold War, which supported NATO cooperation as one of the country's fundamental security tenets. As the 1970 *Supplementary Statement on Defence Policy* argued: "The security of Britain rests on the strength of the North Atlantic Alliance. The maintenance and improvement of our military contribution to NATO remains the first priority of our defence policy."[54]

Britain's involvement in transatlantic collaboration during the Cold War included a number of projects such as joint production of the Sky Flash/AIM-7 medium-range air-to-air missile; the ASRAAM short-range air-to-air missile; and the AV-8B Harrier attack and reconnaissance aircraft. All three involved close cooperation with American defense firms: Raytheon with the Sky Flash, Hughes with the ASRAAM, and McDonnell Douglas with the Harrier. British defense officials argued that procurement collaboration along transatlantic lines was

---

[52] *Jane's Weapons Systems, 1987–88,* pp. 136–7.

[53] Roy Mason, "Setting British Defence Priorities," *Survival,* Vol. 17, No. 5, September/ October 1975, pp. 221–2.

[54] UK Ministry of Defence, *Supplementary Statement on Defence Policy,* Cmnd. 4521 (London: HMSO, 1970). Yet there were some limits. The *Supplementary Statement on Defence Policy* noted, "There are serious threats to stability outside the NATO area" such as Britain's overseas territories, and "Britain will be willing to play her part in countering them." This meant, in turn, that Britain needed "to keep to a minimum" the percentage of weapons bought from abroad to ensure security of supply and to provide a measure of foreign policy independence. See also, for example, UK Ministry of Defence, *Statement on the Defence Estimates, 1981,* Cmnd. 8212–1 (London: HMSO, 1981), p. 47.

important to increase economic and military efficiency, and they were primarily responsible for pushing transatlantic cooperation. George Younger, defense minister for Margaret Thatcher, strongly endorsed greater collaboration to improve NATO's fighting effectiveness. He argued, "There can surely be no greater condemnation of the way in which we have gone about our procurement business in the past than the fact that NATO has not, and will not have for some years yet, an interoperable identification friend or foe system in service."

As a result if we had to go to war tomorrow, or next year, or even the year after that, we should inevitably end up by shooting down numbers of our own aircraft – of which we do not have enough to start with.[55]

Even intra-European projects that Britain was involved in, such as the Tornado fighter aircraft, were built largely for NATO purposes. Two NATO-based procurement agencies, NAMMO and NAMMA, were established to monitor the Tornado program and to facilitate intergovernmental decision-making.[56]

In West Germany, NATO cooperation was particularly important because West Berlin was a major point of contention between the US and the USSR, and West Germany's geographic location meant that a conventional war between NATO and Warsaw Pact countries would likely be fought on its soil.[57] The 1971/1972 *White Paper* noted, "The armament of the Bundeswehr is determined by its mission within the Alliance. The Federal Government considers cooperation with allied partners to be essential" since "standardized weapons systems enable an economical employment of forces."[58] German defense officials pursued

---

[55] Robert Mauthner, "UK Plea for Greater Co-operation on Armaments," *Financial Times*, March 8, 1988, p. 2.

[56] Hayward, *The British Aircraft Industry*, p. 113; Draper, *European Defence Equipment Collaboration*, p. 40.

[57] Marc Trachtenberg, *A Constructed Peace: The Making of the European Settlement, 1945–1963* (Princeton, NJ: Princeton University Press, 1999).

[58] German Federal Minister of Defence, *White Paper 1971/1972: The Security of the Federal Republic of Germany and the Development of the Federal Armed Forces* (Bonn: Federal Minister of Defence, 1971/72), pp. 149–50. As the 1973/1974 *White Paper* explained in more detail: "The weapons and equipment of the Bundeswehr must be adequate to the threat, the security policy objectives of the Federal government, and the strategic defense cooperation of the Western Alliance. The similarity of tasks calls for largely uniform equipment in the Alliance; consequently, inter-allied cooperation must aim at achieving standardization of equipment, above all of the more expensive weapons systems. Cooperation and standardization offer economic advantages to the countries concerned and facilitate the logistic support, training, and operations of the allied armed forces." German Federal Minister of Defense, *White Paper 1973/1974: The Security of the Federal Republic of Germany and the Development of the Federal Armed Forces* (Bonn: Federal Minister of Defence, 1973/1974), p. 179.

coproduction and codevelopment projects within the context of NATO to increase the alliance's military power and fighting effectiveness.[59]

Consequently, West Germany was involved in transatlantic coproduction and codevelopment projects during the Cold War. Germany's Ministry of Defense and its procurement agency, the Bundesamt für Wehrtechnik und Beschaffung (BWB), were largely responsible for deciding, approving, and overseeing transnational collaboration projects – not German defense firms.[60] Notable examples included development of the Seasparrow surface-to-air missile, a joint NATO project to provide ships with an effective surface-to-air anti-missile defense. It also included the Rolling Airframe Missile air defense system, designed by the US and Germany to enable surface ships to engage incoming anti-ship cruise missiles.[61] Germany also participated in some intra-European projects such as the Atlantique aircraft.[62] A number of these efforts failed, such as the Franco-German tank project and the Franco-German observation satellite. But those that survived were generally built to serve NATO functions.[63] For instance, the Atlantique was designed and built under the auspices of the NATO Armaments Committee to supersede the Lockheed P-2 Neptune as a NATO reconnaissance aircraft.[64]

European dependence on the US declined significantly over the course of the Cold War. In the 1960s, European states procured American armaments either directly through exports or indirectly through licensed production. Licensed production includes the domestic manufacture of another state's weapons under license, and is a good indicator of foreign dependence.[65] As Figure 5.2 illustrates, European states were dependent on American armaments in the early Cold War and produced a number of weapons and platforms such as the F-104 aircraft through licensed production. But by 1990, however, the United States granted only a handful of licenses to European states.

---

[59] German Federal Minister of Defence, *White Paper 1985: The Situation and Development of the Federal Armed Forces* (Bonn: Federal Minister of Defence, 1985), p. 367.

[60] Regina H. E. Cowen, *Defense Procurement in the Federal Republic of Germany: Politics and Organization* (Boulder, CO: Westview Press, 1986).

[61] Jane's Defense database.

[62] On French and German discussions about European collaboration, see, for example, Konrad Adenauer's account of discussions with Charles de Gaulle in Adenauer, *Erinnerungen, 1959–1963* (Stuttgart: Deutsche Verlags-Anstalt, 1968), pp. 179, 433.

[63] On the Franco-German tank project see Stephen A. Kocs, *Autonomy or Power? The Franco-German Relationship and Europe's Strategic Choices, 1955–1995* (Westport, CT: Praeger, 1995), p. 172, 159; Moravcsik, "Armaments among Allies," pp. 143–50.

[64] *Jane's All the World's Aircraft, 1971/1972*, pp. 48–9. Draper, *European Defence Equipment Collaboration*, p. 15.

[65] Sandler and Hartley, *The Economics of Defense*, pp. 238–41.

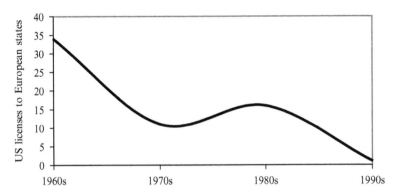

Figure 5.2. European dependence on US arms in the early Cold War.

Mergers and acquisitions

During the Cold War there was little prospect for military cooperation among European states outside NATO because of the central importance of balancing the USSR. Consequently, European states pursued a procurement policy encouraging some transnational mergers and acquisitions along transatlantic lines to combine power and increase fighting effectiveness in response to the Soviet threat. We now turn to the motivations of French, British, and German decision-makers.

Despite de Gaulle's establishment of a nuclear *force de frappe* and partial withdrawal from NATO, French leaders believed that cooperation with NATO was important to balance against the Soviet Union. General Michel Fourquet, chief of staff of the armed forces, noted in March 1969 that a Soviet conventional attack from the east would require a coordinated response from NATO countries: "Engaged along the northern and eastern borders against an enemy coming from the East, the [French] force will normally act in close coordination with the forces of our allies."[66] This recognition of the need for future NATO cooperation was apparent in other sources such as the 1972 *Livre blanc sur la défense nationale* (the French white paper on national defense).

---

[66] See General Michel Fourquet, "Emploi des différents systèmes de forces dans le cadre de la stratégie de dissuasion," *Revue de défense nationale*, Vol. 25, May 1969, pp. 757–67. The translation was drawn from the English version printed as "The Role of the Forces," *Survival*, Vol. 11, No. 7, July 1969, pp. 208. On French military independence also see the "Loi de Programme 1971–1975," in Dominique David, ed., *La politique de défense de la France: Textes et documents* (Paris: Fondation pour les études de défense nationale, 1989).

Defense Minister Michel Debré believed that NATO arms collaboration was important to deter Soviet aggression and to maximize efficiency in a war against the Soviets.[67] One aspect of NATO cooperation involved transatlantic M&As.

Successive French governments played the central role in M&A policies, which owned nearly four-fifths of the French defense industry.[68] As one study on French arms concluded: "The presence of state officials through the [defense] consolidation process has been *pervasive*. Each step toward concentration has been under the prodding or oversight of a host of interested political leaders and civilian and military functionaries."[69] While the primary goal of the government was to pursue consolidation to create French national champions in the defense sector, some transatlantic M&As were encouraged to increase NATO efficiency. For example, Thomson-CSF acquired such US defense firms in the 1980s as Ocean Defense Corporation, which manufactured helicopter sonar and equipment for antisubmarine warfare, and Wilcox Electric, which produced microwave landing systems. In the aerospace industry a series of domestic and transatlantic mergers established Dassault-Breguet as one of NATO's primary producers of military aircraft, including the Mirage series of fighter aircraft and the Atlantique reconnaissance aircraft.

In Britain, there were a limited number of transnational M&As during the Cold War, and most were transatlantic. Examples of transatlantic M&As involving British firms included British Aerospace's acquisition of such US firms as Nanoquest, Sperry Gyroscope, Reflectone, and Steinheil Optronics. Furthermore, Plessey acquired several US firms such as Electronic Systems Division, Sippican, and Singer Electronics. In the wake of British Prime Minister Margaret Thatcher's decision to privatize the British defense industry in the 1980s, firms such as British Aerospace "were encouraged to adopt an international orientation," especially among NATO countries, so that they could "provide less

[67] Michel Debré, "France's Global Strategy," *Foreign Affairs*, Vol. 49, No. 3, April 1971, pp. 400–1.

[68] On the French government and consolidation see André Collet, *Les industries d'armement* (Paris: Presses Universitaires de France, 1988), p. 30; US Congress, Office of Technology Assessment, *Lessons in Restructuring the Defense Industry: The French Experience*, OTA-BP-ISC-96 (Washington, DC: US Government Printing Office, June 1992), p. 8. On nationalization see also Peter A. Hall, *Governing the Economy: The Politics of State Intervention in Britain and France* (New York: Oxford University Press, 1986), p. 149 and 202–6. See also Commissariat Général du Plan, IVe *Plan de développement économique et social 1962–1965* (Paris: Documentation française, 1965); R. Vernon, ed., *Big Business and the State* (Cambridge, MA: Harvard University Press, 1974).

[69] Kolodziej, *Making and Marketing Arms*, p. 237 (emphasis added).

expensive technology and subsystems."[70] Transatlantic M&As were
acceptable because they facilitated NATO's fighting effectiveness.

In West Germany, transatlantic defense consolidation through M&As
was important for efficiency reasons because of the Soviet threat. The
1984 German *White Paper* argued, "The military aim is the standardization of military equipment and procedures."[71] Consequently, the
German government encouraged some transatlantic M&A activity
during the Cold War. For instance, Daimler-Benz acquired the industrial automation systems division of the US firm Gould, and Siemens
acquired US defense firms Bendix and Cardion.[72] However, most
M&As in Germany during the Cold War were domestic, and the
government played an integral role. Perhaps the starkest example was
Daimler Benz's takeover of Messerschmidt-Boelkow-Blohm in 1989,
in which the federal Ministry of Economics in Bonn initiated and
negotiated the merger.[73] In sum, most transnational M&As involving
European defense firms were transatlantic because of the bipolar nature
of the international system and the need to balance Soviet power.

The rise of Europe

The structural shift from bipolarity to unipolarity caused a notable shift
in the European defense industry. As Figure 5.3 illustrates, there has
been a substantial increase in intra-European codevelopment and coproduction weapons projects in the post-Cold War era. This marked a stark
contrast with the Cold War. The percentage of intra-European projects
increased from 42 percent and 43 percent in the 1970s and 1980s,
respectively, to 57 percent in the 1990s. European defense firms have
been almost twice as likely to pursue coproduction and codevelopment
projects with each other than with US firms, and over three times more
likely than with defense firms from other regions. In addition, there has
been a substantial increase in intra-European defense mergers and
acquisitions in the post-Cold War. The percentage of intra-European
M&As increased from 43 percent in the 1980s to 55 percent in the

---

[70] Trevor Taylor, "The British Restructuring Experience," in Michael Brzoska and Peter
Lock, eds., *Restructuring of Arms Production in Western Europe* (New York: Oxford
University Press, 1992), p. 87.
[71] *White Paper 1985*, p. 360.
[72] See, for example, "Gould to Sell Unit to AEG," *New York Times*, May 3, 1988, p. D4;
Michael Farr, "A 'Sleeping Giant' Goes Global," *New York Times*, December 12, 1988,
p. D1.
[73] Brzoska and Lock, "Daimler Benz: The Final Stage of Concentration in German Arms
Production?", in Brzoska and Lock, eds., *Restructuring of Arms Production in Western
Europe*, pp. 118–30.

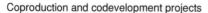

Coproduction and codevelopment projects

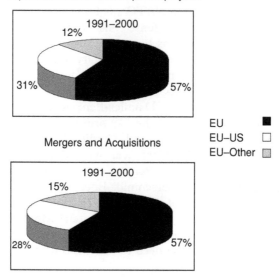

Figure 5.3. Post-Cold War defense cooperation.

1990s, and the percentage of European–American M&As decreased from 55 percent in the 1980s to 32 percent in the 1990s. European defense firms have been nearly twice as likely to pursue M&As with each other than with American defense firms, and nearly three times as likely to pursue M&As with each other than with firms from other regions.

The changing structure of the international system explains the shift to intra-European defense cooperation. In a unipolar system, European Union states led by Germany, France, and Britain have collaborated in the defense industry to decrease reliance on the United States and increase their economic and defense power. To be clear, the US does not present a military threat to Europe. Rather, collaboration decreases reliance on the US and its defense industry, and ensures that European states have autonomous military capabilities. In addition, collaboration increases the global power of European defense firms and allows them to compete more effectively with the United States in such areas as arms sales and the spin-offs that defense industries can produce.

Creating fortress Europe

The structural shift from bipolarity to unipolarity caused a notable shift in the procurement behavior of European states. While most coproduction and codevelopment projects during the Cold War were transatlantic and geared toward NATO cooperation, there was a substantial increase in the number and percentage of intra-European projects in the 1990s. In the absence of the Soviet threat, EU states became increasingly concerned about US dominance of the arms market. Furthermore, procurement collaboration was also necessary to increase military efficiency for use abroad as the EU pushed to develop a CFSP and ESDP. British and French leaders concluded at the 1998 St. Malo summit: "The European Union needs to be in a position to play its full role on the international stage ... To this end, the Union must have the capacity for autonomous action, backed up by credible military forces, the means to decide to use them and a readiness to do so, in order to respond to international crises."[74]

The risk of not collaborating was high. The European Advisory Group on Aerospace, which included such participants as the EU high representative for CFSP and European aerospace industry chairmen, argued in a report titled *Strategic Aerospace Review for the 21st Century* that the failure to pursue intra-European collaboration would lead to US dominance of the European arms market. "Unless Europe maintains these capabilities and develops them further," it contended, "there is a real risk that Europe's ability to act will be determined by the US through its dominance over the supply of certain types of equipment, or support to systems already delivered."[75]

In France the DGA, not French defense firms, played the central role in pushing for intra-European collaboration. As laid out in its yearly *Rapport d'activité*, the DGA argued that collaboration was important to increase European power and military effectiveness.[76] The power of the United States defense industry also provided a critical impetus. As the Ministry of Defense's *Projet de loi* explained: "[The US's] global intention demands a massive reinforcement of the defense effort, which in turns benefits research and development of new defense systems, increasing the technological and military gulf between Europe and the United States." In response to US power, it continued, France and Europe needed to "include an increase in defense effort" in such areas

---

[74] Text of a joint statement by the British and French Governments, Franco-British summit, St. Malo, France, December 4, 1998.

[75] *Strategic Aerospace Review for the 21st Century: Creating a Coherent Market and Policy Framework for a Vital European Industry*, in Burkhard Schmitt, ed., *European Armaments Cooperation: Core Documents*, Chaillot Paper 59 (Paris: Institute for Security Studies, 2003), p. 152.

[76] French General Delegation for Armament, *Rapport d'activité 2000* (Paris: Délégation générale pour l'armement, 2000), p. 38.

as weapons production.[77] This made projects such as the Galileo global navigation satellite system important so that, in the words of France's transport minister, "the European Union [could] liberate itself from dependence on the American GPS system."[78] Consequently, the DGA worked closely with the governments of Britain and Germany to co-ordinate long-term procurement planning, future preparedness, and research and technology.[79] Examples of French involvement in intra-European projects in the post-Cold War era included Galileo, the 140-mm tank gun, PAAMS main missile system, Europatrol combat ship, MU-90 torpedo, and Horizon frigate.

In Britain, Ministry of Defence officials also pushed for intra-European collaboration to build power. As the Ministry of Defence's *Defence Industrial Policy* argued: "The US is the most important creator of new defence technology, and there is an increasing disparity between its defence spending to that of Europe." In response to US power and to the US government's establishment of barriers to entry into its defense market, the British Ministry of Defence argued that "there are significant potential benefits to be gained from a better function-ing European market, a more efficient supplier base, and better prioritization of research and technology budgets in Europe."[80] While British policymakers supported transatlantic collaboration during the Cold War, and have engaged in some projects with US firms, they have favored European codevelopment and coproduction projects in the post-Cold War era. Ministry of Defence documents have been explicit about this.[81] Examples of British involvement in intra-European weapons collaboration included the Storm Shadow land attack cruise missile, Eurofighter Typhoon, and Europatrol maritime patrol aircraft.

German leaders likewise advocated European procurement co-operation to aggregate power and reduce reliance on the US, and they

---

[77] French Ministry of Defence, *Projet de loi de programmation militaire 2003–2008* (Paris: Ministère de la Défense, 2002).

[78] Ian Black, "European Satellite Plan Ruffles US Feathers," *Guardian*, March 27, 2002, p. 17; Thomas Fuller, "EU Positions Its Challenge to GPS," *International Herald Tribune*, March 27, 2002, p. 1.

[79] French General Delegation for Armament, *Rapport d'activité 2001* (Paris: Délégation générale pour l'armement, 2001), pp. 48–51.

[80] UK Ministry of Defence, *Defence Industrial Policy*, Paper No. 5 (London: Ministry of Defence, 2002), p. 9.

[81] See, for example, UK Ministry of Defence, *European Defence Policy*, Paper No. 3 (London: HMSO, 2001); *The Defence White Paper, 1999*, Cm 4446 (London: HMSO, 1999), paras 99–103; *The Strategic Defence Review, 1998*, Cm 3999 (London: HMSO, 1998), paras 162–8.

pushed for greater intra-European collaboration.[82] As German Chancellor Gerhard Schröder argued:

Europe would not have an internationally successful aircraft industry had not some countries shown the will to challenge US dominance. Airbus's success shows the importance of setting strategic priorities. Galileo, the European satellite system agreed at the recent Barcelona European summit, is another such example. In short, Europe needs to become better at pooling resources and working towards a strategic vision.

German Ministry of Defense documents have explicitly argued that intra-European weapons collaboration is critical to improve European economic and military efficiency – particularly in light of the creation of a common foreign and security policy and a European security and defense policy.[83] The army's report *Bundeswehr 2002: Sachstund und Perspektiven* noted that European weapons cooperation is an integral part of the Common Foreign and Security Policy and "occupies a key position in the efforts to consolidate the political unification of Europe."[84] Indeed, Germany has been one of the strongest supporters of European armaments collaboration, and German defense firms have been involved in almost every major coproduction and codevelopment project in the post-Cold War era. Examples include the Boxer armored utility vehicle, Tiger attack helicopter, Taurus precision-guided missile, and Trigate anti-tank guided missile.

In addition, two projects clearly illustrate how the changing structure of the international system created a strong incentive for intra-European collaboration: (1) the Galileo navigation system; and (2) the A400M strategic lift.[85]

First, European governments began development of the Galileo global navigation satellite system in the late 1990s to aggregate power and decrease reliance on the United States.[86] European governments could have continued relying on the US's global positioning system (GPS) for navigation, but they became increasingly concerned about the security of supply. A European Commission's *White Paper* on European

[82] See, for example, Sarotte, *German Military Reform and European Security*, pp. 48–52.
[83] German Federal Minister of Defense, *The Bundeswehr – Advancing Steadily into the 21st Century* (Berlin: Federal Minister of Defense, 2000), para. 48; *White Paper on the Security of the Federal Republic of Germany and the Situation and Future of the Bundeswehr 1994* (Bonn: Federal Minister of Defense, 1994), para. 594.
[84] German Secretary of Defense, *Bundeswehr 2002: Sachstand und Perspektiven* (Berlin: Bundesministerium der Verteidigung, 2002), p. 22.
[85] Seth G. Jones, "Arming Europe," *National Interest*, No. 82, Winter 2005/2006, pp. 62–8.
[86] On Galileo and transatlantic relations see David Braunschvig, Richard L. Garwin, and Jeremy C. Marwell, "Space Diplomacy," *Foreign Affairs*, Vol. 82, No. 4, July/August 2003, pp. 156–64.

transport policy noted, "Only the USA (GPS) and Russia (Glonass) currently have this technology, both being financed for military purposes, with the result that the signals can be blocked or jammed at any moment to protect these countries' own interests. This happened during the Kosovo war, when the United States cut the GPS signal . . . Europe cannot afford to be totally dependent on third countries in such strategic areas."[87] European policymakers initiated negotiations for Galileo in the late 1990s. Consequently, in 1999 European governments began development of Galileo, which is composed of thirty satellites and ground stations to provide information on the positioning of users in such sectors as defense and transport.[88] It launched the first satellite into space in December 2005 from Kazakhstan, as European leaders commented that it signified "independence for the European Union and a scientific success superior to that of the Americans."[89]

Second, European governments agreed to develop and produce the A400M strategic transport plane in the late 1990s to facilitate the undertaking of European military operations autonomous of the US. In the early 1990s policymakers, rather than defense firms, initiated a study of alternative options for replacing their aging fleets of C-130 Hercules and C-160 Transall strategic transport planes. One possibility was to purchase Boeing C-17s and updated Lockheed Martin C-130s, but European military leaders didn't want to rely on the United States for security of supply.[90] Consequently, the armaments directors of several European countries – including France, Germany, and Britain – began a series of feasibility studies to develop a European transport plane. In June 2001 they signed a memorandum of understanding to develop the A400M because "it generates the necessary potential for harmonizing operational and support arrangements and offers a large margin for cost savings by means of cooperation. It also paves the way for greater task sharing in meeting European military air transport demands."[91]

[87] Commission of the EC, *White Paper – European Transport Policy for 2010: Time to Decide,* Com 370/2001 (Luxembourg: Office for Official Publications of the European Communities, September 2001), pp. 94–5. Also see *Inception Study to Support the Development of a Business Plan for the GALILEO Programme,* TREN/B5/23–2001 (Brussels: PricewaterhouseCoopers, 2001), p. 2.
[88] Brooks Tigner, "EU Lays Foundation for MilSpace Presence," *Defense News,* July 19, 2004.
[89] "A System to Make Jove Proud," *Economist,* December 29, 2005; George Parker and John Thornhill, "European Navigation Satellite a Challenge for US Galileo," *Financial Times,* December 29, 2005, p. 6.
[90] Interview with French Ministry of Defense official, Washington, June 19, 2001.
[91] "Press release for the signature ceremony of the A400M program," June 19, 2001, Ministère de la défense de la France (www.defense.gouv.fr).

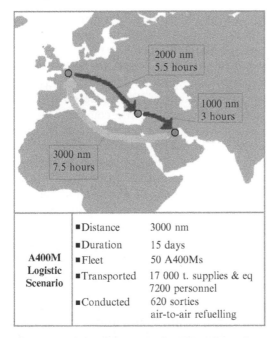

Figure 5.4. A400M scenario for EU military force.

The A400M was specifically designed to meet the cargo load requirements of participating European nations and to include all likely
equipment – such as European armored vehicles, missile systems,
helicopters, and trucks – needed for joint rapid reaction forces. As
British Defence Secretary Geoffrey Hoon noted, "A400M is the best
deal" for Britain because it "delivers clear benefits in interoperability
and shared development and through life costs."[92] Figure 5.4 illustrates
one EU scenario for the A400M: the deployment of a European rapid
reaction military force to the Middle East in response to instability,
consisting of air mobile brigade troops with additional fire support,
helicopters, and fighter squadrons. This scenario would involve 7,200
European personnel, 2,500 wheeled and tracked vehicles (including
artillery and light armor), 23 helicopters, and support material for
twenty-four fighter aircraft. Approximately fifty A400M transport
planes would need to fly the 17,000 tons of equipment to the Gulf

---

[92] "Hoon Welcomes Progress on A400M," December 18, 2001 (www.mod.uk/dpa/
pressoffice).

within fifteen days.[93] In sum, European governments procured the A400M to provide them with an autonomous transport capability and to decrease reliance on the United States.

In addition, several institutional developments have been critical in promoting intra-European collaboration. One was the Letter of Intent (LoI) signed by the defense ministers of France, Germany, Britain, Italy, Spain, and Sweden, which argued that the countries should harmonize the military requirements of their armed forces. It continued by noting that future capabilities should be geared toward future European military operations, including peacekeeping and more demanding missions.[94] As US policymakers quickly realized, the LoI was important because it demonstrated the intentions of European leaders to increase intra-European codevelopment and coproduction projects at the expense of transatlantic ones.

Another development was the establishment of the institution OCCAR (Organisation Conjoint de Coopération en matière d'Armement) by France, Germany, the UK, and Italy to manage a number of important intra-European weapons programs. Defense ministers agreed that collaboration was critical "in order to improve efficiency and reduce costs" because the strengthening of cooperation "in defence equipment will contribute to the establishment of a European security and defense identity."[95] Programs managed by OCCAR included the Boxer armored utility vehicle, ROLAND surface-to-air missile, Tiger attack helicopter, COBRA long-range battlefield radar, A400M strategic airlift, and FSAF surface-to-air anti-missile system.

In addition, the European Council established the European Defense Agency to improve European military capabilities, consolidate defense research and technology, and develop promote armaments cooperation.[96] The high representative for common foreign and security policy

---

[93] *Scenario: Rapid Reaction Force* (Blagnac Cedex, France: Airbus Military, 2005). Also see Damian Kemp, "Strategic Airlift," *Jane's Defence Weekly*, June 15, 2005.

[94] "Letter of Intent between the Minister of Defense of the French Republic, the Federal Minister of Defense of the Republic of Germany, the Minister of Defense of the Republic of Italy, the Minister of Defense of the Kingdom of Spain, the Minister of Defense of the Kingdom of Sweden, and the Secretary of State for Defense of the United Kingdom of Great Britain and Northern Ireland Concerning Measures to Facilitate the Restructuring of the European Defense Industry," July 6, 1998. Published in Schmitt, ed., *Between Cooperation*, p. 149.

[95] Convention on the Establishment of the Organisation for Joint Armament Cooperation, OCCAR, Bonn: OCCAR, 1998, p. 7.

[96] Council Joint Action on the Establishment of the European Defense Agency, 2004/551/CFSP, July 12, 2004; Council of the European Union, *Agency in the Field of Defense Capabilities Development, Research, Acquisition, and Armaments* (Brussels: Council of the EU, May 17, 2004).

is head of the agency, and EU ministers of defense comprise its steering board. With an initial budget of €20 million and a staff of eighty, it had few resources and little power at the outset.[97] It initially managed several major projects:

- *UAVs and ISTAR* – launched ad hoc projects by member states on long endurance unmanned aerial vehicles (UAVs) and wider intelligence, surveillance, target acquisition and reconnaissance (ISTAR) capabilities. The Euroupean Defense Agency was particularly involved in encouraging joint technological developments among European states to increase standardization and interoperability.
- *Command, control, and communication* – improved coordination on command, control, and communiciations technologies; set requirements for future satellite communications; and assessed the scope for a joint civil–military effort regarding software defined radio.
- *Armored fighting vehicles* – developed proposals for collaborative technology development and procurement programs regarding armored fighting vehicles. The European Defense Agency was particularly interested in technologies that led to the establishment of a European family of vehicles.
- *Code of conduct for defence procurement* – assisted in the implementation of a revised code of conduct, including further work on related issues such as security of supply.[98]

The European Defense Agency was also involved in other issues, such as developing network enabled capabilities, solutions to air-to-air refueling challenges, detection and defense against improvised explosive devices, and operational intelligence and network connections for EU battlegroups.[99] A number of European defense officials argued that the European Defense Agency should develop into a legitimate European procurement agency.[100] This would mean integrating such components as OCCAR, LoI, Western European Armaments Group, and industry

[97] European Council, *Second Meeting of the EDA's Steering Board* (Brussels: European Council, November 2004); Martin Aguera, "Execs Blast EU Defense Agency's Slow Start," *Defense News*, November 7, 2005, p. 4.
[98] European Defense Agency, *EDA Bulletin*, Issue 1 (Brussels: EDA, December 2005); Guy Anderson, "EDA Outlines 2006 Objectives," *Jane's Defence Weekly*, January 11, 2006; European Council, *EDA Work Programme for 2006* (Brussels: European Council, November 2005); Nick Witney, "Closing the Capability Gap: The EDA's Role as Catalyst and Coordinator," presentation at the Royal Institute for International Affairs, London, December 6, 2004.
[99] European Council, *EDA Work Programme for 2006*; European Defense Agency, *EDA Bulletin*, Issue 1.
[100] Nick Witney, "Closing the Capability Gap."

bodies such as the AeroSpace and Defence Industries Association of Europe. More importantly, it would mean that the European Defense Agency would have significant power in developing capabilities requirements; determining and promoting defense research, development, and investment projects; and managing land, aerospace, and maritime defense programs. The European Defense Agency would play a significant role in implementing the European Capability Action Plan (ECAP) and remedying European defense shortfalls.[101]

In sum, European weapons development and production behavior is explained by a desire to build power and decrease reliance on the US in a unipolar system. There was little intra-European collaboration in the Cold War because European states were primarily concerned about balancing the USSR through NATO. As one study in 1977 rather bluntly concluded: "Despite a number of successful joint projects involving two or sometimes three countries, all attempts so far to produce a sustained and collective European effort have failed."[102] However, there was a significant change in the post-Cold War era and a notable increase in intra-European coproduction and codevelopment projects.

The race for critical mass

The structural shift from bipolarity to unipolarity at the end of the Cold War marked a significant shift in European M&A activity. European states adopted a procurement policy that stressed intra-European collaboration in the post-Cold War era to decrease reliance on the United States and increase European power abroad. As one study concluded, in the post-Cold War era "the perception of an American 'threat' was widespread in politico-industrial circles in Europe . . . Faced with the new American giants, national champions in Europe were obliged to launch into a race for critical mass."[103] Perhaps the most significant example was the creation of European Aeronautic, Defense, and Space company (EADS). It included the merger of Germany's

---

[101] Council of the European Union, *Military Capability Commitment Conference: Declaration on European Military Capabilities* (Brussels: European Council, November 2004). The European Capability Action Plan was launched at the end of 2001 to remedy shortcomings in the Helsinki Headline Goal. It was based on several principles: enhancing efficiency of European military capability efforts; encouraging a "bottom-up" approach to European defense cooperation; improving coordination between the EU and NATO; and gaining broader public support.

[102] D. C. R. Heyhoe, *The Alliance and Europe: Part VI, The European Programme Group*, Adelphi Paper 129 (London: International Institute for Strategic Studies, 1976/1977), p. 1.

[103] Schmitt, *From Cooperation to Integration*, pp. 25–6.

Daimler-Chrysler Aerospace, Spain's Construcciones Aeronauticas SA, and France's Aérospatiale Matra. Again, national governments played a pivotal role in pushing for a transnational European weapons industry. European defense firms were almost twice as likely to pursue M&As with each other than with American firms, and nearly three times as likely than with firms from other regions.

The US defense industry consolidated in the early 1990s and produced several giant defense firms led by Lockheed Martin and Boeing that threatened to dominate the global arms market and jeopardize other states' security of supply. During what was referred to as the "last supper," Secretary of Defense Les Aspin and Deputy Secretary William Perry invited a small number of defense industry executives to dinner at the Pentagon in 1993. After the dinner, Aspin and Perry announced that at least half the companies at the dinner would not be needed in five years, and warned that the Department of Defense was ready to see some firms exit the market.[104] Since the US defense budget was steadily decreasing in the wake of the Soviet collapse, US government leaders pushed for consolidation to increase efficiency in the US defense market and augment greater global competitiveness. For example, Lockheed acquired the Fort Worth division of General Dynamics in 1993 and then merged with the missile manufacturer Martin Marietta in 1995 to form Lockheed Martin. Grumman was salvaged from near bankruptcy and acquired by Northrop in 1994. Boeing purchased McDonnell Douglas.[105] By the late 1990s Lockheed Martin and Boeing were the dominant arms-producing firms in the world, with arms sales of $18.5 billion and $14.5 billion respectively.[106] Furthermore, US defense firms were the most technologically advanced in the world, and, as one scholar warned: "For the first time in modern history, one country is on the verge of monopolizing the international arms trade."[107]

US consolidation in the 1990s caused deep concern in European capitals. As Thomas Enders, then-CEO of defense and security systems

[104] Norman R. Augustine, "Reshaping an Industry: Lockheed Martin's Survival Story," *Harvard Business Review*, May–June 1997, pp. 83–94; John J. Dowdy "Winners and Losers in the Arms Industry Downturn," *Foreign Policy*, Vol. 107, Summer 1997, pp. 88–101.
[105] Pages, "Defense Mergers," in Markusen and Costigan, eds., *Arming the Future*, pp. 207–223; Oden, "Cashing in, Cashing out, and Converting," in Markusen and Costigan, eds., *Arming the Future*, pp. 74–105.
[106] *SIPRI Yearbook 1999*, p. 413.
[107] Ethan B. Kapstein, "America's Arms-Trade Monopoly," *Foreign Affairs*, Vol. 73, No. 3, May/June 1994, p. 13. Also see Jens Van Scherpenberg, "Transatlantic Competition and European Defence Industries: A New Look at the Trade-Defence Linkage," *International Affairs*, Vol. 73, No. 1, 1997, pp. 99–122.

at EADS and eventually CEO of EADS, argued: "By 1996, in view of the mega-mergers in the US, it was clear to European industry leaders that national consolidation and joint ventures were inadequate counters to the competitive challenge being posed by US industry."[108] In a December 1997 message to European defense firms, French President Jacques Chirac, British Prime Minister Tony Blair, and German Chancellor Helmut Kohl argued that they shared "a vital political and economic interest in an efficient and globally competitive European aerospace industry. This will help to improve Europe's position in the global market, to promote European security, and ensure that Europe will play a full role in its defense." One important step in this direction, they contended, was consolidation of the defense industry along European lines: "We are agreed on the urgent need to restructure the aerospace and defense electronics industries. This should embrace civil and military activities in the field of aerospace, and should lead to European integration based on balanced partnership."[109]

A year later the defense ministers of France, Germany, Britain, Italy, Spain, and Sweden signed the LoI to facilitate the restructuring of the European defense industry.[110] Furthermore, the European Advisory Group on Aerospace argued in its *Strategic Aerospace Review for the 21st Century* of the critical need to compete with the United States:

As regards international competition, US companies operate in the world's single largest home market and benefit from a highly supportive operation framework which is designed to underpin a declared policy aim to maintain US supremacy in aerospace . . . This situation poses a constant challenge to European industry and cannot but affect its competitive position . . . Within Europe major restructuring has taken place in recent years, leading to an industry organized on a European scale, as a competitor and partner of its powerful US counterpart.[111]

[108] Thomas Enders, "Defense Industry Restructuring and the Implications of ESDI/DCI," at XVIIth International Workshop: On Political-Military Decision Making in the Atlantic Alliance, Berlin, Germany, June 2–5, 2000.

[109] "Joint Statement by the President of the Republic and the French Prime Minister, the Chancellor of the Federal Republic of Germany, and the Prime Minister of the United Kingdom," December 9, 1997. Published in Schmitt, ed., *Between Cooperation and Competition*, p. 144.

[110] "Letter of Intent between the Minister of Defense of the French Republic, the Federal Minister of Defense of the Republic of Germany, the Minister of Defense of the Republic of Italy, the Minister of Defense of the Kingdom of Spain, the Minister of Defense of the Kingdom of Sweden, and the Secretary of State for Defense of the United Kingdom of Great Britain and Northern Ireland Concerning Measures to Facilitate the Restructuring of the European Defense Industry," July 6, 1998. Published in Schmitt, ed., *Between Cooperation and Competition*, pp. 146, 149.

[111] *STAR 21: Strategic Aerospace Review for the 21st Century*, cited in Burkard Schmitt, *European Armaments Cooperation: Core Documents*, Chaillot Paper 59 (Paris: Institute for Security Studies, 2003), p. 131.

As Table 5.2 highlights, by 2005 Europe had four of the top ten largest defense firms in the world: BAE Systems, Thales, EADS, and Finmeccanica. This marked a notable change from 1994, when European countries had only two of the top ten firms.

In France, the DGA played the central role in encouraging defense industry consolidation along European lines. As laid out in its *Rapport d'activité*, the DGA argued that intra-European defense consolidation had occurred "with the encouragement of heads of State and government" to aggregate European power.[112] The power and impetus to pursue European consolidation came from the government, which held shares in several major defense firms such as Dassault and SNECMA and exercised decisive clout.[113] French Prime Minister Lionel Jospin noted following the creation of EADS that "in view of the formation of very large-scale international groups, particularly American ones, it was becoming vitally important to group together the European forces."[114] Examples of French involvement in intra-European M&As included Thomson-CSF's acquisition of the defense electronics business of the Philips group – which included the Dutch company Signaal, the Belgian company MBLE, and the French company TRT – and the British firm Racal Electronics. Other examples included SNECMA's acquisition of the Belgian firm FN Moteurs, the Norwegian firm Norsk Jet Motors, and British TI Group's landing gear business. In short, as French Defense Minister Alain Richard summed up, intra-European defense consolidation increased Europe's ability "to gain shares in a highly competitive market."[115]

British Ministry of Defence documents in the post-Cold War era also noted the desire to increase power. The 1999 *White Paper*, for example, stated that "we are working with the Governments of France, Germany, Italy, Spain and Sweden to develop a consistent approach to facilitate restructuring in Europe" for the purposes of "improving the

[112] French Delegation for Armament, *Rapport d'activité 2000*, p. 43.
[113] See the comments by Philippe Humbert, Vice President for International Development of SNECMA, "European before Transatlantic Consolidation", in *European Defense Industrial Consolidation: Implications for U.S. Industry and Policy* (Washington: Center for Strategic and International Studies, December 2001), p. 8. Also see Frédérique Sachwald, *Defence Industry Restructuring: The End of an Economic Exception* (Paris: Institut Français des relations internationals, 1999), p. 45.
[114] "Jospin: Aerospatiale Matra-DASA Merger 'Powerful Tool,'" *Paris AFP*, October 14, 1999.
[115] Alain Richard, "European Defense," Speech at the Annual Defense Dinner of the London Chamber of Commerce and Industry, London, May 17, 2001.

Table 5.2. *Top ten global arms-producing companies*

1994		
Company	Country	Arms Sales (US$ million)
Lockheed	US	10,070
McDonnell Douglas	US	9,050
General Motors	US	6,900
Martin Marietta	US	6,500
British Aerospace	UK	5,950
Raytheon	US	4,500
Northrop	US	4,480
Thomson S.A.	France	4,240
United Technologies	US	4,200
Boeing	US	3,800

2005		
Company	Country	Arms Sales (US$ million)
Lockheed Martin	US	24,910
Boeing	US	24,370
Northrop Grumman	US	22,720
BAE Systems	UK	15,760
Raytheon	US	15,450
General Dynamics	US	13,100
Thales	France	8,350
EADS	Europe	8,010
United Technologies	US	6,210
Finmeccanica	Italy	5,290

Source: SIPRI, *Yearbook 1995*, p. 485 for 1994 data; SIPRI, *Yearbook 2005*, p. 406 for 2005 data.

methodology for harmonising key military requirements."[116] Furthermore, it argued that consolidation would lead to greater European military effectiveness. British Aerospace (renamed BAE Systems in 1999) was particularly active, acquiring a number of European companies like Heckler & Koch (Germany), a 30 percent stake in Saab

[116] UK Ministry of Defence, *The Defence White Paper 1999* (London: Ministry of Defence, 1999), para. 100.

(Sweden), and Muiden Chemie (Netherlands). As noted later in this chapter, BAE Systems closely collaborated with American defense firms through such projects as the Joint Strike Fighter and the ASTOR ground surveillance system. In 2005, it acquired the US firm United Defense Industries, which manufactured the Bradley combat system vehicle.[117] But Europe is still its largest market.

In Germany, defense officials advocated European M&As as a way to increase power.[118] German support for consolidation was apparent in the government's participation in the LoI and the December 1997 joint statement. More importantly, the establishment of the transnational EADS in 1999 left Germany with *no major domestic defense company*. Rheinmetall, which produced ammunition and other defense equipment, was Germany's largest national firm measured in arms sales. That placed it twenty-second among firms from OECD and developing countries, well behind Europe's major defense giants such as British Aerospace, EADS, and France's Thales.[119] As European Defense Minister Rudolf Scharping argued, European governments have taken "major steps to establish new political and military structures and develop more effective military capabilities for the full range of conflict prevention and crisis management tasks defined in the EU Treaty." One of the most important steps, he continued, was "the intensification of co-operation with the European defense industry, with the merger of DASA, Aerospatiale and CASA to form EADS lending the key impetus."[120]

Indeed, two M&A examples highlight the desire of EU states to aggregate resources to decrease reliance on the US and increase European power. First, the establishment of EADS in 2000 was a significant step toward defense consolidation by creating a transnational European defense giant capable of competing with US firms Boeing

---

[117] Damian Kemp, "ASTOR System Passes Another Major Milestone," *Jane's Defense Weekly*, July 6, 2005; Ethan B. Kapstein, "Capturing Fortress Europe: International Collaboration and the Joint Strike Fighter," *Survival*, Vol. 46, No. 3, Autumn 2004, pp. 137–60; Griff Witte, "BAE to Buy Maker of Bradley Vehicles," *Washington Post*, March 8, 2005, p. E1.

[118] Martin Agüera, "German Arms Exporters Eye Mergers for Survival," *Defense News*, September 17–23, 2001, p. 32. At the same time, however, German government officials blocked a French bid in 2005 for EADS to acquire Thales out of concern that the merger would give the French side greater weight in the company. David Mulholland, "German Industry: Feeling the Squeeze," *Jane's Defence Weekly*, March 30, 2005.

[119] Jane's Defense Database.

[120] Rudolf Scharping, "Euro-Atlantic Security and Regional Stability in the 21st Century," Eisenhower lecture, NATO Defense College in Rome, January 11, 2000.

and Lockheed Martin and producing a variety of advanced armaments such as the Eurofighter combat aircraft, Eurocopter, A400M transport aircraft, and strategic weapons. As EADS Joint Executive Chairmen Rainer Hertrich and Philippe Camus acknowledged: "Let us dare to assert it: EADS has, right at its birth, the scale of a European Boeing."[121] Moreover, French Defense Minister Alain Richard and Economy Minister Laurent Fabius jointly noted that the establishment of EADS "goes in line with the European policy promoting an autonomous defense industry that is globally competitive."[122]

Following the December 1997 declaration by French, German, and British leaders for regional consolidation, government and industry negotiations commenced regarding the creation of a European defense company. The defense ministers of Britain, France, Germany, Italy, Spain, and Sweden asked several of Europe's major defense companies to submit a series of reports in March and November 1998 outlining plans for the creation of a European aerospace and defense company.[123] The successive reports submitted by industry officials argued that the target should be a single, integrated European company that could produce weapons in a number of key defense sectors. While the British government placed substantial pressure on British Aerospace to join EADS, company executives defied the government and merged with Marconi. This left German, French, and Spanish companies and government officials to negotiate a merger. In the summer of 1999, secret negotiations between the shareholders of Daimler-Chrysler, the Spanish state holding company SEPI, the Laragardère Group, and the German, Spanish, and French governments eventually led to the creation of EADS.[124] French government officials such as Finance Minister Dominique Strauss-Kahn played a particularly important role in the negotiations. The result was the creation of one Europe's largest defense companies, which produces a number of weapons and systems in such sectors as civil and military transport aircraft, combat and military

---

[121] Rainer Hertrich and Philippe Camus, "EADS or the Ambition to Make Europe Win," *Le Monde*, June 8, 2000.
[122] "Europe to Create World No. 2 Missiles Firm," *Xinhua General News Service*, April 27, 2001.
[123] Schmitt, *From Cooperation to Integration*, pp. 29–56.
[124] A number of government officials were involved in the secret negotiations. John Rossant, "Birth of a Giant," *Business Week*, July 10, 2000, p. 170; Pierre Sparaco, "EADS Completes Europe's Long-Awaited Restructuring," *Aviation Week & Space Technology*, Vol. 153, No. 4, July 24, 2000, pp. 103–9; Yolande Baldeweck and Vianney Aubert, "Aerospatiale Matra et Dasa fusionnent," *Le Figaro*, October 15, 1999.

mission aircraft, helicopters, space launchers, satellites, guided weapons, and defense and aerospace systems.

Second, the creation of MBDA in the late 1990s was a significant step toward consolidating European missile production under one roof and challenging the US missile producer Raytheon.[125] As former Chief Executive Fabrice Brégier argued: "Raytheon is the world leader, and we respect that. But we believe we can challenge that position."[126] It quickly became the second-largest missile firm in the world behind US-based Raytheon. MBDA produces guided weapons for land-based, naval, and airborne requirements such as the Meteor and ASRAAM air-to-air missiles, Storm Shadow/Scalp long-range cruise missile, Brimstone anti-armor weapon, and Exocet anti-ship missile. European governments began pushing for consolidation in missile production in the late 1990s to improve interoperability and decrease reliance on the US. These benefits were particularly important because of the increased prospects for intra-European military cooperation. Following negotiations between executives from British, Italian, and French missile companies and their respective governments, MBDA was established in 1999.

The US's desire to be autarkic has meant that most European defense firms have been unable to penetrate the US market, with the partial exception of BAE Systems. Political obstacles to transatlantic cooperation have included the "Buy American Act," extensive export and technology-transfer controls, and restrictive regulatory processes regarding foreign investment in US firms.[127] For example, Thales sales to North America in 2005 were 10 percent of overall sales.[128] Despite significant efforts by Thales executives to push into the US market in such areas as defense electronics, Thales was unable to improve much from its 9 percent of overall sales to North America in 1999.[129] Finmeccanica's sales to North America also remained remained low

---

[125] See, for example, Katia Vlachos-Dengler, *From National Champions to European Heavyweights: The Development of European Defense Industrial Capabilities across Market Segments*, DB-358-OSD (Santa Monica, CA: RAND, 2002), pp. 63–74.

[126] Daniel Michaels, "European Missile Firm Targets Raytheon," *Wall Street Journal*, August 1, 2000, p. A18. Also see "Interview, Fabrice Brégier: 'Nous avons crée l'Airbus des missiles,'" *Les Echos*, April 27, 2001, p. 14.

[127] On US defense obstacles, see Mark A. Lorell *et al.*, *Going Global? U.S. Government Policy and the Defense Aerospace Industry* (Santa Monica, CA: RAND, 2002); Vlachos-Dengler, *Off Track?*, pp. 106–9; Adams, Cornu, and James, *Between Cooperation and Competition*, pp. 21–49.

[128] Thales Group, *Annual Report 2005* (Paris: Thales Group, 2006), p. 97.

[129] Thomson C. S. F., *Reference Document 1999* (Paris: Thomson C. S. F., 2000), p. 13. On Thales market strategy, also see *Thales Annual Report 2000* (Paris: Thales, 2001).

despite significant efforts to enter the US market. They slightly edged up from 8 percent of total sales in 1999 to 9 percent in 2005.[130] The major exception, however, was BAE Systems, which more than doubled the percentage of exports to North America from 17 percent of overall sales in 1999 to 35 percent in 2005.[131] Indeed, BAE Systems has made a major push to sell to the US market, and has been aided by the UK's close strategic relationship with the United States. Figure 5.5 summarizes 2005 defense sales for Thales, Finmeccanica, and BAE Systems by region. For all of these companies, sales to Europe continue to be the largest percentage of overall sales.

In sum, European M&A activity is best explained by a desire to decrease reliance on the US and increase European power. This marked a striking contrast from the Cold War, when transnational M&As occurred primarily along transatlantic lines. It also contrasted with M&A activity in non-defense sectors, since European companies concentrated more on global than regional consolidation in the post-Cold War era. As with coproduction and codevelopment projects, consolidation has been more frequent in aerospace than in land or naval systems.

Conclusions

The argument laid out in this chapter is strengthened by the absence of persuasive alternatives. First, some might argue that the increasing amount of intra-European collaboration is purely a function of economic interests: it is a result of pressure from domestic actors, especially defense firms, who want to increase profits.[132] Collaboration allows

---

[130] Finmeccanica, *Annual Report 1999* (Rome: Finmeccanica, 2000), p. 44; Finmeccanica, *Annual Report 2005* (Rome: Finmeccanica, 2006), p. 175.

[131] BAE Systems, *Annual Report 1999* (London: BAE Systems, 2000), p. 46; BAE Systems, *Annual Report 2005* (London: BAE Systems, 2006), p. 95.

[132] Andrew Moravcsik, "Arms and Autarky in Modern European History," *Daedalus*, Vol. 120, No. 4, Fall 1991, pp. 23–45; Moravcsik, "Armaments among Allies: European Weapons Collaboration, 1975–1985," in Peter B. Evans, Harold K. Jacobson, and Robert D. Putnam, *Double-Edged Diplomacy: International Bargaining and Domestic Politics* (Berkeley: University of California Press, 1993), pp. 128–67; Moravcsik, "The European Armaments Industry at the Crossroads," *Survival*, Vol. 32, No. 1, January/February 1990, pp. 65–85; Jonathan B. Tucker, "Partners and Rivals: A Model of International Collaboration in Advanced Technology," *International Organization*, Vol. 45, No. 1, Winter 1991, pp. 83–120; Andrew D. James, "The Prospects for a Transatlantic Defence Industry," in Schmitt, ed., *Between Cooperation and Competition*, pp. 93–122; John Lovering, "Which Way to Turn? The European Defense Industry after the Cold War," in Markusen and Costigan, eds., *Arming the Future*, pp. 363–6; Terrence Guay and Robert Callum, "The Transformation and

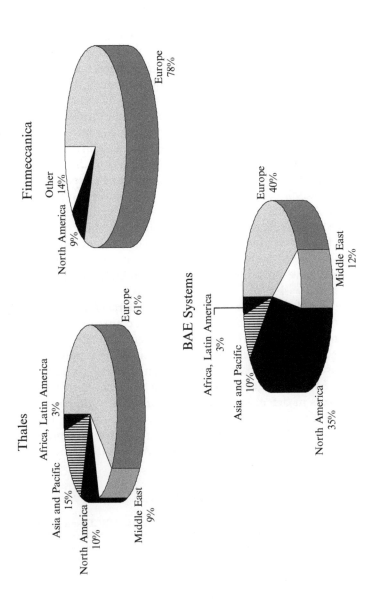

Figure 5.5. Defense sales by region.
Source: Thales Group, *Annual Report 2005* (Paris: Thales Group, 2006), p. 97; Finmeccanica, *Annual Report 2005* (Rome: Finmeccanica, 2006), p. 175; BAE Systems, *Annual Report 2005* (London: BAE Systems, 2006), p. 95.

defense firms to build better weapons and systems, and sell them abroad. Intra-European coproduction, codevelopment, and M&As are less about structural changes than about economics in a highly competitive international market. This argument has its roots in broader liberal theories of international politics, which argue that collaboration is a function of pressure from domestic firms on state preferences.

However, there are several problems with this argument. Perhaps the most significant is that it cannot explain the specific *form* that collaboration took. Why did collaboration occur with other European firms, rather than with firms from other regions? If European states and defense firms were primarily concerned about economic gains, we should expect to see much more collaboration with defense firms from Russia, Asia, or other regions. Yet most collaboration was intra-European. This is particularly puzzling because a number of defense firms outside the US and Europe are much smaller, incapable of self-sufficient production, and hence more likely to pursue collaboration.[133] These conditions should be ripe for greater global collaboration. The existence of a global economy and the speed with which information and goods can travel across the planet have broken down most geographic barriers, making collaboration much easier.[134]

As noted earlier, defense markets are not free markets. Security concerns take precedence over economic ones when it comes to researching, developing, producing, and even selling advanced weapons. States are constrained because of a desire to ensure a security of supply, sustain a strong defense industrial base, and maintain national technological capabilities.[135] Moreover, governments, rather than defense firms, are the central players in defense markets. They are able to determine the size, structure, entry and exit, prices, exports, and ownership of their domestic defense industry.[136] Philippe Humbert, former vice-president of the French defense firm SNECMA, acknowledged that "the role of

Future Prospects of Europe's Defence Industry," *International Affairs*, Vol. 78, No. 4, 2002, pp. 757–76.
[133] Out of the top fifty largest arms-producing companies in the OECD and developing countries, there were only nine firms outside Europe and North America. The list included Mitsubishi Heavy Industries (Japan), Israel Aircraft Industries, Ordnance Factories (India), Mitsubishi Electric (Japan), Kawasaki Heavy Industries (Japan), Singapore Technologies, ST Engineering (Singapore), Elbit Systems (Israel), and Rafael (Israel). SIPRI Arms Industry Database.
[134] John Stopford and Susan Strange, *Rival States, Rival Firms: Competition for World Market Shares* (New York: Cambridge University Press, 1991).
[135] Trevor Taylor and Keith Hayward, *The UK Defence Industrial Base: Development and Future Policy Options* (Washington: Brassey's Defence Publishers, 1989), p. 67.
[136] Sandler and Hartley, *The Economics of Defense*, p. 114.

governments . . . cannot be overstated. Governments hold responsibility over various aspects, including consolidation of demand in the face of constant supply. It is up to policymakers to state the new geopolitical realties of the 21st century, to assess the nature of future threats, and to determine what is needed on the industry side to address those issues most effectively."[137] Economic concerns have played some role in the rise of intra-European collaboration, especially the desire to compete with the United States defense industry. But they have been part of a much broader structural shift in US power in the post-Cold War era.

Second, some might argue that "ideational changes are the key to the Europeanization of defense industry policy" in Europe.[138] The increase in intra-European weapons collaboration is caused by the construction of a European identity, rather than changing structural conditions. Decades of interaction through the European Coal and Steel Community and the European Community caused a change in the interests and identity of European states. German, French, Italian, and other national identities have increasingly been transformed into a collective European identity. However, the empirical evidence does not support this argument. There is no evidence that there was a change in the identity of European states or defense firms in the post-Cold War era. The issue is partly one of timing. If ideational arguments were to explain convincingly the shift in arms production from transatlantic to intra-European, they would have to show that: (a) there was a shift in the identities of European leaders, populations, or defense executives in the late 1980s and early 1990s; and (b) that this shift caused a change in cooperation. I have found little evidence of either.

Indeed, the "Europeanization" of governments and defense executives toward greater collaboration was a result of structural changes, not a constitutive process or solely of economic factors. The empirical evidence strongly indicates that structural changes at the end of the Cold War caused an increase in intra-European M&As, coproduction projects, and codevelopment projects. A preponderant state's defense firms are likely to have global power and reach in an open international trading system. These states will try to expand their arms sales to foreign markets, pursue an arms monopoly, and thereby increase influence over others. These actions create a strong impetus for other states to combine power. In the defense realm, collaboration increases the power and competitiveness of weaker states' defense firms. In the post-Cold War

---

[137] Philippe Humbert, "European before Transatlantic Consolidation," p. 8.
[138] Ulrika Morth and Malena Britz, "European Integration as Organizing: The Case of Armaments," *Journal of Common Market Studies*, Vol. 42, No. 5, 2004, p. 967.

era, the increasing power of the United States and its defense firms, such as Boeing, Lockheed Martin, and Raytheon, had a decisive impact on the actions of European states and firms. US power created deep concern among European government and industry leaders that a failure to collaborate through M&As, coproduction projects, and codevelopment projects might place them in danger of dependence on the US for weapons and platforms.

6   Military forces

Why have European states opted to build forces through the European Union in the post-Cold War era? Furthermore, why have these forces been developed for peacekeeping and humanitarian operations rather than for major theater wars? Since the December 1998 Franco-British summit in St. Malo, France, there has been a significant increase in the construction, organization, and deployment of European military and other crisis response forces. This development marked a substantial change from the Cold War, when European states coordinated their military forces solely through NATO. As William Wallace and Bastian Giegerich argue: "There has been a remarkable increase in the scale, distance and diversity of external operations by European forces – an increase that has scarcely registered in public debate across Europe, let alone the United States."[1]

EU forces have been deployed to Bosnia, the Democratic Republic of Congo, Macedonia, Georgia, Palestinian territory, and Sudan for a range of missions. To conduct these missions, European states have established a rapid reaction capability consisting of up to 60,000 soldiers, deployable within sixty days, sustainable for at least one year, and intended for peacekeeping and humanitarian operations. They have established EU battle groups consisting of 1,500 combat soldiers plus support, as well as gendarmerie and civilian police forces, for international operations. Finally, they have established a permanent political-military structure divided into several levels: a political and security committee that exercises political control and strategic direction of EU military operations; a military committee that provides military advice

---

[1] Bastian Giergerich and William Wallace, "Not Such a Soft Power: The External Deployment of European Forces," *Survival*, Vol. 46, No. 2, Summer 2004, p. 164. Also see Jolyon Howorth, "European Defence and the Changing Politics of the European Union: Hanging Together or Hanging Separately?" *Journal of Common Market Studies*, Vol. 39, No. 4, November 2001, pp. 765–89.

and recommendations on all military matters; and a military staff that conducts EU military operations and provides early warning, situation assessment, and strategic planning for operations.

These developments are striking. This chapter argues that the changing structure of the international system explains the creation and deployment of European Union forces. During the Cold War, the existence of a bipolar international system and the Soviet threat led European states to construct joint military forces through NATO. Following the collapse of the Soviet Union and the emergence of a unipolar international system, EU states began construction of military forces to decrease reliance on the US and increase their ability to project power abroad. Projecting power abroad is important because it allows European states to influence, deter, and coerce others in an anarchic international system. Furthermore, the scope of forces has been a function of the nature of the threat. Since European states do not face a major conventional military threat, the most significant threats consist of small-scale instability in areas such as the Balkans. To meet these threats, low-end military forces are sufficient.

To test this argument, this chapter examines two cases since World War II: the construction of NATO military forces at the beginning of the Cold War, and the creation of EU forces in the post-Cold War era. These cases were chosen for three major reasons: they are the most significant cases of European multilateral military forces since World War II; they ensure variation in the independent variable (the structure of the international system); and they ensure some variation in the dependent variable (the type of military forces). Particular attention will be devoted to understanding the motivations of leaders from the major powers – the United States, France, Britain, and Germany – because they played a determining role in the construction of these forces. Both case studies use primary sources, such as government documents and memoirs, where available to determine the motivations of policymakers. While this is difficult in the post-Cold War era because most primary source data have not been declassified, sufficient primary and secondary information is available to make reliable inferences.

The creation of EU forces has elicited two types of responses. The first is deep skepticism about whether they amount to much – and, for that matter, will *ever* amount to much. As one analysis concludes: "The whole European initiative to develop a more autonomous European Security and Defense Policy (ESDP) offers little that Pentagon analysts would recognize as a serious military contribution – in terms of techno-logically advanced weapon systems and aircraft, or the ability to deploy and maintain substantial numbers of troops at a long range."[2] The second response is disagreement about *why* a rapid reaction force has been constructed. Some argue that it is a function of the establishment of a common European identity; others contend that it is largely a function of the influence of liberal elites.

This chapter is divided into four sections. First, it outlines the major options states have when constructing military forces. Second, it explores the construction of multilateral forces through NATO in the early Cold War period. Third, it examines the establishment of a European Union rapid reaction force in post-Cold War Europe. And fourth, it concludes by evaluating several alternative arguments.

Options for building military forces

This section lays out the options states have when constructing military forces and explains the conditions under which they construct multilateral forces. As used here, a "multilateral force" refers to a joint military force established by states, containing a political-military organizational structure, and intended for repeated use. It can range in scope from small peacekeeping forces to large armies capable of fighting major theater wars. Historical examples include those forces built by the Delian League in ancient Greece, Hanseatic League in northern Europe, NATO, and European Union in the post-Cold War era. This definition excludes coalition forces – such as those used in the Korean War or World War II – that are constructed for single iterations.[3] The distinction is important because the longer time horizon for multilateral forces signifies a greater degree of cooperation.

State options

States can build unilateral and multilateral military forces.[4] First, they construct *unilateral* forces for two broad reasons: to defend their homeland from aggression; and to project power abroad for coercive,

[2] William Wallace, "As Viewed from Europe: Transatlantic Sympathies, Transatlantic Fears," *International Relations*, Vol. 16, No. 2, August 2002, p. 285.
[3] On coalitions see Barry R. Posen, *The Sources of Military Doctrine: France, Britain, and Germany between the World Wars* (Ithaca, NY: Cornell University Press, 1984), pp. 61–3, 73–4, 125–30. Andrew J. Pierre, *Coalitions: Building and Maintenance* (Washington, DC: Institute for the Study of Diplomacy, 2002).
[4] See, for example, Michèle A. Flournoy and Kenneth F. McKenzie, Jr., "Sizing Conventional Forces: Criteria and Methodology," in Flournoy, ed., *QDR 2001: Strategy-Driven Choices for America's Security* (Washington, DC: National Defense University Press, 2001), p. 168.

deterrent, and other purposes.[5] The former rationale is self-evident; states need to build forces to protect their homeland from attack. For example, the United States Department of Defense's *Annual Report to the President and the Congress* notes: "Defending the nation from attack is the first priority."[6] Moreover, as Thomas Schelling argues: "Military forces are commonly expected to defend their homelands, even to die gloriously in a futile effort at defense. When Churchill said that the British would fight on the beaches nobody supposed that he had sat up all night running once more through the calculations to make sure that that was the right policy."[7] States also build unilateral forces to project power abroad to promote national interests. These forces can be used for a range of missions such as noncombatant evacuation operations, peace-keeping deployments, limited aim strikes, or major wars.

Second, states have built *multilateral* military forces on several occasions throughout history. For example, ancient Greek city-states established joint forces to defend themselves against Persia. The Delian League, which was organized by Athens, included a joint treasury at Delos. Members contributed ships and money to the league, as Thucydides explained in *The Peloponnesian War*:

So Athens took over the leadership, and the allies, because of their dislike of Pausanias, were glad to see her do so. Next the Athenians assessed the various contributions to be made for the war against Persia, and decided which states should furnish money and which states should send ships – the object being to compensate themselves for their losses by ravaging the territory of the King of Persia . . . The leadership was Athenian, but the allies were originally independent states who reached their decisions in general congress.[8]

In the thirteenth century, Swiss cantons created a confederal army with a joint political-military structure that included a commanding general and a "council of war" that was responsible for overall military strategy.[9] Beginning in the fourteenth century, members of the Hanseatic League in northern Europe such as Lubeck and Hamburg built multilateral military forces. A general assembly, or diet, helped

---

[5] Thomas C. Schelling, *Arms and Influence* (New Haven: Yale University Press, 1966); Robert J. Art, "To What Ends Military Power?" *International Security*, Vol. 4, No. 4, Spring 1980, pp. 3–35.
[6] US Department of Defense, *Annual Report to the President and the Congress, 2002* (Washington, DC: US Dept of Defense, 2002), p. 20.
[7] Schelling, *Arms and Influence*, pp. 35–6.
[8] Quoted in Michael W. Doyle, *Empires* (Ithaca, NY: Cornell University Press, 1986), p. 55.
[9] Frederick K. Lister, *The Early Security Confederations: From the Ancient Greeks to the United Colonies of New England* (Westport, CT: Greenwood Press, 1999), pp. 67–91; William E. Rappard, *Collective Security in Swiss Experience, 1291–1948* (London: George Allen and Unwin, 1948).

determine the number of ships and soldiers that each member was expected to provide, and the Hansa's naval and land forces fought numerous wars over the next few centuries. In the second half of the fourteenth century, the Hanseatic League became something of a great power, though it remained largely intergovernmental rather than supranational.[10] Finally, in the aftermath of World War II the United States, Canada, and Western European states created NATO to protect Western Europe from a Soviet attack. By the early 1950s NATO had an integrated political-military structure and forces specifically geared to fight the Soviet Union. In sum, states can build either unilateral, or multilateral forces, as well as both types of forces.

Why multilateral forces?

States have traditionally shied away from constructing multilateral forces. Under what conditions, then, will they build these forces? Weaker states have historically built multilateral forces in response to preponderant powers. Greek city-states led by Athens constructed the Delian League in response to Persian power, the Hansa established joint forces to protect themselves against Denmark, Swiss cantons cooperated in response to Hapsburg power, and the United States, Canada, and Western Europe created NATO to counter Soviet power. In some cases, the preponderant power may pose a significant military risk to states and threaten territorial conquest. In other cases, the preponderant power may simply threaten the autonomy and interests of other states. In short, the establishment of multilateral forces has been a response to structural conditions.

In unipolar systems, states should have a particularly strong impetus to aggregate power for two reasons. First, aggregating power and building multilateral forces increases the autonomy of weaker states and decreases the likelihood that the dominant power will impose its will on them in areas of strategic importance. As Castlereagh argued, states may aggregate power to "prevent any of them becoming sufficiently strong to impose its will upon the rest."[11] Hans Morgenthau and Kenneth Thompson wrote that combining power "is a universal instrument of foreign policy used at all times by all nations who wanted to

[10] Lister, *The Early Security Confederations*, pp. 45–66; Phillippe Dollinger, *The German Hansa*, trans. and ed. D. S. Ault and S. H. Steinberg (Stanford, CA: Stanford University Press, 1970).
[11] Quoted in Lenox A. Mills and Charles H. McLaughlin, *World Politics in Transition* (New York: Holt, 1956), pp. 107–8; Inis L. Claude, *Power and International Relations* (New York: Random House, 1962), pp. 13–14.

preserve their independence in their relations with other nations."[12] In a unipolar international system, the dominant power, which by definition possesses superior military and economic capabilities, will use military force to pursue its own interests. In some instances, it may threaten weaker states because it seeks territorial conquest. In other cases, it may simply pose a threat to their interests and autonomy. Aggregating power and building joint military forces is not a matter of principle, but of expediency. States will shun multilateral forces if they believe they are strong enough to counter the preponderant power by themselves.[13] In Europe, the risk for states – including Germany, France, and Britain – is that a failure to aggregate military forces increases the likelihood that they will be dependent on the preponderant power. Some efforts by the US to improve its power position may necessarily erode the power position of others and could reduce their security. Other US initiatives may simply create a more dangerous world in their view.

Second, aggregating power and constructing joint forces increases the ability of weaker states to project power abroad. Deploying military and other crisis response forces can improve the security of European states by increasing their ability to influence, deter, and coerce others. The logic is that weaker states are much stronger when they combine military power than when they act unilaterally. Constructing joint military forces merges military resources (troops, weapons, and technology) and augments their ability to project power abroad. In response to US power, the risk for European states is that a failure to combine resources may decrease their security by jeopardizing their ability to deal with security threats. As the European Security Strategy argued, European states face a number of external security threats, such as terrorism, proliferation of weapons of mass destruction, regional conflicts, state failure, and organized crime. Effectively dealing with them improves European security:

The European Union and Member States have intervened to help deal with regional conflicts and to put failed states back on their feet, including in the Balkans, Afghanistan, and the DRC. Restoring good government to the Balkans, fostering democracy and enabling the authorities there to tackle organized crime is one of the most effective ways of dealing with organized crime within the EU.[14]

---

[12] Hans J. Morgenthau and Kenneth W. Thompson, eds., *Principles and Problems of International Politics: Selected Readings* (New York: Alfred A. Knopf, 1950), p. 104.

[13] Hans J. Morgenthau, *Politics among Nations: The Struggle for Power and Peace* (New York: Alfred A. Knopf, 1963), pp. 181–2.

[14] European Council, *European Security Strategy* (Brussels: European Council, September 2003), p. 6.

Aggregating power to increase autonomy and global power necessitates creating the political-organizational structure to plan, execute, and sustain these operations.[15] Indeed, the process of planning for multilateral operations forces states to coordinate their strategies and doctrines, integrate their forces through training and exercises, and improve the interoperability of their equipment. By establishing a political-military organizational structure, militaries also centralize decision-making and increase efficiency. For example, the creation of a NATO military structure and the appointment of a Supreme Allied Commander Europe (SACEUR) centralized decision-making for the defense of Western Europe and facilitated the compatibility of NATO militaries during the Cold War. Multilateral forces can also relieve states of some of the burdens of supplying troops and assets since it is expensive to buy and maintain military equipment, develop and produce weapons, train and deploy forces, and prepare for and fight wars.[16] States may decrease the costs and burdens of military operations by dividing up various aspects of a military campaign and post-war reconstruction efforts.[17] Of course, multilateral forces also spread "blood costs" because other states are willing to risk the lives of their citizens.[18] The cost of inefficiency can be high. Incompatible strategic objectives, disunity of command and control, and difficulties in communication may lead to costly delays, unnecessary civilian and combat deaths, poorly executed operations, and substantial tension among participant states.

Finally, the scope of military forces is a result of the nature of the threat. "Scope" refers to the type of operations that military forces are used for, ranging from low-end peacekeeping operations to high-end theater wars. The greater the conventional threat, the greater the rationale for high-end military forces to fight major theater wars. Likewise, the

[15] Myron Hura et al., Interoperability: A Continuing Challenge in Coalition Air Operations, MR-1235-AR (Santa Monica, CA: RAND, 2002); Thomas S. Szayna et al., Improving Army Planning for Future Multinational Coalition Operations, MR-1291-A (Santa Monica, CA: RAND, 2001); Wesley K. Clark, Waging Modern War: Bosnia, Kosovo, and the Future of Combat (New York: Public Affairs, 2001); Michele Zanini and Jennifer Morrison Taw, The Army and Multinational Force Compatibility, MR-1154-A (Santa Monica, CA: RAND, 2000).
[16] David A. Lake, Entangling Relations: American Foreign Policy in its Century (Princeton, NJ: Princeton University Press, 1999). Szayna et al., Improving Army Planning for Future Multinational Coalition Operations.
[17] On multilateral cooperation and post-war reconstruction efforts, see James Dobbins, John G. McGinn, Keith Crane, Seth G. Jones, Rollie Lal, Andrew Rathmell, Rachel Swanger, and Anga Timilsina, America's Role in Nation-Building: From Germany to Iraq (Santa Monica, CA: RAND, 2003), especially pp. 87–128.
[18] J. David Singer and Melvin Small, Resort to Arms: International and Civil Wars, 1816–1980 (Beverly Hills, CA: Sage, 1982), pp. 82–95.

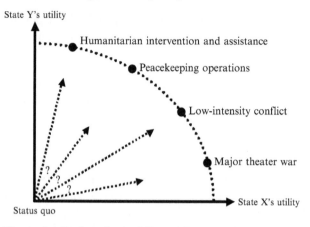

Figure 6.1 Options for multilateral forces.

smaller the conventional threat, the greater the impetus for low-end forces for peacekeeping and other operations. While states may decide to cooperate in the construction of military forces, there are often several potential options for cooperation.[19] As Charles Lipson, Duncan Snidal, and Barbara Koremenos argue: "If actors prefer different outcomes, the range of possibilities creates bargaining problems. Which cooperative outcome should they choose?"[20] Figure 6.1 illustrates that states considering multilateral forces have several choices, ranging from low-end forces for humanitarian operations to high-end forces for major theater wars.

The types of cooperative arrangements established should reflect the relative power of states, and the arrangements should change as the distribution of power changes.[21] We should expect that the scope of

[19] Krasner, "Global Communications and National Power: Life on the Pareto Frontier," *World Politics*, Vol. 43, No. 3, April 1991; James D. Morrow, "Modeling the Forms of International Cooperation: Distribution versus Information," *International Organization*, Vol. 48, No. 3, pp. 387–423; James D. Fearon, "Bargaining, Enforcement, and International Cooperation," *International Organization*, Vol. 52, No. 2, pp. 269–305.

[20] Barbara Koremenos, Charles Lipson, and Duncan Snidal, "The Rational Design of International Institutions," *International Organization*, Vol. 55, No. 4, Autumn 2001, p. 765.

[21] On power and institutions see Krasner, "Global Communications and National Power"; Charles Perrow, *Complex Organizations: A Critical Essay* (New York: Random House, 1986); Jeffrey Pfeffer, *Power in Organizations* (Marshfield, MA: Pitman Publishers, 1981); Charles Perrow, *Organizing America: Wealth, Power, and the Origins of Corporate Capitalism* (Princeton, NJ: Princeton University Press, 2002); Albert O. Hirschman, *National Power and the Structure of Foreign Trade* (Berkeley: University of California Press, 1945).

multilateral forces chosen should be correlated with the interests of major powers. If major powers face a common threat from a powerful neighbor, they will be more likely to build high-end forces capable of fighting major theater wars. If they face less significant threats such as small-scale instability in their periphery, major powers will be more likely to choose low-end forces that can be used for humanitarian, peacekeeping, and peacemaking operations. In contemporary Europe, the most powerful states include Germany, France, and Britain, and these powers should be the primary motors of a military force.

To sum up the hypotheses for Europe, we should expect the following:

- During the Cold War, there would be little intra-European military collaboration. Since the international system was bipolar, European states would be primarily concerned about balancing the USSR and collaborating with the United States.
- During the post-Cold War era, there should be a significant increase in intra-European collaboration. Since the international system is unipolar, European states should be concerned about decreasing their reliance on the US and increasing their power projection capabilities.

The construction of NATO forces

Following the end of World War II and the defeat of Germany and Japan, United States and West European leaders increasingly believed that the Soviet Union presented a grave threat to their security. As the US National Security document NSC-68 noted: "Soviet efforts are now directed toward the domination of the Eurasian land mass. The United States . . . is the principal enemy whose integrity and vitality must be subverted or destroyed by one means or another if the Kremlin is to achieve its fundamental design."[22] Britain's Lord Gladwyn likewise argued: "Not only was the Soviet Government not prepared to cooperate in any real sense with any non-Communist or non-Communist-controlled government, but it was actively preparing to extend its hold over the remaining part of continental Europe and subsequently, perhaps, over the Middle East, and no doubt the bulk of the Far East as well."[23] The evidence demonstrates that multilateral forces were created through NATO because of the structure of the international system.

---

[22] "NSC 68: United States Objectives and Programs for National Security, April 14, 1950," in *Foreign Relations of the United States 1950*, Vol. I, *National Security Affairs; Foreign Economic Policy*, p. 235.

[23] Hubert Gladwyn, *The Memoirs of Lord Gladwyn* (New York: Weybright and Talley, 1972), p. 211.

In a bipolar system, US and Western European leaders had a common interest in protecting themselves from the USSR and increasing their ability to project power in Europe. By the late 1940s, European states had three major options:

• Unilateralism
• European defense community
• NATO.

First, European states could have built only *unilateral* military forces. A brief perusal of European history demonstrates that they have often chosen this option. Despite the rise of Germany in the 1930s, for example, Britain and France not only refused to create multilateral forces, but Britain attempted to pass the buck to France.[24] Britain declined military cooperation with France in the 1930s because of British leaders' belief that war with Germany was not inevitable, their concern that establishing multilateral forces would be a self-fulfilling prophecy, and the country's more secure geographic location. As Barry Posen argues: "Except for some brief and attenuated instances, the British persistently avoided joint military conversations and planning with the French until March 1939, when war seemed all but inevitable . . . They did this out of fear that the advance planning and cooperation with the French might dictate the fact and the form of such intervention."[25] Unilateralism was not an option after World War II. It was unanimously rejected because the United States and Western Europe's major powers believed that the Soviet Union was a significant threat. As indicated by such documents as NSC-68 and Lord Gladwyn's comments, unilateralism and buckpassing were rejected out of concern that it would encourage Soviet expansionism.

Second, European states could have constructed a multilateral *European military force*. As explained in Chapter 3 in more detail, one of the core elements of the proposed European Defense Community (EDC) was a 43-division army with a unified command that integrated the military forces of the Federal Republic of Germany, Belgium, France, Italy, Luxembourg, and the Netherlands. No state could recruit

---

[24] On buckpassing and World War II see Barry R. Posen, *Sources of Military Doctrine*; John J. Mearsheimer, *The Tragedy of Great Power Politics* (New York: W. W. Norton, 2001), pp. 267–333; Thomas J. Christensen and Jack Snyder, "Chain Gangs and Passed Bucks: Predicting Alliance Patterns in Multipolarity," *International Organizations*, Vol. 44, No. 2, Spring 1990, pp. 137–68.

[25] Posen, *The Sources of Military Doctrine*, p. 157. On British foreign policy and entanglement see Josef Joffe, "'Bismarck' or 'Britain'? Toward an American Grand Strategy after Bipolarity," *International Security*, Vol. 19, No. 4, Spring 1995, pp. 94–117.

or retain national forces unless given explicit permission to do so by the organization. However, a major drawback with the European Army was that it did not encompass the set of states that were concerned about the Soviet Union, as well as a revanchist Germany. Neither the United States nor Britain were members of the EDC, yet both were deeply alarmed about the growing Soviet threat. Indeed, British leaders refused to participate in the EDC largely *because* it didn't include the United States. Even the French wanted US and British participation. A resolution in favor of the EDC passed the French National Assembly in February 1952, but only on the condition that it guarantee "the maintenance of sufficient US and British troops on the European Continent as long as appears necessary."[26] In sum, a European army was not a sufficient option because US military power was critical for balancing the Soviet Union and preventing Germany revanchism.

This led to a third option: the creation of multilateral forces through *NATO*. Following the creation of NATO by the Washington Treaty in April 1949, participant countries built an integrated political-military structure designed to coordinate war-fighting efforts against the Soviet Union.[27] The only structure created by the treaty was the North Atlantic Council. But over the next several years a political structure was established that included a NATO Secretary-General, a civilian staff, and a series of committees covering such areas as logistics, armaments, and nuclear planning.

On the military side, a Military Committee composed of the chiefs of staff of member states was created as NATO's highest military authority. Furthermore, the NATO defense area was divided into three separate regional commands – European, Atlantic, and Channel – as well as a regional planning group for Canada and the United States. Consequently, military power was centralized in three regional commanders: the Supreme Allied Commander Europe (SACEUR), responsible for ensuring the security of Western Europe; the Supreme Allied Commander Atlantic (SACLANT), responsible for guarding the sea lanes in the Atlantic and denying their use by enemy forces; and the

---

[26] The National Assembly resolution is reprinted in Denise Folliot, ed., *Documents on International Affairs, 1952* (Oxford: University Press, 1955), pp. 81–3.
[27] On the creation of NATO see Timothy P. Ireland, *Creating the Entangling Alliance: The Origins of the North Atlantic Treaty Organization* (Westport, CT: Greenwood Press, 1981); Sir Nicholas Henderson, *The Birth of NATO* (Boulder, CO: Westview Press, 1983); Lawrence S. Kaplan, *The United States and NATO: The Formative Years* (Lexington: The University Press of Kentucky, 1984); Melvyn P. Leffler, *A Preponderance of Power: National Security, the Truman Administration, and the Cold War* (Stanford, CA: Stanford University Press, 1992).

Commander-in-Chief Channel (CINCHAN), responsible for controlling and protecting the southern area of the North Sea and the English Channel.[28] Military planning for NATO's primary objective – defending the Western European land mass from a Soviet attack – was coordinated through SACEUR and involved joint air, land, and sea operations.[29] As one scholar noted: "By the end of 1953, in sum, NATO had been transformed from a traditional alliance, implying little more than a commitment to stand together, to an integrated . . . army."[30]

Why were multilateral forces constructed through NATO? In a bipolar international system, they were built because NATO countries shared a common interest in responding to Soviet power and improving their ability to project military power in Europe. Furthermore, the scope of forces was a function of the type of threat. Since NATO countries faced a large Soviet military that could overrun Western Europe, they needed a large military to deter Soviet aggression.

First, the US, Canada, and Western European states were motivated to protect themselves from Soviet power in a bipolar international system. Since American and Western European leaders believed that the Soviet Union desired to expand its power through Europe, the Middle East, and Asia, a failure to aggregate power meant a successful Soviet conquest of the continent. Indeed, the military forces left in Europe – and especially in western Germany – in the aftermath of World War II were not organized to conduct large-scale military operations. Samuel Huntington notes that the forces in Europe after the war were poorly trained and equipped, and could operate at barely 50 percent of their wartime efficiency.[31] This left Western Europe

---

[28] For a general outline of NATO's political-military structure see Lord Ismay, *NATO: The First Five Years, 1949–1954* (Netherlands: Bosch-Utrecht, 1954); North Atlantic Treaty Organization, *The North Atlantic Treaty Organization: Facts and Figures* (Brussels: NATO Information Service, 1981).

[29] On the defense of Europe see John J. Mearsheimer, "Why the Soviets Can't Win Quickly in Central Europe," *International Security*, Vol. 7, No. 1, Summer 1982, pp. 3–39; William P. Mako, *U.S. Ground Forces and the Defense of Central Europe* (Washington, DC: The Brookings Institution, 1983).

[30] Roger Hilsman, "NATO: The Developing Strategic Context," in Kraus Knorr, ed., *NATO and American Security* (Princeton: Princeton University Press, 1959), p. 23.

[31] Samuel P. Huntington, *The Common Defense: Strategic Programs in National Politics* (New York and London: Columbia University Press, 1961), pp. 33–9. US Commanders of the European and Pacific theaters argued: "By the Fall and Winter of 1945–1946 the armies and air forces that had been victorious in Europe and in the Pacific were no longer a closely integrated military machine, but rather had disintegrated to little more than large groups of individual replacements." John C. Sparrow, *History of Personnel Demobilization in the United States Army* (Washington, DC: United States Army, 1951), p. 360.

vulnerable to a Soviet attack. As Field Marshall Bernard Montgomery argued in 1950: "As things stand today and the foreseeable future, there would be scenes of appalling and indescribable confusion in Western Europe if we were ever attacked by the Russians."[32]

Furthermore, the establishment of an integrated military structure was a function of relative power, and the United States played the dominant role in organizing and running NATO forces. Indeed, American policymakers were unanimous in their belief that if the United States was going to be involved in multilateral NATO forces, it would have to be the central player. As a State Department policy planning staff paper argued: "If there is to be an effective organization of Europe, it will have to be set in a framework which assures continuous and responsible leadership by the United States."[33] The Joint Chiefs of Staff similarly argued that US policymakers needed to give "vigorous leadership" to ensure the effectiveness of NATO, and the US should be given the "choice of its strategic course and maximum freedom of action in its execution."[34] In a February 1951 letter to President Truman, Dwight D. Eisenhower wrote that "a goodly portion of [NATO's] most serious problems will be purely American. This is because of our country's position of power and leadership, to say nothing of its inescapable function as the principal arsenal of NATO."[35]

Above all, this meant that US military officials would be placed in key positions in the NATO military structure, which would ensure US predominance and allow American policymakers to play a central role in the structure of forces and military planning. American policymakers from the State and Defense Departments were insistent that "an American National be appointed now as Chief of Staff and eventually as a Supreme Commander" of NATO.[36] Furthermore, since roughly 75 percent of Allied naval forces in the Atlantic Ocean in 1951 were American, US policymakers believed it "very important" that SACLANT be an American naval officer and "imperative" that he occupy the same

[32] Ismay, *NATO: The First Five Years*, p. 30.
[33] Paper Prepared by the Policy Planning Staff, "The Current Position in the Cold War," April 14, 1950, *FRUS 1950*, Vol. III, *Western Europe*, p. 859.
[34] Kenneth W. Condit, *The History of the Joint Chiefs of Staff: The Joint Chiefs of Staff and National Policy*, Vol. II, *1947–1949* (Washington, DC: Joint Chiefs of Staff, 1976), p. 385. See also Douglas L. Bland, *The Military Committee of the North Atlantic Alliance: A Study of Structure and Strategy* (Westport, CT: Praeger, 1990), pp. 119–21.
[35] Louis Galambos, *The Papers of Dwight D. Eisenhower*, Vol. XII (Baltimore, MD: Johns Hopkins University Press, 1984), p. 68.
[36] Acheson and Johnson to Truman, September 8, 1950, *FRUS 1950*, Vol. III, p. 276.

command level as SACEUR.[37] Consequently, out of the three major military commands – SACEUR, SACLANT, and CINCHAN – American officers were guaranteed two of them. Because CINCHAN was responsible for the English Channel and the North Sea, it was given to a British commander. US power was also apparent in its control of nuclear weapons. As Acheson told NATO ministers in a 1954 closed-door session, nuclear weapons were a critical component of NATO defense because they helped deter a Soviet attack. While the United States would "consult with its Allies" in the event that nuclear weapons were used, the US would ultimately hold the keys. Acheson warned, "Under certain conditions time would not permit consultation" with NATO allies "without itself endangering the very security we seek to protect."[38]

Britain and France were also ensured substantial influence through such structures as the NATO Standing Group, which was composed of American, British, and French defense officials and was in charge of coordinating and integrating NATO defense plans.[39] Indeed, British and French leaders pushed strongly for prominent positions in NATO. The French "wanted to use North Atlantic Treaty machinery to secure their preeminent position in continental defense strategy and arms assistance," and British leaders lobbied for substantial British and US influence.[40] The British Chiefs of Staff "expressed a strong preference for Anglo-American domination of the NATO military structure, necessarily to be achieved by indirect rather than direct means."[41] While American leaders were willing to accede to some of these demands, they were ultimately unwilling to compromise American preponderance. As Eisenhower, NATO's first SACEUR, noted to Secretary of Defense George Marshall during the initial construction of NATO's military structure: "It has now been my purpose to draw the British and

[37] Walter S. Poole, *The History of the Joint Chiefs of Staff*, Vol. 7 (Washington, DC: Joint Chiefs of Staff, 2000), p. 280.
[38] Statement by Acheson to the North Atlantic Council, April 23, 1954, *FRUS 1952–1954*, Vol. V, *Western European Security*, p. 512. On nuclear weapons and Europe see also Marc Trachtenberg, *A Constructed Peace: The Making of the European Settlement, 1945–1963* (Princeton: Princeton University Press, 1999), pp. 146–200.
[39] On the US Defense Department's push for British, French, and American influence, see Condit, *The History of the Joint Chiefs of Staff*, pp. 382–99. Also see JCS to SecDef, "Proposed Military Organization under the North Atlantic Treaty, 23 June 1949 (derived from JCS 1868/87), same file, sec 23.
[40] Ireland, *Creating the Entangling Alliance*, p. 161.
[41] Condit, *The History of the Joint Chiefs of Staff*, Vol. II, p. 383. Also see UK C of S C.O.S. (49) 92, 18 March 1949, Encl to Memo, Br Jt Services Mission RDC 5/76 to DJS, 24 March 1949, same file, sec 18.

French into prominent posts of command and staff organization."
However, he reassured Marshall, "American interest, prestige, and
doctrine are amply represented in this layout."[42]

Second, NATO countries constructed multilateral forces to increase
efficiency in projecting power in Europe. As NATO's *Strategic Concept
for the Defense of the North Atlantic Area* explained, the effective application of force against the Soviet Union required participant states to
combine military forces and strategic planning. This meant that "a
successful defense of the North Atlantic Treaty nations through maximum efficiency of their armed forces, with the minimum necessary
expenditures of manpower, money and materials, is the goal of the
defense planning."[43] Ensuring maximum efficiency, the document explained, meant taking several important cooperative measures. These
included standardizing military doctrines and procedures of NATO
forces, undertaking joint training exercises, compiling and sharing intelligence information relevant to NATO's military mission, and standardizing military equipment and material as much as possible. NATO's
Standing Group was ordered to "coordinate and integrate the defense
plans" that originated in the organization's regional planning groups in
order to facilitate "the rapid and efficient conduct" of NATO's defense
mission.[44] Indeed, Eisenhower argued that he had two main objectives
as NATO's Supreme Commander in Western Europe. The first was "to
bring about a coordination and greater efficiency in American activity in
this region" by directing all US military activity toward collective defense, and the second was "to produce efficiency in the *Allied* machinery
set up in NATO."[45] As Figure 6.2 demonstrates, NATO's front-line
defense against the Soviet Union in Central Europe required the coordination of Dutch, West German, British, American, and Belgian ground
forces.

The outbreak of the Korean War in June 1950 served as a catalyst for
the creation of multilateral forces through NATO because Western
militaries were deeply skeptical that they could defend Western Europe

---

[42] Galambos, *The Papers of Dwight D. Eisenhower*, Vol. XII, pp. 118, 121.
[43] Strategic Concept for the Defense of the North Atlantic Area, December 1, 1949, *FRUS
1949*, Vol. IV, *Western Europe*, p. 354.
[44] North Atlantic Council Final Communiqué, September 17, 1949, in Ismay, *NATO: The
First Five Years*, p. 173.
[45] Galambos, *The Papers of Dwight D. Eisenhower*, Vol. XII, p. 380.

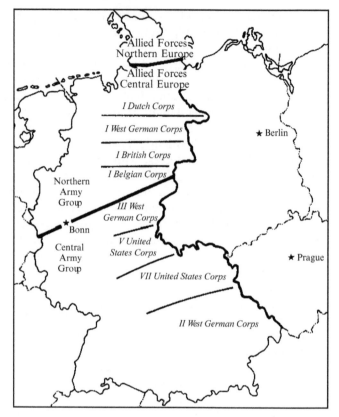

Figure 6.2 NATO ground forces, central Europe.[46]

from a Soviet attack.[47] As a State Department paper on NATO argued: "[I]t has become increasingly more apparent to each nation in Western Europe that their individual efforts . . . cannot effectively defend their own borders. Since the Korean invasion the urge for a 'common defense' has rapidly multiplied."[48] Perhaps most important in establishing an efficient multilateral fighting force was the creation of a unified command. Since Eisenhower was dubious that Western European militaries

[46] Mako, *US Ground Forces and the Defense of Central Europe*, p. 33.
[47] On NATO and the Korean War see Ireland, *Creating the Entangling Alliance*, pp. 183–220. Lawrence S. Kaplan, *The United States and NATO: The Formative Years*, (Lexington, KY: University of Kentucky Press, 1984), pp. 145–75.
[48] "Establishment of a European Defense Force," in Matthews to Burns, August 15, 1950, *FRUS 1950*, Vol. III, p. 213.

could defeat the Soviets, he believed "it vital that we ensure that the very best use is made of the forces now available, and that we set and achieve a very high level of professional efficiency."[49] In particular, this meant that NATO militaries had to develop close cooperation at the command level, and build a centralized command headquarters through the Supreme Headquarters Allied Powers Europe (SHAPE).

In sum, the threat of a massive Soviet conventional invasion of Western Europe explains the scope of multilateral forces. American leaders pushed for a large-scale integrated NATO force because it would be used to fight – and deter – a large Soviet military. By the late 1940s, 12 inefficient and poorly organized Western divisions were believed to face a Soviet force of 25 divisions supported by another 115 to 150 divisions in the Soviet Union.[50] This meant that NATO forces had to be adequately structured to meet this threat; smaller-scale forces would have been doormats in the event of a Soviet attack. As Secretary of State Acheson and Secretary of Defense Johnson argued to President Truman, the objective of NATO countries "should be the early creation of an integrated force adequate to insure the successful defense of Western Europe, including Western Germany, against possible Soviet invasion."[51] NATO multilateral forces persisted throughout the Cold War because of the power of the Soviet Union and the desire to project power in Europe.

European Union forces

With the end of the Cold War and the emergence of a unipolar international system, European leaders became increasingly concerned about the relative power of the United States. The historical evidence strongly suggests that the structural shift to unipolarity at the end of the Cold War caused EU states to create military and other crisis response forces to decrease dependence on the United States and increase their power projection capabilities. Furthermore, the prospect of conflict in North Africa, the Middle East, and the Balkans shifted European attention from major war with the Soviet Union to a joint response to smaller-scale conflicts.

European options

In the post-Cold War era, European states had three major policy options *vis-à-vis* military forces: unilateralism, NATO, and European Union. First, Europe's major powers could have constructed only

---

[49] Galambos, *The Papers of Dwight D. Eisenhower*, Vol. XII, p. 529.
[50] Mako, *US Ground Forces and the Defense of Central Europe*, p. 7.
[51] Acheson and Johnson to Truman, September 8, 1950, *FRUS 1950*, Vol. III, p. 274.

unilateral military forces. This would have meant abandoning NATO
and refusing multilateral cooperation. States are often unwilling to share
responsibility regarding the construction of military forces. The problem
with unilateralism, and the reason Europe's major powers never seriously
considered it, was that it risked continuing dependence on the United
States. The wars in Bosnia and Kosovo were stark reminders that
European countries were largely dependent on US power to conduct
even modest military operations. Moreover, unilateralism and a resort to
"renationalization" might also have increased the possibility of security
competition among Europe's major powers.[52] In short, relying only on
unilateral forces would have caused European states to remain dependent
on American power, even when European security interests diverged.
It also might have jeopardized long-term security on the continent, as
explained in more detail in Chapter 3.

Second, European states could have continued relying solely on
NATO. NATO had existed for half a century, included a well-developed
political-military institutional structure, and was involved in two military
operations in the 1990s: Operation Deliberate Force in Bosnia in 1995,
and Operation Allied Force in Kosovo in 1999. Indeed, some have
argued that NATO's involvement in both wars and its enlargement to
Eastern Europe made it the pivotal forum for coordinating military
forces and tackling the new threats of the twenty-first century.[53]
However, there were several problems with NATO. To begin with, the
shift to unipolarity and the increase in US relative power meant that
relying on NATO would continue to leave European capitals dependent
on the United States military. Furthermore, the collapse of the Soviet
Union caused US leaders to shift their focus to other areas of the world,
such as the Middle East and Asia, and to become reluctant to deploy
military forces to small-scale problems in Europe. As one senior French
diplomat argued: "If there were another Balkan war today, I'm not sure
we would have the same level of American involvement as before."[54]
This created the possibility that if the United States refused to respond
to a crisis that European states believed was in their strategic interest,
Europe would not be capable of acting autonomously of the US.

[52] On renationalization see Jan Willem Honig, "The 'Renationalization' of Western
European Defense," *Security Studies*, Vol. 2, No. 1, Autumn 1992, pp. 122–38. Also
see Seth G. Jones, "The European Union and the Security Dilemma," *Security Studies*,
Vol. 12, No. 3, Spring 2003, pp. 114–56.
[53] Ronald D. Asmus, *Opening NATO's Door: How the Alliance Remade Itself for a New Era*
(New York: Columbia University Press, 2002), p. xxiv.
[54] Craig S. Smith, "For U.S. to Note, Europe Flexes Muscles in Afghanistan," *New York
Times*, September 22, 2004, p. A1.

Indeed, US post-Cold War defense documents shifted their focus from Europe to the Middle East and Asia as the primary theaters of operation for US forces. This marked a substantial change from the Cold War, when both the US and Europe shared a common interest in preparing for a possible war against the Soviet Union. For example, the *National Military Strategy* noted:

As a global power with worldwide interests, it is imperative that the United States be able to deter and defeat nearly simultaneous, large-scale, cross-border aggression in two distant theaters in overlapping time frames, preferably in concert with regional allies. For the time being, we face this challenge in the Arabian Gulf region and in Northeast Asia.[55]

Furthermore, rather than demonstrating growing common interests between Europe and the United States, the NATO operations in Bosnia and Kosovo showed quite the reverse. The United States was deeply reluctant to become involved in military operations in Europe's periphery. Even when it did, US policymakers were unwilling to commit ground forces because the Balkans were not considered strategically important.[56] General Wesley Clark, the American commander who oversaw Operation Allied Force, noted that there was substantial skepticism within the US military that the Balkans were an important region: "The Services were against any commitment [in Kosovo] . . . because it wasn't in our 'national interest.' And any use of forces there would be bad for 'readiness,' which to them meant only readiness for the two Major Regional Contingencies" in the Middle East and Northeast Asia.[57] American reservations about participating in Operation Allied Force and coalition problems during the operation led one defense minister to conclude that the most fundamental lesson was that "we never want to do this again."[58]

This left a third option: build *EU forces*. The first major step toward the creation of a European Union military force came in December 1998 at the Franco-British summit in St. Malo, France. British Prime

---

[55] US Department of Defense, *National Military Strategy* (Washington, DC: US Dept of Defense, 1997), p. SH-1-9; see also *Quadrennial Defense Review Report* (Washington, DC: US Dept of Defense, 2001), pp. 4–5.
[56] On US skepticism *vis-à-vis* Kosovo see Clark, *Waging Modern War*, pp. 46–9, 129, 154, 164–6, 303–4; Ivo H. Daalder and Michael E. O'Hanlon, *Winning Ugly: NATO's War to Save Kosovo* (Washington, DC: Brookings Institution Press, 2000), pp. 53–7, 69–72, 96–100, 190–1; Bruce R. Nardulli, Walt L. Perry, Bruce Pirnie, John Gordon, John G. McGinn, *Disjointed War: Military Operations in Kosovo, 1999*, MR-1406-A (Santa Monica, CA: RAND, 2002).
[57] Clark, *Making Modern War*, p. 165.
[58] Clark, *Making Modern War*, p. 417.

Minister Tony Blair and French President Jacques Chirac agreed that the European Union must have the capacity for joint military action to respond to international crises.[59] This marked a notable shift from the Cold War and jumpstarted the construction of European Union military forces that could act independently of NATO and the United States. The shift was particularly important because the British Government reversed a long-standing position of refraining from EU cooperation in the military realm.[60] To be clear, the EU and NATO were not mutually exclusive options. Both currently exist. Rather, the issue was which institution should have priority in the short and long term when deploying military and crisis response forces.

At the 1999 Helsinki Summit, EU member states officially agreed to establish a rapid reaction military force consisting of up to 60,000 soldiers, deployable within sixty days, and sustainable for at least one year. The forces were intended for low-end military operations such as peacekeeping and humanitarian missions – what have been termed the Petersberg tasks.[61] Furthermore, they were intended to operate as an expeditionary force with necessary sealift, airlift, and amphibious capabilities for rapid deployment to the theater of operation. EU force components include a headquarters and command structure; communications systems; battlefield-surveillance and target-acquisition capabilities; and airpower capabilities such as airborne early warning, command and control, suppression of enemy air defenses, and precision-guided munitions.[62] Under the Headline Goals 2010, European Union states also established rapidly deployable battle groups: high readiness, battalion-sized units with a deployable force headquarters and associated strategic lift and logistics.[63] In addition, France, Italy, Spain, Portugal, and the Netherlands launched a European gendarmerie force for international policing tasks. Key functions include performing security and public order missions; conducting public surveillance, traffic regulations, border policing, and general intelligence; performing criminal investigation work, which covered detection of offenses, tracing of offenders,

---

[59] Franco-British Summit, St. Malo, France, December 3–4, 1998 in Maartje Rutten, ed., *From St-Malo to Nice, European Defence: Core Documents*, Chaillot Paper 47 (Paris: Institute for Security Studies, 2001), p. 8.
[60] Hunter, *The European Security and Defense Policy*, pp. 29–32; Gilles Andréani, Christoph Bertram, and Charles Grant, *Europe's Military Revolution* (London: Centre for European Reform, 2001), pp. 8–11.
[61] European Council, Helsinki, December 10–11, 1999.
[62] "The 'European Rapid Reaction Force,'" *The Military Balance, 2001–2002* (London: Oxford University Press, 2001), pp. 283–191.
[63] Council of the European Union, *ESDP Presidency Report* (Brussels: European Council, December 2004).

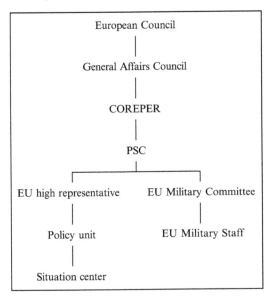

Figure 6.3 EU political–military structure.

and their transfer to the appropriate judicial authorities; and training police and instructors.[64]

As Figure 6.3 illustrates, European states also established a multi-tiered political-military structure that was approved at the Nice European Council. At the top of the institutional structure is the European Council, which is composed of the leaders of EU states and is the main decision-making body for EU foreign policy and defense matters. The decision to place power in the European Council, rather than the supranational European Commission, suggests that military affairs will continue to remain intergovernmental for the foreseeable future. In order to enable the European Union fully to assume its responsibilities for crisis management, the European Council established three permanent political and military structures at Nice: a Political and Security Committee, European Union Military Committee, and European Union Military Staff. The Political and Security Committee

(PSC)'s major function is to monitor international crises and exercise political control and strategic direction of EU military operations.[65] It proposes political objectives and military options to EU member states when crises occur, and sends guidelines to the EU Military Committee. The Military Committee, which includes the defense ministers of EU states, provides the Political and Security Committee with military advice and recommendations on all military matters within the EU.[66] It is also responsible for maintaining an official military relationship with non-EU European NATO members and organizations. Finally, the Military Staff is responsible for conducting EU military operations and providing early warning, situation assessment, and strategic planning.[67]

European Union missions

Despite the existence of some shortfalls such as insufficient airlift, sealift, and aerial refueling capabilities, the first EU forces were deployed in 2003. During the Cold War, there were no European Community military or crisis response forces. A decade and a half after the end of the Cold War, there were nearly a dozen military, civilian police, and other missions to a range of countries such as the former Yugoslav Republic of Macedonia, Democratic Republic of Congo, Bosnia and Herzegovina, Georgia, Iraq, and Palestinian territory. This section outlines the core missions in the post-Cold War era.

A small EU military mission, Operation Concordia, was deployed to the former Yugoslav Republic of Macedonia in 2003. Its task was to provide security and protection for international monitors from the European Union and Organization for Security and Cooperation in Europe (OSCE), who were overseeing implementation of the 2002 peace agreement and monitoring the reentry of security forces into former crisis areas.[68] European leaders had become deeply concerned about the stability of Kosovo, which had increasingly experienced unrest as members of the National Liberation Army, who represented the armed wing of the ethnic Albanian rebels, attacked police and army

[65] Council Decision 2001/78/CFSP, January 22, 2001; Zdzislaw Lachowski, "The Military Dimension of the European Union," in *SIPRI Yearbook 2002: Armaments, Disarmament and International Security* (New York: Oxford University Press, 2002), pp. 151–73.
[66] Council Decision 2001/79/CFSP, January 22, 2001.
[67] Council Decision 2001/80/CFSP, January 22, 2001.
[68] Council of the European Union, *Political and Security Committee Decision Setting up the Committee of Contributors for the EU-Led Operation in FYROM* (Brussels: European Council, February 18, 2003); *Council Decision Relating to the Launch of the EU Military*

units in such areas as Tetovo.[69] The EU force was based in Skopje, Macedonia, and took over from NATO with the broad goal of contributing to a stable security environment in Macedonia. The force incorporated both heavy and light forces, as well as support elements that included an air component, medical evacuation teams, and an explosive ordnance disposal team. The Concordia chain of command remained under the political and strategic direction of the EU, though close links were maintained with NATO at all levels.[70]

The prime minister of the former Yugoslav Republic of Macedonia also invited the EU to deploy a police mission. In response, the EU sent several hundred police experts to monitor, mentor, and advise the country's police to help fight organized crime, referred to as Operation Proxima. EU police were deployed to Skopje, Tetovo, Kumanovo, Gostivar, and Ohrid. As the *European Security Strategy* noted, the Balkans were a key strategic interest since "90 percent of the heroin in Europe comes from poppies grown in Afghanistan – where the drugs trade pays for private armies. Most of it is distributed through Balkan criminal networks which are also responsible for some 200,000 of the 700,000 women victims of the sex trade world wide."[71] EU civilian police assisted Macedonian police officials by improving investigations skills in the areas of serious and organized crime, as well as strengthening counter-intelligence capacity. EU personnel also helped reform the Ministry of Interior, created a border police to promote integrated

Operation in the Former Yugoslav Republic of Macedonia (Brussels: European Council, March 18, 2003); Council Joint Action, 2003/92/CFSP, January 27, 2003.

[69] Catriona Mace, "Operation Concordia: Developing a 'European' Approach to Crisis Management," *International Peacekeeping*, Vol. 11, No. 3, Autumn 2004, pp. 474–90.

[70] Philippe Gelie, "Alors que l'Union deploie une force d'intervention en RD Congo; Les Quinze rodent leur 'diplomatie globale' en Macedoine," *Le Figaro*, June 16, 2003; "Feuerprobe in Kongo; Die EU-Truppe hat sich beim ersten Einsatz in Mazedonien bewährt," *Süddeutsche Zeitung*, May 30, 2003, p. 10; Judy Dempsey, "Operation in Macedonia Will Test European Security Policy," *Financial Times*, March 31, 2003, p. 12; Ambrose Evans-Pritchard, "Euro Army on its First Mission," *Daily Telegraph*, April 1, 2003, p. 14; Eric Jansson, "Greater Role Sought in 'Europe Project,'" *Financial Times*, June 10, 2003, p. 4; Giovanna Bono, "Operation Concordia: The first steps towards a new EU–NATO strategic relationship?" *Deutsche Gesellschaft fuer Auswaertige Politik*, June 2003. The EU forces had access to NATO assets and planning, and relied on NATO to send in extra reinforcements if needed for emergency purposes such as search and rescue missions.

[71] *A Secure Europe in a Better World*, p. 5. On the Afghan drug trade, see also UN office on Drugs and Crime, *Afghanistan: Opium Survey 2004* (Vienna: United Nations Office on Drugs and Crime, 2004); UN office on Drugs and Crime, *The Opium Economy in Afghanistan: An International Problem*, 2nd edn (Vienna: UN Office on Drugs and Crime, 2003); *Afghanistan: Opium Survey 2003*, pp. 1–10; Barnett R. Rubin, *Road to Ruin: Afghanistan's Booming Opium Industry* (New York: Center on International Cooperation, October 2004).

border management, and enhanced cooperation with neighboring states in the field of policing.[72]

The EU deployed a French-led EU military force of approximately 1,400 troops, codenamed Operation Artemis, to protect UN personnel and civilians in Bunia, Congo.[73] Bunia had experienced inter-ethnic clashes between members of the Lendu and Hema communities, which led to the death of several hundred civilians and created concerns of further instability. Consequently, the EU deployed a force to provide security in the area. The operation was planned and conducted by France's Centre Planification et Conduite des Opérations, rather than NATO, and was supported with artillery and fixed-wing Mirage 2000 ground attack jets.[74] The theater-level force command headquarters was situated at Entebbe, Uganda, with an advance party in Bunia. Most of the forces were drawn from the French 9th Brigade légère blindée de marine, such as the 3rd Marine infantry regiment, the 11th Marine artillery regiment, the 6th Marine engineer regiment, and the 1st Hussars parachute regiment. EU forces were involved in initial skirmishes with Lendu militia in June 2003, and then encountered more serious resistance from Union of Congolese Patriots forces in early July. They killed at least twenty militia members, demonstrating a willingness to use force when necessary. Ultimately, European forces reestablished security in Bunia, weakened the military capabilities of the rival Lendu and Hema militias, and then handed responsibility back to United Nations forces.[75]

Operation Artemis was followed by two additional EU missions to the Congo: a European police mission, and a security sector reform operation. First, the EU's Political and Security Committee agreed in December 2003 to establish an EU police mission to Congo to rehabilitate and refurbish a police-training center; provide basic equipment; train Congolese police; and monitor and mentor the police after the

---

[72] Council Joint Action 2003/681/CFSP, September 29, 2003; Council Joint Action 2004/789/CFSP, November 22, 2004.

[73] Council Common Position 2003/319/CFSP, May 8, 2003; Council Decision 2003/432/CFSP June 12, 2003.

[74] Corine Lesnes, "Quel mandat pour une force internationale?" Le Monde, September 8, 2003; Michèle Alliot-Marie, "La mission de l'union en république démocratique du Congo etait une 'première,'" Le Figaro, September 2, 2003; Helen Vesperini, "French Fighter Jets Overfly Powderkeg DR Congo Town," Agence France Presse, June 11, 2003; Nicholas Fiorenza, "EU Force Seeks New Mission after Congo," Defense News, September 8, 2003, p. 42.

[75] UN Peacekeeping Best Practices Unit, Operation Artemis: The Lessons of the Interim Emergency Multinational Force (New York: United Nations Peacekeeping Best Practices Unit, October 2004); Stale Ulriksen, Catriona Gourlay, and Catriona Mace, "Operation Artemis: The Shape of Things to Come?" International Peacekeeping, Vol. 11, No. 3, Autumn 2004, pp. 508–25.

initial training phase was complete.[76] Second, the EU decided in 2005 to provide advice and assistance for security sector reform in the Democratic Republic of Congo. The European Council believed that "the current security situation in the DRC may deteriorate, with potentially serious repercussions for the process of strengthening democracy, the rule of law and international and regional security. A continued commitment of EU political effort and resources will help to embed stability in the region."[77] The EU consequently deployed security personnel to the private office of the Minister of Defense, combined general staff, army general staff, Joint Operational Committee, and National Committee for Disarmament, Demobilization and Reintegration.[78]

The European Union deployed a military force of 7,000 troops to Bosnia, codenamed Operation Althea. The objective was to maintain a secure environment in Bosnia and ensure continued compliance of the Dayton peace agreement. Establishing a secure environment included combating organized criminal groups, collecting weapons, and helping rebuild Bosnia's security forces.[79] The European Union force replaced NATO's stabilization force, which had been deployed to Bosnia since 1996 when it took over from NATO's implementation force.[80] The EU's Political and Security Committee exercised political control and strategic direction of Operation Althea, under the responsibility of the European Council.[81] The operation was carried out with recourse to NATO assets and capabilities through the Berlin Plus arrangements. EU force commanders divided Bosnia into three military areas of operation: Multinational Task Forth North, headquartered in Tuzla; Multinational Task Force Southeast, headquartered in Mostar; and Multinational Task Force Northwest, headquartered in Banja Luka.

The EU also deployed a police mission to Bosnia to increase the competency of the police by helping mentor and assess Bosnian police.

---

[76] Council Joint Action 2004/494/CFSP, May 17, 2004; Council Joint Action 2004/847/ CFSP, 9 December 9, 2004.

[77] Council Joint Action 2005/355/CFSP, May 2, 2005.

[78] Council of the European Union, *Council Establishes Mission to Provide Advice and Assistance for Security Sector Reform in the Democratic Republic of Congo* (Brussels: European Council, May 2005), press release.

[79] Council of the European Union, *EU Military Operation in Bosnia and Herzegovina* (Brussels: EU Council Secretariat, November 29, 2004); Council Decision 2004/803/ CFSP, November 25, 2004; Council Joint Action 2004/569/CFSP, July 12, 2004; United Nations Security Council Resolution 1575 (2004), S/RES/1575, November 22, 2004.

[80] NATO's implementation force was first deployed to Bosnia in December 1995, NATO's stabilization force took over in December 1996, and the European Union's follow-on force was launched in December 2004.

[81] Political and Security Committee Decision BiH/2/2004, September 24, 2004.

EU units were co-located with Bosnian state- and district-level police, and served as advisers to the Ministry of Security and Ministry of Interior for the Bosnian-Croat Federation and the Republika Srpska.[82] The EU police mission monitored, advised, and inspected Bosnian police in the context of seven major programs. These were developed in partnership with the Police Steering Board in Bosnia, which comprises the highest-ranking police officials of the country.[83] Key programs included:

- Enhancing the investigation capacities of the crime police
- Streamlining the Bosnian police training and education system
- Developing the necessary procedures and institutions to manage disciplinary and criminal cases involving police officers
- Strengthening the police as an institution through increased capacity in managing finances, human resources, logistics, and cooperation with the media
- Advancing the abilities of Traffic Units, Support Units, and Anti-terrorist Units
- Improving investigation techniques to fight drug smuggling and human trafficking
- Developing the State Investigation and Protection Agency, which deals with major and organized crime.

The European Union launched an EU Rule of Law Mission to Georgia in the context of the European Security and Defense Policy.[84] It deployed European experts to support, mentor, and advise Georgian ministers and senior officials at the level of the central government. Key issues included providing guidance for the new criminal justice reform strategy; supporting the coordinating role of the relevant Georgian authorities in the field of judicial reform and anti-corruption; and supporting the development of international as well as regional cooperation in the area of criminal justice. EU personnel were co-located in Georgian ministries and governmental bodies in the national capital. This objective was important since European states had identified the promotion of

---

[82] Council Joint Action 2002/210/CFSP, March 11, 2002; Council Decision 2002/845/ CFSP, September 30, 2002; Marco Nesse, "Intervista del Ministro della Difesa Prof. Antonio Martino," *Corriere della Sera*, October 13, 2003.

[83] Council Joint Action 2003/681/CFSP, September 29, 2003; Council Joint Action 2004/ 789/CFSP, November 22, 2004; Political and Security Committee Decision Proxima/2/ 2004; Kari M. Osland, "The EU Police Mission in Bosnia and Herzegovina," *International Peacekeeping*, Vol. 11, No. 3, Autumn 2004, pp. 544–60.

[84] Council Joint Action 2004/523/CFSP, June 28, 2004; European Union, *Facts on EUJUST THEMIS* (Tbilisi, Georgia: European Union Rule of Law Mission to Georgia, 2004).

"a ring of well governed countries to the East of the European Union and on the borders of the Mediterranean with whom we can enjoy close and cooperative relations" as a strategic objective.[85] And EU leaders identified significant and urgent challenges in Georgia's rule of law system, ranging from the courts, through the Procuracy, to the penitentiary system.

Similarly, the European Union launched a rule-of-law mission to Iraq in 2005 in the context of the European Security and Defense Policy. The mission consisted of integrated training in the fields of management and criminal investigation for senior officials and executive staff from the judiciary, police, and penitentiary systems.[86] The Political and Security Committee exercised political control and strategic direction of the mission. The mission was established in support of the European Union's Iraq strategy laid out in *A Framework for EU–Iraq Engagement*.[87]

The European Union also deployed a border assistance mission and police mission to Palestinian territory in 2005 and 2006. The EU's border assistance mission began in November 2005 at the Rafah border crossing on the Gaza–Egyptian border. It monitored, verified, and evaluated Palestinian performance; improved Palestinian capacities regarding border management; and helped improve liaison arrangements between the Palestinian, Israeli, and Egyptian authorities on management of the Rafah border crossing. In January 2006, the European Union also launched a police mission to Palestinian territory to help the Palestinian Authority establish sustainable and effective policing arrangements. Key tasks included assisting in the implementation of the Palestinian Civil Police Development Plan, advising and mentoring senior members of the Palestinian Civil Police and criminal justice system, and coordinating EU and other international assistance to the Palestinian civil police.[88] Both missions were part of a broader EU effort to help the Palestinian Authority improve its ability to establish law and order in Palestinian territory.

In sum, there was a significant increase in the deployment of European Union military and civilian forces and personnel in the post-Cold War era.

---

[85] *A Secure Europe in a Better World*, p. 8.

[86] Council Joint Action 2005/190/CFSP, March 7, 2005; Council Joint Action 2005/190/CFSP, March 7, 2005; Council of the EU, *European Union Factsheet: EU Support for Iraq* (Brussels: European Union, 2005).

[87] Commission of the EC, *A Framework for EU–Iraq Engagement* (Brussels: European Commission, 2004).

[88] Council of the EC, *Presidency Report on ESDP*, 15678/05 (Brussels: Council of the European Union, December 2005); Council of the EU, *Council Establishes EU Police Mission in the Palestinian Territories* (Brussels: Council of the European Union, November 2005).

In addition to those missions mentioned in Macedonia, Congo, Bosnia, Georgia, Iraq, and Palestinian territory, EU states also conducted additional missions such as a civilian-military support to the African Union in the Darfur region of Sudan.[89] This brings us to an important question: why was there a significant increase in the construction and use of EU forces? And what explains the scope of forces built? Europe's major powers created a multilateral EU force to decrease reliance on the US and increase their ability to project power abroad. Moreover, the scope of forces has been a function of the type of threat: since European states were concerned about small-scale instability in their periphery, they required low-end forces capable of peacekeeping and humanitarian operations rather than high-end forces. In order to understand the motivations of European leaders, the rest of this section is divided into two segments. The first examines the European desire to decrease dependence on the United States; the second explores the desire to project power abroad.

Increasing autonomy

The creation of European Union forces has partly been caused by a desire to decrease dependence on the United States and increase European autonomy in a unipolar international system. The cost of continuing to rely on a preponderant US is straightforward: it increases the possibility that the US will impose its will on Europe in areas of strategic importance. This would be the consequence of a bandwagoning strategy. As Barry Posen argues: "Some consequential powers will nevertheless find bandwagoning uncomfortable . . . Some efforts by the US to improve its power position may necessarily erode the power position of others and could indeed reduce their security. Other US initiatives may simply create a more dangerous world in the eyes of other states." Posen continues that "consequential states will at a minimum act to buffer themselves against the caprices of the US and will try to carve out an ability to act autonomously, should it become necessary."[90] Indeed, since the collapse of the Soviet Union, which tied Europe and the United States together during the Cold War, differences in strategic interests have become magnified.

---

[89] Council Joint Action 2005/556/CFSP, July 18, 2005; Council Joint Action 2005/557/CFSP, July 18, 2005.
[90] Barry R. Posen, "ESDP and the Structure of World Power," *The International Spectator*, January–March 2004, Vol. 39, No. 1, p. 9.

At least three wars in the post-Cold War era – Bosnia, Kosovo, and Iraq – were critical in raising concerns about US power and persuading European capitals to decrease their dependence on the US. First was the 1995 war in Bosnia, in which European states were dependent on the US military for combat operations. As David Owen, European envoy to Bosnia in the early 1990s, argued, the EU's inability to coordinate a military response was largely attributable to the fact that "they did not have sufficient power to exercise without the participation of the United States."[91] European states lacked the military capabilities and political-military structure to act autonomously, and were forced to rely on the United States to conduct the air operation. The United States Air Force flew two-thirds of the sorties during the air war. Britain flew 9 percent, France 8 percent, the Netherlands 6 percent, and an amalgam of other European countries the final 11 percent.[92]

The second was the 1999 war in Kosovo. Much like in Bosnia, the US nearly declined to become involved. When it did agree to participate, however, the US military demanded control of the operation and placed some of its assets such as B-2s and F-117s under US, rather than NATO, command. The British House of Commons Defence Committee concluded in its report on the lessons of Kosovo that "Operation Allied Force demonstrated just how far the European NATO nations are from having a capability to act without massive US support. This deficit is recognized and acknowledged by the European Allies." This meant that Europe's ability to decrease dependence on the US demanded "a high level of European political cooperation."[93] Moreover, the British Ministry of Defence's document *European Defence* noted that Operation Allied Force in Kosovo offered at least two lessons: European states lacked the institutional structure and military capabilities to act autonomously

[91] David Owen, *Balkan Odyssey* (New York: Harcourt Brace, 1995), p. 402.
[92] North Atlantic Treaty Organization, *Operation Deliberate Force: AFSOUTH Fact Sheet* (Brussels: NATO, 2002). On Operation Deliberate Force, also see Robert C. Owen, "Balkans Air Campaign Study: Part 1," *Airpower Journal*, Vol. 11, Summer 1997, pp. 4–25; Owen, "Balkans Air Campaign Study: Part 2," *Airpower Journal*, Vol. 11, Fall 1997, pp. 6–26; Michael O. Beale, *Bombs over Bosnia* (Maxwell AFB, AL: School of Advanced Airpower Studies, 1997); Ivo H. Daalder, *Getting to Dayton: The Making of America's Bosnia Policy* (Washington, DC: Brookings Institution Press, 2000).
[93] UK House of Commons, Defence Committee, *Lessons of Kosovo*, Fourteenth Report (London: HMSO, 2000), para. 313. Also see Elizabeth Pond, "Kosovo: Catalyst for Europe," *Washington Quarterly*, Vol. 22, No. 4, pp. 77–92; Christopher Layne, "Death Knell for NATO? The Bush Administration Confronts the European Security and Defense Policy," *Policy Analysis*, No. 394, April 4, 2001; Mary Elise Sarotte, *German Military Reform and European Security*, Adelphi Paper 340 (London: International Institute for Strategic Studies, 2001), p. 54; Gilles, Bertram, and Grant, *Europe's Military Revolution*, pp. 8–11.

of the US and NATO; and United States participation in future crises in
Europe and its periphery could not always be guaranteed. "As the
lessons of Kosovo showed . . . European nations need significantly to
improve their military capabilities. They should not continue to depend
so heavily on the United States in dealing with crises in and around
Europe. Europe needs to improve its ability to act in circumstances
where NATO is not engaged."[94] German Chancellor Gerhard Schröder
presciently noted that "it was above all the experience of the wars in
Bosnia and Kosovo that led us to adopt in Cologne during the German
Presidency a plan for the development of an autonomous European
Security and Defense Policy."[95]

Third, the 2003 US war in Iraq increased the incentive of EU states to
pursue a multilateral EU military force.[96] Of particular concern for
states such as Germany and France was the US's unilateral willingness
to use force despite deep concern in European capitals. The war was a
stark reminder of US power and a further indication that the United
States was not a status quo power.[97] German Chancellor Gerhard
Schröder argued that US unilateralism provided an important impetus
for "emancipating" Germany from its historical relationship with the US
and continuing in the direction of "core Europe" or "more Europe" –
including the development of a rapid reaction force.[98] As Robert Art
summed up: "Just as the Kosovo War crystallized for Europeans their
long-standing dependence on the United States to solve conflicts on
their periphery, so, too, the second Gulf War drove home to them, even

[94] UK Ministry of Defence, *European Defence*, Paper No. 3 (London: Ministry of Defence,
2001). On British policymakers and the US/NATO commitment, also see Andréani,
Bertram, Grant, *Europe's Military Revolution*, p. 11; UK Ministry of Defence, *Defence
Policy 2001* (London: HMSO, 2001), para. 19; Miskimmon, "Recasting the Security
Bargains," p. 90.
[95] Policy Statement by Gerhard Schröder, Berlin, December 12, 2001 (Berlin: The
Federal Press Office, 2001).
[96] Stale Ulriksen, "Requirements for Future European Military Strategies and Force
Structures," *International Peacekeeping*, Vol. 11, No. 3, Autumn 2004, pp. 457–73. See
also the *Financial Times* series on the Divided West. "War in Iraq: How the Die Was Cast
before Transatlantic Diplomacy Failed," *Financial Times*, May 27, 2003, p. 11; "The Rift
Turns Nasty: The Plot that Split Old and New Europe Asunder," *Financial Times*, May
28, 2003, p. 13; "Blair's Mission Impossible: The Doomed Effort to Win a Second
Resolution," *Financial Times*, May 29, 2003, p. 11; "The US Has Come to See the
Status Quo as Inherently Dangerous," *Financial Times*, May 30, 2003, p. 13.
[97] Martin Wolf, "A Partnership for a Destructive Separation," *Financial Times*, May 21,
2003, p. 23.
[98] Elaine Sciolino, "Europe Assesses Damage to Western Relationships and Takes Steps to
Rebuild," *New York Times*, April 2, 2003, p. B12; William Boston, "Rifts over Iraq:
How Deep?" *Christian Science Monitor*, April 14, 2003, p. 8; John Vinocur, "What
'Emancipation' is Schroeder After?" *International Herald Tribune*, May 8, 2003, p. 3.

including those who supported US policy toward Iraq, their inability to restrain Washington's growing unilateralist impulses."[99]

In sum, Bosnia, Kosovo, and Iraq were critical events that caused deep concern in European capitals about the dominance of US power and the paucity of European power. In particular, German, French, and British policymakers were active in constructing EU forces.[100] Agreement among the great powers has generally been reached *before* the critical EU bargaining events such as Cologne, Helsinki, and Nice. The first clear example was the Franco-British summit in St. Malo in December 1998, in which Chirac and Blair agreed that the EU "must have the capacity for *autonomous* action, backed up by credible military forces, the means to decide to use them, and a readiness to do so, in order to respond to international crises."[101]

German policymakers supported the St. Malo agreement and used their six-month EU Presidency in early 1999 to push forward the establishment of an EU multilateral force.[102] German, French, and British policymakers engaged in a series of high-level meetings to negotiate the details of a rapid reaction force leading to the June 1999 Cologne and December 1999 Helsinki European Council meetings. They agreed to establish target goals for an EU military force at the May 1999 Franco-German summit in Toulouse, November 1999 Anglo-French summit in London, and November 1999 Franco-German summit

[99] Robert J. Art, "Europe Hedges its Security Bets," in T. V. Paul, James J. Wirtz, and Michael Fortmann, *Balance of Power Revisited: Theory and Practice in the 21st Century* (Stanford, CA: Stanford University Press, 2004), pp. 199–200.

[100] As German Foreign Minister Joschka Fischer noted in an interview with the German magazine *Der Spiegel*: "We do not want to dance alone, but rather be the driver of further integration." Joschka Fischer, "Wir wollen kein Soli tanzen," *Der Spiegel*, No. 48, November 23, 1998. Furthermore, the French Ministry of Defense's *La défense nationale* argues: "The ability to maintain France's position in the world will be closely related to its ability to influence the European construction and future developments in Europe . . . The gradual restructuring of Europe is leading to the definition of a political identity which would be incomplete if it were not also expressed in the context of defense." French Ministry of Defence, *La défense nationale* (Paris: Ministère de la Défense, 2002).

[101] Franco-British Summit, St. Malo, France, December 3–4, 1998 in Maartje Rutten, ed., *From St. Malo to Nice, European Defence: Core Documents*, Chaillot Paper 47 (Paris: Institute for Security Studies, 2001), p. 8. Emphasis added. The diplomatic language used at St. Malo tried to smooth over concerns about US participation by noting that a European military force was necessary for acting "where the [NATO] Alliance as a whole is not engaged." Franco-British Summit, St. Malo, France, December 3–4, 1998 in Rutten, ed., *From St. Malo to Nice*, p. 8. See also Hunter, *The European Security and Defense Policy*, pp. 29–32.

[102] "German Presidency Paper," February 24, 1999, in Rutten, *From St. Malo to Nice*, pp. 14–16; "German Proposal at the Informal Meeting of EU Foreign Minister," Eltville, March 13–14, 1999, in Rutten, ed., *From St. Malo to Nice*, pp. 17–19.

in Paris.[103] These objectives officially became the "Headline Goals" and included the construction, deployment, and sustainment of EU military forces of up to 60,000 troops.[104] European leaders were clear that their objective was to create forces that were autonomous of the United States. At Toulouse, for example, Chirac and Schröder stated that their "two countries reaffirm their determination to put their full weight behind the effort to secure for the European Union the necessary autonomous assets it needs to be able to decide and act in the face of crises."[105]

The major powers continued to discuss various aspects of the EU military force before the December 2000 Nice European Council meeting. France, Britain, Germany, and Italy proposed the establishment of a political-military structure to facilitate the conduct of EU military operations in a draft document initiated by Richard Hatfield of the British Ministry of Defense. As noted in the final version of the document, known as the "Toolbox Paper," they argued that in order "to have an autonomous capacity to take decisions" and to "conduct EU-led military operations in response to international crises," it was necessary for European Union states to "establish new political and military structures."[106] Furthermore, a December 2000 French Presidency Report on ESDP argued that the motivation to build a rapid reaction force was "to give the European Union the means of playing its role fully on the international stage and of assuming its responsibilities in the face of crises by adding to the range of instruments already at its disposal an autonomous capacity to take decisions and action in the security and defense field."[107] These efforts led to the approval at the Nice summit of a political and security committee, military committee, and military staff.[108] In sum, European Union states have created a rapid reaction force that can be deployed

---

[103] Franco-German Summit, Toulouse, May 29, 1999 (Washington: Embassy of France, 1999); Anglo-French Summit, London, November 25, 1999, in Rutten, ed., *From St. Malo to Nice*, pp. 77–9; Tom Buerkle, "EU Force No Threat to NATO, Allies Say," *International Herald Tribune*, November 26, 1999, p. 1; Rupert Cornwell, "Blair and Chirac Call for 60,000 EU Troops," *The Independent*, November 26, 1999, p. 4; "Germany and France Act to Strengthen European Defence," *Deutsche Press-Agentur*, November 30, 1999.

[104] Helsinki European Council, December 10–11, 1999.

[105] Franco-German Summit, Toulouse.

[106] "Toolbox Paper," in Rutten, ed., *From St. Malo to Nice*, p. 94.

[107] Report of the Presidency on the European Security and Defence Policy, Annex VI of the Conclusions of the French Presidency of the European Council, December 9, 2000.

[108] Negotiations among the major powers – particularly France and Germany – continued over the next several years, though the Cologne, Helsinki, and Nice European Council meetings have been the most critical in the establishment of an EU military force. Examples include the Franco-German summits at Mayence (June 9, 2000), Vittel (November 10, 2000), Freibourg (June 12, 2001), Nantes (November 23, 2001), and Schwerin (July 30, 2002).

and sustained independently of NATO in order to increase autonomy and decrease reliance on the United States.

Increasing global power

The creation of European Union forces has also been caused by a desire to increase European power projection capabilities around the globe. This marks a stark contrast from the Cold War, when European states shared a common interest with the United States in defending Western Europe from a Soviet attack. Aggregating resources increases the ability of European states to influence, deter, and coerce others – and ultimately to improve their own security. As Tony Blair elaborated a few months after St. Malo: "We Europeans should not expect the United States to have to play a part in every disorder in our own back yard. The European Union should be able to take on some security tasks on our own, and we will do better through a common European effort than we can by individual countries acting on their own." Consequently, he argued that Europeans need to "restructure our defense capabilities so that we can project force, can deploy our troops, ships and planes beyond their home bases and sustain them there, equipped to deal with whatever level of conflict they may face."[109] In addition, as President Chirac argued in the French journal *Défense nationale*, "the creation of permanent bodies within the European Union will enable it to make decisions and act completely autonomously, whether or not it uses NATO assets, to prevent or manage crises affecting its security."[110] The cost of not increasing Europe's power projection capabilities was high: EU leaders believed it would severely hamper the ability of European states to respond quickly and effectively to regional crises, and could ultimately decrease Europe's security. EU External Relations Commissioner Christopher Patten argued, "Too often in the past, take the Balkans for example, we have just not been able to respond with the efficiency or timeliness that developments in the real world demand."[111]

Increasing global power has been a significant impetus among French, German, and British policymakers. French leaders have repeatedly noted that the most effective way for EU states to project power abroad

---

[109] Tony Blair, "NATO, Europe, and Our Future Security," Speech at NATO's 50th Anniversary Conference, Royal United Services Institute, London, March 8, 1999.

[110] Jacques Chirac, "Politique de défense et de sécurité," *Défense nationale*, No. 57, July 2001, p. 10.

[111] Christopher Patten, "Remarks in the European Parliament," January 17, 2001. Available at: (europa.eu.int/comm/external_relations/news/patten/rrf_17_01_01.htm).

is to combine military forces.[112] No European power, including France, had the capability to match US power on its own. Indeed, a major reason that the French supported EU missions, such as Operation Artemis in the Congo, was that it was critical to begin developing the EU as a major international actor. The French proposals for Artemis were in line with the proactive EU role in peacekeeping and conflict prevention in Africa called for at the Franco-British summit in Le Touquet in February 2003.[113] As French President Chirac argued: "The multipolar world that France is seeking will provide balance and harmony. But it will not be feasible unless Europe is organized and able to play its role on the international stage . . . To do so, it will need diplomatic and military instruments."[114] As one senior French defense official argued, in areas such as the Balkans and the Mediterranean where Europe's major powers share a strategic interest, "it is much more efficient to create multilateral forces than to try to put them together piecemeal when a crisis occurs."[115] This meant that an EU political-military structure was critical to coordinate military strategies and doctrines; command, control, and communications (C^3); and intelligence, surveillance, and reconnaissance (ISR). Indeed, not only was it important to aggregate resources, but it was also important to establish a permanent political-military organizational structure to oversee European Union deployments.

German leaders have shared this rationale. A European military force and integrated political-military structure would increase EU power projection capabilities. As noted in the Ministry of Defense's *Bundeswehr 2002*: "The central goal of the European Security and Defense Policy (ESDP) is to provide the instruments it takes to render the CFSP efficient."[116] Furthermore, the Franco-German *Common Concept for Security and Defense* noted that coordination was critical in creating effective multilateral forces.[117] Consequently, the Bundeswehr

---

[112] Chirac, "Politique de défense et de sécurité," pp. 5–20; Lionel Jospin, "La politique de défense de la France," *Défense nationale*, No. 56, November 2000, pp. 5–16; Alain Richard, "L'Europe de la défense," *Défense nationale*, No. 57, January 2001, pp. 7–15.

[113] Ulriksen, Gourlay, and Mace, "Operation Artemis: The Shape of Things to Come," pp. 512–13; Gorm Rye Olsen, "EU and Conflict Management in African Emergencies," *International Peacekeeping*, Vol. 9, No. 3, Autumn 2002, pp. 87–102.

[114] Jacques Chirac, "European Defense," Address to the Presidential Committee of the WEU Parliamentary Assembly and the Visiting Fellows, May 30, 2000.

[115] Interview with French defense official, Washington, DC, December 12, 2002.

[116] German Federal Minister of Defense, *Bundeswehr 2002: Sachstand und Perspektiven* (Berlin: Bundesministerium der Verteidigung, 2002), p. 16.

[117] Quoted in Christoph Bertram, Joachim Schild, Francois Heisbourg, and Yves Boyer, *Starting Over: For a Franco-German Initiative in European Defense* (Berlin: Stiftung Wissenschaft und Politik, 2002), p. 37.

restructured its armed forces in the post-Cold War era around German participation in multilateral operations, especially future EU operations. It is remarkable that German military planners have focused almost exclusively on preparing for multilateral – rather than unilateral – combat operations. They have concentrated on creating forces capable of sustaining either one major multilateral operation involving 60,000 troops for up to one year or two medium-sized operations involving up to 10,000 troops each for several years.[118] This includes setting up an EU political-military structure, coordinating strategic reconnaissance and intelligence, establishing a mobile joint theater command, and perhaps creating joint courses at national training establishments.

British leaders have also supported the establishment of an EU rapid reaction force because it increased European power projection capabilities. As Defence Secretary Geoff Hoon argued: "We need flexible forces that can get to a crisis more quickly, efficiently, and effectively."[119] If EU states were going to create an autonomous military capability to act in areas of strategic importance, they had a strong impetus to make it effective. This meant coordinating military strategies and doctrine through a joint political-military structure, performing joint training and exercises, and improving interoperability.

The scope of military forces has been a function of the type of threat. European leaders have supported low-end forces for peacekeeping and humanitarian operations – rather than for major wars – because they are intended for small-scale conflicts. As Britain's *Defence Policy 2001* noted: "On the periphery of Europe (and in the Balkans) there are instabilities and tensions which are likely to remain . . . problems for European security."[120] During the Cold War European powers established multilateral forces to deal with their primary threat: a war with the Soviet Union. In the post-Cold War era, however, European states have been primarily concerned about instability in such regions as the Balkans, Mediterranean, and North Africa.[121] This meant the construction of

[118] American Institute for Contemporary German Studies, *Redefining German Security: Prospects for Bundeswehr Reform*, German Issues No. 25 (Washington, DC: AICGS, 2001). See also German Federal Minister of Defence, *Bundeswehr 2002*.
[119] Cornwell, "Blair and Chirac Call for 60,000 EU Troops," p. 4. On multilateral forces and efficiency see UK Ministry of Defence, *Multinational Defence Co-operation*, Paper No. 2 (London: Ministry of Defence, 2001).
[120] Ministry of Defence, *Defence Policy 2001* (London: HMSO, 2001), para. 7.
[121] François Bujon de l'Estaing, "Defense and Security Projects in Europe," Address to the National War College, January 24, 2001; Chirac, "European Defense"; Mark Oakes, *Common European Security and Defence Policy: A Progress Report*, Research Paper 00/84 (London: House of Commons, 2000); AICGS, *Redefining German Security*.

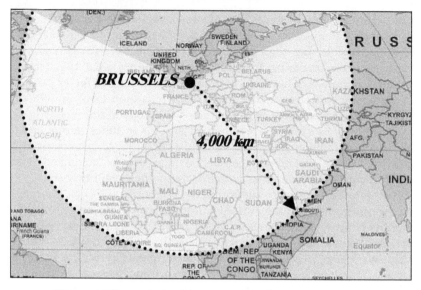

Figure 6.4 Europe's 4,000km strategic radius.

low-end military forces to conduct humanitarian and peacekeeping missions. As Figure 6.4 highlights, the most likely area of deployment consists of an one that is within a 4,000 km radius of Brussels.[122] Indeed, conflict erupted in the 1990s in Bosnia, Kosovo, Macedonia, and Albania, but EU states lacked an EU multilateral force to respond to them. The French Ministry of Defense's *Loi de Programmation Militaire 2003–2008* noted that similar conflicts will inevitably occur in the future: "The transitional societies at the borders of Europe will still be marked by severe tension, aggravated by economic difficulties, and extensive migration. The security interests of European countries will be affected."[123] Consequently, this has created an incentive to build an EU multilateral force that can respond to potential small-scale crises.

---

[122] Mikkel-Vedby Rasmussen, "Turbulent Neighbourhoods: How to Deploy the EU's Rapid Reaction Force," *Contemporary Security Policy*, Vol. 23, No. 2, August 2002, pp. 51–3; Alfred van Staden, Kees Homan, Bert Kreemers, Alfred Pijpers, and Rob de Wijk, *Toward a European Strategic Concept* (The Hague: Netherlands Institute of International Relations, November 2000); Hans-Christian Hagman, *European Crisis Management and Defense: The Search for Capabilities*, Adelphi Paper 353 (London: International Institute for Strategic Studies, 2002), pp. 35–59.

[123] French Ministry of Defence, Loi de Programmation Militaire 2003–2008, Paris, 2002.

Conclusion

In sum, the construction of EU military and rapid response forces has been caused by the structural shift to unipolarity in the post-Cold War era. In a unipolar international system, EU states have been motivated by a desire to decrease reliance on the US and increase power abroad. There are several alternative explanations for the emergence of a European Union force, though none of them are persuasive. Some might argue that they have been built because of the preferences of liberal domestic elites. Others may contend that they have emerged because of the construction of a European identity. Finally, numerous skeptics have argued that a meaningful EU force has not been – nor will likely be – created.

First, some might argue that the creation of an EU force is largely a function of the influence of liberal elites. This argument has its roots in broader liberal theories of international politics.[124] As John Owen argues, an EU force has been motivated by the desire of liberal elites "to carry out liberal foreign policy more efficiently."[125] The assumption is that if EU leaders wish to pursue such liberal policies as humanitarian intervention and peacekeeping, and the United States does not want to participate, it makes sense to build EU forces. This logic is problematic, however. If European countries were only interested in carrying out liberal foreign policy more efficiently, there would be no reason to build military forces outside of NATO. Indeed, NATO has sufficient military assets and operational and defense planning capabilities to support European-led operations, as US policymakers have long argued.[126] This is true whether the United States chooses to participate in a

---

[124] On liberal theory see Moravcsik, "Liberal International Relations Theory: A Scientific Assessment," in Colin Elman and Miriam Fendius Elman, eds., *Progress in International Relations Theory* (Cambridge, MA: MIT Press, 2003); Moravcsik, "Taking Preferences Seriously: A Liberal Theory of International Politics," *International Organization*, Vol. 51, No. 4, Autumn 1997, pp. 513–53; John M. Owen, IV, *Liberal Peace, Liberal War: American Politics and International Security* (Ithaca, NY: Cornell University Press, 1997), ch. 1; Michael W. Doyle, *Ways of War and Peace: Realism, Liberalism, and Socialism* (New York: W. W. Norton, 1997); Lisa L. Martin, *Democratic Commitments: Legislatures and International Cooperation* (Princeton, NJ: Princeton University Press, 2000).

[125] John M. Owen, IV, "Transnational Liberalism and US Primacy," International Security, Vol. 26, No. 3, Winter 2001, 2002, p. 142.

[126] For instance, James Jones, Supreme Allied Commander, Europe, has contended that "there's no mission which can't be addressed by the alliance." Fiorenza, "EU Force Seeks New Mission after Congo," p. 42. On US reactions to ESDP also see Hunter, *The European Security and Defense Policy*, pp. 99–108, 117–24; Isabelle Ioannides, *The European Rapid Reaction Force: Implications for Democratic Accountability*, Paper 24 (Bonn: Bonn International Center for Conversion, September 2002), pp. 32–4.

NATO mission or not. The evidence strongly suggests that EU states have built an EU multilateral force to decrease dependence on the United States and build an autonomous military capability. This is more than a desire to prepare for military operations in case the United States chooses not to participate. The benefit of an EU force is that it provides European Union states with the ability to project power abroad *even if the United States objects*.

Second, others might argue that the construction of EU forces is caused by the internalization of a common European identity.[127] The logic is that decades of interaction through the European Community and European Union have led to the construction of a common identity and common strategic culture among European states. Rather than being caused by such factors as liberal elites or structural factors, European states have built military and other rapid response forces because they have internalized common norms and values.[128] The independent variable is a change in identity, not a change in power. However, there are good reasons to believe that constructivist accounts are problematic. As noted in Chapter 2, if EU forces have been caused by the construction of a European identity, we should expect to find a change in the degree of "Europeanness" in the post-Cold War era. Unfortunately, there is little evidence.

Third, perhaps the most serious alternative argument is that a veritable European Union force is a pipedream that will exist largely on paper.[129] As one study contends: "European defence is failing because, in the absence of a transnational strategic concept shared and agreed upon by the European great powers, there are no guidelines for the application of European coercive power – be it within the EU or beyond." This leaves the rapid reaction force "in danger of being 'WEU-ized': that is, left to

[127] For constructivist arguments on the EU and military power see Henrik Larsen, "The EU: A Global Military Actor?" *Cooperation and Conflict*, Vol. 37, No. 3, September 2002, pp. 283–302; Paul Cornish and Geoffrey Edwards, "Beyond the EU/NATO Dichotomy: The Beginnings of a European Strategic Culture," *International Affairs*, Vol. 77, No. 3, July 2001, pp. 587–603; Ian Manners, "Normative Power Europe: A Contradiction in Terms?" *Journal of Common Market Studies*, Vol. 40, No. 2, June 2002, pp. 235–58.

[128] Alexander Wendt, *Social Theory of International Politics* (New York: Cambridge University Press, 1999); Ole Waever, "Insecurity, Security, and Asecurity in the West European Non-War Community," in Emanuel Adler and Michael Barnett, *Security Communities* (New York: Cambridge University Press, 1998), pp. 69–118.

[129] For skeptical views of ESDP see Julian Lindley-French, "In the Shade of Locarno? Why European Defence is Failing," *International Affairs*, Vol. 78, No. 4, October 2002, pp. 789–811; Michael Clarke and Paul Cornish, "The European Defence Project and the Prague Summit," *International Affairs*, Vol. 78, No. 4, October 2002, pp. 777–88; James Graff, "Ready, Aim . . . React," *Time*, Vol. 156, No. 23, December 4, 2000.

quietly rot in the corner of the EU institutional framework, never to be used."[130] As some have noted, the inability of EU states to coordinate military policy has created a division of labor in which the Americans "make the dinner" and Europeans "do the dishes."[131] The logic is that nationalism and a desire to protect state sovereignty and autonomy will prevent EU states from attaining the same degree of military cooperation that they have achieved in the economic realm. Since EU forces are at a nascent stage, it is conceivable that they will never be used for major combat operations, let alone operations that require 60,000 soldiers envisioned in the Headline Goal. However, the evidence since 1998 strongly suggests the opposite: the trend and the political momentum is toward greater EU military cooperation rather than less. Indeed, the creation of a rapid reaction force and battle group, the development of an EU political-military institutional structure, and the deployment of EU forces to Macedonia, Bosnia, Congo, and other countries demonstrate that EU states have increasingly deepened cooperation in the military realm. We now turn to the future of Europe.

---

[130] Lindley-French, "In the Shade of Locarno?" p. 791.
[131] Robert Kagan, *Of Paradise and Power: America and Europe in the New World Order* (New York: Alfred A. Knopf, 2003), p. 23.

7 The tragedy of US–European relations

What are the future prospects for security cooperation among EU states? What are the implications for European–American relations? A large body of opinion assumes that European security cooperation is – and will be – more fiction than fact. Europeans have a predilection to talk about greater security cooperation, but little stomach to actually do it. As one pessimist concludes: "This is old continental European-style political grandstanding – full of sound and fury, but signifying nothing."[1] For many, the French and Dutch rejection of the European constitution signified "an insurrection, a democratic intifada," which make the idea of meaningful security cooperation seem risible and naïve.[2]

However, there is substantial evidence that this pessimistic view is wrong. Thus far, this book has examined empirical evidence from both the past and the present. Past evidence strongly indicates that structural factors discouraged European states from pursuing widespread security collaboration through the European Community during the Cold War. European states were concerned about balancing the Soviet Union, and most cooperation was therefore transatlantic. Recent evidence suggests that changing structural conditions in the post-Cold War caused a significant rise in intra-European security cooperation in several areas, such as economic sanctions, arms production, and military forces. There has also been an increase in cooperation in numerous other areas not examined in detail in this book. One example is counter-terrorism cooperation, especially in the aftermath of such attacks as those in 2001 in Washington and New York, 2004 in Madrid, and 2005 in London.

The future, by contrast, is much less clear. Predicting the future is a tenuous business. As former New York Yankees' catcher Yogi Berra once

---

[1] Wolfgang Munchau, "Time to Abandon the 'Core Europe' Fantasy," *Financial Times*, November 3, 2003, p. 21.
[2] Richard Bernstein, "Two 'No' Votes in Europe: The Anger Spreads," *New York Times*, June 2, 2005, p. 1. See also Martin Walker, "Walker's World: The EU's Grim Year," *United Press International*, December 31, 2005.

wryly remarked: "It's tough to make predictions, especially about the future." It is impossible to know with certainty what the future holds for Europe. But past and current evidence suggests that European security cooperation will deepen over the next decade. Much will depend on the structure of the regional and international systems. In particular, a further withdrawal of US forces from Europe, a strong Germany, and a continuation of US global preponderance will lead to greater security cooperation among EU states and perhaps greater US–European friction. The aggregation of power by European Union states will increase their ability and embolden their willingness to disagree with the United States and project power abroad. This was demonstrated rather neatly by the Franco-German decision to oppose the US war in Iraq. Table 7.1 summarizes one Central Intelligence Agency prediction about great power politics over the next decade. The CIA's Strategic Assessment Group predicted that the European Union may be a unified political, military, and economic actor by 2015. Indeed, the EU may be the second most powerful actor in the international system behind the US, based on a national power index that combines gross domestic product, defense spending, population, and technological capabilities.[3]

The remainder of this chapter is organized as follows. First, it reviews the competing arguments and evidence. Second, it examines the impact of structural factors on European security. Third, it explains how these changes might translate into developments in three areas: economic sanctions for foreign policy goals, arms production, and military forces. Fourth, it discusses the United States response to greater European security cooperation. And fifth, it argues that the aggregation of power among EU states will likely result in more policy disagreement and tension with the United States, rather than less.

Theory and European security cooperation

The empirical evidence over the last sixty years strongly suggests that *structural factors* go a long way in explaining the significant increase in European security cooperation since the end of the Cold War. Building

[3] The model is based on a national power index that combines GDP, defense spending, population, and a technology factor weighted at 1.1, 0.9, 0.8, and 0.3. Central Intelligence Agency, *Modeling International Politics in 2015: Potential U.S. Adjustments to a Shifting Distribution of Power* (Washington, DC: Strategic Assessments Group, CIA, 2004).

Table 7.1. *CIA projections about major powers in 2015*

Rank	Country	2015 Power Score
1	United States	20.0
2	European Union	14.9
3	China	14.0
4	India	8.7
5	Japan	4.3
6	Brazil	2.4
7	South Korea	2.1
8	Russia	1.9
9	Indonesia	1.8
10	Mexico	1.4

on the assumptions of political realism, this book argues that substantial security cooperation among EU states has occurred because of the changing structure of the international and regional systems. The international system shifted from a bipolar structure during the Cold War to a unipolar structure in the post-Cold War era characterized by US preponderance. This shift caused European states to cooperate in the security realm for two reasons: to increase Europe's ability to project power abroad, and to decrease reliance on the United States. Power is important because it can make states more secure in an anarchic international system, and it can increase their ability to influence, deter, and coerce others. In addition, the regional system in Europe shifted from one with a divided Germany and a significant US presence during the Cold War, to one with a rapidly declining US presence and a reunified Germany. This shift caused European leaders in the early 1990s to adopt a "binding" strategy to ensure peace on the continent and prevent Germany from becoming a potential hegemon.

Each of the alternative arguments offers some useful insights into why European states are increasingly cooperating in the security realm. But none ultimately offers a better explanation. Evaluating theories is, of course, never dichotomous. The objective of this book is not to prove that one theory can entirely explain European security cooperation since World War II. Rather, it is to assess the relative importance of various theories.

No theory offers a complete explanation. My structural theory of European cooperation has several problems. For example, it can offer at best a rough prediction of which states will combine capabilities against a dominant power. Changing structural conditions in both the international and regional systems help explain why European states have a significant *impetus* to cooperate. But unit-level factors help determine whether – and with whom – a state will aggregate resources.[4] In Europe, this includes common historical, cultural, political, economic, and other factors. In addition, my theory can't explain why Britain has been less enthusiastic in pursuing intra-European cooperation than other European powers, especially France and Germany. The Franco-British decision to establish a rapid reaction force at St. Malo was critical to jumpstarting European military cooperation, and Britain has played a key role in pursuing intra-European arms production and sanctions cooperation. But Britain also retains a close security relationship with the United States.[5] Britain and the United States have cooperated in the deployment of military forces to such countries as Iraq, and British defense companies have pursued more arms collaboration with the United States than any other European country. Britain's stance on the European Union is a function of unit-level factors, such as the deep historical ties between Britain and America, a common language, and similar cultures. Still, these unit-level factors are at best intervening variables, and structural factors have exerted a powerful influence on European state behavior. Consequently, focusing predominantly on structure tells us a substantial amount about security cooperation.

We now turn to the alternative theories. First, there is a significant amount of evidence that contradicts the argument that meaningful security cooperation has been *illusory*. The establishment of a security arm of the European Union and the increase in sanctions cooperation, arms production, and military forces largely discredits this argument. In addition, public opinion polls in Europe strongly support a viable security arm of the European Union. As Figure 7.1 illustrates, for example, Eurobarometer polls show that a majority of French, British, and Germans have consistently supported a common security policy among European Union member states since 1992. In addition, support has been extremely high across the European Union: approximately

---

[4] Christopher Layne, "The Unipolar Illusion: Why New Great Powers Will Rise," *International Security*, Vol. 17, No. 4, Fall 1993, p. 9; Mearsheimer, *Tragedy of Great Power Politics*, p. 335.

[5] UK Ministry of Defence, *Delivering Security in a Changing World: Future Capabilities*, Cm 6269 (London: Ministry of Defence, 2004), p. 3.

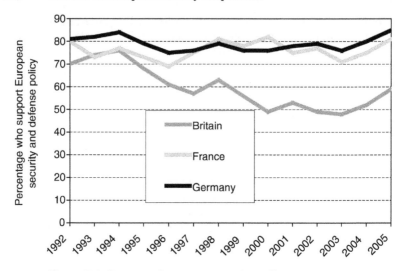

Figure 7.1. Support of common security policy.
Note: "Question: irrespective of other details of the Maastricht Treaty, what is your opinion on a common defence and security/military policy among the European Union member states? Please tell me whether you are for it or against it." Polls were conducted between 1992 and 2005. *Eurobarometer Interactive Search System* (Brussels: European Commission, 2005).

77 percent of the EU population supports a common defense and security policy. Eastern European countries, which are often perceived as the most transatlantic countries in the European Union, are among the strongest supporters of EU security cooperation. Support was 88 percent in Latvia, 88 percent in Slovakia, 87 percent in the Czech Republic, 85 percent in Slovenia, 84 percent in Poland, and 83 percent in Hungary.[6]

However, some may correctly point out that European states have not established viable power projection capabilities to fight major wars, with the possible exception of Britain and France. The EU rapid reaction force and battle groups are largely geared toward peacekeeping missions, not major theater wars. Europe does not have a veritable army – at least not yet. European states have also disagreed about major policy decisions. The French and Dutch rejection of the European Constitution in

[6] Commission of the EC, *Eurobarometer 64: Public Opinion in the European Union* (Brussels: European Commission, 2005), p. 34.

2005 demonstrated that nationalism had not entirely disappeared from the continent. But, as this book shows, the evidence overwhelmingly indicates that there has been a significant increase in European security cooperation.

Second, the historical evidence demonstrates that *domestic actors* had remarkably little impact and influence on European states. Security cooperation is thus not a function of domestic politics. This argument is also unable to explain the variation in cooperation over time. Why was there a significant increase in cooperation in the post-Cold War era, and why was there little intra-European cooperation during the Cold War? Perhaps the strongest evidence for this argument is in the arms industry, where European defense firms have pushed for greater intra-European cooperation through M&As and coproduction and codevelopment projects. But governments nonetheless played the lead role for greater intra-European arms cooperation in response to structural changes.

Third, *institutional arguments* are largely unable to explain the rise of European security cooperation since the end of the Cold War. There is little evidence that the European Union has had an independent impact on European governments, especially its major powers such as Germany, France, and Britain. Indeed, security cooperation has been intergovernmental rather than supranational. In addition, the timing of cooperation does not correlate with the establishment of European political cooperation beginning in 1969, as some institutionalists such as Michael Smith have argued. The evidence presented in Chapter 3 suggests that European political cooperation was largely a gentlemen's club, rather than an example of significant cooperation. Finally, most institutionalists believe that European states should not be alarmed by American power because it has been "institutionalized" through Western security institutions such as NATO. Again, the evidence indicates that European states have been deeply concerned about the United States.

Fourth, there is also insufficient evidence to support the argument that cooperation has primarily occurred because of the development of a *European identity*. Indeed, there is little indication of a significant shift in "European-ness" in the late 1980s and early 1990s. If anything, data show that for two of Europe's most significant powers – Germany and France – sentiments of Europeanness among their populations and elites actually *decreased* by the early 1990s. With little or no variation in the independent variable, how can constructivist arguments explain change? As one author pointedly argues: "Unfortunately, there is little consensus on how to define and measure identity in empirical terms, nor have many analysts applied these arguments to the EU in any systematic way."[7] In addition, primary sources clearly indicate that European states – including France and Britain – were deeply concerned about a reunified Germany in the early 1990s. This had a significant impact on the creation of a common foreign and security policy in the Maastricht Treaty.

Constructivist arguments about Europe are strongest on the subject of EU enlargement, which is not the primary focus of this book. As Frank Schimmelfennig argues, for example, EU enlargement is partly explained by a desire to spread liberal values, ideas, and norms across Eastern Europe. On the one hand, Eastern European communities were motivated to join the European Union by a mixture of security and economic reasons. EU membership served as a protection against a future revanchist Russia (as did NATO membership), and Eastern European economies were likely to benefit from participation in the European economic market. On the other hand, constructivist arguments provide a plausible explanation of the motivation of EU member states. As Schimmelfennig notes, "the EU embarked upon Eastern enlargement because its fundamental values and norms had spread to and taken root in Central and Eastern Europe since the Eastern European revolutions of 1989 and 1990."[8] The pro-enlargement coalition strategically used arguments based on the identity, ideology, values, norms, and past practices of the EU to shame member states that did not support enlargement because they expected net losses.

Europe and Pax Americana

Over the next decade, the degree of European security cooperation, as well as the state of the US–European strategic relationship, will be significantly influenced by the structure of the international and regional systems.

International system

The current evidence suggests that the United States will remain the preponderant global power for the foreseeable future. As William Wohlforth and others have argued, the international system is unambiguously

---

[7] Michael E. Smith, *Europe's Foreign and Security Policy* (New York: Cambridge University Press, 2004), p. 257.

[8] Frank Schimmelfennig, *The EU, NATO and the Integration of Europe: Rules and Rhetoric* (New York: Cambridge University Press, 2003), p. 282.

unipolar.[9] The United States has an unprecedented quantitative and qualitative margin of superiority over the next most powerful state. It enjoys decisive preponderance in all major underlying components of power: economic, military, technological, and geopolitical. Even if one accepts Paul Kennedy's argument that the United States will inevitably decline in power, as great powers have historically done, it is difficult to conceive of this happening anytime soon.[10] One of the most significant implications of US preponderance is its willingness and ability to project power unilaterally. Perhaps the clearest example is the 2003 war in Iraq. Despite substantial protest from a range of great powers that included Russia, France, Germany, India, China, and Japan, the Bush Administration nevertheless went to war with Iraq. United States preponderance and foreign policy behavior have led to a sharp decline in European views of the United States. As Figure 7.2 illustrates, the British, French, and German populations have increasingly viewed the United States unfavorably.

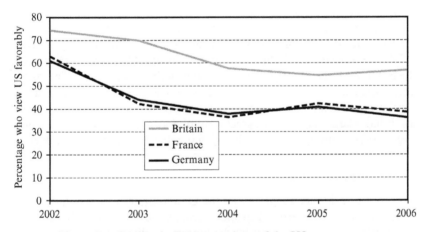

Figure 7.2. Decline in European views of the US.

Source: The Pew Research Center for the People and the Press, America's Image Slips, But Allies Share U.S. Concerns over Iran, Hamas (Washington, DC: Pew Research Center for the People and the Press, 2006).

[9] William C. Wohlforth, "The Stability of a Unipolar World," International Security, Vol. 24, No. 1, Summer 1999, pp. 5–41.
[10] Paul Kennedy, The Rise and Fall of the Great Powers (New York: Vintage Books, 1989). See also Robert Gilpin, War and Change in World Politics (New York: Cambridge University Press, 1981).

Assuming the United States remains the preponderant global power, this structural condition will cause EU states to continue aggregating power. A global hegemon in a unipolar system tends to acquire an enormous stake in world order, as does the scope of what constitutes its "national interest." While most countries are primarily interested about what occurs in their immediate neighborhood, for a hegemon most of the world is its neighborhood. This tends to bring it into conflict with the interests of other states. As Robert Jervis argues: "The large European states have every reason to be concerned about US hegemony and seek to constrain it; they understandably fear a world in which their values and interests are served only at Washington's sufferance."[11] To be clear, this is not traditional balancing. The United States does not pose a military threat to Europe. However, a hegemonic United States that enjoys unchecked power and is increasingly assertive around the globe will cause deep concern among EU states. Indeed, the response among Europeans will likely be to aggregate power to decrease dependence on the US and increase their ability to project power abroad.

For example, an opinion poll conducted by the Pew Research Center showed that 85 percent of French, 58 percent of British, and 73 percent of Germans believed that it would be much better if another power, such as the EU, rivaled US military power. In addition, majorities in every country in Western Europe – including France, Britain, and Germany – believe that the EU should take a more independent approach to security and diplomatic affairs than it has in the past.[12] As Figure 7.3 illustrates, when Europe combines power it is able to compete with the United States in most categories. It has a larger population, greater number of active military forces, and larger gross domestic product – though a notably smaller defense budget.

Regional system

The current evidence suggests that the United States will withdraw most of its ground forces from Europe, perhaps leaving only a handful of prepositioned forces that can be deployed quickly to areas of instability such as the Middle East and Central Asia.[13] This includes a significant

---

[11] Robert Jervis, "The Compulsive Empire," *Foreign Policy*, Vol. 137, July/August 2003, p. 85.
[12] Pew Research Center for the People and the Press, *American Character Gets Mixed Reviews*. (Washington, DC: The Pew Global Attitudes Project, 2005).
[13] Thom Shankler, "Plan to Shift Army Units is Complete, Officials Say," *New York Times*, July 27, 2005, p A6; Congressional Budget Office, *Options for Changing the Army's Overseas Basing* (Washington, DC: Congressional Budget Office, May 2004); John Diamond, "U.S. Lays Groundwork in Eastern Europe," *USA Today*, July 18, 2005, p. 4A; Demetri Sevastopulo, "Pentagon Backs Closing 33 Military Bases," *Financial*

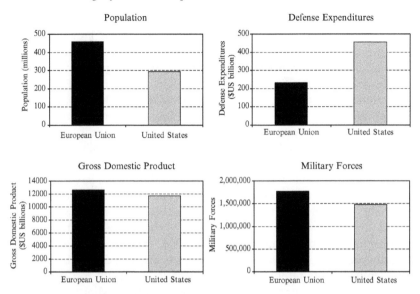

Figure 7.3. EU vs. US power.
Source: IISS, *The Military Balance, 2005–2006*, pp. 13–150.

decrease in US forces in Germany, which make up over-three quarters of US troops in Europe.[14] However, these numbers are likely to decrease substantially. The US Department of Defense is engaged in a significant reposturing of its global forces, relocating them from traditional Cold War installations in Germany to countries in Central Asia and the Middle East.

Current US deliberations over withdrawing forces from Europe are largely a function of changing security threats to the United States.[15] There are no major security threats to the United States originating from Europe. The terrorist attacks in Madrid and London were reminders that terrorism is a threat to Western countries, and the September 11, 2001 terrorists spent significant time in Germany. But the primary terrorist threat to the US originates from such areas as the Middle East. Since the end of the Cold

Times, May 14, 2005, p. 8; Andrew Koch, "U.S. Overseas Basing Moves Face Budget Crunch," *Jane's Defence Weekly*, May 18, 2005.
[14] In 2005, there were 90,700 US forces in Europe (69,790 – or 77 percent – in Germany). IISS, *The Military Balance, 2004–2005* (London: Taylor and Francis, 2005), pp. 30–1.
[15] The US withdrawal from Western Europe may also be partly a response by piqued US policymakers to such "Old Europe" policies as French and German opposition to the United States war in Iraq and refusal to support the US during the post-conflict insurgency. But this probably had only a marginal impact on the decision.

War and the terrorist attacks of September 2001, United States policymakers have become increasingly concerned about an "arc of instability" that stretches from North Africa to Southeast Asia, and covering such areas as the Middle East in between.[16] The United States engaged in sustained combat missions in such locations as Iraq, Afghanistan, and the Philippines. This shift is also evident in such documents as the *Quadrennial Defense Review* and *National Strategy of the United States of America*, which argued that the Middle East and Asia should increasingly become the central areas of American security policy.[17] Consequently, this means shifting US forces to countries and regions that are closer to future areas of operation.

Assuming the United States continues to withdraw military forces from Europe, we should see an increase in EU security cooperation as part of a "binding" strategy over the long run. The reason is that a withdrawal would largely remove the American pacifier, which ameliorated the security dilemma in Europe during the Cold War. Indeed, absent substantial security cooperation, EU states would risk provoking a destabilizing security dilemma in the future. While this scenario is difficult to contemplate today, the deep concern expressed by British Prime Minister Margaret Thatcher and French President François Mitterrand in the early 1990s suggests that a Germany that "opted out" of the European Union could trigger substantial concern. In sum, security cooperation through the European Union will be inversely correlated with American power in Europe: the further withdrawal of US forces from Europe should increase the incentive for cooperation through the European Union.

The argument that the United States is likely to withdraw its forces from Europe, yet remain a preponderant global power, may seem contradictory. But it is not. In fact, the two are quite complementary. A US withdrawal from Europe will likely be caused by a desire to preposition American troops and equipment closer to potential combat areas such as the Middle East and Asia. For US policymakers, withdrawing troops from Europe and repositioning them in other countries will be viewed as

---

[16] Yasuhiro Nakasone, "Insights into the World," *The Daily Yomiuri* (Tokyo), May 15, 2005, p. 10; Donna Miles, "Jones Outlines NATO, EUCOM Transformations," *American Forces Press Service*, November 23, 2004; Jim Garamone, "Jones Discusses Changing Troop 'Footprint' in Europe," *American Forces Press Service*, October 10, 2003; Robert Schlesinger, "US Remaking Look, Locations of Bases Abroad," *Boston Globe*, July 7, 2003, p. A1.

[17] US Department of Defense, *Quadrennial Defense Review* (Washington, DC: Dept of Defense, September 2001), pp. 2–7; White House, *National Strategy of the United States of America* (Washington, DC: White House, 2002), pp. 5–16; George Tenet, *The Worldwide Threat in 2003: Evolving Dangers in a Complex World* (Washington, DC: Central Intelligence Agency, 2003); Central Intelligence Agency, *Mapping the Global Future: Report of the National Intelligence Council's 2020 Project* (Washington, DC: CIA, 2004);

a way to facilitate and augment – not weaken – US power around the globe.

The European response

What specific steps might European states take in response to these structural factors? In order to answer this question, this section briefly explores European developments in three areas: economic sanctions for foreign policy goals, defense production, and military forces.

Economic Sanctions

Based on their post-Cold War behavior, EU states will likely continue to impose economic sanctions predominantly through the European Union, rather than unilaterally or multilaterally through other forums. These sanctions might include a variety of objectives such as terminating a target state's weapons of mass destruction program, establishing or restoring democracy, and ending civil or interstate war. EU states have a significant incentive to aggregate power when imposing sanctions because it increases their ability to project power and influence abroad, and it decreases their reliance on the United States. Based on past trends, EU states are likely to impose sanctions on a range of countries in Africa, the Middle East, and Asia, rather than such areas as Latin America.

Arms production

Recent developments suggest that European states and defense firms will continue to collaborate with each other through mergers and acquisitions, codevelopment projects, and coproduction projects. The likely result will be increasing competition between European and US firms in building arms and selling them abroad. As the European Advisory Group on Aerospace argued in its *Strategic Aerospace Review for the 21st Century*: "Operating in a global market place, the European aerospace industry faces strong competition from companies located in other parts of the world, mainly in the US."[18] The establishment of such transnational European defense companies as EADS and missile-maker MBDA is a testament to the increase in consolidation of Europe's defense industry. It also reflects a view that regional consolidation increases European competitiveness against such powerful American defense firms as Boeing and Lockheed Martin. There

---

[18] Commission of the EC, *STAR21: Strategic Aerospace Review for the 21st Century* (Brussels: European Commission, July 2002), p. 18.

are a number of market segments, such as land and sea systems, where there may be increased European consolidation in the future.[19] A continuation of US political obstacles to transatlantic defense cooperation will also create friction and provide an impetus for European states to collaborate in the defense industry. US obstacles have included the "Buy American Act," extensive export and technology transfer controls, and restrictive regulatory processes regarding foreign investment in US firms.[20]

EU states have also made substantial progress in collaborating to develop and produce missiles, helicopters, satellites, and other aerospace systems. This will likely continue in the future. European defense firms will produce some of the most advanced weapons and military systems in the world, including in such areas as command, control, communications, computers, intelligence, surveillance, and reconnaissance (C4ISR). Even today, Europe has a technological base capable of meeting modern C4ISR and other requirements.[21] While there is some truth to the argument that a "capabilities gap" exists between between the United States and Europe, it is largely a function of defense spending rather than technological prowess. In addition, it is not as large as many US defense planners perceive, especially vis-à-vis such countries as Britain. Most European states are planning to continue developing digital communications; cross-server command and control systems; and several types of intelligence, surveillance, and reconnaissance platforms. The most advanced development programs will likely be in France and Britain, which currently devote more resources to C4ISR capabilities.[22]

---

[19] Joris Janssen Lok, "Jean-Georges Malcor: Senior Vice President, Thales Naval Division," *Jane's Defence Weekly*, May 4, 2005; David Mulholland, "German Industry: Feeling the Squeeze," *Jane's Defence Weekly*, March 30, 2005; Andrew Chuter, Tom Kington, and Pierre Tran, "Consolidate or Fail? Europe's Fractured Industry Faces Crisis," *Defense News*, Vol. 18, No. 23, June 9, 2003, pp. 1; Andrew Chuter, "Armor Industry Consolidation Certain, But Scope Unclear," *Defense News*, September 8, 2003, p. 46.

[20] On US defense obstacles, see Mark A. Lorell *et al.*, *Going Global? U.S. Government Policy and the Defense Aerospace Industry* (Santa Monica, CA: RAND, 2002); Vlachos-Dengler, Katia, *Off Track? The Future of the European Defense Industry* (Santa Monica, CA: RAND, 2004), pp.106–9; Gordon Adams, Christophe Cornu, and Andrew D. James, *Between Cooperation and Competition: The Transatlantic Defence Market* (Paris: Institute for Security Studies, 2001), pp. 21–49.

[21] Gordon Adams, Guy Ben-Ari, John Logsdon, and Ray Williamson, *Bridging the Gap: European C4ISR Capabilities and Transatlantic Interoperability* (Washington, DC: National Defense University Center for Technology and National Security Policy, 2004).

[22] Vlachos-Dengler, *Off Track?*, pp. 89–97; Council of the EU, *Capability Improvement Chart 2004* (Brussels: European Council, May 2004); Adams, Ben-Ari, and Logsdon, *Bridging the Gap*; Nick Cook, Christopher Foss, and Richard Scott, "Briefing: UK Defence Industry," *Jane's Defence Weekly*, Vol. 41, No. 34, August 24, 2004, pp. 21–8.

Perhaps the most significant aerospace developments will be in space research and development, such as the Galileo global navigation satellite system and Global Monitoring of Environment and Safety programs.[23] European space technology is already highly advanced, and these developments will likely cause European militaries to utilize and fit platforms with global navigation satellite capabilities. They may also trigger an increase in space-based capabilities, such as satellite receivers for information awareness, positioning services, and weapons guidance to improve strike effectiveness.[24] Major collaboration will also likely occur in naval and land systems.[25] As one EU document notes, the failure to develop a European space capability would "lead to a rapid decline in European industrial capacities and would not therefore enable Europe to acquire the space infrastructures that are vital to a political power, as demonstrated by the US policy."[26]

European developments in weapons, platforms, and systems will improve the ability of European states to conduct autonomous action abroad and decrease dependence on the United States. For example, European militaries lack strategic airlift for out-of-area missions. EU countries possess a number of C-160 Transall and C-130 Hercules transport planes. But their payloads are less than a quarter of the C-17 Globemaster. Britain has also leased C-17s from Boeing, and other European governments such as Germany have rented Ukrainian Antonov-124 transport planes.[27] But any EU military mission over the next five to ten years will be forced to rely on US strategic lift to transport troops and equipment to the theater of operations. To overcome this deficiency, European states have begun development of the Airbus A-400M strategic airlift, which is expected to come off the production lines by the end of the decade. European militaries also lack the capability to conduct all-weather, precision-strike air operations such as those in Bosnia and Kosovo in the 1990s. In order to rectify this problem, European militaries are developing such precision weapons as the

---

[23] Gustav Lindstrom, *The Galileo Satellite System and its Security Implications*, No. 44 (Paris: Institute for Security Studies, April 2003).

[24] Adams, Ben-Ari, and Logsdon, *Bridging the Gap*.

[25] Guy Anderson, "France and UK Prepare for Cooperation Over Aircraft Carriers," *Jane's Defence Industry*, June 21, 2005; Richard Scott, "Navy Sees Cuts Across Fleet," *Jane's Defence Weekly*, Vol. 41, No. 30, July 28, 2004, p. 14; Nick Cook, Christopher Foss, and Richard Scott, "Briefing: UK Defence Industry," *Jane's Defence Weekly*, Vol. 41, No. 34, August 24, 2004, pp. 21–8.

[26] European Space Agency, *Agenda 2007: A Document by the ESA Director General*, BR-213 (Noordwijk, Netherlands: ESA, 2003), p. 8.

[27] Bastian Giegerich and William Wallace, "Not Such a Soft Power: The External Deployment of European Forces," *Survival*, Summer 2004, Vol. 46, No. 2, pp. 163–82.

Storm Shadow/Scalp cruise missile and the Taurus long-range stand-off missile.[28] Galileo will provide EU states with a number of military capacities – monitoring troop movements, facilitating logistics planning, and improving targeting and munitions guidance – that can be performed independently of the US monopoly of GPS.[29] In order to monitor these activities, there may also be progress in the development of the European Defense Agency to improve the coordination of European military capabilities, armaments, technology, and research and development.[30]

Military forces

The current evidence suggests that European states will continue to develop joint military forces to project power abroad. Concrete developments first began at the December 1998 Franco-British summit in St. Malo, France when British Prime Minister Tony Blair and French President Jacques Chirac agreed that the European Union "must have the capacity for autonomous action, backed up by credible military forces."[31] At the 1999 Helsinki summit, European states established a permanent political-military structure to oversee future military operations in support of the Common Foreign and Security Policy and to reinforce and extend the European Union's external role. The structure includes a political and security committee, military committee, and military staff. In 2003 EU states agreed to the construction of a military planning capability independent of NATO. As an internal document approved by Germany, France, and Britain noted, the European Union "should be endowed with a joint capacity to plan and conduct operations without recourse to NATO resources and capabilities."[32] While Britain, France, and Germany have national military planning

---

[28] Martin Aguera, "German Vehicle, Missile Programs Move Ahead," *Defense News*, January 2, 2006.

[29] On Galileo's military applications see Lindstrom, *The Galileo Satellite System*.

[30] Council Joint Action on the Establishment of the European Defense Agency, 2004/551/ CFSP, Brussels, July 12, 2004; Council of the EU, *Agency in the Field of Defense Capabilities Development, Research, Acquisition, and Armaments* (Brussels: European Council, May 17, 2004).

[31] Franco-British Summit, St. Malo, France, December 3–4, 1998 in Maartje Rutten, ed., *From St-Malo to Nice, European Defence: Core Documents*, Chaillot Paper 47 (Paris: Institute for Security Studies, 2001), p. 8.

[32] Bertrand Benoit and Ben Hall, "Europe's Big Three Closer on Defense," *Financial Times*, September 22, 2003, p. 2. See also Ambrose Evans-Pritchard and Kate Connolly, "Blair 'Backs Plan' to Give EU Army More Power," *Daily Telegraph*, September 22, 2003, p. 1; Judy Dempsey, "'Big Three' Discuss EU Military Planning Unit," *Financial Times*, November 27, 2003, p. 3.

headquarters, a coordinated operational planning capability improves their ability to act autonomously. Under the Headline Goal 2010, EU defense ministers established European battle groups for international intervention and tasks reaching up to full-combat situations. Each battle group will be composed of 1,500 combat soldiers plus support.[33]

European Union military cooperation will also include the establishment and development of joint paramilitary "gendarmerie" to help stabilize countries during peacekeeping operations and train local police.[34] This has already started to occur. France, Italy, the Netherlands, Portugal, and Spain created a European Gendarmerie Force with a permanent headquarters in Vicenza, Italy. Its *raison d'être* is to ensure security and public order, fight organized crime, advise and train local police forces and fill the security gap during peacekeeping and stability operations.[35] In addition, the EU deployed a police mission to Bosnia to help mentor and assess Bosnian police. EU units were co-located with Bosnian state- and district-level police, and served as advisors to the Ministry of Security and Ministry of Interior for the Bosnian-Croat Federation and the Republika Srpska. European leaders have argued that the development and deployment of EU paramilitary police in the future would help project EU power and supplement military forces during peacekeeping and nation-building operations.[36]

In sum, the evidence suggests that EU states will continue to develop an autonomous military force that can be used for peacekeeping and perhaps some peace enforcement missions, and that will include an independent military planning capability. The result will likely be increasing EU tension with the United States in areas such as the Middle East and Asia where their strategic interests do not overlap.

United States dominance

How will the United States respond to increasing European security cooperation? Based on US policy over the past decade, the likely response will be to resist increasing EU security cooperation. This should not be significantly affected by whether a Republican or Democratic

---

[33] Council of the EU, *Headline Goal 2010* (Brussels: European Council, June 2004).
[34] Dempsey, "Paris Seeks EU 'Gendarme' Force for Peace Missions," *Financial Times*, October 6, 2003, p. 2; Giegerich and Wallace, "Not Such a Soft Power," p. 172.
[35] Enrique Esquivel Lalinde, *The New European Gendarmerie Force* (Madrid: Real Institute Elcano, 2005); Interview given by French Minister of Defense Michèle Alliot-Marie, September 19, 2004 (Paris: French Ministry of Defense, 2004).
[36] Marco Nesse, "Intervista del Ministro della Difesa Prof. Antonio Martino," *Corriere della Sera*, October 13, 2003.

administration sits in the White House, nor ultimately by whether a Republican or Democratic administration adopts a "unilateral" or "multilateral" foreign policy. Specifically, a preponderant US will likely view an increasingly powerful and cooperative European Union as a challenge to its hegemony. This is the logical response by the most powerful state in the international system to a rising power.[37]

Perhaps the clearest indication of the US response is in the area of military forces. Since the end of the Cold War, United States officials have advocated a "NATO first" policy.[38] The US is willing to facilitate the creation of a European Union defense arm, but not as an independent entity from NATO. Indeed, the grand bargain reached at NATO's Berlin and Brussels foreign and defense ministerial meetings in June 1996 permitted the existence of an EU military arm, but only within NATO. This was reinforced by the "Berlin Plus" arrangements, which reaffirmed NATO's primacy for military action and argued that there should be no "unnecessary duplication" between the EU and NATO. The use of NATO assets and capabilities by the European Union had to be approved by NATO's North Atlantic Council, and NATO resources could be returned or recalled if needed for a competing crisis or conflict. Furthermore, EU countries had to rely on NATO for military planning and exercises. As President George W. Bush argued: "A strong, capable European force *integrated with NATO* would give us more options for handling crises when NATO, as a whole, chooses not to engage."[39] In short, US policymakers have insisted on NATO – and United States – primacy. This preserves US power and influence in Europe and ensures stability on the continent.

United States policymakers have two related concerns with an independent European defense arm: decoupling and duplication. First, US officials worry that an autonomous European organization with independent capabilities would lead to a *decoupling* of transatlantic cooperation. The logic is that the United States and Europe share a common interest in ensuring security and stability within Europe and its periphery, and NATO plays the pivotal role. The concern is that decoupling would decrease US influence over Europe and threaten US hegemony.

---

[37] On power transitions, see Dale Copeland, *The Origins of Major War* (Ithaca, NY: Cornell University Press, 2001); Robert Gilpin, *War and Change in International Politics* (Cambridge: Cambridge University Press, 1981); Stephen Van Evera, *Causes of War: Power and the Roots of Conflict* (Ithaca, NY: Cornell University Press, 1999).

[38] See, for example, Robert E. Hunter, *The European Security and Defense Policy: NATO's Companion or Competitor?* MR-1463-NDRI/RE (Santa Monica, CA: RAND, 2002).

[39] "Press Availability with President Bush and NATO Secretary General Lord Robertson at NATO Headquarters, Brussels" (Washington, DC: White House, June 13, 2001). Emphasis added.

Second, American policymakers have also expressed concern about *duplication*. This has partly reflected a desire that European militaries refrain from spending precious resources on a second set of capabilities that they could easily obtain from NATO or the US. Why waste money on constructing the A-400M strategic airlift when Europeans can buy C-17s from Boeing? Why build the Galileo global navigation satellite system when they can use the US's global positioning system (GPS)? Under what conceivable scenario, some might argue, would the United States be unwilling to share these resources? US policymakers have also noted concern about duplication because many are deeply skeptical that the EU will ever have the capability or political will to act autonomously of NATO. Since any significant use of military force will *ipso facto* involve the United States, it makes little sense to devote resources to a pipe-dream. Most importantly, however, duplication could lead to a decoupling of the transatlantic alliance. Both the US Senate and the House of Representatives adopted a nonbinding resolution which stated that EU efforts should "complement, rather than duplicate NATO efforts and institutions, and be linked to, rather than decoupled from NATO structures."[40] Similarly, US Secretary of Defense Donald Rumsfeld argued that "actions that could reduce NATO's effectiveness by confusing duplication or by perturbing the transatlantic link would not be positive. Indeed, they run the risk of injecting instability into an enormously important Alliance."[41]

As Christopher Layne argues, Washington has historically responded to European security cooperation by engaging in a strategy of "divide and rule" in Europe.[42] Future US steps to pursue this strategy and undermine greater EU security cooperation might include:

• Resisting development of such European Union programs as the rapid reaction force and military planning unit that give EU states an independent capability. This means trying to ensure that NATO remains the preponderant defense institution for European states.
• Encouraging EU states to individually carve out "niche" functions – such as conducting peacekeeping operations or providing

[40] H. Res. 59, adopted November 2, 1999.
[41] Roger Cohen, "Shifts in Europe Pose Prickly Challenge to US," *New York Times*, February 11, 2002, p. 4; Tony Harnden and Toby Helm, "Warning Shot on EU Army by White House," *Daily Telegraph*, February 5, 2001, p. 1; Roger Boyes, "Moscow Exploits Europe Fears over US Weapon," *Times*, February 5, 2001.
[42] See, for example, Christopher Layne, "America as European Hegemon," *National Interest*, No. 72, Summer 2003, pp. 17–29.

development assistance – that will complement US power rather than challenge it.[43]

- Utilizing a bilateral "divide and rule" strategy. In particular, this means using the US's special friendship with Britain to encourage divisions in Europe on specific policy issues. It might also mean pressuring pro-American states in Eastern Europe, such as Poland and Hungary, to support US interests.[44]

In short, each US administration in the post-Cold War era – George H. W. Bush, Bill Clinton, and George W. Bush – has adopted a "NATO first" defense policy. This response is not likely to change in the future if EU security cooperation increases. Future US administrations will continue to believe that NATO must remain the bedrock of European security. The establishment of a viable defense arm of the European Union with the structures and capability to act independently of NATO and the US would reduce American influence by causing decoupling and duplication.

Trouble ahead

The future of the US–European strategic relationship will be significantly influenced by power considerations. Assuming that the US remains the preponderant global power, increasingly withdraws its military forces from Europe, and asserts its power across the globe, EU states will have an enormous incentive to aggregate power. US steps to curb cooperation through such tactics as "divide and rule" will likely increase – rather than decrease – EU efforts to combine power in the foreign policy and defense realms. Consequently, future transatlantic relations will be characterized by increasing tension. What does "increasing tension" mean? To begin with, it does *not* mean military conflict between the United States and Europe, at least not in the foreseeable future. Nor does it preclude the two from cooperating in a number of

---

[43] Andrew Moravcsik, "How Europe Can Win Without an Army," *Financial Times*, April 3, 2003, p. 19. Andrew Moravcsik, "Lessons from Iraq," in *One Year On: Lessons from Iraq*, Chaillot Paper 68 (Paris: Institute for European Studies, 2004), pp. 185–93.

[44] See, for example, US attempts to divide Europe before the 2003 war in Iraq. Quentin Peel, James Harding, Judy Dempsey, and Robert Graham, "The Rift Turns Nasty: The Plot that Split Old and New Europe Asunder," *Financial Times*, May 28, 2003, p. 13. One of the most divisive issues was the January 2003 opinion piece in the *Wall Street Journal*, which divided European states on support for the United States. José María Aznar, José Manuel Durão Barroso, Silvio Berlusconi, Tony Blair, Václav Havel, Medgyessy Péter, Leszek Miller, Anders Fogh Rasmussen, "Europe and America Must Stand United," *Wall Street Journal*, January 30, 2003.

important areas. But increasing tension does mean that they will disagree more often on major foreign policy and defense issues. It also means that Europe will increasingly possess the capability and willingness to act independently of – and, at times, contrary to – the United States.

It is impossible to predict what specific issues will cause tension between Europe and the United States in the future. However, the 2003 dispute over the US-led war in Iraq offers an interesting preview. Of particular interest was the January 22, 2003, joint declaration by French President Jacques Chirac and German Chancellor Gerhard Schröder to oppose the Bush Administration in Iraq.[45] The date commemorated the fortieth anniversary of the Franco-German Treaty negotiated by Charles de Gaulle and Konrad Adenauer as a bulwark against American hegemony. During his 2002 reelection campaign, Schröder ran on a political platform that emphasized German opposition to the US war against Iraq.[46] When the United States and Britain pushed for a second United Nations Security Council resolution in March 2003 that would effectively authorize military action against Iraq, Berlin and Paris stated they would oppose it. As Chirac explained on French television, his government would oppose the resolution "quelles que soient les circonstances" (whatever the circumstances).[47] Both countries also refused to offer significant political and military support to the reconstruction effort after major combat ended, when US casualties began to mount. As one member of the German Bundestag noted: "Why should we bail the United States out of a conflict that we never supported to begin with?"[48] This view remained consistent in Paris and Berlin despite changes in government. In Germany, for example, Chancellor Angela Merkel's government strongly supported the decision to stand up to the United States regarding Iraq, and similarly refused to deploy troops.[49]

---

[45] See, for example, Layne, "America as European Hegemon," pp. 17–29.
[46] Elizabeth Pond, *Friendly Fire: The Near-Death of the Transatlantic Alliance* (Washington, DC: Brookings Institution Press, 2004), pp. 56–62; Laurent Cohen-Tanugi, *An Alliance at Risk: The United States and Europe since September 11* (Baltimore: Johns Hopkins University Press, 2004), p. 82.
[47] Claire Trean, "La guerre contre l'Irak se fera sans le feu vert des Nations unies," *Le Monde*, March 12, 2003; Luc de Barochez, "Alors que la date du prochain vote du Conseil de sécurité n'est pas encore fixée," *Le Figaro*, March 11, 2003; "Paris rejetera une deuxième résolution au conseil de securité," *La Tribune*, March 11, 2003, p. 4.
[48] Author's interview with Bundestag member, Washington, DC, September 30, 2003.
[49] See, for example, the speech by Foreign Minister Frank-Walter Steinmeier to the German Bundestag, Berlin, December 14, 2005. "Speech by Foreign Minister Steinmeier in the German Bundestag" (Berlin: Federal Foreign Office, December 2005). See also Merkel's objections to the US prison in Guantanamo Bay in Jens Tartler and Olaf Gersemann, "Merkel fordert Ende von Guantanamo," *Financial Times Deutschland*, January 9, 2006.

There was a nearly universal consensus that the clash over Iraq was one of the gravest crises between Europe and the United States since the formation of NATO. "The road to Iraqi disarmament has produced the gravest crisis within the Atlantic Alliance since its creation five decades ago," concluded former Secretary of State Henry Kissinger. US Secretary of State Colin Powell similarly remarked: "Who's breaking up the alliance? . . . The alliance is breaking itself up because it will not meet its responsibilities." Philip Gordon and Jeremy Shapiro argued: "The US–Europe clash over Iraq led to the most serious deterioration of transatlantic relations in recent memory." Ivo Daalder went even further, noting that one consequence of the war in Iraq "is the effective end of Atlanticism – American and European foreign policies no longer center around the transatlantic alliance." US–European tension over Iraq also spilled into the human rights realm. European governments accused the United States of torturing detainees in several US-run prisons, such as in Afghanistan, Iraq, and at Guantanamo Bay, Cuba. For example, British Attorney General Lord Goldsmith declared that "the existence of Guantanamo Bay remains unacceptable," and German Chancellor Angela Merkel told President George W. Bush in a frank meeting in Washington that Guantanamo Bay "should not exist."[50]

One of the most significant areas of future tension may be over China, where the United States and Europe have different strategies and interests. One example is European technology transfers to such adversaries as China.[51] A closer European–Chinese economic and political partnership would almost inevitably lead to European military and dual-use technology transfers to China. This development could increase China's military capabilities by accelerating important components of military

[50] Henry A. Kissinger, "Role Reversal and Alliance Realities," *Washington Post*, February 10, 2003, p. A21; Patrick E. Tyler, "Threats and Responses: Old Friends," *New York Times*, February 12, 2003, p. A1; Philip H. Gordon and Jeremy Shapiro, *Allies at War: America, Europe, and the Crisis over Iraq* (New York: McGraw-Hill, 2004), p. 2; Ivo H. Daalder, "The End of Atlanticism," *Survival*, Vol. 45, No. 2, Summer 2003, pp. 147–8. Also see Samuel F. Wells, "The Transatlantic Illness," *Wilson Quarterly*, Vol. 27, No. 1, Winter 2003, pp. 40–6; James B. Steinberg, "An Elective Partnership: Salvaging Transatlantic Relations," *Survival*, Vol. 45, No. 2, Summer 2003, pp. 113–46. Holger Schmale, "USA Merkel und Bush bekräftigen Freundschaft Guantanamo Thema beim Treffen im Weißen Haus," *Berliner Zeitung*, 14 January 2006, p. 1; Daniel Dombey and Sarah Laitner, "Attorney-General Demands that U.S. Close Guatanamo Bay," *Financial Times*, 11 May 2006, p. 2. On European public views of the US treatment of prisoners during the war in Iraq, see Pew Research Center for the People and the Press, *America's Image Slips, But Allies Share U.S. Concerns Over Iran, Hamas* (Washington, DC: Pew Research Center for the People and the Press, 2006).
[51] On China's policy toward the European Union, see "Full Text of China's EU Policy Paper," *Xinhua News Service*, October 13, 2003.

modernization, and ultimately impede America's ability to sustain deterrence in Asia. China has a rich history of using foreign technology and assistance to improve its military capabilities. Over the past decade, for example, China's military has had access to limited amounts of foreign military equipment and technical assistance, especially from Russia and Israel. This aid has increased China's ability to copy weapon systems, integrate advanced technologies into China's production lines, and raise the technical expertise of Chinese workers involved in defense production.[52]

Indeed, European governments and firms have increasingly exported military and dual-use technology to China. According to EU data, the value of licenses for weapons exports increased from 54 million euros in 2001 to more than 400 million euros in 2004 – an increase of nearly 700 percent.[53] As Table 7.2 highlights, examples of European exports include British micro- and nano-satellite technology for anti-satellite weapon systems, British airborne early warning radar for Y-8 AEW aircraft, German engines for Song-A conventional submarines, and French and Italian technology for attack helicopters.[54] China reached

Table 7.2. *Selected European technologies transferred to China*

Weapon system	European content
Anti-satellite, direct ascent	British micro- and nano-satellite technology
Y-8 airborne early warning (AEW) aircraft	British Racal/Thales Skymaster AEW radar
Song-A submarine	German engine
Medium transport/attack helicopter	French design assistance for rotor head; Italian design assistance
Type-98 main battle tank	British or German influenced engine
JH-7 fighter bombers	Rolls Royce turbofan engine technology
Satellites	Chinese participation in Galileo global navigation satellite system

[52] Evan S. Medeiros, Roger Cliff, Keith Crane, and James C. Mulvenon, *A New Direction for China's Defense Industry* (Santa Monica, CA: RAND, 2005).
[53] Evan S. Medeiros and Seth G. Jones, "Heading off European Arms to China," *The Hill*, March 2, 2005.
[54] Author interviews were with senior executives at EADS, Thales, BAE Systems, and the defense ministries of Britain, France, and Germany from January to July 2005. Also see Eugene Kogan, *The European Union Defence Industry and the Appeal of the Chinese*

a deal with Eurocopter in December 2005 to build a new medium-lift helicopter, raising concerns that China might use systems on these helicopters – such as dynamic systems – for its medium-lift attack helicopter program, the Z-10.[55]

In addition, China invested several hundred million dollars in the Galileo navigation satellite system. China Galileo Industries Ltd, a Chinese state-run company, is developing Galileo's satellite and remote sensing technologies and application systems. According to a cooperation agreement signed by the National Remote Sensing Center of China and the Galileo Joint Undertaking, China pledged to invest in research and development on space technologies, ground equipment, and application systems for the Galileo Project.[56] European officials have welcomed Chinese participation in Galileo. "China should remain part of the Galileo project until the end," European Commission vice-president Jacques Barrot has argued, adding he was delighted by the "strategic partnership which is starting to take shape with China."[57]

It is unlikely that European defense firms will sell weapons or platforms directly to China because of political concerns and Code of Conduct restrictions.[58] Nor is wholesale licensing probable. Rather, the most likely concern will be military and dual-use technology transfers. The United States has several options in response to European military and dual-use technology transfers to China. Examples include

Market (Vienna: Studien und Berichte zur Sicherheitspolitik, 2005); US General Accounting Office, *China: U.S. and European Union Arms Sales since the 1989 Embargoes* (Washington, DC: General Accounting Office, 1998); *Hearing on Military Modernization and Cross Straight Balance, Hearing before the U.S.-China Economic and Security Review Commission, February 6, 2004* (Washington, DC: US Government Printing Office, 2004); Daniel Byman, Mark Burles, Roger Cliff, and Robert Mullins, *China's Arms Purchases: Understanding the Danger* (Santa Monica, CA: RAND, 1999); Paul Betts and Justine Lau, "EADS Moves to Boost Ties with China," *Financial Times*, October 21, 2003, p. 31; "Europe's Companies Urge Removal of Ban on High-Tech Exports to China," *Xinhua News Agency*, November 26, 2003.

[55] Michael A. Taverna, "Chinese Ink Deals with Eurocopter, Safran, and Alcatel Alenia Space," *Aviation Week and Space Technology*, Vol. 163, No. 23, December 12, 2005, p. 32.

[56] "Chinese State Company Obtains Contract to Develop Galileo Satellite Technology," *Xinhua News Agency*, March 9, 2005; Raphael Minder, "China's Focus on Galileo Pinpoints U.S. Security Fears," *Financial Times*, February 24, 2005.

[57] "China Urged to Take Full Part in Europe's Galileo Space Project," *Agence France Presse*, July 1, 2005.

[58] On the European code of conduct, see Raul Romeva Rueda, *Report on the Council's Sixth Annual Report According to Operation Provision 8 of the European Code of Conduct on Arms Control*, A6-0292/2005 (Brussels: European Parliament, 2004). See also Raul Romeva Rueda, *Report on the Council's Fifth Annual Report According to Operation Provision 8 of the European Code of Conduct on Arms Control*, A6-0022/2004 (Brussels: European Parliament, 2004).

curbing business with European companies that export military or dual-use technologies that are used by China for military purposes, and erecting fire walls to make it more difficult for European companies to acquire sensitive US technologies through collaborative programs.[59] Future areas of concern include:

- Navigation satellite technology, including through Chinese participation in Europe's Galileo global navigation satellite system
- Stealth technology
- Missile technology, such as air-to-air missiles or land attack cruise missiles
- Helicopter and aircraft technology, such as dynamic systems
- Micro- and nano-satellite technology
- Airborne early warning technology
- Engine technology
- Communications technology
- Naval systems.

The European opposition to the US-led war in Iraq and simmering debates over China offer a taste of the future. There will likely be an increasing number of disagreements as EU states – especially France and Germany – become more willing to stand up to American power. In the absence of a major security threat that binds Europe and America together, like the Soviet Union during the Cold War, they are destined to clash over international politics. As Jacques Chirac acknowledged: "We want to live in a multipolar world, one with a few large groups enjoying as harmonious relations as possible with each other, a world in which Europe, among others, will have its full place."[60] The tragic future of the US–European strategic relationship is unfortunate. But it is the logical result of the structure of the regional and international systems.

[59] Jon Kyl, *European Union Likely to End Arms Embargo on the People's Republic of China* (Washington, DC: Republican Policy Committee, 2005); Guy Dinmore, "U.S. Warns Europeans Against Resuming Arms Sales to China," *Financial Times*, December 14, 2004, p. 6.
[60] Peter Ford, "Europe's Fears of US Domination," *Christian Science Monitor*, March 14, 2003, p. 6.

Appendix A

Coproduction and Codevelopment Involving European Defense Firms, 1961–2000 N=283

Program start period	Regions	Countries	Companies	System name
1961–1970	EU	GE FR	Dornier, Dassault	Atlantique – reconnaissance aircraft
		GE FR	MBB, Aerospatiale	C-160 Transall – military transport
		UK FR	Rolls-Royce, SNECMA	M-45 – engines
		FR UK GE	SNECMA, Rolls-Royce, MTU	Tyne Mk 21-22 – turboprop engines
		FR GE	Aerospatiale, MBB (DASA)	HOT-1 – anti-tank guided weapons
		GE FR	MBB, Thomson, Aerospatiale	Kormoran – anti-ship missiles
		UK FR	Hawker Siddley, Matra	Martel – air-to-ground missiles
		FR GE	Aerospatiale, MBB (DASA)	Milan-1 – anti-tank guided weapons
		FR GE	Aerospatiale, MBB (DASA)	Roland – surface-to-air missiles
		UK FR	BAe, Dassault	Sepecat/Jaguar – fighters
		FR UK	Turbomeca, Rolls-Royce	Adour – engines
		FR GE	Dassault, Dornier	Alpha Jet trainers – reconnaissance aircraft
		FR UK	Aerospatiale, Westland	Gazelle – helicopters
		FR GE	Snecma, Turbomeca, MTU, Siemens	Larzac – aeroengines
		UK FR	Westland, Aerospatiale	Lynx – helicopters
		FR UK	Aerospatiale, Westland	Puma – helicopters
		IT UK	FIAT, GEC	Viper 600 – engines
		GE IT UK	Rheinmetall, OTO Melara, Vickers	FH-70 – 155-mm towed howitzers
		UK BE	BAC, FN	Atlas – missiles
		IT FR	OTO Melara, Matra	Otomat – anti-ship missiles
1961–1970	EU US	US GE	US, German government agencies	MBT-70 – tanks
		US EU	NATO countries	Hawk – surface-to-air missiles
		UK US	Rolls-Royce, Allison	Spey TF-41 – engines
		US GE NL NOR BE DE Canada	Raytheon	Seasparrow – surface-to-air missiles

Program start period	Regions	Countries	Companies	System name
1961–1970	EU EE	GE Switzerland	Krauss-Maffei, Contraves	Gepard AAA
		UK IT Switzerland	Hawker Siddley, Contraves	Indigo – missiles
1971–1980	EU	FR GE IT UK	Aerospatiale, DASA	ESA/Ariane launcher
		GE IT UK	DASA, Alenia, BAe	Panavia/Tornado – fighters
		GE IT UK	MTU, FIAT, Rolls-Royce	RB-199 – engines
		UK GE IT	Rheinmetall, OTO Melara, Vickers	SP-70 – howitzers
		GE FR	Lorenz, LMT	RATAC – radar
		FR BE	Thomson-CSF	RITA – communication systems
		BE FR NL	Beliard, CMN, Van der Giesse	Tripartite MCMV – minesweeper
		FR GE	Aerospatiale, MBB (DASA)	Euromissile
		FR IT	Aerospatiale, Alenia	ATR-42/-72 – transport
		FR GE	Thomson, Thyssen	Dragon AA gun
		UK GE NOR	BAe, BGT, NFT	ASRAAM – air-to-air missiles
1971–1980	EU US	US GE	LTV, VFW	USAF – trainers
		NATO	NATO government agencies	AWACS – airborne early warning
		US FR	GE, Snecma	CFM engines (for KC-135s)
		US UK GE	Hughes, GEC, BAe Dynamics, MBB	AMRAAM – air-to-air missiles
		FR NL NOR UK GE US	Aerospatiale, BAe, GEC, MBB	ASSM – anti-ship missiles
		US BE DE NL NOR	SABCA, Fokker, GD(Lockheed)	F-16 – fighters
		US GE	GD, BGT, DASA	RAM – surface-to-air missiles
		US UK	Raytheon, Hawker Siddley (BAe)	Skyflash/AIM-7 – air-to-air missiles
		US GE	Boeing, MBB	Armburst – anti-tank weapons
		US UK	ITT Gilfillan, Plessey	AD radar systems
		US UK	Martin Marietta, BAe	IR guidance systems
		UK GE US	BAe, MBB, MDC	SOM – air-to-ground missiles
1971–1980	EU AS	GE Japan	MBB, Kawasaki Heavy Industries	BK-117 – helicopters

Period		Countries	Companies	Product
1971–1980	EU LA	UK Brazil	Vickers, Verolme	AS-90 – howitzers
		IT Brazil	Alenia, Aermacchi, Embraer	AMX – fighters
1981–1990	EU	IT UK	Westland, Agusta	EHI/EH-101 – helicopters
		GE IT SP UK	DASA, Alenia, CASA, BAe	Eurofighter/EFA – fighters
		SP Austria	Santa Barbara, Steyr	ASCOD – armored personnel carriers
		GE IT	MaK, OTO Melara	AV-90 – armored personnel carriers
		GE NL	Krauss-Maffei	Bueffel ARV
1981–1990	EU	UK GE IT	BAe, MBB, Aeritalia	EAP – fighter techdemos
		FR GE	Aerospatiale, DASA	Tiger – helicopters
		GE IT SP UK	DASA, Siemens, FIAR, INISEL, GEC	ECR-90 – radar
		UK IT	Marconi, Alenia	EMPAR – radar
		FR UK GE IT	Turbomeca, RR, DASA, Plaggio	RTM-322 – engines
		FR GE UK	Aerospatiale, MBB, BAe Dynamics	EMDG/Trigat – anti-tank guided weapons
		FR IT	Aerospatiale, Thomson, Alenia	Eurosam/Aster – surface-to-air missiles
		FR GE	Thomson, BGT, DASA	Astrid seeker – air-to-air missiles
		UK SP FR IT	BAe, GEC, Ibermisil, Eurosam	LAMS – surface-to-air missiles
		FR GE	Matra, BGT	MICA-ASRAAM – air-to-air missiles
		FR UK	Matra, Dassault, GEC	MICA-ASRAAM – air-to-air missiles
		IT GE	Aermacchi, DASA	PTS-2000 – training systems
		FR GE	Thomson-Brandt, Diehl, Rheinmetall	ACED – anti-ship missiles
		UK GE	Hotspur, Rheinmetall	20mm AAA
1981–1990	EU	FR GE	Aerospatiale, DASA	ANL – anti-ship missiles
		UK GE	BAe, GEC, DASA, Bayern Chemie	ALARM – air-to-ground missiles
		FR GE	Euromissile (Aerospatiale, DASA)	ANNG – anti-ship missiles
		FR GE	Matra, Aerospatiale, DASA	APACHE/CWS – air-to-ground missiles
		FR GE	GIAT, Rheinmetall	General cooperation
		FR GE	GIAT, BAe Royal Ordnance	General cooperation
		UK GE	ML Aviation, Rheinmetall	Damocles cluster bomb
		UK SWE	BAe Dynamics, Marconi, SAAB	Active Skyflash – air-to-air missiles
		FR IT SP	Aerospatiale, Matra, Alenia, CASA	Helios 1 – reconnaissance satellites

Program start period	Regions	Countries	Companies	System name
		GE FR	Dornier, Diehl, Ae, Thomson	SRSOM – stand-off missiles
		FR UK	Thomson-Sintra, BAe Dynamics	ATAS – sonar
		GE FR	MBB, Siemens, AEG	MFS2000/SAM 90 – surface-to-air missiles
1981–1990	EU	FR GE	Ae, Thomson, Dornier, Diehl	Mobidic – air-to-ground missiles
		GE IT SP UK	DASA, FIAT, Sener, Rolls Royce	EJ-2000 – engines
		FR IT	Matra, OTO-Melara	Milas – anti-ship missiles
		FR IT SP GE UK	Ae, Ag, Alenia, CASA, Eurocop, West	Eurofar – transport
		UK NL SP IT	Westland, Fokker, CASA, Agusta	LAH Tonal – helicopters
		BE NL	Bellard, Van der Giesse	MSC
		GE FR	DASA, Matra	Eurodrone/Brevel – UAV
		FR GE UK	Turbomeca, DASA, Rolls-Royce	MTR-390 engine – aeroengines
		FR GE	Aerospatiale, DASA	Polyphem ATW
		FR UK	Giat, Vickers	Tank technology
		FR GE	Matra, Euromissile	RM-5 – surface-to-air missiles
		FR GE IT NL	Aerospatiale, DASA, Agusta, Fokker	NH-90 – helicopters
1981–1990	EU US	UK US	BAe, GD	General cooperation
		SWE US	SAAB Missiles, Hughes	Missile cooperation
		US FR	Lockheed, Aerospatiale	General cooperation
		US GE IT SWE	UTC, DASA, FiatAvio, Volvo Aero	PW-2000 – engines (C-17)
		UK GE FR IT US	MLRS-EPG, Vought	MLRS
1981–1990	EU US	US UK FR GE	MM, Thorn EMI, Thomson, Diehl	MLRS-TGW warhead
		US IT	Westinghouse, FIAT	Airborne radar
		UK IT US	BAe, FIAR, Bendix	HELRAS – radar
		FR BE US	Thomson, GTE	RITA (US Army)
		US UK	E-Systems, Royal Ordnance	Vehicular Intercom
		US UK	MDC, BAe	AV-8B Harrier – fighters
		BE IT NL UK GE US	Gov'ts of BE, IT, NL, UK, GE, US	SRARM – anti-radar missiles

Period	Region	Countries	Companies	Product
		US GE TU NL GR	Dornier, General Dynamics, Aselsan, Rocketsan, Fokker, SEH	Stinger – surface-to-air missiles
1981–1990	EU US	US UK	MDC, BAe, Northrop	ASTOVL/JAST – fighters
		US NL BE NO DE	GD, Fokker, SABCA	Agile Falcon – fighters
		GE US	Grob, E-Systems, Garrett	Egrett – surveillance aircraft
		US UK GE IT SP	Lockheed, BAe, DASA, Ale, CASA	FIMA – transport
		US GE	Rockwell, DASA	Fan Ranger JPATS – trainers
		US SP IT UK	MDC, CASA, Alenia, BAe	Harrier II Plus – fighters
		US IT	Lockheed, Aermacchi	MB-339 JPATS – trainers
		GE US	DASA, Lockheed	MPA-90 – patrol aircraft
		US IT	Grumman, Agusta	S.211 JPATS – trainers
		GE US	DASA, Rockwell	X-31A – fighters
		FR US	Lohr, Oshkosh	PLS
		UK US	Vickers, FMC	VFM-5 – tanks
		UK US	BAe, FMC	155mm – howitzers
		UK US	Royal Ordnance, Harsco	Light towed howitzers
		US FR	Hughes, Thomson-Sintra	ALFS – sonar systems
		US UK FR GE IT	Bendix, Ray, GEC, Thomson, Siemens	NIS IFF system
		FR US	Thomson, Rockwell	RAN – sub combat systems
		Canada FR GE IT NL TU US	GD, OTO Melara, Matra, Dornier	APGM warhead
1981–1990	EU US	UK US	BAe, Hughes	ASRAAM – air-to-air missiles
		GE IT Canada SP UK FR US	Dornier, Hunting, GD, Aero, Agusta	MSOW (Team 1) – air-to-ground missiles
		GE IT Canada SP UK FR US	MBB, BAe, GEC, Boeing, Rockwell	MSOW (Team 2) – air-to-ground missiles
		US Canada NL GE SP	Two consortia	NAAWS – surface-to-air missiles
		US NOR	Hughes, NFT	NASAMS – surface-to-air missiles
		US FR	Hughes, LTV, Thomson	THAAD – surface-to-air missiles
		US GE	Lockheed, Litton, Rockwell, DASA	THAAD – surface-to-air missiles
		UK US	BAe, Honeywell, Plessey	Adv. Sea Mine I

Program start period	Regions	Countries	Companies	System name
		UK US	Marconi, Loral	Adv. Sea Mine II
		Canada FR GE IT SP	Government agencies, FR, GE, IT, SP, Canada	NATO Frigate 90 (NFR-90) – frigates
1981–1990	EU US	UK US	BAe, Martin Marietta, Hughes	Ship Torpedo Defense
		UK US	Ferranti, Dowty, AT&T, Westinghouse	Ship Torpedo Defense
		UK US	GEC, Alliant, GE	Ship Torpedo Defense
		Canada FR GE	Canadair, Snecma, DASA	CL-289 RPV
		NL GE Canada	HSA, DASA, NTL	APAR – radar
		US FR GE SP IT Canada	Plessey, Thomson, Siemens, INISEL	MIDS – communication. systems
1981–1990	EU EE	UK Switzerland	Plessey, Contraves, Oerlikon	Seaguard CIWS
		FR, Yugoslavia	Dassault, Soko	Novi Avion – fighters
1981–1990	EU AS	FR China	Chinese, French government agencies	Q-5K – fighters
		IT China	Chinese, Italian government agencies	A-5M – fighters
		GE India	DASA, HAL	ALH – helicopters
		FR Malaysia	Aerospatiale, OFEMA, AIROD	Aircraft servicing
		KO SWI UK	ADD, Daewoo, Pilatus, Cranfield	KTX-1 – basic trainers
		IT PRC	Alenia	A-5M – fighters
		PRC UK	Norinco, Vickers	NVH-1 MICV
1981–1990	EU LA	UK Brazil	BAe, Orbita	MSS-3.1 AGM
		IT Brazil	Orbita, OTO Melara	MSS-1.1 – air-to-ground missiles
1991–2000	EU	FR IT GE	Ae, Dassault, Alenia, DASA	Eurohermespace
		BE DE NL NOR	SABCA, Fokker, etc (Lockheed–prime)	F-16 MLU
		FR UK GE SP IT	Ae, BAe, DASA, CASA, Alenia	FLA/Airbus – transport aircraft
		FR GE IT	SNECMA, MTU, FiatAvio	M-138 – engines (FLA)
		SP GE	Ceselsa, Dornier	SIVA – UAVs
		FR UK GE	GIAT, RO, Rheinmetall	140mm tank gun/ammo
		FR GE	Krauss-Maffei, Lohr	Folding Roadway Systems

Period	Region	Countries	Companies	Program
1991–2000	EU	GE NL	DAF, Wegmann	Light armed recce vehicles
		FR GE UK	GIAT, Panhard, Krauss, Mercedes, GKN	VBM/GTK – armored personnel carriers
		FR GE	Panhard, Mercedes Benz	VBM/GTK – armored personnel carriers
		GE FR	Dornier(DASA), CNIM	Eurobridge
		FR SWE	GIAT, Bofors	155-mm artillery gun
		NOR SWE	Raufoss, Bofors	Artillery ammo
		UK FR	Dassault, BAe	Future fighters
		UK FR	BAe/Aerospatiale	General cooperation
		FR UK	Snecma, Rolls-Royce	A/C engines
		FR SWE	GIAT, Bofors	BONUS – artillery shells
		UK FR GE	GTAR consortium, DASA	AMSAR radar – phased-ray airborne radar
		NOR SWE	NFT, Ericsson	Arthur – artillery-seeking radar
		GE NL	Siemens, HSA	Army comm. system
		UK FR	GEC, Thomson	Bowman comm. system
		FR SWE	Thomson-CSF, Bofors	MCM – sonar
		FR UK	BAe, Thomson	Active Skyflash II – air-to-air missiles
		UK FR	BAe Dynamics, Matra	Apache-C CASOM (UK)
		FR GE	Dassault, DASA, BGT	Aramis ARM
		FR SWE	Matra, Ericsson	MICA 0 – air-to-air missiles
		FR SWE	GIAT, Hagglunds	ARV (Leclerc-based)
		UK FR IT	GEC, Eurosam	MSAM (UK) – surface-to-air missiles
		UK FR IT	BAe, Eurosam (for Horizon FFG program)	PAAMS – surface-to-air missiles (Horizon)
1991–2000	EU	UK SWE IT	BAe, SAAB, Alenia, GEC-Marconi	S-225X – air-to-air missiles
		NL SP	Royal Schelde, Bazan	Amphib. transport
		GE NL SP	ARGE, Royal Schelde, Bazan	Common frigate
		UK FR IT	DCN, GEC, Orizzonte	Horizon FFG
		FR SP	DCN, Bazan	New submarines
		NL SP	Royal Schelde, Bazan	Small combat ships
		FR NL BE	Thomson-Sintra	Tripartite MCM upgrade
		GE SP UK IT FR	Alenia, BAE Systems, Dassault, EADS, Fokker	Europatrol – maritime patrol aircraft

Program start period	Regions	Countries	Companies	System name
		UK GE	Alvis, MAK, Krauss-Maffei	MRAV/GTK – armored vehicles
		SWE FI	Alvis, Patria	Patria-Hagglunds – armored vehicles
		UK IT	AMS	EMPAR – surveillance and tracking radar
		FR GE UK IT	Astrium	Galileo – military navigation satellite system
1991–2000	EU	UK GE SP FR	BAE Systems, EADS, EMAC, Tusas, Flabel, IAEP	A400M – transport aircraft
		UK GE SP FR	BAE Systems, EADS, ENOSA, FIAR	ECR90 – Eurofighter radar
		UK FR	BAE Systems, GIAT	CTA International – 45-mm case telescoped ammo
		UK FR GE	BAE Systems, GIAT, Rheinmetall	RGR – tank ammunition
		UK IT SP GE FR	BAE Systems, Alenia, Inisel, EADS	Automatic test systems
		UK SP IT	BAE Systems, Ensa, Elettronica	Eurodass – defensive aids subsystem
		FR UK	Dassault, BAE Systems	European Aerosystems – fighter concepts
		FR SP	DCN, Izar	Scorpion – submarines
		FR IT	DCN, Thales, Whitehead Alenia	Eurotorp/MU-90 – torpedos
		FR IT	DCN, Fincantieri, Finmeccanica	Horizon FFG – frigates
		FR GE SP SWE IT NOR	EADS, Saab, Alenia, Kongsberg	IRIS-T – short-range air-to-air missiles
1991–2000	EU	GE NL SP FR Canada	EADS, HSA, Northern Telecom	Multifunction radar
		FR SWE	GIAT, Bofors	BONUS – guided artillery rounds
		FR UK	GIAT, Hunting Engineering	GIAT/Hunting Shelters – shelters
		SWE FR	Hagglunds, GIAT	CV90105 – light tank version of CV90 IFV
		SWE FI	Hagglunds, Patria	AMOS – mortar systems
		SWE DE NOR	Kockums, Danyard, Kongsberg	Viking – submarines
		NOR FR	Kongsberg, MBDA	NSM – anti-ship missiles
		FR UK	Dassault Elect, GEC-Ferranti	CLARA nav pod

Period	Region	Country	Company	Product
		GE SWE	LFT, Saab	Taurus – guided weapons, LACMs
		FR IT	MBDA	Milas – ASW torpedo missiles
		FR UK	MBDA	Storm Shadow – land attack cruise missile
		UK FR GE	MBDA	Euromissile Dynamics/Trigate – anti-tank guided missiles
1991–2000	EU	UK IT	GEC, Alenia	Guided missile systems
		FR IT UK	MBDA, Thales, BAE Systems	Europaams – naval surface-to-air missiles
		UK GE IT SP	Rolls-Royce, MTU, Fiat, ITP	Eurojet – Eurofighter aeroengines
		UK FR BE GE	Rolls-Royce, Snecma, FN Moteurs, MTU	Tyne – turboprop engines
		UK GE IT SP	Rolls-Royce, MTU, Fiat	Turbounion – Tornado engines
		FR IT	Snecma, Fiat	Europropulsion – solid rocket boosters
		GE SP	TDA, Santa Barbara	DEFTEC – anti-tank missile warheads
		FR GE	TDA, Diehl	RTG Euromunition – submunitions
		FR GE IT NL	Thales, EADS, FIAR, Alenia, TNO Applied Physics	SOSTAR – surveillance and target acq. radar
		FR UK	Thales, Astrium	Spartacus – satcom systems
1991–2000	EU US	US NOR UK	Hughes, NFT, Siemens	AdSAMS – surface-to-air missiles
		US GE UK	MM, Aerojet, BAe, DASA	Corps-SAM
		US UK	MDC, Hunting	Grand SLAM CASOM (UK
		US GE FR	2 int'l consortia envisioned	MEADS/Corps-SAM
		US IT UK	GE, FiatAvio, Alfa Romeo Avio, GEC	T-700/T6E – engines
		UK US	BAe, Martin Marietta	Corps-SAM (Rapier)
		US UK	MDC, Westland	Apache – helicopters
		UK US	Siemens-Plessey, Hughes	Aster surveil a/c
		UK US	Thorn-EMI, Loral Fed Systems	Aster surveil a/c
		GE US	Thyssen, General Dynamics	Fuchs – NBC vehicles
		UK US	BAe, Raytheon	MSAM/Patriot (UK)
		UK US	BAe, ITT Defense	Bowman comm. system
		SWE US	Ericsson, Rodale Electronics	ECCM/ECM equipment
		UK US FR	GEC, Westinghouse, Thomson-CSF	Aster surveil a/c
		GE US	CMS(DASA), Rockwell Autonetics	Submun dispenser a/c

Program start period	Regions	Countries	Companies	System name
		UK US	GEC, Bell	Cobra Venom – helicopters
		UK US	Westland, Loral Fed Systems	EH-101 Merlin – helicopters
		UK IT US	Agusta Westland, Lockheed Martin	EH-101 Merlin – helicopters
		US UK	Hughes, TI, BAe	AIM-9X
		US FR	MDC, Aerospatiale	Anti-ship missiles
		UK US	BAE Systems, Boeing	Brimstone – anti-tank guided weapons
1991–2000	EU US	FR US	Lockheed, Matra	AD systems cooperation
		FR US	GIAT, Alliant	Ammunition
		UK US	BAE Systems, Boeing	Tanker aircraft
		GE US	Alliant, Rheinmetall	Tank ammunition
		UK US	BAE Systems, Alvis, Raytheon, United Defense	Tracer – recce vehicles
		UK US	BAE Systems, Vickers, Lockheed Martin, GDLS	Tracer – recce vehicles
		UK US NL DE	Boeing, BAE Systems, Dowty Aerospace, Rolls-Royce, Fokker, Terma	Joint Strike Fighter (X-32) – fighter aircraft
		UK US	BAE Systems, Rolls-Royce, Lockheed Martin	Joint Strike Fighter (X-35) – fighter aircraft
		GE US	Diehl, Raytheon	Rolling airframe missiles
		GE SP FR US	EADS, Boeing	X-31 Program
		FR US	Thales, Raytheon	Thoray – sonar
		GE IT US	MBDA, Lockheed Martin	MEADS
1991–2000	EU US	FR GE SP UK SWE US	MBDA, Saab, Boeing	Meteor – medium-range air-to-air missiles
		FR GE Canada	Thomson, Dynamit Nobel, Bristol	Area Defense Weapon
		FR Canada	SAT, Bombardier	CL-289 – UAVs
1991–2000	EU EE	FR Switz	GIAT, Pyrotech	Ammunition
1991–2000	EU ME	BE Israel	Elta	EL/M-2140 – radar

1991–2000	EU AS	FR Russia	SNECMA, Sextant, MiG MAPO	MiG-AT – trainer jets
		FR GE Russia	Eurocopter, Mil, Kazan Helo, Klimov	Euromil/Mi-38 – helicopters
		Russia IT	Yakolev, Aermacchi	Yak-130UT – trainer jets
		UK Singapore	Royal Ordnance, ODE	Light towed howitzer
		GE FR SP Indonesia	EADS, IPTN	CN-235 – transport aircraft
		GE FR SP Singapore China	EADS, ST Aerospace, CATIC	EC-120 – helicopters
1991–2000	EU AS	GE S.Korea China	DASA, Samsung, AVIC	Regional fighters
		GE FR SP Russia	EADS, MiG RSK	MiG-29 upgrades
		BE Russia	Promavia, MiG MAPO	ATTA-3000 trainer
		GE Israel	Dynamit Nobel, Rafael	Panzerfaust-3LR ATGW
		GE Malaysia	Dornier, Aerospace Ind. of Malaysia	Seastar amphibian – amphibious aircraft
		SWE Singapore	Saab, ST Marine	Naval vessels
		FR S.Korea	Thales, LG	Chonma – surface-to-air missiles
		UK Singapore	Vickers, ST Engineering	Armored vehicles, artillery
1991–2000	EU LA	SWE Brazil	Ericsson, Embraer	EMB-145 AEW
		UK Chile	BAE Systems, FAMAE	Ordnance, multiple rocket launchers
		SWE Brazil	Ericsson, Embraer	Landing gear
1991–2000	EU AF	South Africa UK	Denel, Marshalls	Rooivalk – helicopters

Appendix B

Mergers and Acquisitions (M&As) Involving European Defense Firms, 1961–2000 N=195

Program start period	Regions involved	Countries involved	Companies involved	Explanation
1961–1970	EU	GE NL	VFW, Fokker	VFW>Fokker (later dissolved)
1971–1980	EU US	FR US	Aerospatiale, Vought Helicopter	Aerospat>Vought Helicopter
1981–1990	EU	UK SP	Rolls Royce, Soc Espaniola de Motores	RR>45% SEM
		BE FR	SABCA, Dassault Belgique	SABCA>Dassault Belgique
		FR NOR	SNECMA, Norsk Jetmotor	SNECMA>Norsk Jetmotor
		BE FR	Snecma, FN Moteurs	Snecma>FN Moteurs
		FR NL	Thomson-CSF, Hollandse Signaalapparat	Thomson-CSF>HSA
		FR UK	Thomson-CSF, Link-Miles	Thomson-CSF>Link-Miles
		FR NL	Thomson-CSF, Philips MBLE	Thomson-CSF>MBLE
		FR NL	Thomson-CSF, Philips TRT	Thomson-CSF>TRT
		UK NL	Thorn-EMI, MEL (from Phillips)	Thorn>MEL
		GE FR	MBB, Matra	DASA>5% Matra
1981–1990	EU	FR UK	Thomson, BAe	Eurodynamics
		FR UK	Matra, GEC	GEC>5% Matra
		FR GE	Matra, BGT	Matra>20% BGT
		FR SWE	Matra, Wallenberg	Wallenberg>2% Matra
		FR UK	Thomson-Lucas, Bendix France	Thomson-Lucas>Bendix
		GE IT	Daimler-Benz, ENASA	Daimler-Benz>ENASA
		IT SP	FIAT, ENASA	FIAT>ENASA
		GE Austria	MAN, Steyr Daimler Puch	MAN>Steyr Daimler Puch
		UK BE	Astra, PRB	Astra>PRB
		FR BE	French Suez, SGB	French Suez>SGB
		FR GE	GIAT, Heckler & Koch	GIAT>Heckler & Koch
		FR BE	GIAT, PRB (from Astra)	GIAT>PRB
		UK FR	CAP Group, Sema-Matra	CAP>Sema-Matra
		FR NL BE	Dassault, Fokker, SABCA	Dassault, Fokker>SABCA

Program start period	Regions involved	Countries involved	Companies involved	Explanation
1981–1990	EU	GE FR	Daimler, MHA (from Matra)	Daimler>MHS
		IT FR	Finmeccanica, CSEE Defense Systems	Finmecc>49% CSEE
		IT UK	Finmeccanica, Ferranti Italiana	Finmecc>Ferranti Italiana
		IT SWE	Finmeccanica, FIAR (from Ericsson)	Finmeccanica>FIAR
		FR GE	Aerospatiale, DASA	Aerospatiale>8% DASA
		GE UK	Siemens, GEC, Plessey Radar	Siemens, GEC>Plessey
		SWE NL	Nobel, Phillips Electronik AB	Nobel>Phillips Electronik AB
		FR BE	Thomson Brandt, Forges de Zeebrugge	Thomson>Forges de Zeebrugge
		FR BE	Alcatel, ACEC Space, Defense	Alcatel>ACEC
1981–1990	EU US	GE US	Daimler-Benz, Gould Ind. Automation	Daimler>Gould
		FR US	Thomson, Ocean Defense (AlliedSignal)	Thomson>Ocean Defense
		UK US	ASA, RJO Enterprises	ASA>RJO Enterprises
		UK US	Astra, Walters	Astra>Walters
		GE US	Diehl, BGT (from Perkin Elmer)	Diehl>BGT
		UK US	Hunting, Irvin Industries	Hunting>Irvin Industries
		FR US	Thomson, Wilcox Electric	Thomson>Wilcox Electric
		UK US	BAe, Reflectone	BAe>Reflectone
1981–1990	EU US	UK US	BAe, Steinheil Optronics(Lear Siegr)	BAe>Steinheil Optronics
		US UK	BEI, Systron Donner (from Thorn-EMI)	BEI>Systron Donner
		US UK	UTC (Sikorsky), Westland	UTC>27% Westland
		UK US	Brit Telecom, Tymnet (from MDC)	Brit Telecom>Tymnet
		FR US	Dassault, Midway Aircraft Instruments	Dassault>Midway
		UK US	Dowty, Palmer Chenard Industries	Dowty>Palmer Chenard
		UK US	Dowty, Resdel Industries	Dowty>Resdel
		IT US	Elsag, Bailey Controls	Elsag>Bailey Controls
		UK US	Ferranti, Adv Laser Tech Group	Ferranti>Adv Laser
		UK US	Ferranti, Int'l Signal & Control	Ferranti>ISC
		UK US	GEC, Lear Astronics	GEC>Lear Astronics

Period	Region	Countries	Companies	Abbreviation
		UK US	GEC, Plessey (acq. Singer holdings)	GEC>Plessey USA
		US UK	GM, Rediffusion Simulation	GM Hughes>Rediffusion
		FR US	Groupe Bull, Honeywell Fed Systems	Groupe Bull>Honeywell
		FR US	Groupe Bull, Zenith Data Systems	Groupe Bull>Zenith
1981–1990	EU US	UK US	Lucas, EPSCO	Lucas>EPSCO
		UK US	Lucas, Lear Siegler Power Systems	Lucas>Lear Siegler Power Syst.
		UK US	Lucas, Zeta Laboratories	Lucas>Zeta Laboratories
		UK US	Plessey, Elect. Systems Div.	Plessey>ESD
		UK US	Plessey, Leigh Instruments	Plessey>Leigh Instr
		UK US	Plessey, Nash Engineering	Plessey>Nash Eng
		UK US	Plessey, Singer Electronics	Plessey>Singer Ele
		UK US	BAe, Sperry Gyroscope	BAe>Sperry
		US UK	MDC, Applied Research of Cambridge	MDC>Applied Research
		UK US	Racal, Megapulse	Racal>Megapulse
		FR IT US	Aerospatiale, Alenia, DeHavilland	Aero/Ale> DeHavilland
		UK US	BAe, Nanoquest Ltd	BAe>Nanoquest Ltd
		FR US	Matra, Fairchild	Matra>Fairchild
		UK US	Systems Designers, Scicon	Systems Designers>Scicon
		GE US	Siemens, Bendix (from AlliedSignal)	Siemens>Bendix
		GE US UK	Siemens, Cardion (from Ferranti)	Siemens>Cardion
		UK US	Smith, Lear Siegler systems integration division	Smith>Lear Siegler
1981–1990	EU US	UK US	Plessey, Sippican	Plessey>Sippican
1981–1990	EU CA	FR Canada	GIAT, Belcan	GIAT> Technologies Belcan
1981–1990	EU Switz	UK Switz	Astra, BMARC (from Oerlikon)	Astra>BMARC
		IT GE Switz	Fincantieri; Bremer Vulkan, Sulzer	Fincan, Brem>Sulzer
1991–2000	EU	FR GE SP	Aerospatiale-Matra, DASA, CASA	Merger (EADS)
		GE SWE	HDW, Kockums	Merger (HDW Group)
		UK SWE	Alvis, Hagglunds	Alvis>Hagglunds
		SWE NOR	Alvis, Hagglunds Moelv	Alvis>Hagglunds
		UK SWE	BAE Systems, Saab	BAE>35% Saab
		UK GE	BAE Systems, STN Atlas	BAE>49% STN Atlas

Program start period	Regions involved	Countries involved	Companies involved	Explanation
		UK GE	BAE Systems, Heckler & Koch	BAE>Heckler & Koch
		UK NE	BAE Systems, Muiden Chemie	BAE>Muiden Chemie
		FR BE	Dassault, SABCA	Dassault>53% SABCA
		GE FR SP FI	EADS, Patria	EADS>27% Patria
		SW DE	Ericsson, TERMA Electronik	Ericsson>40% TERMA
		FR BE	GIAT, FN Herstal	GIAT>FN Herstal
		FR BE	GIAT, PRB	GIAT>PRB
		NOR UK	Kvaerner, Govan Yards	Kvaerner>Govan Yards
1991–2000	EU	GE FR SP	MBDA, BGT	MBDA>20% BGT
		GE FR SP	MBDA, LFK	MBDA>30% LFK
		GE NL	Rheinmetall, NwM de Kruithoorn	Rheinmetall>NwM de Kruithoorn
		GE NL	Rheinmetall, Eurometall	Rheinmetall>Eurometall
		UK SP	Rolls-Royce, ITP	Rolls-Royce>49%ITP
		SWE NOR	Saab, Raufoss	Saab>15% Raufoss
		SWE FI	Saab, Nexplo	Saab>60% Nexplo
		FR BE	Snecma, FN Moteurs	Snecma>FN Moteurs
		FR NOR	Snecma, Norsk Jet Motors	Snecma>11% Norsk Jet Motors
		FR UK	Snecma, TI Group's landing gear business	Snecma>TI Group's landing
		NE BE	Stork Fokker, SABCA	Stork Fokker>43% SABCA
		FR GE	Thales, Bayern Chemie	Thales>50% Bayern Chemie
		FR IT	Thales, Elettronica	Thales>33% Elettronica
		FR NL	Thales, Signaal	Thales>99% Signaal
		FR NL	Thales, MBLE	Thales>MBLE
		FR NL	Thales, TRT	Thales>TRT
1991–2000	EU	FR NL	Thales, Sestrel Observation	Thales>Sestrel Observation
		FR POR	Thales, Edisoft	Thales>33.3% Edisoft
		FR SP	Thales, Indra	Thales>13% Indra
		FR SP	Thales, Indra Espacio	Thales>49% Indra Espacio

Period		Country	Transaction	Result
		FR SP	Thales, SAES	Thales>49% SAES
		FR UK	Thales, Pilkington	Thales>Pilkington
		FR UK	Thales, Racal	Thales>Racal
		FR UK	Thales, Redifon	Thales>Redifon
		FR UK	Thales, Shorts Missiles	Thales>Shorts Missiles
		FR UK	Thales, Thorn EMI	Thales>Thorn EMI
		FR UK	Thales, Link-Miles	Thales>Link-Miles
		FR UK	Thales, Rediffusion	Thales>Rediffusion
		FR UK	Thales, MEL	Thales>MEL
		FR UK	Thales, Ferranti Syseca	Thales>Ferranti Syseca
		IT NL	Finmeccanica, Fokker	Finmecc>6% Fokker
		FR GE	Thales, Siemens TWT business	Thales>Siemens TWT
		UK FI	Vickers, Aquamaster Rauma	Vickers>Aquamaster Rauma
		GE NL	DASA, Fokker	DASA>Fokker
		FR UK	Matra Marconi Space, BAe Space	MMS>BAe Space
		UK SWE	Vickers, KaMeWa	Vickers>KaMeWa
1991–2000	EU	SWE	Foreign investors own 40% of Celsius	Celsius (Bofors)
		FR BE	GIAT, FN Herstal	GIAT>FN Herstal
		UK GE	Royal Ordnance, Heckler & Koch	Royal Ord>Heckler & Koch
		UK NL	Royal Ordnance, Muiden Chemie	Royal Ord>Muiden Chemie
		GE FR	BGT, Sextante Avionique, VDO-Luft	BGT/SexAv>VDO-Luft
		UK, FR NL	GEC Alsthom, HSA (from Thomson-CSF)	GEC Alsthom>HSA
		SWE NOR	Volvo, Volvo Aero Norge	Volvo>78% Volvo Aero Norge
		NOR UK	Sinrad, Osprey	Simrad>Osprey
		FR SP	Thomson-CSF, Indra (Ceselsa+Inisel)	Thomson>25% Indra
		FR SP	T-Sintra, SAES (from Inisel)	Thomson>49% SAES
		FR SP	Thomson, Kyat	Thomson>Kyat
		FR UK	Thomson CSF, Thorn-EMI fusing div.	Thomson>Thorn fuses
		FR UK	CMN, Swan Hunter	CMN>Swan Hunter
		FR UK	Thomson, MEL (from Thorn)	Thomson>MEL
1991–2000	EU	FR UK	Thomson-TRT, Pilkington Optics	Thomson>Pilkington Optics
		GE NL	Wegman & Co., SP Aerospace and Vehicles	Wegman>SP Aerospace

Program start period	Regions involved	Countries involved	Companies involved	Explanation
1991–2000	EU US	US GE	Raytheon, Anschuetz	Raytheon>Anschuetz
		UK US	BAE Systems, Marconi Hazeltine	BAE Systems>Marconi Hazeltine
		UK US	BAE Systems, Tracor	BAE Systems>Tracor
		UK US	BAE Systems, LM Controls	BAE Systems>LM Controls
		UK US	BAE Systems, LM Sanders	BAE Systems>LM Sanders
		UK US	BAE Systems, Reflectone	BAE Systems>Reflectone
		UK US	BAE Systems, Plessey USA	BAE Systems>Plessey USA
		UK US	BAE Systems, Lear Astronics	BAE Systems>Lear Astronics
		UK US	GKN, Interlake	GKN>Interlake
		US UK	TRW, LucasVarity	TRW>LucasVarity
		US GE	TRW, Pierburg Luftfahrtgerate Union	TRW>Pierburg Luftfahrtgerate
		FR US	Renault, Mack Trucks	Renault>Mack Trucks
		UK US	Rolls-Royce, Allison Engines	Rolls-Royce>Allison Engines
1991–2000	EU US	US SWE	United Defense, Saab's Bofors Weapons Division	United Defense>Saab's Bofors
		US SP	General Dynamics, Santa Barbara	General Dynamics>Santa Barbara
		UK US	Smiths Industries, Envir. Technologies Group	Smiths> Envir. Technologies
		UK US	Smiths Industries, Strategic Technology System	Smiths>Strategic Technology
		UK US	Smiths Industries, Leland Electro Systems	Smiths>Leland Electro Systems
		UK US	Smiths Industries, Lear Siegler Instr. & Avionics	Smiths>Lear Siegler
		US Austria	General Dynamics, Steyr-Daimler-Puch	General Dynamics> Steyr-Daimler-Puch
		FR US	Thales, Allied Signal Aerospatiale Canada	Thales>Allied Signal
		UK US	Ultra Electronics, Raytheon's sonobuoy business	Ultra>Raytheon's sonobuoy bus.
		FR US	Alcatel, Rockwell Transmission	Alcatel>Rockwell Transmission
1991–2000	EU US	NL US	Carlyle, Magnavox (from Philips)	Carlyle>Magnavox El
		GE US	DASA, Loral satellites division	DASA>Loral satellites division
		UK US	GKN, Westland (from UTC, Sikorsky)	GKN>27% Westland

		Countries	Companies	Relationship
		UK US	Lucas Aerospace, Tracor Aviation	Lucas>Tracor Aviation
		US FR	Orbital Sci, Fairchild (Matra)	Orbital>Fairchild
		UK US	Rolls Royce, Allison (from GM)	RR>Allison
		US UK	Raytheon, Hawker (from BAe)	Raytheon>Hawker
		US BE	UTC (P&W), FN Moteurs	UTC>19% FN Moteurs
		US GE	UTC, MTU (DASA)	UTC>25% MTU
		US UK	Rockwell, GEC Plessey Semiconductors	Rockwell>Plessey Semiconductors
		FR US	Sextant Avionique, AlliedSignal	Sextant, AlliedSignal
		FR UK US	Thomson-CSF, Rediffusion (from GM)	Thomson>Rediffusion
		FR US	Thomson-CSF, LTV missiles division	Thomson> LTV missiles division
1991–2000	EU AS	SWE Australia	Saab, Hawker Pacific	Saab>Hawker Pacific
1991–2000	EU AS	FR Australia	Thales, Australian Defense Industries (ADI)	Thales>50% ADI
		FR Singapore	Thales, Avimo	Thales>42% Avimo
		FR S.Korea	Thales, Samsung Electronics	Thales>50% Samsung Electronics
		FR Australia	Thales, Wormald Technology	Thales>50% Wormald Technology
		UK Australia	BAE Systems, Land Rover Australia	BAE Systems>Land Rover Australia
1991–2000	EU LA	FR GE SP Brazil	Dassault, Thales, EADS, Snecma, Embraer	Dassault, Thales, EADS, Snecma>20% Embraer
1991–2000	EU AF	FR S.Africa	Thales, Altech Defense Systems	Thales>Altech
		UK S.Africa	BAE Systems, Paradigm Systems	BAE Systems>Paradigm Systems
		UK S.Africa	BAE Systems, ATE	BAE Systems>20% ATE
		FR GE SP S.Africa	EADS, Reutech Radar Systems	EADS>Reutech Radar Systems
		UK S.Africa	Pains Wessex Defence, Denel Swartklip	Pains>Denel Swartklip
		FR S.Africa	Turbomeca, Denal Airmotive	Turbomeca>Denal Airmotive
		UK S.Africa	Vickers, Reumech OMC	Vickers>Reumech OMC

ABBREVIATIONS

AF – Africa
AS – Asia
BE – Belgium
CA – Canada
DE – Denmark
EE – Eastern Europe

EU – European Union/European Community
FI – Finland
FR – France
GE – Germany
IT – Italy
LA – Latin America
ME – Middle East
NOR – Norway
NL – Netherlands
SP – Spain
SWE – Sweden
SWI – Switzerland
UK – United Kingdom
US – United States
> – Acquire
Source: DBP Globalization Database (© Richard A. Bitzinger, 2001).

Select Bibliography

Achen, Christopher, "Social Psychology, Demographic Variables, and Linear Regression: Breaking the Iron Triangle in Voting Research," *Political Behavior*, Vol. 14.

Acheson, Dean, *Present at the Creation: My Years in the State Department* (New York: W.W. Norton, 1969).

Adams, Gordon, Christophe Cornu, and Andrew D. James, *Between Cooperation and Competition: The Transatlantic Defence Market* (Paris: Institute for Security Studies, 2001).

Adams, Gordon, Guy Ben-Ari, John Logsdon, and Ray Williamson, *Bridging the Gap: European C4ISR Capabilities and Transatlantic Interoperability* (Washington, DC: National Defense University Center for Technology and National Security Policy, 2004).

Adenauer, Konrad, *Erinnerungen, 1959–1963* (Stuttgart: Deutsche Verlags-Anstalt, 1968).

Adenauer, Konrad, *Memoirs, 1945–53* (Chicago: Henry Regnery, 1966).

Adler, Emanuel and Michael Barnett, eds., *Security Communities* (New York: Cambridge University Press, 1998).

Allen, David, Reinhardt Rummel, and Wolfgang Wessels, *European Political Cooperation: Towards a Foreign Policy for Western Europe* (Boston: Butterworth Scientific, 1982).

American Institute for Contemporary German Studies, *Redefining German Security: Prospects for Bundeswehr Reform*, German Studies No. 25 (Washington, DC: AICGS, 2001).

Amnesty International, *Tools of Repression for the Likes of Amin?* (London: Amnesty International, July 1979).

Anderson, Benedict, *Imagined Communities: Reflections on the Origin and Spread of Nationalism* (New York: Verso, 1991).

Anderson, Jeffrey J. and John B. Goodman, "Mars or Minerva? A United Germany in a Post-Cold War Europe," in Robert O. Keohane, Joseph S. Nye, and Stanley Hoffman, eds., *After the Cold War: International Institutions and State Strategies in Europe, 1989–1991* (Cambridge, MA: Harvard University Press, 1993).

Andréani, Gilles, Christoph Bertram, and Charles Grant, *Europe's Military Revolution* (London: Centre for European Reform, 2001).

Anthony, Ian, "Sanctions Applied by the European Union and the United Nations," *SIPRI Yearbook 2002: Armaments, Disarmament and International Security* (New York: Oxford University Press, 2002).

265

Armitage, David T., Jnr., and Anne M. Moisan, *Constabulary Forces and Post-conflict Transition: The Euro-Atlantic Dimension*, No. 218 (Washington, DC: Institute for National Strategic Studies, National Defense University, 2005).

Art, Robert J., "Europe Hedges its Security Bets," in T.V. Paul, James J. Wirtz, and Michael Fortmann, *Balance of Power Revisited: Theory and Practice in the 21st Century* (Stanford, CA: Stanford University Press, 2004).

"To What Ends Military Power?" *International Security*, Vol. 4, No. 4, Spring 1980.

"Why Western Europe Needs the United States and NATO," *Political Science Quarterly*, Vol. 111, No. 1, Spring 1996.

Arthur, Brian, "Competing Technologies, Increasing Returns, and Lock-In by Historical Events," *Economic Journal*, Vol. 99, March 1989.

Ash, Timothy Garton, "Is Britain European?" *International Affairs*, Vol. 77, No. 1, January 2001.

Asmus, Ronald D., *Opening NATO's Door: How the Alliance Remade Itself for a New Era* (New York: Columbia University Press, 2002).

Attali, Jacques, *Verbatim: Tome 3, Chronique des années 1988–1991* (Paris: Fayard, 1995)

Augustine, Norman R., "Reshaping an Industry: Lockheed Martin's Survival Story," *Harvard Business Review*, May–June 1997.

Avirgan, Tony, and Martha Honey, *War in Uganda: The Legacy of Idi Amin* (Westport, CN: Hill, 1982).

Axelrod, Robert, *The Evolution of Cooperation* (New York: Basic Books, 1984).

Axelrod, Robert and Robert O. Keohane, "Achieving Cooperation under Anarchy: Strategies and Institutions," *World Politics*, Vol. 38, No. 1, October 1985.

BAE Systems, *Annual Report 1999* (London: BAE Systems, 2000).

Annual Report 2005 (London: BAE Systems, 2006).

Baker III, James A., *The Politics of Diplomacy* (New York: G.P. Putnam's Sons, 1995).

Baldwin, David A., *Economic Statecraft* (Princeton, NJ: Princeton University Press, 1985).

"The Sanctions Debate and the Logic of Choice," *International Security*, Vol. 24, No. 3, Winter 1999/2000.

Bayard, Thomas O., Joseph Pelzman, and Jorge Perez-Lopez, "Stakes and Risks in Economic Sanctions," *The World Economy*, Vol. 6, No. 1, March 1983.

Beale, Michael O., *Bombs over Bosnia* (Maxwell AFB, AL: School of Advanced Airpower Studies, 1997).

Berger, Thomas U., "Norms, Identity, and National Security in Germany and Japan," in Katzenstein, ed., *The Culture of National Security: Norms and Identity in World Politics* (New York: Columbia University Press, 1996)

Bertram, Christoph, Joachim Schild, Francois Heisbourg, and Yves Boyer, *Starting Over: For a Franco-German Initiative in European Defense* (Berlin: Stiftung Wissenschaft und Politik, 2002).

Birkler, John, *et al.*, *Assessing Competitive Strategies for the Joint Strike Fighter: Opportunities and Options*, MR-1362-OSD/JSF (Santa Monica, CA: RAND, 2001).

Bitzinger, Richard A., *Towards a Brave New Arms Industry?* Adelphi Paper 356 (London: Oxford University Press, 2003).

"Globalization in the Post-Cold War Defense Industry: Challenges and Opportunities," in Ann R. Markusen and Sean S. Costigan, eds., *Arming the Future: A Defense Industry for the 21st Century* (New York: Council on Foreign Relations, 1999).

Bland, Douglas L., *The Military Committee of the North Atlantic Alliance: A Study of Structure and Strategy* (Westport, CT: Praeger, 1990).

Bloes, Robert, *Le "Plan Fouchet" et le problème de l'Europe politique* (Bruges: Collège d'Europe, 1970).

Bodenheimer, Susanne J., *Political Union: A Microcosm of European Politics, 1960–1966* (Leiden: A.W. Sijthoff, 1967).

Bohr, Sebastian, "Sanctions by the United Nations Security Council and the European Community," *European Journal of International Law*, Vol. 4, No. 2, 1993.

Bozo, Frédéric, *Two Strategies for Europe: De Gaulle, the United States, and the Atlantic Alliance* (New York: Rowman and Littlefield, 2001).

"The Effects of Kosovo and the Danger of De-coupling," in Jolyon Howarth and John T. S. Keeler, eds., *Defending Europe: The EU, NATO and the Quest for European Autonomy* (New York: Palgrave Macmillan, 2003).

Brandt, Willy, *People and Politics: The Years 1960–1975* (Boston, MA: Little, Brown and Company, 1976).

Braunschvig, David, Richard L. Garwin, and Jeremy C. Marwell, "Space Diplomacy," *Foreign Affairs*, Vol. 82, No. 4, July/August 2003.

Brooks, Stephen G., *Producing Security: Multinational Corporations, Globalization, and the Changing Calculus of Conflict* (Princeton, NJ: Princeton University Press, 2005);

Brooks, Stephen G. and William C. Wohlforth, "Hard Times for Soft Balancing," *International Security*, Vol. 30, No. 1, Summer 2005, 72–108.

Brown, Harold, press conference on May 6, 1977. Reprinted in *Survival*, Vol. 19, No. 4 , July/August 1977.

Brzezinski, Zbigniew, "Living with a New Europe," *The National Interest*, No. 60, Summer 2000.

Brzoska, Michael and Peter Lock, eds., "Restructuring of Arms Production in Western Europe: Introduction," in Brzoska and Lock, eds., *Restructuring of Arms Production in Western Europe* (New York: Oxford University Press, 1992).

Bullen, Roger and M.E. Pelly, eds., *Documents on British Policy Overseas* (London: HMSO, 1986).

Burg, Steven L. and Paul S. Shoup, *The War in Bosnia-Herzegovina: Ethnic Conflict and International Intervention* (Armonk, NY: M.E. Sharpe, 1999).

"The International Community and the Yugoslav Crisis," in Milton J. Esman and Shibley Telhami, eds., *International Organizations and Ethnic Conflict* (Ithaca, NY: Cornell University Press, 1995).

Byman, Daniel, Mark Burles, Roger Cliff, and Robert Mullins, *China's Arms Purchases: Understanding the Danger* (Santa Monica, CA: RAND, 1999).

Campbell, David, *Writing Security* (Minneapolis: University of Minnesota Press, 1992).

Caporaso, James A., Gary Marks, Andrew Moravcsik, and Mark A. Pollack, "Does the European Union Represent an *n* of 1?" *ECSA Review*, Vol. 10, No. 3, Fall 1997.

Carr, E.H., *The Twenty Years' Crisis: 1919–1939* (New York: Harper & Row, 1964).

Cauchie, Marc, "Coopération internationale dans le domaine des armaments," *Défense nationale*, June 1980.

Central Intelligence Agency, *Mapping the Global Future: Report of the National Intelligence Council's 2020 Project* (Washington, DC: CIA, 2004).

Modeling International Politics in 2015: Potential U.S. Adjustments to a Shifting Distribution of Power (Washington, DC: Strategic Assessments Group, CIA, 2004).

Cerny, Philip G., *The Politics of Grandeur: Ideological Aspects of De Gaulle's Foreign Policy* (New York: Cambridge University Press, 1980).

Checkel, Jeffrey T., "Social Construction and Integration," *Journal of European Public Policy*, Vol. 6, No. 4, 1999.

Chenais, Francois, Gracia Ietto-Gillies, and Roberto Simonetti, eds., *European Integration and Global Corporate Strategies* (New York: Routledge, 2000).

Chirac, Jacques, "European Defense," Address to the Presidential Committee of the WEU Parliamentary Assembly and the Visiting Fellows, May 30, 2000.

"Politique de défense et de sécurité," *Défense nationale*, No. 57, July, 2001.

Christensen, Thomas J. and Jack Snyder, "Chain Gangs and Passed Bucks: Predicting Alliance Patterns in Multipolarity," *International Organization*, Vol. 44, No. 2, Spring 1990.

Christiansen, Thomas, Knud Erik Jorgensen, and Antje Wiener, "The Social Construction of Europe," *Journal of European Public Policy*, Vol. 6, No. 4, 1999.

Churchill, Winston S., *The Gathering Storm* (Boston: Houghton Mifflin, 1948).

Cimbalo, Jeffrey L., "Saving NATO From Europe," *Foreign Affairs*, Vol. 83, No. 6, November/December 2004.

Clark, Wesley K., *Waging Modern War: Bosnia, Kosovo, and the Future of Combat* (New York: Public Affairs, 2001).

Clarke, Duncan, "Israel's Unauthorized Arms Transfers," *Foreign Policy*, No. 99, Summer 1995.

Clarke, Michael and Paul Cornish, "The European Defence Project and the Prague Summit," *International Affairs*, Vol. 78, No. 4, October 2002.

Claude, Inis L., *Power and International Relations* (New York: Random House, 1962).

Cohen-Tanugi, Laurent, *An Alliance at Risk: The United States and Europe since September 11* (Baltimore: Johns Hopkins University Press, 2004).

"The End of Europe?" *Foreign Affairs*, Vol. 84, No. 6, November/December 2005.

Collet, André, *Les industries d'armement* (Paris: Presses Universitaires de France, 1988).

Collier, David, "The Comparative Method: Two Decades of Change," in Dankwart A. Rustow and Kenneth Paul Erickson, eds., *Comparative Political Dynamics: Global Research Perspectives* (New York: Harper Collins, 1991).

Collier, David and James Mahoney, "Insights and Pitfalls: Selection Bias in Qualitative Research," *World Politics*, Vol. 49, No. 1, October 1996.

Commission of the European Communities, *Communication from the Commission on Conflict Prevention* (Brussels: European Commission, November 2001).

Common Foreign and Security (CFSP) Sanctions (Brussels: European Commission, 2004).

Eurobarometer 64: Public Opinion in the European Union (Brussels: European Commission, 2005).

"European Union Sanctions Applied to Non-Member States" (Washington, DC: Delegation of the EC to the US, 2002); see: (www.eurunion.org/ legislat/Sanctions.htm).

A Framework for EU – Iraq Engagement (Brussels: European Commission, 2004).

Galileo: The European Project on Radio Navigation by Satellite (Brussels: European Commission, Directorate general for Energy and Transport, March 2002).

Space: A New Frontier for an Expanding Union (Brussels: European Commission, 2003).

Towards an EU Defence Equipment Policy, COM (2003) 113 Final (Brussels: Commission of the EC, March 2003).

White Paper – European Transport Policy for 2010: Time to Decide, COM 370/ 2001 (Luxembourg: Office for Official Publications of the European Communities, September 2001).

Commission Général du Plan, *Ive Plan de développement économique et social 1962–1965* (Paris: Documentation française, 1965).

Condit, Kenneth W., *The History of the Joint Chiefs of Staff: The Joint Chiefs of Staff and National Policy, Vol. II, 1947–1949* (Washington, DC: Joint Chiefs of Staff, 1976).

Congressional Budget Office (US Congress), *Options for Changing the Army's Overseas Basing* (Washington, DC: Congressional Budget Office, May 2004).

Convention on the Establishment of the Organisation for Joint Armament Cooperation, OCCAR (Bonn: OCCAR, 1998).

Conybeare, John C., *Trade Wars: The Theory and Practice of International Commercial Rivalry* (New York: Columbia University Press, 1987).

Copeland, Dale C., *The Origins of Major War* (Ithaca, NY: Cornell University Press, 2000).

"Trade Expectations and the Outbreak of Peace," *Security Studies*, Vol. 9, Nos. 1–2, Autumn 1999-Winter 2000.

Corbett, Richard, *Treaty of Maastricht: From Conception to Ratification: A Comprehensive Reference Guide* (Harlow: Longman Group, 1993).

Cornish, Paul and Geoffrey Edwards, "Beyond the EU/NATO Dichotomy: The Beginnings of a European Strategic Culture," *International Affairs*, Vol. 77, No. 3, July 2001.

Cornu, Christopher, "Fortress Europe – Real or Virtual?" in Burkard Schmitt, ed., *Between Cooperation and Competition: The Transatlantic Defence Market*, Chaillot Paper 44 (Paris: Institute for Security Studies, 2001).

Cortright, David and George A. Lopez, *Economic Sanctions: Panacea or Peacebuilding in a Post-Cold War World?* (Boulder, CO: Westview, 1995).

270   Select Bibliography

The Sanctions Decade: Assessing UN Strategies in the 1990s (Boulder, CO: Lynne Rienner, 2000).

Council of the European Union, *Agency in the Field of Defense Capabilities Development, Research, Acquisition, and Armaments* (Brussels: European Council, May 2004).

Basic Principles for an EU Strategy against Proliferation of WMD (Brussels: European Council, June 2003).

Capability Improvement Chart 2004 (Brussels: European Council, May 2004).

Council Decision Relating to the Launch of the EU Military Operations in the Former Yugoslav Republic of Macedonia (Brussels: European Council, March 18, 2003).

Council Establishes EU Police Mission in the Palestinian Territories (Brussels: European Council, November 2005).

Council Establishes Mission to Provide Advice and Assistance for Security Sector reform in the Democratic Republic of Congo (Brussels: European Council, May 2005).

EDA Work Programme for 2006 (Brussels: European Council, November 2005).

ESDP Presidency Report (Brussels: European Council, December 2004).

European Union Factsheet: EU Suppport for Iraq (Brussels: European Union, 2005).

EU Military Operation in Bosnia and Herzegovina (Brussels: EU Council Secretariat, November 29, 2004).

Guidelines on Implementation and Evaluation of Restrictive Measures, (Sanctions) in the Framework of the EU Common Foreign and Security Policy, 15579/03 (Brussels: European Council, December 2003).

Headline Goal 2010 (Brussels: European Council, June 2004).

Military Capability Commitment Conference: Declaration on European Military Capabilities (Brussels: European Council, November 2004).

Political and Security Committee Decision Setting up the Committee of Contributors for the EU-Led Operation in FYROM (Brussels: European Council, February 18, 2003).

A Secure Europe in a Better World: European Security Strategy (Brussels: European Council, December 2003).

Presidency Report on ESDP, 15678/05 (Brussels: European Council, December 2005).

Second Meeting of the EDA's Steering Board (Brussels: European Council, November 2004).

Cowen, Regina H.E., *Defense Procurement in the Federal Republic of Germany: Politics and Organization* (Boulder, CO: Westview Press, 1986).

Crawford, Neta C. and Audie Klotz, *How Sanctions Work: Lessons from South Africa* (New York: St. Martin's Press, 1999).

Crémieux, Alain, *Quand les 'Ricains' repartiront: Le journal imaginaire du nouveau millénaire* (Boofzheim, France: ACM, 2000).

Daalder, Ivo H., *Getting to Dayton: The Making of America's Bosnia Policy* (Washington, DC: Brookings Institution Press, 2000).

"The End of Atlanticism," *Survival*, Vol. 45, No. 2, Summer 2003.

Dagi, Ihsan D., "Democratic Transition in Turkey, 1980–93: The Impact of European Diplomacy," *Middle Eastern Studies*, Vol. 32, No. 2, April 1996.

Daoudi, M.S. and M.S. Dajani, *Economic Sanctions: Ideals and Experience* (Boston, MA: Routledge & Kegan Paul, 1983).

Dashti-Gibson, Jaleh, Patricia Davis, and Benjamin Radcliff, "On the Determinants of the Success of Economic Sanctions: An Empirical Analysis," *American Journal of Political Science*, Vol. 41, No. 2, April 1997.

David, Dominique, ed., *La politique de défense de la France: Textes et documents* (Paris: Fondation pour les études de défense nationale, 1989).

Debré, Michel, "France's Global Strategy," *Foreign Affairs*, Vol. 49, No. 3, April 1971.

Defourneaux, Marc, "France and a European Armament Policy," *NATO Review*, No. 5, 1979.

"Coopération et indépendance technologique," *Défense nationale*, March 1983.

"Indépendance nationale et coopération internationale en matière d'armements," *Défense nationale*, February 1979.

[de Gaulle, Charles], *Major Addresses, Statements and Press Conferences of General Charles de Gaulle, May 19, 1958 – January 31, 1964* (New York: French Embassy, 1964).

Memoirs of Hope: Renewal 1958–62, Endeavour 1962– (London: Weidenfeld and Nicolson, 1971).

Deutch, John, Arnold Kanter, and Brent Scowcroft, "Saving NATO's Foundation," *Foreign Affairs*, Vol. 78, No. 6, November/December 1999.

Deutsch, Karl W. et al., *Political Community and the North Atlantic Area: International Organization in the Light of Historical Experience* (Princeton, NJ: Princeton University Press, 1957).

Deutsch, Karl W. and J. David Singer, "Multipolar Power Systems and International Stability," *World Politics* Vol. 16, No. 3, April 1964.

Divis, Dee Ann, "Military Role for Galileo Emerges," *GPS World*, Vol. 13, No. 5.

Dobbins, James, John G. McGinn, Keith Crane, Seth G. Jones, Rollie Lal, Andrew Rathmell, Rachel Swanger, and Anga Timilsina, *America's Role in Nation-Building: From Germany to Iraq* (Santa Monica, CA: RAND, 2003).

Dollinger, Phillippe, *The German Hansa*, trans. and ed. by D.S. Ault and S.H. Steinberg (Stanford, CA: Stanford University Press, 1970).

Dowdy, John J., "Winners and Losers in the Arms Industry Downturn," *Foreign Policy*, Vol. 107, Summer 1997.

Doyle, Michael W., *Empires* (Ithaca, NY: Cornell University Press, 1986).

Ways of War and Peace: Realism, Liberalism, and Socialism (New York: W.W. Norton, 1997).

Draper, Alan G., *European Defence Equipment Collaboration: Britain's Involvement, 1957–87* (New York: St. Martin's Press, 1990).

Drezner, Daniel W., *The Sanctions Paradox: Economic Statecraft and International Relations* (New York: Cambridge University Press, 1999).

"Bargaining, Enforcement, and Multilateral Sanctions: When is Cooperation Counterproductive?" *International Organization*, Vol. 54, No. 1, Winter 2000.

"The Hidden Hand of Economic Coercion," *International Organization*, Vol. 57, Summer 2003.

Drown, Jane Davis, "European Views on Arms Cooperation," in Jane Davis Drown, Clifford Drown, and Kelly Campbell, eds., *A Single European Arms Industry? European Defence Industries in the 1990s* (London: Brassey's, 1990).

Duchesne, Sophie and André-Paul Frognier, "Is There a European Identity?" in Oskar Niedermayer and Richard Sinnott, eds., *Public Opinion and Internationalized Governance* (New York: Oxford University Press, 1995).

Eden, Anthony, *Full Circle: The Memoirs of Anthony Eden* (Boston, MA: Houghton Mifflin, 1960).

Eisenhower, Dwight D., *The White House Years: Mandate for Change, 1953–1956* (Garden City, NY: Doubleday, 1963).

Eland, Ivan, "Economic Sanctions as Tools of Foreign Policy," in David Cortright and George Lopez, eds., *Economic Sanctions: Panacea or Peacebuilding in a Post-Cold War World?* (Boulder, CO: Westview Press, 1995).

Elbe, Frank and Richard Kiessler, *A Round Table with Sharp Corners: The Diplomatic Path to German Unity* (Baden-Baden, Germany: Nomos Verlagsgesellschaft, 1996).

Enders, Thomas, "Defense Industry Restructuring and the Implications of ESDI/DCI," at XVIIth International Workshop: On Political-Military Decision Making in the Atlantic Alliance, Berlin, Germany, June 2–5, 2000.

English, Robert D., *Russia and the Idea of the West: Gorbachev, Intellectuals, and the End of the Cold War* (New York: Columbia University Press, 2000).

European Advisory Group on Aerospace, STAR21: *Strategic Aerospace Review for the 21st Century: Creating a Coherent Market and Policy Framework for a Vital European Industry* (Brussels: European Commission, July 2002).

European Defense Agency, *EDA Bulletin*, Issue 1 (Brussels: EDA, December 2005).

European Parliament, Political Committee, *Towards Political Union: A Selection of Documents* (General Directorate of Parliamentary Documentation and Information, 1964); see: ⟨http://aei.pitt.edu/944/⟩.

European Space Agency, *Agenda 2007: A Document by the ESA Director General*, BR-213 (Noordwijk, Netherlands: ESA, 2003).

European Union, *Facts on EUJUST THEMIS* (Tbilisi, Georgia: European Union Rule of Law Mission to Georgia, 2004).

Evans, Tony and Peter Wilson, "Regime Theory and the English School of International Relations: A Comparison," *Millennium: Journal of International Studies*, Vol. 21, No. 3, Winter 1992.

Farmer, Richard D., "Costs of Economic Sanctions to the Sender," *The World Economy*, Vol. 23, No. 1, January 2000.

Fauvet, Jacques, "Birth and Death of a Treaty," in Daniel Lerner and Raymond Aron, *France Defeats the EDC* (New York: Frederick A. Praeger, 1957).

Fearon, James D., "Bargaining, Enforcement, and International Cooperation," *International Organization*, Vol. 52, No. 2, Spring 1998.

"Domestic Political Audiences and the Escalation of International Disputes," *American Political Science Review*, Vol. 88, No. 3, September 1994.

"Signaling Foreign Policy Interests: Tying Hands versus Sinking Costs," *Journal of Conflict Resolution*, Vol. 41, No. 1, February 1997.

Finmeccanica, *Annual Report 1999* (Rome: Finmeccanica, 2000).

Annual Report 2005 (Rome: Finmeccanica, 2006).

Finnemore, Martha, *National Interests and International Society* (Ithaca, NY: Cornell University Press, 1996).

Fischer, Fritz, *War of Illusions: German Policies from 1911 to 1914* (New York: Norton, 1975).

Fischer, Joschka, "From Confederacy to Federation: Thoughts on the Finality of European Integration," Berlin, May 12, 2000 (www.germany-info.org).

Flamm, Kenneth, "Redesigning the Defense Industrial Base," in Ann R. Markusen and Sean S. Costigan, eds., *Arming the Future: A Defense Industry for the 21st Century* (New York: Council on Foreign Relations Press, 1999).

Flournoy, Michèle A. and Kenneth F. McKenzie, Jr., "Sizing Conventional Forces: Criteria and Methodology," in Flournoy, ed., *QDR 2001: Strategy-Driven Choices for America's Security* (Washington, DC: National Defense University Press, 2001).

Folliot, Denise, ed., *Documents on International Affairs, 1952*, (Oxford: University Press, 1955).

Forsberg, Thomas, "Power, Interests, and Trust: Explaining Gorbachev's Choices at the End of the Cold War," *Review of International Studies*, Vol. 24, No. 4, October 2000.

Fouchet, Christian, *Mémoires d'hier et de demain: Au service du Général de Gaulle* (Paris: Plon, 1971).

Fourquet, General Michel, "Emploi des différents systèmes de forces dans le cadre de la stratégie de dissuasion," *Revue de défense nationale*, Vol. 25, May 1969.

Fredman, Steven J., "U.S. Trade Sanctions against Uganda: Legality under International Law," *Law and Policy in International Business*, Vol. 11, No. 3, 1979.

French General Delegation for Armament, *Rapport d'activité 2000* (Paris: Délégation générale pour l'armement, 2000).

Rapport d'activité 2001 (Paris: Délégation générale pour l'armement, 2001).

French Ministry of Defense, *La défense nationale* (Paris: Ministère de la Défense, 2002).

Livre blanc sur la défense nationale (Paris: Ministère de la Défense Nationale, June 1972).

Projet de loi de programmation militaire 2003–2008 (Paris: Ministère de la Défence, 2002).

Friedberg, Aaron L., *In the Shadow of the Garrison State: America's Anti-Statism and its Cold War Grand Strategy* (Princeton, NJ: Princeton University Press, 2000).

Friedman, James W., "A Non-cooperative Equilibrium for Supergames," *Review of Economic Studies*, Vol. 38, No. 1.

Fudenberg, Drew and David K. Levine, *The Theory of Learning in Games* (Cambridge, MA: MIT Press, 1998).

Fursdon, Edward, *The European Defence Community: A History* (New York: St. Martin's Press, 1980).

Gaddis, John Lewis, *Strategies of Containment: A Critical Appraisal of Postwar American National Security Policy* (New York: Oxford University Press, 1982). *We Now Know: Rethinking Cold War History* (New York: Oxford University Press, 1997).

Galtung, John, "On the Effects of International Economic Sanctions: With Examples from the Case of Rhodesia," *World Politics*, Vol. 19, No. 3, April 1967.

Gansler, Jacques, *Defense Conversion: Transforming the Arsenal of Democracy* (Cambridge, MA: MIT Press, 1995). "Needed: A U.S. Defense Industrial Strategy," *International Security*, Vol. 12, No. 2, Autumn 1987.

Gardner, Grant W. and Kent P. Kimbrough, "The Economics of Country-Specific Tariffs," *International Economic Review*, Vol. 31, No. 3.

Garton Ash, Timothy, "Is Britain European?" *International Affairs*, Vol. 77, No. 1, January 2001.

Gary Clyde Hufbauer, Jeffrey J. Schott, and Elliot Kimberly Ann, *Economic Sanctions Reconsidered*, 3rd edn (Washington, DC: Institute for International Economics, forthcoming).

Gellner, Ernest, *Nations and Nationalism* (Ithaca, NY: Cornell University Press, 1983).

Genscher, Hans-Dietrich, *Rebuilding a House Divided: A Memoir by the Architect of Germany's Unification* (New York: Broadway Books, 1998).

George, Alexander L., "Case Studies and Theory Development: The Method of Structured, Focused Comparison," in Paul Gordon Lauren, ed., *Diplomacy: New Approaches in History, Theory, and Policy* (New York: Free Press, 1979).

George, Alexander L. and Timothy J. McKeown, "Case Studies and Theories of Organizational Decision Making," in Robert F. Coulam and Richard A. Smith (eds.), *Advances in Information Processing in Organizations: A Research Annual*, Vol. II (Greenwich, CT: JAI Press, 1985).

Gerber, Alan and Donald P. Green, "Rational Learning and Partisan Attitudes," *American Journal of Political Science*, Vol. 42, No. 3, July 1998.

Gerbert, Pierre, "In Search of Political Union: The Fouchet Plan Negotiations (1960–62)," in Roy Pryce, ed., *The Dynamics of European Union* (New York: Croom Helm, 1987).

German Federal Minister of Defense, *The Bundeswehr – Advancing Steadily into the 21st Century* (Berlin: Federal Ministry of Defense, 2000). *White Paper 1970: The Security of the Federal Republic of Germany and the Development of the Federal Armed Forces* (Bonn: Federal Ministry of Defense, 1970). *White Paper 1971/1972: The Security of the Federal Republic of Germany and the Development of the Federal Armed Forces* (Bonn: Federal Ministry of Defense, 1971/72). *White Paper 1973/1974: The Security of the Federal Republic of Germany and the Development of the Federal Armed Forces* (Bonn: Federal Ministry of Defense, 1973/74).

White Paper 1985: The Situation and Development of the Federal Armed Forces (Bonn: Federal Ministry of Defense, 1985).

White Paper on the Security of the Federal Republic of Germany and the Situation and Future of the Bundeswehr (Bonn: Federal Ministry of Defense, 1994).

German Secretary of Defense, *Bundeswehr 2002: Sachstand und Perspektiven* (Berlin: Bundesministerium der Verteidigung, 2002).

Giergerich, Bastian and William Wallace, "Not Such a Soft Power: The External Deployment of European Forces," *Survival*, Vol. 46, No. 2, Summer 2004.

Gill, Bates and Taeho Kim, *China's Arms Acquisitions from Abroad: A Quest for 'Superb and Secret Weapons'* (New York: Oxford University Press, 1995).

Gilpin, Robert, *War and Change in World Politics* (New York: Cambridge University Press, 1981).

"Economic Interdependence and National Security in Historical Perspective," in Klaus Knorr and Frank N. Trager, eds., *Economic Issues and National Security* (Lawrence, KA: Allen Press, 1977).

Ginsberg, Roy H., *Foreign Policy Actions of the European Community: The Politics of Scale* (Boulder, CO: Lynne Reimer, 1989).

Gladwyn, Hubert, *The Memoirs of Lord Gladwyn* (New York: Weybright and Talley, 1972).

Glarbo, Kenneth, "Wide-Awake Diplomacy: Reconstructing the Common Foreign and Security Policy of the European Union," *Journal of European Public Policy*, Vol. 64, No. 4, 1999.

Glaser, Charles L., "Realists as Optimists: Cooperation as Self-Help," *International Security*, Vol. 19, No. 3, Winter 1994/95.

"The Security Dilemma Revisited," *World Politics*, Vol. 50, No. 1, October 1997.

"Why NATO is Still Best: Future Security Arrangements for Europe," *International Security*, Vol. 18, No. 1, Summer 1993.

Glenny, Misha, *The Fall of Yugoslavia: The Third Balkan War* (New York: Penguin, 1999).

Global Witness, *Conflict Diamonds: Possibilities for the Identification, Certification and Control of Diamonds* (London: Global Witness, May 2000).

Goldstein, Judith and Robert O. Keohane, eds., *Ideas and Foreign Policy: Beliefs, Institutions, and Political Change* (Ithaca, NY: Cornell University Press, 1993).

Goldthorpe, John H., "Current Issues in Comparative Macrosociology: A Debate on Methodological Issues," in Lars Mjoset *et al.*, *Comparative Social Research: Methodological Issues in Comparative Social Science*, Vol. XVI (Greenwich, CT: JAI Press, 1997).

Gompert, David C., "The United States and Yugoslavia's Wars," in Richard H. Ullman, ed., *The World and Yugoslavia's Wars* (New York: Council on Foreign Relations, 1996).

Gordon, Philip H., *A Certain Idea of France: French Security Policy and the Gaullist Legacy* (Princeton, NJ: Princeton University Press, 1993).

"Europe's Uncommon Foreign Policy," *International Security*, Vol. 22, No. 3, Winter 1997/98.

Gordon, Philip H. and Jeremy Shapiro, *Allies at War: America, Europe, and the Crisis Over Iraq* (New York: McGraw-Hill, 2004).

Gow, James, *Triumph of the Lack of Will: International Diplomacy and the Yugoslav War* (New York: Columbia University Press, 1997).

Grahame, Iain, *Amin and Uganda: A Personal Memoir* (New York: Granada, 1980).

Grieco, Joseph M, "Anarchy and the Limits of Cooperation: A Realist Critique of the Newest Liberal Institutionalism," *International Organization*, Vol. 42, No. 3, Summer 1988.

Guay, Terrence R., *At Arm's Length: The European Union and Europe's Defence Industry* (New York: St. Martin's Press, 1998).

Guay, Terrence R. and Robert Callum, "The Transformation and Future Prospects of Europe's Defence Industry," *International Affairs*, Vol. 78, No. 4, 2002.

Haas, Ernst B., *The Obsolescence of Regional Integration Theory* (Berkeley, CA: Institute of International Studies, 1975).

The Uniting of Europe: Political, Social, and Economic Forces, 1950–1957 (Stanford, CA: Stanford University Press, 1958).

"The Balance of Power: Prescription, Concept, or Propaganda?" *World Politics*, Vol. 5, No. 4, July 1953.

Haass, Richard N., ed., *Economic Sanctions and American Diplomacy* (New York: Council on Foreign Relations, 1998).

"Sanctioning Madness," *Foreign Affairs*, Vol. 76, No. 6, November/December 1997.

Haftendorn, Helga, Robert O. Keohane, and Celeste Wallander, eds., *Imperfect Unions: Security Institutions over Time and Space* (New York: Oxford University Press, 1999).

Hagman, Hans-Christian, *European Crisis Management and Defense: The Search for Capabilities*, Adelphi Paper 353 (London: International Institute for Strategic Studies, 2002).

Hall, Peter A., *Governing the Economy: The Politics of State Intervention in Britain and France* (New York: Oxford University Press, 1986).

Hallstein, Walter, *Europe in the Making* (London: George Allen & Unwin, 1972).

Hamilton, Alexander, "Report on the Subject of Manufacturers," in Harold C. Syrett, ed., *The Papers of Alexander Hamilton* (New York: Columbia University Press, 1966).

Hartley, Keith, *NATO Arms Co-operation: A Study in Economics and Politics* (London: Allen & Unwin, 1983).

Hardin, Russell, "Collective Action as an Agreeable n-Prisoners' Dilemma," *Behavior Science*, Vol. 16, September 1971.

Hayward, Keith, "The Globalisation of Defence Industries," *Survival*, Vol. 42, No. 2, Summer 2001.

Heath, Edward, *The Course of My Life: My Autobiography* (London: Hodder and Stoughton, 1998).

Hébert, Jean-Paul and Laurence Nardon, *Concentration des industries d'armement américaines: modèle ou menace?* Cahiers d'Etudes Stratégiques No. 23 (Paris: CIRPES, 1999).

Henderson, Sir Nicholas, *The Birth of NATO* (Boulder, CO: Westview Press, 1983).

Herman, Robert G., "Identity, Norms, and National Security: The Soviet Foreign Policy Revolution and the End of the Cold War," in Peter J. Katzenstein, ed., *The Culture of National Security: Norms and Identity in World Politics* (New York: Columbia University Press, 1996).

Herz, John, "Idealist Internationalism and the Security Dilemma," *World Politics*, Vol. 2, No. 2, January 1950.

Heyhoe, D.C.R., *The Alliance and Europe: Part VI, The European Programme Group*, Adelphi Paper 129 (London: International Institute for Strategic Studies, 1976/1977).

Hill, Christopher, ed., *National Foreign Policies and European Political Cooperation* (London: Royal Institute of International Affairs, 1983).

Hill, Christopher and Karen E. Smith, *European Foreign Policy: Key Documents* (New York: Routledge, 2000).

Hilsman, Roger, "NATO: The Developing Strategic Context," in Klaus Knorr, ed., *NATO and American Security* (Princeton: Princeton University Press, 1959).

Hirschman, Albert O., *National Power and the Structure of Foreign Trade* (Berkeley: University of California Press, 1945).

Hitchcock, William, *France Restored: Cold War Diplomacy and the Quest for Leadership in Europe, 1944–1954* (Chapel Hill, NC: University of North Carolina Press, 1998).

Hoffmann, Stanley, "Obstinate or Obsolete? The Fate of the Nation-State and the Case of Western Europe," in Joseph S. Nye, ed., *International Regionalism: Readings* (Boston: Little, Brown and Company, 1968).

Holbrooke, Richard, *To End a War* (New York: Random House, 1998).

Honig, Jan Willem, "The 'Renationalization' of Western European Defense," *Security Studies*, Vol. 2, No. 1, Autumn 1992.

Hoover, Herbert, *Addresses upon the American Road: 1948–1950* (Stanford, CA: Stanford University Press, 1951).

Howorth, Jolyon, "European Defence and the Changing Politics of the European Union: Hanging Together or Hanging Separately?" *Journal of Common Market Studies*, Vol. 39, No. 4, November 2001.

Howorth, Jolyon and John Keeler, eds., *Defending Europe: The EU, NATO and the Quest for European Autonomy* (New York: Palgrave, 2003).

Human Rights Watch, *Angola Unravels: The Rise and Fall of the Lusaka Peace Process* (New York: Human Rights Watch, 1999)

Humbert, Philippe, "European before Transatlantic Consolidation," in *European Defense Industrial Consolidation: Implications for U.S. Industry and Policy*, Conference Report (Washington, DC: Center for Strategic and International Studies, December 2001).

Hunter, Robert E., *The European Security and Defense Policy: NATO's Companion or Competitor?* MR-1463-NDRI/RE (Santa Monica, CA: RAND, 2002).

Huntington, Samuel, *The Common Defense: Strategic Programs in National Politics* (New York and London: Columbia University Press, 1961).

"Why International Primacy Matters," *International Security*, Vol. 17, No. 4, Spring 1993.

Hura, Myron, et al., *Interoperability: A Continuing Challenge in Coalition Air Operations*, MR-1235-AF (Santa Monica, CA: RAND, 2000).

Hyde-Price, Adrian, and Charlie Jeffery, "Germany in the European Union: Constructing Normality," *Journal of Common Market Studies*, Vol. 39, No. 4, November 2001.

Ietto-Gillies, Grazia, Meloria Meschi, and Roberto Simonetti, "Cross-Border Mergers and Acquisitions: Patterns in the EU and Effects," in Francois Chesnais, Grazia Ietto-Gillies, and Roberto Simonetti, eds., *European Integration and Global Corporate Strategies* (New York: Routledge, 2000).

Ifestos, Panayiotis, *European Political Cooperation: Towards a Framework for Supranational Diplomacy?* (Brookfield, VT: Avebury, 1987).

Ikenberry, G. John, *After Victory: Institutions, Strategic Restraint, and the Rebuilding of Order after Major Wars* (Princeton, NJ: Princeton University Press, 2001).

America Unrivaled: The Future of the Balance of Power (Ithaca, NY and London: Cornell University Press, 2002).

International Monetary Fund, *Direction of Trade, Annual 1971–77* (Washington, DC: IMF, 1971).

Direction of Trade Statistics Yearbook, 1998 (Washington, DC: IMF, 1998).

Direction of Trade Yearbook 1980 (Washington, DC: IMF, 1980).

International Institute for Strategic Studies, *The Military Balance, 1962–63* (London: IISS, 1963).

The Military Balance, 1974–1975 (London: IISS, 1974).

The Military Balance, 1988–1989 (London: IISS, 1988).

The Military Balance, 2004–2005 (London: Taylor and Francis, 2004).

The Military Balance, 2005–2006 (London: Taylor and Francis, 2005).

Ioannides, Isabelle, *The European Rapid Reaction Force: Implications for Democratic Accountability*, Paper 24 (Bonn: Bonn International Center for Conversion, September 2002).

Ireland, Timothy P., *Creating the Entangling Alliance: The Origins of the North Atlantic Treaty Organization* (Westport, CT: Greenwood Press, 1981).

Ismay, Lord, *NATO: The First Five Years, 1949–1954* (Netherlands: Bosch-Utrecht, 1954).

Jane's Aero-Engines (London: Jane's Information Group, 2002).

Jane's All the World's Aircraft, 2002–2003 (London: Jane's Information Group, 2003).

Jane's Weapons Systems, 1987–88 (London: Jane's Publishing, 1988).

Jervis, Robert, *The Meaning of the Nuclear Revolution: Statecraft and the Prospect of Armageddon* (Ithaca, NY: Cornell University Press, 1989).

Perception and Misperception in International Politics (Princeton, NJ: Princeton University Press, 1976).

"From Balance to Concert: A Study of International Security Cooperation," *World Politics*, Vol. 38, No. 1, October 1985.

"The Compulsive Empire," *Foreign Policy*, Vol. 137, July/August 2003.

"Cooperation under the Security Dilemma," *World Politics*, Vol. 30, No. 2, January 1978.

Joffe, Josef, "'Bismarck' or 'Britain'? Toward an American Grand Strategy after Bipolarity," *International Security*, Vol. 19, No. 4, Spring 1995.

"Collective Security and the Future of Europe: Failed Dreams and Dead Ends," *Survival*, Vol. 34, No. 1, Summer 1992.

"Europe's American Pacifier," *Foreign Policy*, No. 54, Spring 1984.

"Gulliver Unbound: Can America Rule the World?" Twentieth Annual John Bonython Lecture, Sydney, Australia, August 5, 2003.

Jones, Seth G., "Arming Europe," *National Interest*, No. 82, Winter 2005/2006, pp. 62–68.

"The European Union and the Security Dilemma," *Security Studies*, Vol. 12, No. 3, Spring 2003.

Jospin, Lionel, "La politique de défense de la France," *Défense nationale*, No. 56, November 2000.

Kaempfer, William and Anton Lowenberg, "Unilateral versus Multilateral International Sanctions: A Public Choice Perspective," *International Studies Quarterly*, Vol. 43 1999.

Kagan, Robert, *Of Paradise and Power: America and Europe in the New World Order* (New York: Alfred A. Knopf, 2003).

Kalbermatter, André, *Sanctions Practice of the EC* (Zurich: Wenger Vieli Belser, 1999).

Kaplan, Lawrence S., *The United States and NATO: The Formative Years* (Lexington: The University Press of Kentucky, 1984).

Kapstein, Ethan B., "America's Arms-Trade Monopoly," *Foreign Affairs*, Vol. 73, No. 3 May/June 1994.

"Capturing Fortress Europe: International Collaboration and the Joint Strike Fighter," *Survival*, Vol. 46, No. 3, Autumn 2004.

Katzenstein, Peter J., ed., *Tamed Power: Germany in Europe* (Ithaca, NY: Cornell University Press, 1997).

Kaufmann, J.E. and H.W. Kaufmann, *The Maginot Line: None Shall Pass* (Westport, CT: Praeger, 1997).

Kemp, Anthony, *The Maginot Line: Myth and Reality* (New York: Stein and Day, 1982).

Kennedy, Gavin, *Defense Economics* (New York: St. Martin's Press, 1983).

The Economics of Defence (London: Faber and Faber, 1975).

Kennedy, Paul, *The Rise and Fall of the Great Powers* (New York: Vintage Books, 1989).

Keohane, Robert O., *After Hegemony: Cooperation and Discord in the World Political Economy* (Princeton, NJ: Princeton University Press, 1984).

King, Gary, Robert O. Keohane, and Sidney Verba, *Designing Social Inquiry: Scientific Inference in Qualitative Research* (Princeton, NJ: Princeton University Press, 1994).

Kirshner, Jonathan "The Microfoundations of Economic Sanctions," *Security Studies*, Vol. 6, No. 3, Spring 1997.

Kissinger, Henry A., *Does America Need a Foreign Policy? Toward a Diplomacy for the 21st Century* (New York: Simon & Schuster, 2001).

Years of Upheaval (Boston: Little, Brown and Company, 1982).

"A Memo to the Next President," *Newsweek*, September 19, 1988.

Knorr, Klaus and Frank N. Trager, eds., *Economic Issues and National Security* (Lawrence, KA: Allen Press, 1977).

Kocs, Stephen A., *Autonomy or Power? The Franco-German Relationship and Europe's Strategic Choices, 1955–1995* (Westport, CT: Praeger, 1995).

Kofos, Evangelos, "Greek Policy Considerations over FYROM Independence and Recognition," in James Pettifer, ed., *The New Macedonian Question* (New York: St. Martin's Press, 1999).

Kogan, Eugene, *The European Union Defence Industry and the Appeal of the Chinese Market* (Vienna: Studien und Berichte zur Sicherheitspolitik, 2005).

Kolodziej, Edward A., *Making and Marketing Arms: The French Experience and Its Implications for the International System* (Princeton, NJ: Princeton University Press, 1987).

Koremenos, Barbara, Charles Lipson, and Duncan Snidal, "The Rational Design of International Institutions," *International Organization*, Vol. 55, No. 4, Autumn 2001.

Koslowski, Rey and Friedrich Kratochwil, "Understanding Change in International Politics: The Soviet Empire's Demise and the International System," in Richard New Lebow and Thomas Risse-Kappen, eds., *International Relations Theory and the End of the Cold War* (New York: Columbia University Press, 1995).

Krasner, Stephen D., "Global Communications and National Power: Life on the Pareto Frontier," *World Politics*, Vol. 43, No. 3, April 1991.

Kupchan, Charles A., *The End of the American Era: US Foreign Policy and the Geopolitics of the Twenty-First Century* (New York: Alfred A. Knopf, 2002).

"Reconstructing the West: The Case for an Atlantic union," in Kupchan, ed., *Atlantic Security: Contending Visions* (New York: Council on Foreign Relations, 1998).

"The Travails of Union: The American Experience and its Implications for Europe," *Survival*, Vol.46, No. 4, Winter 2004/5.

"Hollow Hegemony or Stable Multipolarity?" in G. John Ikenberry, ed., *America Unrivaled: The Future of the Balance of Power* (Ithaca and London: Cornell University Press, 2002).

Kupchan, Charles A. and Clifford A. Kupchan, "Concerts, Collective Security, and the Future of Europe," *International Security*, Vol. 16, No. 1, Summer 1991.

Kydd, Andrew, "Sheep in Sheep's Clothing: Why Security Seekers Do Not Fight Each Other," *Security Studies*, Vol. 7, No. 1, Autumn 1997.

Kyemba, Henry, *A State of Blood: The Inside Story of Idi Amin* (London: Corgi Books, 1977).

Kyle, Jon, *European Union Likely to End Arms Embargo on the People's Republic of China* (Washington, DC: Republican Policy Committee, 2005).

Lachowski, Zdzislaw, "The Military Dimension of the European Union," in *SIPRI Yearbook 2002: Armaments, Disarmament and International Security* (New York: Oxford University Press, 2002).

Lacouture, Jean, *De Gaulle: The Ruler, 1945–1970* (New York: W.W. Norton, 1991).

Lakatos, Imre, "Falsification and the Methodology of Scientific Research Programmes," in Lakatos and Alan Musgrave, eds., *Criticisms and the Growth of Knowledge* (New York: Cambridge University Press, 1970).

Lake, David A., *Entangling Relations: American Foreign Policy in Its Century* (Princeton, NJ: Princeton University Press, 1999).

Lalinde, Enrique Esquivel, *The New European Gendarmerie Force* (Madrid: Real Institute Elcano, 2005).

Larsen, Henrik, "The EU: A Global Military Actor?" *Cooperation and Conflict*, Vol. 37, No. 3, September 2002.

Layne, Christopher, "America as European Hegemon," *National Interest*, No. 72, Summer 2003.

"Death Knell for NATO? The Bush Administration Confronts the European Security and Defense Policy," *Policy Analysis*, No. 394, April 4, 2001.

"The Unipolar Illusion: Why New Great Powers Will Rise," *International Security*, Vol. 17, No. 4, Fall 1993.

Lebow, Richard Ned and Thomas Risse-Kappen, eds., *International Relations Theory and the End of the Cold War* (New York: Columbia University Press, 1995).

Leffler, Melvyn P., *A Preponderance of Power: National Security, the Truman Administration, and the Cold War* (Stanford, CA: Stanford University Press, 1992).

Lemke, Douglas, "Great Powers in the Post-Cold War World: A Power Transition Perspective," in T. V. Paul, James J. Wirtz, and Michael Fortmann, *Balance of Power: Theory and Practice in the 21st Century* (Stanford: Stanford University Press, 2004).

Lerner, Daniel, "Reflections on France in the World Arena," in D. Lerner and R. Aron, *France Defeats the EDC* (New York: Praeger, 1957).

Levy, Jack, "Learning and Foreign Policy: Sweeping a Conceptual Minefield," *International Organization*, Vol. 48, No. 2, Spring 1994.

Liberman, Peter, *Does Conquest Pay? The Exploitation of Occupied Industrial Societies* (Princeton, NJ: Princeton University Press, 1996).

Lindberg, Leon, *The Political Dynamics of European Economic Integration* (Stanford: Stanford University Press, 1963).

Lindberg, Leon and Stuart A. Scheingold, *Regional Integration: Theory and Research* (Cambridge, MA: Harvard University Press, 1971).

Lindberg, Tod, ed., *Beyond Paradise and Power: Europe, America and the Future of a Troubled Partnership* (New York and London: Routledge, 2004).

Lindley-French, Julian, "In the Shade of Locarno? Why European Defence is Failing," *International Affairs*, Vol. 78, No. 4, October 2002.

Lindsay, James M., "Trade Sanctions as Policy Instruments: A Re-Examination," *International Studies Quarterly*, Vol. 30, 1986.

Lindstrom, Gustav, *The Galileo Satellite System and Its Security Implications*, No. 44 (Paris: Institute for Security Studies, April 2003).

Lister, Frederick K., *The Early Security Confederations: From the Ancient Greeks to the United Colonies of New England* (Westport, CT: Greenwood Press, 1999).

Loi de Programmation Militaire 2003–2008, Paris, Ministère de la Défense, 2002.

Lorell, Mark A., et al., *Going Global? U.S. Government Policy and the Defense Aerospace Industry* (Santa Monica, CA: RAND, 2002).

Lorell, Mark A. and Julia Lowell, *Pros and Cons of International Weapons Procurement Collaboration*, MR-565-OSD (Santa Monica, CA: RAND, 1995).

Lovering, John, "Which Way to Turn? The European Defense Industry after the Cold War," in Ann R. Markusen and Sean S. Costigan, eds., *Arming the Future: A Defense Industry for the 21st Century* (New York: Council on Foreign Relations Press, 1999).

Lukic, Reneo and Allen Lynch, *Europe from the Balkans to the Urals: The Disintegration of Yugoslavia and the Soviet Union* (New York: Oxford University Press, 1996).

Mace, Catriona, "Operation Concordia: Developing a 'European' Approach to Crisis Management," *International Peacekeeping*, Vol. 11, No. 3, Autumn 2004.

Mackinder, Halford J., "The Geographical Pivot of History," *Geographic Journal*, Vol. 23, No. 4, April 1904.

Major, John, *John Major: The Autobiography* (New York: HarperCollins Publishers, 1999).

Mako, William P., *U.S. Ground Forces and the Defense of Central Europe* (Washington: The Brookings Institution, 1983).

Mamdani, Mahmood, *Imperialism and Fascism in Uganda* (Nairobi: Heinemann Educational Books, 1983).

Manners, Ian, "Normative Power Europe: A Contradiction in Terms?" *Journal of Common Market Studies*, Vol. 40, No. 2, June 2002.

Mansfield, Edward, "International Institutions and Economic Sanctions," *World Politics*, Vol. 47, No. 4, July 1995.

Marcussen, Martin, Thomas Risse, *et al.*, "Constructing Europe? The Evolution of French, British, and German Nation State Identities," *Journal of European Public Policy*, Vol. 6, No. 4, 1999.

Markovits, Andrei S. and Simon Reich, *The German Predicament: Memory and Power in the New Europe* (Ithaca, NY: Cornell University Press, 1997).

Martin, Lisa L., *Coercive Cooperation: Explaining Multilateral Economic Sanctions* (Princeton, NJ: Princeton University Press, 1992).

Democratic Commitments: Legislatures and International Cooperation (Princeton, NJ: Princeton University Press, 2000).

"Interests, Power, and Multilateralism," *International Organization*, Vol. 46, No. 4, Autumn 1992.

Martin, Lisa L. and Beth A. Simmons, "Theories and Empirical Studies of International Institutions," *International Organization*, Vol. 52, No. 4, Autumn 1998.

Mason, Roy, "Setting British Defence Priorities," *Survival*, Vol. 17, No. 5, September/October 1975.

Mastanduno, Michael, *Economic Containment: CoCom and the Politics of East–West Trade* (Ithaca, NY: Cornell University Press, 1992).

"Economic Statecraft, Interdependence, and National Security: Agendas for Research," in Jean-Marc F. Blanchard, Edward D. Mansfield, and Norrin M. Ripsman, eds., *Power and the Purse: Economic Statecraft, Interdependence, and National Security* (Portland, OR: Frank Cass, 2000).

"Preserving the Unipolar Moment: Realist Theories and US Grand Strategy after the Cold War," *International Security*, Vol. 21, No. 4, Spring 1997.

Mattli, Walter, *The Logic of Regional Integration: Europe and Beyond* (New York: Cambridge University Press, 1999).

"Ernst Haas's Evolving Thinking on Comparative Regional Integration: Of Virtues and Infelicities," *Journal of European Public Policy*, Vol. 12, No. 12, April 2005, pp. 327–348.

Mazzucelli, Colette, *France and Germany at Maastricht: Politics and Negotiations to Create the European Union* (New York: Garland Publishing, 1997).

Mearsheimer, John J., *The Tragedy of Great Power Politics* (New York: W.W. Norton, 2001).

"Back to the Future: Instability in Europe after the Cold War," *International Security*, Vol. 15, No. 1, Summer 1990.

"The False Promise of International Institutions," *International Security*, Vol. 19, No. 3, Winter 1994/95.

"The Future of the American Pacifier," *Foreign Affairs*, Vol. 80, No. 5, September/October 2001.

"Why the Soviets Can't Win Quickly in Central Europe," *International Security*, Vol. 7, No. 1, Summer 1982.

Mead, Walter Russell, "American Endurance," in Tod Lindberg, ed., *Beyond Paradise and Power: Europe, America and the Future of a Troubled Partnership* (New York and London: Routledge, 2004).

Medeiros, Evan S., Roger Cliff, Keith Crane, and James C. Mulvenon, *A New Direction for China's Defense Industry* (Santa Monica, CA: RAND, 2005).

Mendès-France, Pierre, *Oeuvres complètes III: Gouverner c'est Choisir 1954–1955* (Paris: Gallimard, 1986).

Mercer, Jonathan, "Anarchy and Identity," *International Organization*, Vol. 49, No. 2, Spring 1995.

Merlingen, Michael, Cas Mudde, and Ulrich Sedelmeier, "The Right and the Righteous? European Norms, Domestic Politics and the Sanctions against Austria," *Journal of Common Market Studies*, Vol. 39, No. 1, March 2001.

Méry, General Guy, "French Defence Policy," *Survival*, Vol. 18, No. 5, September/October 1976.

"Une armée pour quoi faire et comment?" *Défense Nationale*, June 1976.

Mezerik, A.G., *Rhodesia and the United Nations*, Vol. XII (New York: International Review Service, 1966).

Miers, Anne C., and T. Clifton Morgan, "Multilateral Sanctions and Foreign Policy Success: Can Too Many Cooks Spoil the Broth?" *International Interactions*, Vol. 28, 2002.

Milgrom, Paul R., Douglass C. North, and Barry R. Weingast, "The Role of Institutions in the Revival of Trade: The Law Merchant, Private Judges, and the Champagne Fairs," *Economics and Politics*, Vol. 2, No. 1.

Miller, Judith, "When Sanctions Worked," *Foreign Policy*, No. 39, Summer 1980.

Mills, Lenox A. and Charles H. McLaughlin, *World Politics in Transition* (New York: Holt, 1956).

Milner, Helen V., *Interests, Institutions, and Information: Domestic Politics and International Relations* (Princeton, NJ: Princeton University Press, 1997).

Mitrany, David, *The Functional Theory of Politics* (New York: St. Martin's Press, 1975).

284   Select Bibliography

A Working Peace System (Chicago: Quadrangle Books, 1966).

Monnet, Jean, *Memoirs* (Garden City, NY: Doubleday, 1978).

Moran, Theodore H., "The Globalization of America's Defense Industries: Managing the Threat of Foreign Dependence," *International Security*, Vol. 15, No. 1, Summer 1990.

Moravcsik, Andrew, *The Choice for Europe: Social Purpose and State Power from Messina to Maastricht* (Ithaca, NY: Cornell University Press, 1998).

"Armaments among Allies: European Weapons Collaboration, 1975–1985," in Peter B. Evans, Harold K. Jacobson, and Robert D. Putnam, *Double-Edged Diplomacy: International Bargaining and Domestic Politics* (Berkeley: University of California Press, 1993).

"Arms and Autarky in Modern European History," *Daedalus*, Vol. 120, No. 4, Fall 1991.

"De Gaulle between Grain and Grandeur: The Political Economy of French EC Policy, 1958–1970 (Parts I and II)," *Journal of Cold War Studies*, Spring and Fall 2000.

"The European Armaments Industry at the Crossroads," *Survival*, Vol. 32, No. 1, January/February 1990.

"The European Constitutional Compromise and the Neofunctionalist Legacy," *Journal of European Public Policy*, Vol. 12, No. 12, April 2005.

"Liberal International Relations Theory: A Scientific Assessment," in Colin Elman and Miriam Fendius Elman, eds., *Progress in International Relations Theory* (Cambridge, MA: MIT Press, 2003).

"Taking Preferences Seriously: A Liberal Theory of International Politics," *International Organization*, Vol. 51, No. 4, Autumn 1997.

Morgan, T. Clifton and Valerie L. Schwebach, "Fools Suffer Gladly: The Use of Economic Sanctions in International Crises," *International Studies Quarterly*, Vol. 41, No. 1, March 1997.

Morgenthau, Hans J., *Politics among Nations: The Struggle for Power and Peace* (New York: Alfred A. Knopf, 1963).

Morgenthau, Hans J. and Kenneth W. Thompson, eds., *Principles and Problems of International Politics: Selected Readings* (New York: Alfred A. Knopf, 1950).

Morrow, James D., *Game Theory for Political Scientists* (Princeton, NJ: Princeton University Press, 1994).

"Modeling the Forms of International Cooperation: Distribution versus Information," *International Organization*, Vol. 48, No. 3, Summer 1994.

Morth, Ulrika and Malena Britz, "European Integration as Organizing: The Case of Armaments," *Journal of Common Market Studies*, Vol. 42, No. 5, 2004.

Nardulli, Bruce R., Walt L. Perry, Bruce Pirnie, John Gordon, John G. McGinn, *Disjointed War: Military Operations in Kosovo, 1999*, MR-1406-A (Santa Monica, CA: RAND, 2002).

Neal, Derrick J. and Trevor Taylor, "Globalisation in the Defence Industry: An Exploration of the Paradigm for US and European Defence Firms and Implications for Being Global Players," *Defence and Peace Economics*, Vol. 12, 2001.

Nelson, Daniel J., *A History of U.S. Military Forces in Germany* (Boulder, CO: Westview Press, 1987).

North Atlantic Treaty Organization, *The North Atlantic Treaty Organization: Facts and Figures* (Brussels: NATO Information Service, 1981).

Operation Deliberate Force: AFSOUTH Fact Sheet (Brussels: NATO, 2002).

North, Douglas C., *Institutions, Institutional Change, and Economic Performance* (New York: Cambridge University Press, 1990).

Nuttall, Simon J., *European Political Co-operation* (New York: Oxford University Press, 1992).

Nye, Joseph S., *Bound to Lead: The Changing Nature of American Power* (New York: Basic Books, 1990).

The Paradox of American Power (New York: Oxford University Press, 2002).

Peace in Parts: Integration and Conflict in Regional Organization (Boston: Little, Brown, and Company, 1971).

"Comparing Common Markets: A Revised Neo-Functionalist Model," *International Organization*, Vol. 24, No. 4, Autumn 1970.

Oakes, Mark, *Common European Security and Defence Policy: A Progress Report*, Research Paper 00/84 (London: House of Commons, 2000).

Olson, Mancur, *The Logic of Collective Action: Public Goods and the Theory of Groups* (Cambridge, MA: Harvard University Press, 1965).

Omara-Otunnu, Amii, *Politics and the Military in Uganda, 1890–1985* (New York: St. Martin's Press, 1987).

Organisation for Economic Cooperation and Development, *Quarterly Labour Force Statistics, No.4* (OECD, 2001).

Organization for Security and Co-operation in Europe, *OSCE Handbook* (Vienna: OSCE, 2000).

Osland, Kari M., "The EU Police Mission in Bosnia and Herzegovina," *International Peacekeeping*, Vol. 11, No. 3, Autumn 2004.

O'Sullivan, Meghan L., *Shrewd Sanctions: Statecraft and State Sponsors of Terrorism* (Washington, DC: Brookings Institution Press, 2003).

Owen, David, *Balkan Odyssey* (New York: Harcourt Brace, 1995).

Owen, John M., IV, *Liberal Peace, Liberal War: American Politics and International Security* (Ithaca, NY: Cornell University Press, 1997).

"Transnational Liberalism and U.S. Primacy," *International Security*, Vol. 26, No. 3, Winter 2001/02.

Owen Robert C., "Balkans Air Campaign Study: Part 1," *Airpower Journal*, Vol. 11, Summer 1997.

"Balkans Air Campaign Study: Part 2," *Airpower Journal*, Vol. 11, Fall 1997.

Oye, Kenneth, "Explaining Cooperation under Anarchy: Hypotheses and Strategies," *World Politics*, Vol. 38, No. 1, October 1985.

Pages, Erik, "Defense Mergers: Weapons Cost, Innovation, and International Arms Industry Cooperation," in Anne R. Markusen and Sean Costigan, eds., *Arming the Future: A Defense Industry for the Twenty-First Century* (New York: Council on Foreign Relations Press, 1999).

Palmer, Fiona, "European Sanctions and Enforcement: European Law Meets the Individual," *The Cambrian Law Review*, No. 28, 1997.

Pape, Robert A., "Soft Balancing against the United States," International Security, Vol. 30, No. 1, Summer 2005, pp. 7–45.

"Why Economic Sanctions Do Not Work," *International Security*, Vol. 22, No. 2, Fall 1997.

"Why Economic Sanctions Still Do Not Work," *International Security*, Vol. 23, No. 1, Summer 1998.

Paul, T.V., James J. Wirtz, and Michel Fortmann, *Balance of Power: Theory and Practice in the 21st Century* (Stanford, CA: Stanford University Press, 2004).

"Soft Balancing in the Age of U.S. Primacy," *International Security*, Vol. 30, No. 1, Summer 2005, pp. 46–71.

Parsons, Craig, *A Certain Idea of Europe* (Ithaca, NY: Cornell University Press, 2003).

Perrow, Charles, *Complex Organizations: A Critical Essay* (New York: Random House, 1986).

Organizing America: Wealth, Power, and the Origins of Corporate Capitalism (Princeton, NJ: Princeton University Press, 2002).

Pew Research Center for the People and the Press, *American Charter Gets Mixed Reviews* (Washington, DC: Pew Global Attitudes Project, 2005).

America's Image Slips, But Allies Share U.S. Concerns Over Iran, Hamas (Washington, DC: Pew Research Center for the People and the Press, 2006).

Pfeffer, Jeffrey, *Power in Organizations* (Marshfield, MA: Pitman Publishers, 1981).

Pierre, Andrew J., *Coalitions: Building and Maintenance* (Washington, DC: Institute for the Study of Diplomacy, 2002).

Pierson, Paul, "When Effect Becomes Cause: Policy Feedback and Political Change," *World Politics*, Vol. 45, No. 4, July 1993.

Pijpers, Alfred, Elfriede Regelsberger, and Wolfgang Wessels, *European Political Cooperation in the 1980s: A Common Foreign Policy for Western Europe?* (Boston: Martinus Nijhoff, 1988).

Pitman, Paul, "France's European Choices," Ph.D dissertation, University of Columbia, New York, 1998.

Pond, Elizabeth, *Friendly Fire: The Near-Death of the Transatlantic Alliance* (Washington, DC: Brookings Institution Press, 2004).

"Kosovo: Catalyst for Europe," *Washington Quarterly*, Vol. 22, No. 4.

Posen, Barry R., *The Sources of Military Doctrine: France, Britain, and Germany between the World Wars* (Ithaca, NY: Cornell University Press, 1984).

"ESDP and the Structure of World Power," *The International Spectator*, Vol. 39, No. 1, January – March 2004, pp. 5–17.

PricewaterhouseCoopers, *Inception Study to Support the Development of a Business Plan for the GALILEO Programme*, TREN/B5/23–2001 (brussels: PricewaterhouseCoopers, 2001).

Ragin, Charles C. "Comparative Sociology and the Comparative Method," *International Journal of Comparative Sociology*, Vol. 22, Nos. 1–2, March–June 1981.

Rappard, William E., *Collective Security in Swiss Experience, 1291–1948* (London: George Allen and Unwin, 1948).

Rasmussen, Mikkel-Vedby, "Turbulent Neighbourhoods: How to Deploy the EU's Rapid Reaction Force," *Contemporary Security Policy*, Vol. 23, No. 2, August 2002.

Reiter, Dan "Learning, Realism, and Alliances: The Weight of the Shadow of the Past," *World Politics*, Vol. 46, No. 4, July 1994.

Renwick, Robin, *Economic Sanctions*, No. 45 (Cambridge, MA: Center for International Affairs, 1983).

Révay, Paul, *After the "No's": Getting Europe Back on Track* (Brussels: Friends of Europe, 2005).

Rich, Norman, *Great Power Diplomacy, 1814–1914* (Boston, MA: McGraw-Hill, 1992).

Richard, Alain, "L'Europe de la défense," *Défense nationale*, No. 57, January 2001.

Risse, Thomas, "A European Identity? Europeanization and the Evolution of Nation-State Identities," in Maria Green Cowles, James, Caporaso and Thomas Risse, *Transforming Europe: Europeanization and Domestic Change* (Ithaca, NY: Cornell University Press, 2001).

"Neofunctionalism, European Identity, and the Puzzles of European Integration," *Journal of European Public Policy*, Vol. 12, No. 2, April 2005, pp. 291–309.

Rosamond, Ben, *Theories of European Integration* (New York: St. Martin's Press, 2000).

Roudometof, Victor, "Nationalism and Identity Politics in the Balkans: Greece and the Macedonian Question," *Journal of Modern Greek Studies*, Vol. 14, No. 2, 1996.

Rowe, David M., *Manipulating the Market: Understanding Economic Sanctions, Institutional Change, and the Political Unity of White Rhodesia* (Ann Arbor, MI: University of Michigan Press, 2001).

"Economic Sanctions Do Work: Economic Statecraft and the Oil Embargo of Rhodesia," in Jean-Marc F. Blanchard, Edward D. Mansfield, and Norrin M. Ripsman, *Power and the Purse: Economic Statecraft, Interdependence, and National Security* (London: Frank Cass, 2000).

Rowe, Vivian, *The Great Wall of France: The Triumph of the Maginot Line* (New York: G.P. Putnam's Sons, 1961).

Rubin, Barnett, R., *Road to Ruin: Afghanistan's Booming Opium Industry* (New York: Center on International Cooperation, October 2004).

Rueda, Raul Romeva, *Report on the Council's Fifth Annual Report according to Operation Provision 8 of the European Code of Conduct on Arms Control*, A6-0022/2004 (Brussels: European Parliament, 2004).

Report on the Council's Sixth Annual Report according to Operation Provision 8 of the European Code of Conduct on Arms Control, A6-0292/2005 (Brussels: European Parliament, 2004).

Ruggie, John Gerard, "What Makes the World Hang Together? Neo-utilitarianism and the Social Constructivist Challenge," *International Organization*, Vol. 52, No. 4, Autumn 1998.

Rutten, Maartje, ed., *From St. Malo to Nice: European Defence, CoreDocuments*, Chaillot Paper 47 (Paris: Institute for Security Studies, May 2001).

Sachwald, Frédérique, *Defence Industry Restructuring: The End of an Economic Exception* (Paris: Institut Français des relations internationals, 1999).

Sandler, Todd and Keith Hartley, *The Economics of Defense* (New York: Cambridge University Press, 1995).

The Political Economy of NATO: Past, Present, and into the 21st Century (New York: Cambridge University Press, 1999).

Sarotte, Mary Elise, *German Military Reform and European Security*, Adelphi Paper 340 (London: International Institute for Strategic Studies, 2001).

Schelling, Thomas C., *Arms and Influence* (New Haven: Yale University Press, 1966).

The Strategy of Conflict (Cambridge, MA: Harvard University Press, 1960).

Scherer, Frederic M., *The Weapons Acquisition Process: Economic Incentives* (Boston: Division of Research, Graduate School of Business Administration, Harvard University, 1964).

Schimmelfennig, Frank, *The EU, NATO and the Integration of Europe: Rules and Rhetoric* (New York: Cambridge University Press, 2003).

Schmitt, Burkard, *From Cooperation to Integration: Defence and Aerospace Industries in Europe*, Chaillot Paper 40 (Paris: Institute for Security Studies, 2000).

European Armaments Cooperation: Core Documents, Chaillot Paper 59 (Paris: Institute for Security Studies, 2003).

Schmitter, Philippe, "Three Neo-Functional Hypotheses about International Integration," *International Organization*, Vol. 23, No. 1, Winter 1969.

Schröder, Gerhard, "Shaping Industry on the Anvil of Europe," *Financial Times*, April 29, 2002.

Schroeder, Paul W., *The Transformation of European Politics, 1763–1848* (New York: Oxford University Press, 1994).

"Alliances, 1815–1945: Weapons of Power and Tools of Management," in Klaus Knorr, ed., *Historical Dimensions of National Security Problems* (Lawrence, KA: University Press of Kansas, 1976).

Schwartz, Thomas A., *America's Germany: John J. McCloy and the Federal Republic of Germany* (Cambridge, MA: Harvard University Press, 1991).

Schweller, Randall L., *Deadly Imbalances: Tripolarity and Hitler's Strategy of World Conquest* (New York: Columbia University Press, 1998).

"Neorealism's Status-Quo Bias: What Security Dilemma?" *Security Studies*, Vol. 5, No. 3, Spring 1996.

Schweller, Randall L. and David Priess, "A Tale of Two Realisms: Expanding the Institutions Debate," *Mershon International Studies Review*, Vol. 41, 1997.

Searle, John R., *The Construction of Social Reality* (New York: Free Press, 1995).

Shea, John, *Macedonia and Greece: The Struggle to Define a New Balkan Nation* (Jefferson, NC: McFarland & Company, 1997).

Silber, Laura and Allan Little, *Yugoslavia: Death of a Nation* (New York: Penguin Books, 1997).

Silj, Alessandro, *Europe's Political Puzzle: A Study of the Fouchet Negotiations and the 1963 Veto* (Cambridge, MA: Center for International Affairs, 1967).

Singer, J. David and Melvin Small, *Resort to Arms: International and Civil Wars, 1816–1980* (Beverly Hills, CA: Sage, 1982).

Skocpol, Theda and Margaret Somers, "The Uses of Comparative History in Macrosocial Inquiry," *Comparative Studies in Society and History*, Vol. 22, No. 2, 1980.

Smith, Anthony D., "National Identity and the Idea of European Unity," *International Affairs*, Vol. 68, No. 1, January 1992.

Smith, Michael E., *Europe's Foreign and Security Policy* (New York: Cambridge University Press, 2004).

Snidal, Duncan, "Coordination versus Prisoners' Dilemma: Implications for International Cooperation and Regime," *American Political Science Review*, Vol. 79, No. 4, December 1985.

Snyder, Glenn H., *Alliance Politics* (Ithaca, NY: Cornell University Press, 1997).

Snyder, Jack, *Myths of Empire: Domestic Politics and International Ambition* (Ithaca, NY: Cornell University Press, 1991).

Spaak, Paul-Henri, *The Continuing Battle: Memoirs of a European, 1936–1966* (London: Weidenfeld and Nicolson, 1971).

Sparrow, John C., *History of Personnel Demobilization in the United States Army* (Washington, DC: United States Army, 1951).

Spence, A.M., "Job Market Signaling," *Quarterly Journal of Economics*, Vol. 87, No. 3, August 1973.

Steinberg, James B., "An Elective Partnership: Salvaging Transatlantic Relations," *Survival*, Vol. 45, No. 2, Summer 2003.

Stikker, Dirk U., *Men of Responsibility: A Memoir* (New York: Harper & Row, 1965).

Stockhom International Peace Research Institute, *SIPRI Yearbook 1972, 1974, 1976, 1977, 1995* and *2005* (New York: SIPRI, 1972; 1974; 1976; 1977; 1995, 2005).

Stopford, John and Susan Strange, *Rival States, Rival Firms: Competition for World Market Shares* (New York: Cambridge University Press, 1991).

Strack, Harry R., *Sanctions: The Case of Rhodesia* (Syracuse, NY: Syracuse University Press, 1978).

Sulzberger, C.L., *The Last of the Giants* (New York: Macmillan, 1970).

Suny, Ronald Grigor, *The Revenge of the Past: Nationalism, Revolution, and the Collapse of the Soviet Union* (Stanford, CA: Stanford University Press, 1993).

Szayna, Thomas S. *et al.*, *Improving Army Planning for Future Multinational Coalition Operations*, MR-1291-A (Santa Monica, CA: RAND, 2001).

Taft, Robert A., *A Foreign Policy for Americans* (Garden City, NY: Doubleday, 1951).

Tams, Carsten, "The Functions of a European Security and Defence Identity and its Institutional Form," in Helga Haftendorn, Robert O. Keohane, and Celeste A. Wallander, eds., *Imperfect Unions: Security Institutions over Time and Space* (New York: Oxford University Press, 1999).

Taverna, Michael A., "European Union's New Space Role Could Help Meet Military Goals," *Aviation Week & Space Technology*, Vol. 153, No. 22, November 27, 2000.

Taylor, Trevor and Keith Hayward, *The UK Defence Industrial Base: Development and Future Policy Options* (Washington: Brassey's Defence Publishers, 1989).

Tenet, George, *The Worldwide Threat in 2003: Evolving Dangers in a Complex World* (Washington, DC: Central Intelligence Agency, February 2003).

Thales Group, *Annual Report 2005* (Paris: Thales Group, 2006).

Thatcher, Margaret, *The Downing Street Years* (New York: HarperCollins, 1993).

Thomson, C.S.F., *Reference Document 1999* (Paris: Thomson C.S.F., 2000).

Tilly, Charles, "Means and Ends of Comparison in Macrosociology," in Lars Mjoset, *et al.*, *Comparative Social Research: Methodological Issues in Comparative Social Science*, Vol. XVI (Greenwich, CT: JAI Press, 1997).

Tindemans, Léo, "Report on European Union," December 29, 1975, in Christopher Hill and Karen E. Smith, eds., *European Foreign Policy: Key Documents* (New York: Routledge, 2000).

Toko, Gad W., *Intervention in Uganda: The Power Struggle and Soviet Involvement* (Pittsburgh: University Center for International Studies, 1979).

Trachtenberg, Marc, *A Constructed Peace: The Making of the European Settlement, 1945–1963* (Princeton: Princeton University Press, 1999).

Tsouderos, Virginia, "Greek Policy and the Yugoslav Turmoil," *Mediterranean Quarterly*, Vol. 4, No. 2, Spring 1993.

Tucker, Jonathan B., "Partners and Rivals: A Model of International Collaboration in Advanced Technology," *International Organization*, Vol. 45, No. 1, Winter 1991, pp. 83–120.

Ullman, Richard H., ed., *The World and Yugoslavia's Wars* (New York: Council on Foreign Relations, 1996).

Ulriksen, Stale, Catriona Gourlay, and Catriona Mace, "Operation Artemis: The Shape of Things to Come?" *International Peacekeeping*, Vol. 11, No. 3, Autumn 2004.

"Requirements for Future European Military Strategies and Force Structures," *International Peacekeeping*, Vol. 11, No. 3, Autumn 2004.

United Kingdom Foreign and Commonwealth Office, *Documents on British Policy Overseas (DBPO)*, ed. Roger Bullen and M. E. Pelly (London: Her Majesty's Stationery Office, 1986).

Cabinet Meeting held at 10 Downing Street, 16 November 1950, *DBPO, 1950*, Series II, Vol. III.

Jebb to Younger, 12 September 1950, *DBPO, 1950*, Series II, Vol. III.

United Kingdom House of Commons, Defence Committee, *Lessons of Kosovo*, Fourteenth report (London: HMSO, 2000).

United Kingdom Ministry of Defence, *Defence Industrial Policy*, Paper No. 5 (London: Ministry of Defence, 2002).

Defence Policy 2001 (London: HMSO, 2001).

The Defence White Paper, 1999, Cm 4446 (London: HMSO, 1999).

Delivering Security in a Changing World: Future Capabilities, Cm 6269 (London: Ministry of Defence, 2004).

European Defence Policy, Paper No. 3 (London: HMSO, 2001).

Multinational Defence Co-operation, Policy Paper No. 2 (London: Ministry of Defence, 2001).

Report of the Committee of Inquiry into the Aircraft Industry, Cmnd 2853 (London: HMSO, 1985).

Statement on the Defence Estimates, 1981, Cmnd. 8212–1 (London: HMSO, 1981).

The Strategic Defence Review, 1998, Cm 3999 (London: HMSO, 1998).

Supplementary Statement on Defence Policy, Cmnd. 4521 (London: HMSO, 1970).

United Nations, *Afghanistan: Opium Survey 2004* (Vienna: UN Office on Drugs and Crime, 2004).

Final Report of the Monitoring Mechanism on Angola Sanctions, S/2000/1225 (New York: UN, December 2000).

Final Report of the UN Panel of Experts on Violations of Security Council Sanctions against Unita: The "Fowler Report," S/2000/203 (New York: UN, March 2000).

Operation Artemis: the Lessons of the Interim Emergency Multinational Force (New York: UN Peacekeeping Best Practices Unit, October 2004).

The Opium Economy in Afghanistan: An International Problem, 2nd edn (Vienna: UN Office on Drugs and Crime, 2003).

United States Congress, Department of Defense, *Annual Report to the President and the Congress, 2002* (Washington, DC: US Dept of Defense, 2002).

Final Report of the Defense Science Board Task Force on Globalization and Security (Washington, DC: US Dept of Defense, 1999).

National Military Strategy (Washington, DC: Dept of Defense, 2002).

Quadrennial Defense Review (Washington, DC: Dept of Defense, September 2001).

Report on the Bottom-Up Review (Washington, DC: US Dept of Defense, October 1993).

Responsibility Sharing Report (Washington, DC: US Dept of Defense, June 2002).

United States Congress, Department of State, Acheson to Diplomatic Offices, January 29, 1951, in *Foreign Relations of the United States (FRUS) 1951*, Vol. III.

Acheson and Johnson to Truman, September 8, 1950, *FRUS 1950*, Vol. III.

Acheson and Lovett to Truman, July 30, 1951, in *FRUS 1951*, Vol. III.

American Foreign Policy 1950–1955: Basic Documents, Vol. I (Washington, DC: Government Printing Office, 1957).

Chiefs of Mission meeting, October 2, 1952, in *FRUS 1952–4*, Vol. III.

Conant to Dulles, November 13, 1953, in *FRUS 1952–4*, Vol.VII.

"Establishment of a European Defense Force," in Matthews to Burns, August 15, 1950, *FRUS 1950*, Vol. III.

The European Defense Community Treaty, May 27, 1952, in *American Foreign Policy 1950–1955, Basic Documents*, Vol. I (Washington, DC: Government Printing Office, 1957).

Hearing on Military Modernization and Cross Straight Balance, Hearing before the U.S.–China Economic and Security Review Commission, February 6, 2004 (Washington, DC: Government Printing Office, 2004).

Meeting between Truman and Pleven, January 30, 1951, in *FRUS 1951*, Vol. IV.

Meeting of United States ambassadors at Rome, March 22–24, 1950, in *FRUS 1950*, Vol. III, *Western Europe*.

Memorandum by Acheson, July 6, 1951, in *FRUS 1951*, Vol. III, *European Security and the German Question*.

Memorandum of National Security Council discussion, August 13, 1953, in *FRUS 1952–4*.

Memorandum of conversation between Lewis and Krekeler, November 18, 1953, in *FRUS 1952–4*, Vol. VII.

Minutes of Meeting between French, British, and United States foreign ministers and their High Commissioners for Germany, September 14, 1950, in *FRUS 1950*, Vol. III, *Western Europe*.

Paper Prepared by the Policy Planning Staff, "The Current Position in the Cold War," April 14, 1950, *FRUS 1950*, Vol. III, *Western Europe*.

Report on Greek Enforcement of UN Sanctions against Serbia, 95/06/02 (Washington, DC: US Dept of State, 1995).

Report by the North Atlantic Military Committee, December 1950, in *FRUS 1950*.

Semiannual Report of the Secretary of Defense, January 1 to June 30, 1954 (Washington, DC: Government Printing Office, 1955).

Spofford to Acheson, July 8, 1951, in *FRUS 1951*, Vol. III.

Statement by Acheson to the North Atlantic Council, April 23, 1954, *FRUS 1952–1954*, Vol. V, *Western European Security*.

Strategic Concept for the Defense of the North Atlantic Area, December 1, 1949, *FRUS 1949*, Vol. IV, *Western Europe*.

United States Position with Respect to Germany, August 17, 1953, in *FRUS 1952–1954*, Vol. VII, *Germany and Austria* (Washington, DC: Government Printing Office, 1986).

UN *Sanctions against Belgrade: Lessons Learned for Future Regimes* (Washington, DC: US Dept of State, June 1996).

United States General Accounting Office, *China: U.S. and European Union Arms Sales since the 1989 Embargoes* (Washington, DC: General Accounting Office).

Military Presence: U.S. Personnel in NATO Europe, Report to the Chairmen and Ranking Minority Members, Senate and House Committees on Armed Services, GAO/NSIAD-90-04 (Washington, DC: General Accounting Office, October 1989).

US Congress, Office of Technology Assessment, *Lessons in Restructuring Defense Industry: The French Experience*, OTA-BP-ISC-96 (Washington, DC: US Government Printing Office, June 1992).

Van Evera, Stephen, *Causes of War: Power and the Roots of Conflict* (Ithaca, NY: Cornell University Press, 1999).

Guide to Methods for Students of Political Science (Ithaca, NY: Cornell University Press, 1997).

"Primed for Peace: Europe after the Cold War," International Security, Vol. 15, No. 3, Winter 1990/91.

"The Cult of the Offensive and the Origins of the First World War," *International Security*, Vol. 9, No. 1, Summer 1984.

Van Scherpenberg, Jens, "Transatlantic Competition and European Defence Industries: A New Look at the Trade-Defence Linkage," *International Affairs*, Vol. 73, No. 1, 1997.

van Staden, Alfred, Kees Homan, Bert Kreemers, Alfred Pijpers, and Rob de Wijk, *Toward a European Strategic Concept* (The Hague: Netherlands Institute of International Relations, November 2000).

Védrine, Hubert, *France in an Age of Globalization* (Washington, DC: Brookings Institution Press, 2001).

Vernon, R., ed., *Big Business and the State* (Cambridge, MA: Harvard University Press, 1974).

Virginia Tsouderos, "Greek Policy and the Yugoslav Turmoil," *Mediterranean Quarterly*, Vol. 4, No. 2, Spring 1993.

Vlachos-Dengler, Katia, *From National Champions to European Heavyweights: The Development of European Defense Industrial Capabilities across Market Segments*, DB-358-OSD (Santa Monica, CA: RAND, 2002).

Off Track? The Future of the European Defense Industry (Santa Monica, CA: RAND, 2004).

Waever, Ole, "Insecurity, Security, and Asecurity in the West European Non-War Community," in Emanuel Adler and Michael Barnett, eds., *Security Communities* (New York: Cambridge University Press, 1998).

"Integration as Security: Constructing a Europe at Peace," in Charles A. Kupchan, ed., *Atlantic Security: Contending Visions* (New York: Council on Foreign Relations, 1998).

Wallace, William, "As Viewed from Europe: Transatlantic Sympathies, Transatlantic Fears," *International Relations*, Vol. 16, No. 2, August 2002.

Wallace, William and David Allen, "Political Cooperation: Procedure as Substitute for Policy," in Helen Wallace, William Wallace, and Carole Webb, eds., *Policy-Making in the European Communities* (London: John Wiley & Sons, 1977).

Wallander, Celeste, "Institutional Assets and Adaptability: NATO after the Cold War," *International Organization*, Vol. 54, No. 4, Autumn 2000.

Walt, Stephen M., *The Origins of Alliances* (Ithaca, NY: Cornell University Press, 1987).

Taming American Power: The Global Response to U.S. Primacy (New York: W.W. Norton, 2005).

"Rigor or Rigor Mortis? Rational Choice and Security Studies," *International Security*, Vol. 23, No. 4, Spring 1999, pp. 5–48.

"The Ties that Fray: Why Europe and America are Drifting Apart," *The National Interest*, No. 54, Winter 1998/99.

Waltz, Kenneth N., *Theory of International Politics* (New York: McGraw-Hill, 1979).

"The Emerging Structure of International Politics," *International Security*, Vol. 18, No. 2, Fall 1993.

"The Stability of a Bipolar World," *Daedalus*, Vol. 93, No. 3, Summer 1963.

"Structural Realism after the Cold War," in G. John Ikenberry, ed., *America Unrivaled: The Future of the Balance of Power* (Ithaca: Cornell University Press, 2002).

"Structural Realism after the Cold War," *International Security*, Vol. 25, No. 1, Summer 2000.

Watt, D.C. and James Mayall, *Current British Foreign Policy: Documents, Statements, Speeches 1972* (London: Temple Smith, 1972).

Wells, Samuel F., "The Transatlantic Illness," *Wilson Quarterly*, Vol. 27, No. 1, Winter 2003.

Wendt, Alexander, *Social Theory of International Politics* (New York: Cambridge University Press, 1999).

"Anarchy is What States Make of It: The Social Construction of Power Politics," *International Organization*, Vol. 40, 1987.

Western European Union Assembly, "Communiqué issued after the conference in the Hague," *A Retrospective View of the Political Year in Europe, 1969* (Paris: General Affairs Committee, Western European Union Assembly, 1970).

White House, *National Security Strategy of the United States of America* (Washington, DC: White House, 2002).

Wilber, Donald N., *Overthrow of Premier Mossadeq of Iran* (Washington: Central Intelligence Agency, March 1954).

Williamson, Oliver E., *The Economic Institution of Capitalism: Firms, Markets, Relational Contracting* (New York: Free Press, 1985).

Wohlforth, William C., *The Elusive Balance: Power and Perceptions during the Cold War* (Ithaca, NY: Cornell University Press, 1993).

"The Stability of a Unipolar World," *International Security*, Vol. 21, No. 1, Summer 1999, pp. 1–36.

Woodward, Susan L., *Balkan Tragedy: Chaos and Dissolution after the Cold War* (Washington, DC: Brookings Institution, 1995).

"The Use of Sanctions in Former Yugoslavia: Misunderstanding Political Realities," in David Cortright and George A. Lopez, eds., *Economic Sanctions: Panacea or Peacebuilding in a Post-Cold War World?* (Boulder, CO: Westview Press, 1995).

Yost, David S., "Transatlantic Relations and Peace in Europe," *International Affairs*, Vol. 78, No. 2, April 2002.

Zahariadis, Nikolaos, "Nationalism and Small-State Foreign Policy: The Greek Response to the Macedonian Issue," *Political Science Quarterly*, Vol. 109, No. 4, Autumn 1994.

Zanini, Michele and Jennifer Morrison Taw, *The Army and Multinational Force Compatibility*, MR-1154-A (Santa Monica, CA: RAND, 2000).

Zelikow, Philip and Condoleezza Rice, *Germany Unified and Europe Transformed: A Study in Statecraft* (Cambridge, MA: Harvard University Press, 1995).

Zimmermann, Warren, *Origins of a Catastrophe* (New York: Random House, 1996).

Index

For EU product safety concerns, contact us at Calle de José Abascal, 56–1°,
28003 Madrid, Spain or eugpsr@cambridge.org.

www.ingramcontent.com/pod-product-compliance
Ingram Content Group UK Ltd.
Pitfield, Milton Keynes, MK11 3LW, UK
UKHW042154130625
459647UK00011B/1322